PASOLINI

The Sacred Flesh

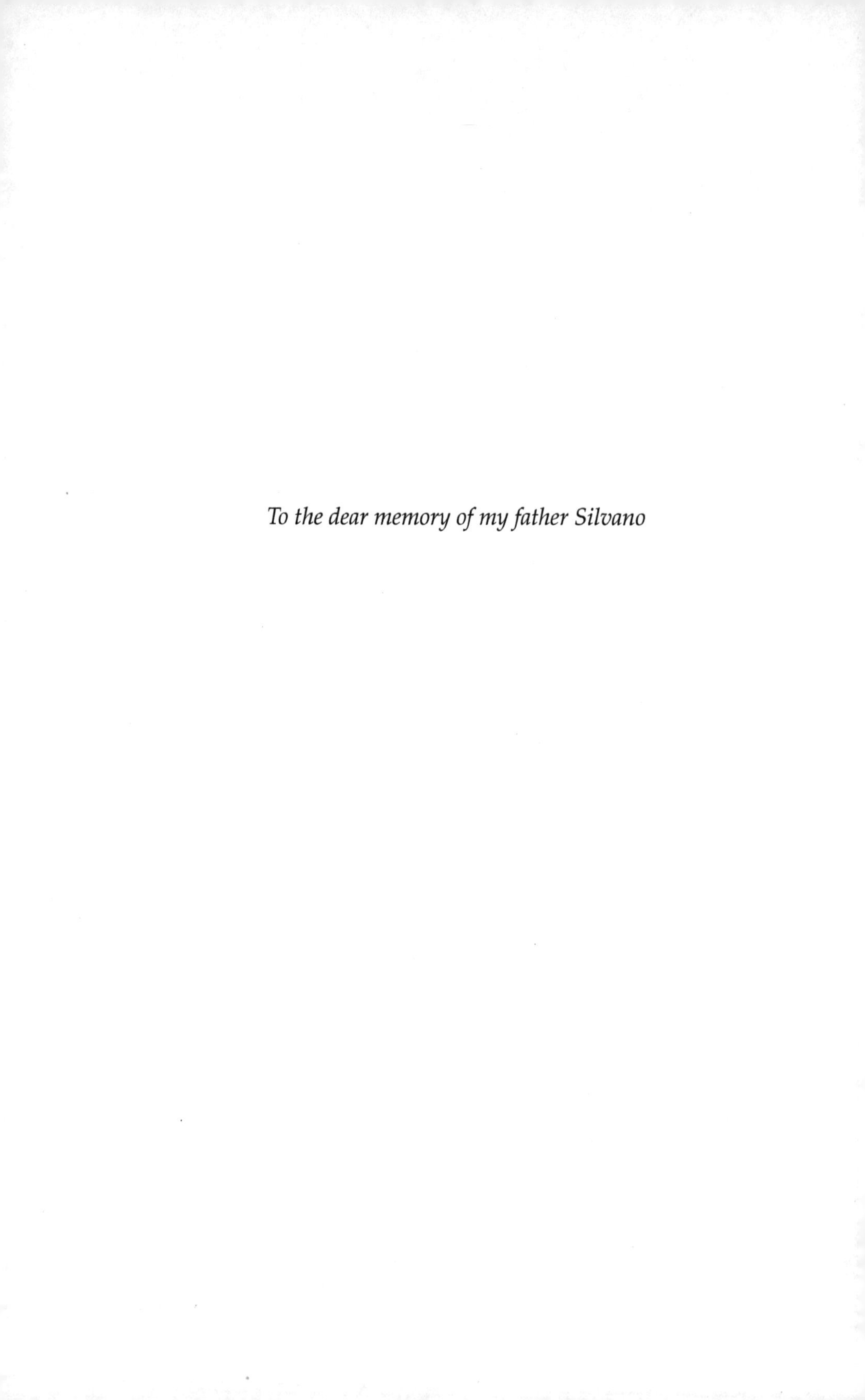

To the dear memory of my father Silvano

STEFANIA BENINI

Pasolini

The Sacred Flesh

UNIVERSITY OF TORONTO PRESS
Toronto Buffalo London

Toronto Buffalo London
www.utppublishing.com

ISBN 978-1-4426-4806-7

Toronto Italian Studies

Library and Archives Canada Cataloguing in Publication

Benini, Stefania, 1964–, author
Pasolini : the sacred flesh / Stefania Benini.

(Toronto Italian studies)
Includes bibliographical references and index.
ISBN 978-1-4426-4806-7 (bound)

1. Pasolini, Pier Paolo, 1922–1975 – Criticism and interpretation.
2. Religion in motion pictures. I. Title. II. Series: Toronto Italian studies

PN1998.3.P37B45 2015   791.4302'33092   C2015-901799-8

University of Toronto Press acknowledges the financial assistance to its publishing program of the Canada Council for the Arts and the Ontario Arts Council, an Ontario government agency.

Funded by the Government of Canada
Financé par le gouvernement du Canada

Contents

Acknowledgments vii
Permissions and Credits ix
Abbreviations xi

Introduction 3

1 The Sense of the Sacred 18
A Brief History of the Sacred 18
The Sense of the Sacred in Pasolini 22
Pasolini between Eliade and De Martino 28
The Archaic and the Christian Sacred 35
Religiosity: *Caritas* 36
Three Popes 45

2 The Passion and the Incarnation: *Ricotta* and *The Gospel according to Matthew* 52
La Ricotta 52
Il Vangelo secondo Matteo 62

3 The Words of the Flesh: *Blasphemy* 78
Bestemmia: Barbaric Christology 78
Bestemmia: The Words of the Flesh 93
Ethical Constellations: Example and Martyrdom 106

4 The Mad Saint and the Anchorite: *Theorem* 111
Pasolini's *Teorema* 112
Emilia and Paolo 125

5 The Franciscan Model 147
Tragic and Comic Franciscanism in Pasolini's Work 147
Bestemmia 156
Uccellacci e uccellini 172

6 The Pauline Model 187
San Paolo: 1966 to 1974 187
The Poetic Idea between Relevance to the Present (*Attualità*) and Sanctity 195
The Scandal of the Cross, the Scandal of Sickness: Homosexuality and *Caritas* 203
Parodies of Saintliness: From *Sant'Infame* to *Petrolio's* "Prima Fiaba sul Potere" 215

Conclusion 221

Notes 227

Bibliography 305

Index of Names 319

Index of Films and Screenplays 323

Index of Subjects 325

Acknowledgments

A number of people and institutions have helped me to transform this book project into reality. First of all, I thank the Center for Italian Studies and its director, Fabio Finotti, who granted me a Salvatori Award that allowed me to do research at the Pasolini Foundation in Bologna and at the Gabinetto Viesseux in Florence, where I had access to material crucial for my research in the Fondo Pier Paolo Pasolini. I also thank Graziella Chiarcossi for giving me permission to consult the original documents at the Fondo Pasolini in Florence, and Roberto Chiesi for his assistance and support of my research in Bologna.

I am grateful to the University of Pennsylvania and to my wonderful colleagues there – Fabio Finotti, Kevin Brownlee, Jonathan Steinberg, Timothy Corrigan, Karen Beckman, Kate McMahon, Michele Richman, Christine Poggi, and Ann Matter – as well as my mentors from my *alma mater* – Jeffrey Schnapp from Harvard University and Hans Ulrich Gumbrecht from Stanford University – for the incredible support they gave me during this complex period. I am also indebted to the colleagues who constitute a model for my research, from Gaetana Marrone Puglia to Millicent Marcus, and to my graduate students in my courses on Pasolini, who have for years been my research guinea pigs.

I want to thank the friends who helped me to prepare this manuscript: Marina Della Putta Johnston, who has been a precious critical eye and a formidable reader, as well as Kenneth Parker and Jessica Otey.

Great gratitude goes to my first editor, Ron Schoeffel, who passed away while I was drafting the manuscript and was wonderfully kind and supportive throughout the early stages of publication. I also want to thank Siobhan McMenemy, who took on Ron's role as editor with the same spirit, and all the staff at the University of Toronto Press who made this book possible. A special thanks goes to the Press readers, whose insightful comments allowed me to make significant improvements to this volume.

In addition, I want to remember all the friends who have given me the strength and resilience to pursue this project, among them Alberta Ferrario, Daniela De Pau, Nicola Gentili, Sabrina Ferri, Ilaria Scaglia, Noelle Plat, Marta Baldocchi, Marco Jacquemet, Meredith Ray, Maria Ludovica Putignano, Meriel Tulante, Letizia Modena, Cristina Gragnani, Rita di Lello, Isabella De Vita, Enzo Lavagnini, and Lillyrose Veneziano Broccia. Invaluable help came from my family: my mother Annamaria and my father Silvano, my sister Marina and particularly my sister Tiziana. I will always be grateful for the gift of their presence in my life.

Finally, I want to thank my partner Thomas France for being at my side during this gestation with love, encouragement, and pride. I am deeply grateful for having been surrounded by so much love and support.

Permissions and Credits

Abbreviations

I employ the following abbreviations for the editions of Pier Paolo Pasolini's works used in this study. First edition is also indicated.

CG	*Le ceneri di Gramsci*. 1957. Milan: Garzanti.
DD	*Descrizioni di descrizioni*. 1979. Turin: Einaudi.
DIAL	*I dialoghi*. 1992. Rome: Editori Riuniti.
EE	*Empirismo eretico*. 1972. Milan: Garzanti.
HE	*Heretical Empiricism*, 2005. Edited by Louise Barnett. Translated by Ben Lawton and Louise Barnett. Washington, DC: New Academia.
LL	*Lettere luterane*. 1976. Turin: Einaudi.
NG	*La nuova gioventù*. 1975. Turin: Einaudi.
PETR	*Petrolio*. 1992. Turin: Einaudi. Translated from the Italian by Ann Goldstein, 1997. New York: Pantheon.
PFR	*Poesia in forma di rosa*. 1964. Milan: Garzanti.
PPC1 and *PPC2*	*Pasolini per il cinema*. 1999. Edited by Walter Siti and Franco Zabagli. 2 vols. Milan: Mondadori.
RILL	*Le regole di un'illusione*. 1996. Edited by Laura Betti and Michele Gulinucci. Rome: Associazione Pier Paolo Pasolini.
RR1 and *RR2*	*Romanzi e racconti*. 1998. Edited by Walter Siti and Silvia De Laude. 2 vols. Milan: Mondadori.
RT	*La religione del mio tempo*. 1961. Milan: Garzanti.
SC	*Il sogno del centauro*. 1983. Edited by Jean Duflot. Rome: Editori Riuniti.
SCOR	*Scritti Corsari*. 1975. Milan: Garzanti.
SLA1 and *SLA2*	*Saggi sulla Letteratura e sull'Arte*. 2003. Edited by Walter Siti and Silvia De Laude. 2 vols. Milan: Mondadori.
SP	*Appunti per un film su San Paolo*. 1977. Turin: Einaudi.

SPS	*Saggi sulla politica e sulla società.* 1999. Edited by Walter Siti and Silvia De Laude. Milan: Mondadori. © Mondadori 1999
TO	*Trasumanar e organizzar.* 1971. Milan: Garzanti.
TP1 and *TP2*	*Tutte le poesie.* 2003. Edited by Walter Siti. 2 vols. Milan: Mondadori.
USI	*L'Usignolo della Chiesa Cattolica.* 1958. Milan: Longanesi.

PASOLINI

The Sacred Flesh

Introduction

Forty years after Pier Paolo Pasolini's brutal assassination, Italian scholars on both the Left and Right still debate the legacy of one of the most controversial intellectuals of the Italian *Novecento*, each side attempting to claim it as its own. As Giacomo Marramao wrote, "Bitter is the fate of disorganic intellectuals, the only intellectuals worthy of the name: to be the cause of scandal for the Right as well as for the Left, even after having provided both with the weapons of criticism against any type of reification" (Baldoni and Borgna 2010, 10).[1] Indeed, Pasolini's body of work remains a monument to the disorganic intellectual who cannot be assimilated by the body of the nation: like his own violated body, Pasolini's oeuvre represents an uncanny source of inspiration and uneasiness, a haunting presence in Italy's cultural landscape.

As poet, novelist, dramatist, polemicist, filmmaker, and polymorphous intellectual, Pasolini recorded – and significantly moulded – the dynamics of thirty years of Italian culture and history. With his writing, his cinematic eye, and his visceral engagement with the socio-political reality of the nation, he probed Italy and the Italians, playing the roles of apocalyptic prophet, nostalgic aesthete, and even scandalous scapegoat.

Italy has been unable to mourn his death: like a Shakespearean ghost, Pasolini continues to haunt political and cultural discourse. He has resurfaced in novels, graphic novels, television debates, and court documents as an enigma no one seems able to solve. Yet attempts to do so proliferate, rivaling the number of pages in his own monumental *opera omnia*.

The body of Pasolini, according to Pasolini scholars today, appears as the erotic, the sodomitical, the initiated body. His writings and his films were completely enmeshed with his corporeality and its desires. He was consumed by his passion for reality as incarnated in life, in young men, in the poor. His *corpus* was cinematic, literary, and poetic: he was his filmic eye as much as his writing hand, his many languages, his fascination with signs. Moreover, the body was central to his poetics: it was a poetics of Incarnation.

In this volume I explore the incarnational matrix of Pasolini's oeuvre, addressing his immanent and corporeal vision of the sacred in his works in cinema and literature between the late 1950s and the late 1960s, in the years of the Italian economic boom.

In a 1969 interview with Giuseppe Cardillo, Pasolini expressed his immanent vision of the sacred in the clearest of terms (Cardillo, in Chiesi and Mancini 2007, 89–90):

> [GC]: *Hmmm. You're a secularist, an agnostic.*
>
> [PP]: … and an atheist. I am agnostic on the question of God. I don't make an issue of defining who he is. That would be dishonest for someone who does not believe in God.
>
> [GC]: *But you're religious. You believe in the divine and say that your works are religious and divine. So there is a contradiction when you say that you believe in the objective and not in the substantive.*
>
> [PP]: There's no contradiction. Ancient, preindustrial man could feel the presence of the sacred in any object, in an event, at any level of his life. Divine manifestations in the stones, the trees, the neighbors, anything.
>
> [GC]: *So what do you mean by the sacred? The root of all things?*
>
> [PP]: Nowadays the sacred world of the peasant has obviously fallen. It's a world I was born into, but as I grew up, I entered another world, an industrial world, dominated by reason, secularism. The contradiction in me is that I still see reality as an apparition. I could explain this contradiction in terms taken from a philosophy manual by saying that my religion is a form of immanentism. I don't believe in a transcendental God, but since reality is a divine apparition, then reality itself is God. […]
>
> The point is that reality is a language. So for me – sentimentally, intuitively – reality is a divine apparition. Through this line of reasoning, reality becomes not an apparition of the divine, but rather a sacred language. But the sacred language of who?
>
> [GC]: *In* The Gospel According to Saint Matthew, *it says "in principio erat verbum …"*
>
> [PP]: You could write a whole book giving linguistic analyses of the word *verbum.* Since I am not a believer, reality is the language of itself. Reality is divine in and of itself. For a believer, my theory is very evocative […].

Recent scholarship on Pasolini has identified some constant elements within his poetics of the sacred. One is indeed the link between the sacred and language, as developed in Giuseppe Conti Calabrese's 1994 *Pasolini e il sacro,* the first book to bring full attention to the sacred dimension of Pasolini's work. In it Calabrese reconstructed Pasolini's approach to this theme with a reading that sought, using the director's own terms and words, "to think *with* Pasolini *beyond* Pasolini" (14).

> There is in Pasolini a primordial, ancestral link between life and language that is grounded in and receives nourishment from that mysterious and obscure source from which corporeality and sex blossom ... The trace that surfaces is that of a thinking poetry which, in the awareness of the loss of the sacred ..., invokes its new advent, disquieted and stimulated from the necessity to rethink it [the sacred] as the unity of presence and absence." (10–11)[2]

Sam Rohdie developed another meditation on the connection among language, the sacred, and reality in Pasolini in his 1995 *The Passion of Pier Paolo Pasolini,* in which he commented that "Pasolini's regressions were ways to go forward ... [He] was trying to disrupt representational forms with poetic ones. He wanted ... to revive a sense of sacredness" (9). Pasolini's violation of reality, Rhodie argued, was a way for him to create a "linguistic simulacrum of it," a language that would allow him to proclaim a reality beyond that same language, which for him was the site both of the alienation of reality and the celebration of its becoming real, of its loss and its recovery.

Conti Calabrese was the first to investigate the sources of Pasolini's interpretation of the sacred, and in particular the influence on him of the thought of Mircea Eliade and George Bataille. Tommaso Subini, in his *La necessità di morire: Il cinema di Pasolini e il sacro* (2008), followed suit, recognizing the impact of Italian ethno-anthropologist Ernesto De Martino's historicist theories on Pasolini's earlier works (in addition to the Eliadian irrationalist interpretation of the sacred, voiced in Pasolini's late productions). Eliade's and De Martino's "sacred" are also at the core of Armando Maggi's study *The Resurrection of the Body: Pier Paolo Pasolini from Saint Paul to Sade* (2009). According to Maggi, however, Pasolini misinterprets De Martino's thought when he attempts to distinguish between the angst of the primitive individual and that of the modern individual provoked by what De Martino conceptualized as a "crisis of presence." In Maggi's opinion, both De Martino's primitives and moderns confront the same crisis of a "void threatening the subject," the difference being that the old apparatuses of myth and the sacred no longer work as ways to overcome the "void" of history in the context of modernity (9).

Scholars have also considered a third aspect of Pasolini's sacred, its relationship with traditional religious discourse, especially in the context of his revival of central Christian themes. For example, in his *Vital Crises in Italian Cinema* (1995), Paul Adam Sitney characterized Pasolini's *Accattone* as a form of hagiography and Accattone himself as a parodic saint. Around the same time, in the 1995 proceedings of a conference on Pasolini and the sacred held in Venzone, Italy, Remo Cacitti pointed out the parallel between Pasolini's vision of the sacred and the theological debate on the "death of God" in the 1960s. More recently, the sacrificial paradigm of the scapegoat as a central feature of Pasolini's sacred was the focus of Stefania Rimini's *La ferita e l'assenza* (2007). Rimini investigated the theme of martyrdom in Pasolini's work, interpreting it as a phenomenon caught between the word's etymological meaning, that is, witnessing, and its embodiment in the figures of fate, violence, redemption, ritual, and holocaust. Her reading was based on a "transcendent" interpretation of Pasolini's sacred, an interpretation that also guided Tommaso Subini's *La necessità di morire*, in which the author centred his inquiry on death as the crucial image of Pasolini's sacred, and on the myth of the death and resurrection of Christ as the antidote to the crisis of presence death provokes.

A fourth element of Pasolini's vision of the sacred developed by recent scholarship is the role of forces operating on the margins of history. In *Sex, the Self and the Sacred* (2007), Colleen Ryan-Scheutz highlighted the connection between sacred and authenticity in Pasolini, analysing the general process of desecration in the global configuration of neo-capitalism, and identifying the signifiers of this threatened or lost authenticity (especially in terms of the sacred) in women and in "the female sphere." Also important is Armando Maggi's *The Resurrection of the Body: Pier Paolo Pasolini from Saint Paul to Sade*, which considered Pasolini's later productions in literature and film, exploring his apocalypticism, focusing on his homosexuality, and discussing his "sodomitical flesh" as the flesh that, according to St Paul, "needs to die and resurrect," "arising at the end of time" (12).

In my analysis, I shift the existing interpretations of Pasolini's sacred from the perspective of the resurrection – either of the sodomitical flesh or of the sacrificial Christ – to that of the Incarnation and to the immanent dimension of "the Sacred Flesh," as exemplified by the Crucifixion and by the death of God.

The Incarnation, sanctity, the concept of *agape,* or *caritas,* and the Apocalypse are aspects of Christian doctrine that still influence contemporary thought, not only in theology but also in radical and materialist philosophy, as proof of the centrality and relevance of the debate about the sacred today. Many theorists of the sacred, such as Ernesto De Martino, Mircea Eliade, Jean-Luc Nancy, Alain Badiou, Giorgio Agamben, and Slavoj Žižek, have made these themes a central axis of investigation. Pasolini's exploration and appropriation of Christian themes anticipated by thirty years contemporary radical theology and its reading of Christian tropes as a crucial critique of late capitalism. This perspective appears, for instance, in Žižek's thought, which is inscribed in the theological tradition that follows Hegel's critique of transcendence through Thomas J.J. Altizer and the "theology of the death of God" he developed in the 1960s. As Boscalijon explained in distinctly "Pasolinian" terms:

> Altizer's innovation was to reinterpret the Christian passion in terms of a Godhead who dies, absolutely, pouring himself out kenotically and resurrected in and as the material universe ... The powerful declaration of the death of the transcendental God is unique as it eliminates the divine work of serving as an external guarantor of meaning; combined with a theologically grounded respect for a divinization of the world in which things mean only themselves (having nothing to point toward), Altizer can be seen as preparing a new way to think of all objects as potential hierophanies. (2010, 4)

Žižek returned to Altizer's claims and his absolute *kenosis* to establish what has been defined as his "atheist theology." "My claim here is not that I am a materialist through and through, and that the subversive kernel of Christianity is accessible also to a materialist approach," he wrote in *The Puppet and the Dwarf* (2003); "my thesis is much stronger: this kernel is accessible *only* to a materialist approach – and vice versa: to become a true dialectical materialist, one should go through the Christian experience" (6).

The God of philosophy dies, as does his role as the "overarching system of meaning" (Boscalijon 2010, 8). It is a God that cannot stop human suffering, but watches it with compassion. It is the suffering Christ of the theology of Dietrich Bonhoeffer (1906–1945). It is a God that offers the only gift he can offer: the gift of himself.

> God doesn't give what he has, he gives what he is, his very being ... From a proper theological perspective, God is the poorest of them all: he "has" only

his being to give away. His whole wealth is already out there, in creation. (Žižek 2009, 59)

God takes our suffering seriously and engages in our history, participating in it with his Passion. His *kenosis* entrusts humanity with the gift of radical freedom – the freedom "to choose death" would say Pasolini. No longer grounded in the "God of Beyond," we are given love, *agape*, which Žižek defined in a political key: "*Agape* as political love means that unconditional, egalitarian love for one's neighbour can serve as the foundation for a new order" (2011, 2).

For Žižek, Christ dies and his resurrection is the Holy Spirit, which consists of the love for our neighbour, since in Boscalijon's explanation, "the bodies of the believers become the immanent, material reality of the resurrected Godhead" (2010, 10). The "politics of love" predicated by Žižek becomes, in the reading of Lorenzo Chiesa and Alberto Toscano inspired by Pasolini, an interpretation of *agape* as a "politics of poverty" against the hedonistic world of neo-capitalism (2007, 116).

In light of these theories, Pasolini's immanent vision of the sacred anticipated – and at times served as an inspiration for – the dialogue between immanence and transcendence and between philosophy (in particular materialist thought) and theology. A fundamental aspect of Pasolini's political, poetical, and philosophical project, this immanent vision contributes to the founding of a materialist notion of the sacred and can be mobilized in contemporary theory to identify a Christian political legacy within the spectrum of anticapitalist subversion and leftist militancy and as the core of an atheist theology. Pasolini's theory of the sacred could be seen as a key contribution to this specific debate. In turn, these philosophers are crucial to understanding Pasolini's theory of the sacred.

According to Pasolini, the sacred does not belong to a transcendental horizon but, rather, pertains to a *hic et nunc* corporeal dimension, which inscribes in the flesh – in its *eros* and even more in its *thanatos*, in its scandalous finitude – the presence of the real. The flesh is the site "of pleasure and pain, suffering and *jouissance*, passivity and mortality" (Caputo 2010, 9), distinct from the body considered as the site of agency, action, and movement. "Flesh aches with hunger but flesh ... is also eaten, flesh is meat, flesh is corpulence, flesh is inseparable from blood, flesh is voluptuous, and when we die, it is flesh that rots (first) and stinks (10).

In my inquiry into Pier Paolo Pasolini's engagement with the sacred, I examine his tragic subproletarian "Sacred Flesh" as an expression of the central scandal of Christian theology, the scandal of the Incarnation, the shocking corporeality of Christ in Passion and death, and the self-annihilation of God. The body at the centre of Pasolini's work is the incarnated body of Christ stripped of any hope for resurrection or redemption. Christ becomes the subproletarian flesh, agonizing in a commodified, hopeless world. The flesh that dies also embodies, on its surface, the full presence of life in all its vitality and energy, in total exposure. Pasolini's understanding of the sacred as a heretical vision, expressed in the sacredness of the Flesh, focuses specifically on the mystery of the Incarnation as a foundational model. The only possible fate is the cross, with no other reality than the tragedy and the epic grandeur of human mortality, which makes a story, a destiny, a human life out of our inconclusive actions and incomprehensible trajectories.

Furthermore, Pasolini's vision of the "incarnated body" participates in a longstanding interpretation of the theme of the Incarnation in Italian literature and culture embodied, for example, in the works of writers such as Clemente Rebora and David Maria Turoldo, discussed by Fabio Finotti (1993, 1997, 2007). However, there is an important difference: Pasolini's immanent and atheistic perspective excludes any intervention of grace. Christ's death is thus connected with the Pasolinian heroes' fate, without promise of salvation. As Fabio Vighi's reading of *Accattone* highlights,

> Accattone dies like Hegel's Christ: behind his death there is no suprasensible bliss, no transcendental salvation, but rather the universalization of humanity through the sublation of negativity ... Accattone's "Christ-like" sacrifice is significant precisely because it fully endorses negativity as immanent substance, quite differently from the Christian dogma of transcendence and sublimation. (2003, 116)

In light of a poetics of the Incarnation, in my discussion of Pasolini's "theology of image" – a concept I borrow from Noah Steimatsky (2008) – I show how the filmmaker searched for an effect of transubstantiation within the cinematic frame. In Pasolini, film becomes like the very first icon, a direct imprinting of Christ's body into an image. The theology of the image focuses precisely on the *acheiropoietic* icon, the ultimate indexical proof of Christ's Incarnation, through the emanation of an image of his body. Rather than reading the Crucifixion as an icon of a transcendent reality that generates a genealogy of devotional images, as Steimatsky does, I interpret it as an immanent structure that creates space for the event of the Incarnation through a "production of presence." This concept, elaborated by Hans Ulrich Gumbrecht (2004, xiii), refers to "a spatial relationship to the world and its objects." Both the etymology of *presence* – from the Latin *prae-esse,* to be in front of us, "in reach of and tangible for our bodies" – and of *production* – from the Latin *pro-ducere,* "to bring forth," "to pull forth" (17) – allude to an effect of tangibility that is based on the materialities of communication, on movements of variable proximity and intensity.

As an alternative to *meaning,* Gumbrecht drafts a different typology, defining four kinds of world appropriation by humans: eating, penetrating, mysticism, and deliberate openness to possession. These modalities are reminiscent of Pasolini's vision of cinema as the "Eye-Mouth"[3] device that cannibalistically devours reality, and of a reality as if perceived through a mechanism of violent possession of and by reality itself.

The writer-director is on the front line of fire in these explosive encounters, this monumental wrestling between the feeling subject and the devouring, all-encompassing reality. The Incarnation is the epitome of this phenomenon: it is where God is substantiated into the dying body of Christ, his dying flesh. For Pasolini there is no resurrection, only the tragic greatness of death on the cross.

The Incarnation is also the sacred matrix of Pasolini's stylistic choices, particularly his persistent interest in contamination. It is at the root of contaminating practices such as free indirect discourse and the cinematic free, indirect point-of-view shot, typical features of Pasolini's poetics of *synoeciosis* (Fortini 1993), a rhetoric figure in which one simultaneously gives expression to opposite meanings that operate in tension with one another. The incarnated body comes back to life in Pasolini's crucified Christs or in his heretical, mad, or criminal saints – representations of what I call "subversive hagiographies," or a series of twisted *Imitationes Christi.* In my retracing of Christian themes within Pasolini's oeuvre, I identify two specific models of sainthood – the Franciscan and the Pauline – as exemplified in a collection of films and scripts, from *Bestemmia* (*Blasphemy,* 1962–67) and *Uccellacci e uccellini* (*The Hawks and the Sparrows,* 1967) to *San Paolo* (*Saint Paul,* 1968–74). They incorporate the human lesson of *agape,* in which Marxism and Catholicism converge, embracing the non-believing other.

I focus mainly on Pasolini's poetic and cinematic production during the age of the Italian economic miracle (the late 1950s and 1960s), but I also refer to the last period of Pasolini's work (early 1970s), produced in what he defined as the "horrendous universe" of neo-capitalism. Other scholars, such as Serafino Murri, inspired by the Frankfurt School's theorists – from Walter Benjamin to Theodor Adorno – and their critique of the effects of industrial society, have provided a Marxist interpretation of Pasolini and his work. However, as this study demonstrates, for Pasolini this new industrial order represented first and foremost the worst enemy of the sacred: the commodification of objects and relationships that had replaced the sacredness of life. In Pasolini, the sacred is repressed under a new, omnipresent consumerism: the miracle has become the economic miracle, and the sacred is configured as a return to origins, a passion for the past that is not nostalgia but becomes a revolutionary memento for the present.

During the years of the economic boom, Pasolini shifted from the national-popular cinema of his Roman films (*Accattone*, 1961; *Mamma Roma*, 1962; *La Ricotta*, 1963) to the *cinema d'elite*, and drafted his film theory and his general semiology of reality in a series of essays, later published in the volume *Empirismo eretico* (*Heretical Empiricism*, 1972). These theoretical formulations about cinema and semiology intersected his evolving and contradictory notion of the sacred, caught between a strong immanent perspective and occasional temptations of transcendence. These are the years of the dialogue between Marxists and Catholics, particularly in Italy and France, of the Second Vatican Council, and of John XXIII. Pasolini represents the corporeal arena of this debate, embodying its ascent with *Il Vangelo secondo Matteo* (*The Gospel According to Matthew*, 1964), and its sudden interruption with *Teorema* (*Theorem*, 1968) and with the failed production of his project on St Paul.

Here I trace Pasolini's path by analysing his films, scripts, poems, and interviews and by reconstructing his poetics through his continuous and insistent declarations of intent. I quote extensively from Pasolini's works, not only to map out these authorial interpretations but also to make these documents available to an English-speaking audience.

Chapter 1, "The Sense of the Sacred," sets the theoretical foundation of this work, examining Pasolini's concept of the sacred through his interviews and films, in particular *Medea* (1969). Pasolini's archaic vision of the sacred – which draws on Mircea Eliade's and Ernesto De Martino's anthropological theories, from both a transcendent and an immanent standpoint – contrasts and at the same time converges with the Christian sacred. It retains the violence in the archaic sacred while adopting the Christian focus on the victims, placing them in dialogue with Marxist ideals. In the Johannine age of Vatican II, Pasolini finds a point of contact between Marxism and Catholicism in the concept of *caritas*, or *agape*, while rejecting the other two Christian dimensions of hope and faith. In this context, I note how his immanent vision of the sacred is aligned with the recent debates in radical theology and materialist thought, particularly with Žižek's interpretation of Christianity as the true core of materialist philosophy, according to which "to become a true dialectical materialist, one should go through the Christian experience" (Žižek 2003, 6). The chapter also delineates the relationship between Pasolini and the Vatican through his depiction of three different popes (Pius XII, John XXIII, and Paul VI) as a reflection of the contemporary debate between Marxists and Catholics in Italy. I chart the course of this relationship from initial hostility, through open reciprocity, to a final diffidence and separation.

Chapter 2, "The Passion and the Incarnation," focuses on different Pasolinian Christs and analyses the Incarnation at the moment of the Crucifixion. I concentrate on the Crucifixion scenes of Pasolini's Christs in *La Ricotta* (*Ricotta*, 1963) and *Il Vangelo secondo Matteo.* Here the Christ figures are caught between the consecration of a starving subproletarian "Good Thief" who dies on the cross on the set of a cinematic rendition of Christ's Passion, and the analogical reconstruction of the life, death, and resurrection of the Christian Saviour, seen through the eyes of a believer and the camera of an atheist director. In this context, I analyse Pasolini's "contaminated" cinematic style, based on the subjective, indirect point-of-view shot, and the nature of his "aesthetic" sense of spirituality. Accused by the Vatican of demonstrating contempt for state religion in *La Ricotta* while being praised by the Church for *Il Vangelo,* Pasolini continued to oscillate between the stake and the altar through the obscenely hungry "Christ" embodied by the film extra Stracci in *La Ricotta* and the revolutionary, "Leninist" Christ portrayed in *Il Vangelo.* In one, the Crucifixion scene reverberates with the tragic fate of the poor, in the other with the desperate cry of abandonment of Christ on the cross. Shot sometimes frontally, sometimes with zooms and lenses normally used to film bike races, *Il Vangelo* resonates like a Mozart mass, while Stracci's death in *La Ricotta* is commented upon by the music of a frantic twist, reduced to a still life with a wheel of ricotta cheese – the instrument of martyrdom – in the foreground. The God of *La Ricotta* observes in impotence, while the God of *Il Vangelo* watches at a distance. Christ is all too human, whether poor subproletarian flesh or parrhesiastes preacher,[4] equally condemned by mocking crowds.

Chapter 3, "The Words of the Flesh," investigates the "barbaric" Christology offered in Pasolini's verse script, *Bestemmia* (*Blasphemy*), which occupied the director's imagination for five years (1962–67) but was never produced as a film. Here Pasolini imagines the protagonist, the scoundrel Bestemmia, having a vision of the Passion after an orgy, and writes a long digression about it. I compare this Crucifixion scene with the erotic one Pasolini described in his poem "Crucifixion" in *L'usignolo della Chiesa cattolica* (The nightingale of the Catholic Church, 1958), where the eroticized spectacle of the publicly displayed sacrifice is all about the intensity and exposure of the Flesh. As Michael Hardt points out, highlighting the vitality of its immanent transcendence in "Exposure: Pasolini in the Flesh" (2002), Pasolini's Christology of the Flesh is dedicated to revealing the humanity of Christ, the kenotic self-emptying into an agonizing body. Through the Passion evoked in the verses of Bestemmia's vision, Pasolini claims a cinematic presence – again a production of presence – that actualizes the Event, that is, the encounter of humankind with the Death of the God/Man.

This production of presence calls into question the semiotic status of cinema: it is not by chance that these were the years of Pasolini's meditations on film in *Empirismo eretico.* His "words of the Flesh" suggest a preverbal and pregrammatical world where bodies speak, a world resembling the vision of cinema proposed by Gilles Deleuze. As Giuliana Bruno and Noah Steimatsky have stated, the corporeality of Pasolini's cinematic signs represents his legacy to contemporary semiotics.

A pervasive aspect of Pasolini's Passions is his fascination with violent images. Jean-Luc Nancy in *The Ground of the Image* (2005) has argued that such violent content corresponds to the violence embedded in the production of presence that constitutes the image itself. Through reflection on the Passion, we may come to understand the importance of death in Pasolini's poetics and cinema: death is what transforms our illegibility into destiny, into a story. It is like montage in cinema; it is what makes us human. Also, it may be argued that art is created inscribed within a horizon of death, more precisely, in response to the death-drive. The artist and his accomplices, the spectators, are inspired by the "freedom to choose death" (*SLA1*, 1600; *HE*, 267), always positioning themselves on the battlefield, always causing scandal. Eroticism and the death-drive return to the centre of Pasolini's incarnational imagination.

In Chapter 4, "The Mad Saint and the Anchorite," I trace the devastating impact of the "encounter" with the sacred in the five protagonists of *Teorema* (*Theorem*, 1968), in both the film and the novel. These characters correspond to figures of expulsion: the madwoman, the saint, the prostitute, the artist, and the prophet. They take on these roles after their encounter with a sixth character – at once a mysterious guest, a visiting figure, a kind of "exterminating Angel" on a mission against the inauthenticity of the Italian bourgeoisie. Drawing on the Girardian theory of mimetic desire, I focus on the maid Emilia and on the rich industrialist and patriarch of the bourgeois family, Paolo. Emilia and Paolo are both on a sacred path, the first as a crazy saint and the latter as an anchorite in the desert of the real. After their encounter with the guest and his eventual departure, they suffer a crisis resulting from the loss of the sacred he embodied: Emilia embraces a destiny of liquefaction in a miraculous fountain of tears, as the fluid sacrificial subtext of a residual peasant and proletarian world; Paolo faces the petrification of his own deserted and annihilated bourgeois subjectivity, transfixed by his transition into a nothingness that awaits a return of the sacred, invoked but indefinitely revoked.

I present one of Pasolini's models of sanctity in Chapter 5, "The Franciscan Model," where I contextualize Pasolini's work from 1962 to 1967. The chapter begins by comparing other films on St Francis produced in Italy, such as Roberto Rossellini's *Francesco Giullare di Dio* (*God's Jester*, 1950) and Liliana Cavani's *Francesco di Assisi* (*Francis of Assisi*, 1966). My analysis establishes a parallel between Pasolini's meditation on the Franciscan model and his cinematic essays of the 1960s, later published in the volume *Empirismo eretico* (1972). I concentrate on comparing Pasolini's "own" realism with the neo-realist tradition. I also compare Pasolini's comic and tragic Franciscanism in *Bestemmia* and *Uccellacci e uccellini* with the Franciscan model proposed by Hardt and Negri, which interprets Francis as the ultimate militant communist subject.

The final chapter, entitled "The Pauline Model," explores Pasolini's appropriation of the apostle as his own cinematic alter ego, as evidenced by his unfilmed project *San Paolo* (*Saint Paul*, 1966–68, 1974; published posthumously in 1977). For Pasolini, St Paul has a schizophrenic personality: he is both saint and priest. As a saint, he is tormented by his homosexuality, but it is precisely through this sexual difference that his saintliness manifests itself as the union of *eros* and *agape*. As the priest who will help to found the Church, he is an unwitting agent of satanic forces.

Another paradox in Pasolini's St Paul is the ultimate irrelevance of his sacred word, despite the fact that its real, relevant, absolute meaning still resonates in the disenchanted, alienated world of neo-capitalism. Paul dies, but his bleeding heart is aflame with charity, an apotheosis that materialist thought (Žižek and Badiou,[5] for instance) still interrogates and re-elaborates. Paul embodies both the scandal of the cross and the scandal of power: he is a man of the Church as an institution and – through the "sickness" and "weakness" of his sexual difference – he is a revolutionary saint, a possible paradigm for the modern militant.

Pasolini also plays on the ambivalence of saintliness, writing stories of criminal saints, cheaters, and pretenders of the sacred who achieve saintliness despite their dishonesty and cynicism. His parodies of the Pauline model play with satanic investitures. The result is always the victory of the sacred – either benign or demonic – and the defeat of the cynical protagonist through his/her own sacrifice.

Overall, in these chapters I investigate the incarnational matrix of Pasolini's imagination, both in cinema and in literature, and as it develops in theoretical writings and interviews. I demonstrate that the self-emptying god, the dying god without any hope of a possible *eschaton,* is at the centre of Pasolini's sacred, caught between the violent sacred of the pagan past and the Christian sacred interpreted in an immanent heretical key. The sacred emerges as a threatened but powerful hidden reality. It inhabits the foundations of our world and resurfaces ghostlike through the cracks of global neo-capitalism. It re-emerges in the sacred flesh of the underprivileged, who, as forgotten Christs, die every day in obscurity. It resurfaces in the body of Pasolini himself, the intellectual sacrificed for his own courageous difference, his dangerous solitude, his ideological independence, his passion for truth, his vital yet destructive desire to choose his own death.

If his death-drive moulded his art, Pasolini nevertheless did not choose to die on the night between 1 and 2 November 1975. Officially, there was only one killer, the "ragazzo di vita" (street youth) Pino Pelosi. In reality, in Ostia that night there was a virtual public execution, repeated in the interpretations of that death by many intellectuals, including some of Pasolini's supporters. The painter Giuseppe Zigaina, a close friend of Pasolini, wrote five books insisting on the story of a liturgical deadly script that Pasolini enacted of his own free will that night, a sacrificial script retraceable throughout his oeuvre. That reading of Pasolini's murder is undermined by Carla Benedetti and Giovanni Giovannetti in their 2012 pamphlet emblematically titled *Frocio e basta,* (*Faggot, that's it*), in which the two authors propose the hypothesis of a political assassination. Pasolini may have been aware of uncomfortable truths about the homicide of Enrico Mattei, director of ENI (Ente Nazionale Idrocarburi), who died in 1962 when a bomb likely exploded on his plane. Eugenio Cefis, Mattei's successor, is one of the protagonists of Pasolini's *Petrolio,* the mastermind of the new power that would turn Italy into "a horribly dirty country."

Pasolini troubles Italians with his inassimilable body-corpse: a tragic reminder of the agony of a nation born out of the Resistance and deeply wounded by the state terrorism known as the "strategy of tension," which was as deadly, according to Pasolini, as the nation's devotion to consumerism. As much as Pasolini's corpse haunts the conscience of Italy, the body of his work constitutes a reservoir of lucid awareness, of prophetic clairvoyance, and, quoting Pasolini, of a "desperate vitality" (*PFR, TP1*, 1182). It is a meditation on our past, our present, our future, a vital legacy for all of us.

Finally, I understand the risk of interpreting Pasolini's vision of the sacred from within his own theoretical horizon. Nevertheless, I consider Pasolini a crucial interpreter of the sacred in Italian culture who grounded his vision, as he describes it, in an agrarian and archaic civilization, from the *contadini* (peasants) of his beloved Friuli, to the uprooted peasantry of Rome's subproletarian peripheries, to the masses of the Mediterranean and the Third World. Maybe Pasolini's dystopian vision of a fully bourgeois future society could be read as too apocalyptic, predicated as it was on his idiosyncratic nostalgia for the peasant world tied to his youth and deeply transformed by modernity. Nevertheless, I believe that Pasolini investigated the anthropological fabric of the Italian society of his time – and gave voice and representation to social groups that were obscured or silenced on the cinematic screen as well as on the political scene – like no other director. Pasolini expressed the archaic sacred embodied in these remnants of the Italian peasantry, their tragic fatalism, and their innocent violence with an evangelical and visceral *flatus* that was unique in the Italian cultural landscape of the time. In the war's aftermath, neo-realism had brought the hardships of the lower classes onto the screen; Pasolini's cinema stressed their outcast role in the social map of the affluent Italy of the economic boom, and their destiny as designated victims of history. His films are both homage to and requiem for a disappearing civilization that still inhabits Italy's social dynamics.

From this anthropological mapping, Pasolini created unforgettable artistic interpretations of that impossible combination of archaic and modern that constitutes Italian culture. In his recent pamphlet, significantly entitled *Dimenticare Pasolini* (*Forgetting Pasolini*, 2013), Pierpaolo Antonello interrogates Pasolini's contemporary intellectual legacy. Antonello interprets the "hagiographical" turn of some studies on Pasolini as the expression of a vertical and elitist revival of the traditional figure of the "*vate*" (prophet) intellectual. The role of the prophet of the nation, even when conceived within the framework of an apocalyptic ethics of *rifiuto* – the refusal of modern and postmodern transformations of society – is, according to Antonello, an impossible model to follow in our times, particularly in Pasolini's sacrificial modality of martyrdom.

In these pages, I provide reasons to remember Pasolini not as an icon invoked *ex parte* by the whole spectrum of political forces to support their claims, but as a foundational figure in mapping and representing marginal subjects who call into question the homogenization of modern subjectivity with their radical difference and their sense of the sacred. Pasolini traces the anthropological roots of national and transnational social outcasts who can embody a critique of global capitalism and become instrumental for a revolutionary use of nostalgia. Through his films and his literary works, as well as through his own political persona, Pasolini acts as the spokesperson of an archaic civilization that is still ingrained in our reality. He is the agent of a tragic but evangelical, immanent, and corporeal sacred that, while disappearing, still permeates Italy in its landscapes and bodies traumatized by modernity.

Like the guest in his film *Teorema*, in his own violent death Pasolini leaves the legacy of a radical quest we still pursue. Like the characters in that movie, whether as isolated monads or clustered in social networks, we keep on wandering a deserted horizon, tantalized, in terror, or in awe, looking for a lost utopia, for a sacred meaning, for a blessing or a curse.

Chapter One

The Sense of the Sacred

An etymological history of the word "sacred" from its Latin foundations traces the two lexical forms *sacer* and *sanctus* to a common root, *sac*. What is interesting is the ambivalence of the word *sacer*, which can refer to buildings, people, or laws and can mean either "consecrated to a divinity" or, conversely, "consecrated to an infernal divinity to be destroyed," "offered as a victim," and thus "cursed" or "cast out from the group."[1] In fact, in its Indo-European form, "sacred" means "separated." According to the definition given by Umberto Galimberti in his volume *Orme del Sacro* (2000), the sacred is a quality that pertains to the relationship and contact with superior powers, an "other" dimension that is above the human, apart from it, and cannot be controlled by human forces. It is a dimension that powerfully attracts humankind, inspiring fascination and awe, and repels us, arousing horror and fear – hence comes religion, which regulates the relationship with the sacred by processing contact and separation, preserving purity, and avoiding contagion and contamination.

A Brief History of the Sacred

Galimberti maps the history of the sacred from the French Sociological School of Èmile Durkheim and Marcel Mauss, through the theories of Lucien Levy-Bruhl and Rudolf Otto, to Carl Jung, Mircea Eliade, and René Girard, all theorists whom I often cite in this volume either because they provide a framework for interpreting Pasolini's work or because they influenced Pasolini as he matured in his own understanding of the sacred. The modern discussion of the concept of the sacred begins with Durkheim (1858–1917) and Mauss (1872–1950), who identify its two main features: its superiority and its heterogeneity in comparison with the profane. This opposition is radical and can be defined as a mutual exclusion, a rivalry between the two dimensions. Things are sacred in religious thought because society sets them apart: they are not inherently related to divinity. The sacred belongs to a superior state: things that are sacred are replete with *mana* – a Polynesian word that indicates influence and power – and they can be accessed through sacrifice. Sacrifice allows a fissure to open between the different levels of experience and creates a contact between the two spheres of the sacred and the profane.

In contrast, for French anthropologist Lucien Levy-Bruhl (1857–1939), a theorist Pasolini read in the 1960s, the sacred belongs to the primitive pre-logical mentality, which interprets mystical participation as an omnipresent factor in its understanding of the real.

Another important reference for Pasolini's vision of the sacred is German theologian Rudolf Otto (1869–1937), who, in his foundational work *Das Helige* (*The Idea of the Holy*, 1917), claims the non-rational aspect within the sphere of the divine. Pasolini knew Otto's theories from works by religious historian Mircea Eliade, and he applied them in his own works through an immanent lens. Otto identifies the sacred in the *numinous*, which is a feeling of intoxicating awe and terror in the face of the *mysterium tremendum*, the sublime contact with the *Ganz Andere*, the Wholly Other, a dimension that is impossible to define conceptually. When one faces the Wholly Other, the sense of belonging to the profane dimension becomes a creatural feeling. Art can express the numinous through various means: from the sublime to darkness, from silence to emptiness, all realities that express the terrifying and overwhelming feeling towards the *mysterium tremendum* in negative terms.

Dutch historian of religion Gerardus van der Leeuw (1890–1950) – another essential thinker in this context – contends in *Sacred and Profane Beauty* (1932) that in the beginning art and religion were one but over time became separated. Originally, the artistic act was not only beautiful but also holy. Van der Leeuw distinguishes between sacred art and traditionally religious art, pointing out how sacred art does not need to be on a religious subject: "Whoever truly serves beauty, serves God" (1963, 335). Though it is not clear whether Pasolini was acquainted with Van der Leeuw's theories of the sacred, the Dutch historian's interpretation is foundational for an analysis of the relationship between cinema and the sacred.[2]

An essential reference for Pasolini's sense of the sacred is the Romanian historian of religion Mircea Eliade (1907–86), for whom the sacred is "the ultimate reality" from which the power of life comes; the whole of reality can be read as sacred. In his book *The Sacred and the Profane* (1956), Eliade investigates the sacred through its manifestations, which he calls *hierophanies.* These manifestations of the sacred appear in the realm of the profane and through a profane object that is itself but also becomes something else, something that transcends its dimension. The highest example of these hierophanies for Christians is God's incarnation in Christ.

In my interpretation of the sacred in Pasolini, I also make reference to the theories of Carl Gustav Jung, Georges Bataille, and René Girard. From a psychological standpoint, Jung (1875–1961) considers the God image as an archetype, as the deepest manifestation of the collective unconscious. The experience of the God image thus represents a numinous occurrence, with primordial, universal, and eternal qualities that bring on "a revelation of the immanent-transcendent, ... 'God within us'" (Palmer 1997, 141). It is a psychic reality that reveals wholeness and is equivalent to the Self. A Jungian reading of Pasolini's art has been given by his lifelong friend, the painter Giuseppe Zigaina, in his volume *Hostia* (1995), where he testifies to Pasolini's enduring interest in Jung and his alchemic vision, mediated and read through the lens of Mircea Eliade's analysis of myths and rites.

The history of the sacred finds another important figure in Georges Bataille (1897–1962), who inverts the association of order with the sacred and disorder with the profane. For Bataille, the sphere of the profane belongs to the world of work and reason, following an economy of utility. The sacred, instead, goes against purpose through the two primary forces of *eros* and *thanatos,* sexuality and death, and follows an economy (or rather an anti-economy) of *dépense* /expenditure. Against the homogeneity of philosophy, Bataille develops a theory of the sacred defined as "heterology," or "the science of what is completely other" (2004, 102n2).

French thinker René Girard (1923–) is also crucial for his notion of the core of the sacred as the violent act of foundation of a community purged through the sacrifice of a scapegoat. With its death, the scapegoat transfers the violence of the founding act from the community to the sacred dimension. Society then tries to suppress violence and, thus, the sacred, but total erasure of the sacred produces a backlash of immanent violence that threatens society again. The Scriptures have revealed the scapegoat mechanism at the foundation of society, but the modern world lives between this awareness and the threat of increasing violence that cannot find a defusing device.

Finally, a seminal reference for the sense of the sacred in Pasolini is the interpretation of the Incarnation as it appears in important figures of Italian Christian poetry and philosophy of the *Novecento*, such as Clemente Rebora (1885–1957) and David Maria Turoldo (1916–92). Rebora and Turoldo were priests and poets who focused their Christian poetics on the image of the cross. As Fabio Finotti's studies have demonstrated, these two Catholic intellectuals gave voice to the sense of annihilation and dismay of the faithful as well as to the salvific touch of grace (Finotti 1997, 2007, 1993). Father David Maria Turoldo – a charismatic figure in the dialogue between Marxists and Catholics in the 1960s – was a very close friend and admirer of Pier Paolo Pasolini, and embodied similar impulses and tensions within the Catholic world. In 1962 he wrote and made the movie *Gli Ultimi* (*The Least Ones*), the autobiographical story of a poor Friulian peasant boy and his community, in collaboration with Marxist director Vito Pandolfi. Pasolini admired the movie, which triggered much controversy in Catholic circles:

> There is no frame shot in sunlight: the light is always wintery with high and compact clouds, which, in their own way, are as absolute as a clear sky. And the village is always still, in the purest black and white, and the countryside naked, drawn with an iron point ... Little by little, the *suite* of life in the piedmont village, with its grey stone houses and its white roads in the blinding light of the snowy air, becomes iteration, litany: the series of episodes becomes obsessive, and the meanings of our poor human life trespass into a symbology that is as poor in ornaments as it is rich in almost physical pain. (*SLA2*, 2393–4)[3]

Pasolini's vision of Turoldo's Friuli was shaped by his recognition of Turoldo's "absolute aesthetical severity," whereas Turoldo's vision of Pasolini's *Il Vangelo secondo Matteo* (*The Gospel according to Matthew*, 1964) would be permeated by a messianic reading. In 1967, referencing *Il Vangelo*, Turoldo claimed, "Pasolini cannot but believe: he is an ancestral projection of his mother, above all! ... And his mother is the people, she is humankind conceived, born, kneaded Christian, like the Friulian people she comes from really is – my own people, sorrowful and unhappy ... Pasolini is an eschatological phenomenon, that's it" (Subini 2010, xvii).[4]

It is with an eye to such theorists of the sacred that we can now move on to explore Pasolini's work and his specific sense of the sacred, from his cinema to his theoretical writings, in relation to his readings of Eliade and the tradition of Italian anthropology.

The Sense of the Sacred in Pasolini

An analysis of the sacred in Pier Paolo Pasolini's oeuvre must begin with a dream; specifically, with *Il sogno del centauro* (*The Dream of the Centaur*),[5] a long, detailed, and controversial interview given – with much reticence – by Pier Paolo Pasolini to Jean Duflot in 1969. It was first published in French in 1970, with a "Preface by the Interviewee" and numerous captions interposed with the dialogue, so as to convey a possible verbal translation of Pasolini's body language, his facial expressions, and the tone of his voice. Duflot prompts the writer to analyse his own poetic and intellectual trajectory, beginning with his Friulian and Roman debut in the 1940s and 1950s up to his complex cinematic conversion and the "cinema of poetry"[6] of the following decade. In the interview, Pasolini introduces a series of interpretive keys that are essential to understanding his reading of the sacred, particularly in his cinematic oeuvre.

The director answers the accusation of being a "desecrator" and a "scandal-monger" by taking a diametrically opposed position. He claims his role is in fact that of defender of the sacred, taking offence at his contemporaries' indifference to it, and accusing the institutional churches and powers of profanation – even if he is aware of the contradictions of such a stance, the risks, and the potential misunderstandings. He states:

> I defend the sacred because it is that part of man which offers least resistance to profanation by power and is the most threatened by Church institutions ... On the other hand, I realize that my longing for an idealized sacred that may never have existed – since the sacred has always been institutionalized, at the beginning by shamans, for example, and then by priests – I realize that in this nostalgia, as I was saying, there is something wrong, irrational, traditionalistic. (*SC*, *SPS*, 1480)[7]

Pasolini is fully aware of the contemporary irrelevance of the sacred. Nevertheless, he is alienated by technology and contemporary society, with its excessive rationality that has basically erased the irrational aspect of the sacred from its horizon. He claims to be allergic to the technological society of his time and asks, "So, what else can I do other than express the reflection of the past? [*As if compelled to be sincere*]" (*SC*, *SPS*, 1481).[8]

The sacred imagined by Pasolini is a spontaneous, "anarchic," non-institutional sacred, a "forza del Passato" (force of the Past)[9] that is identified with the "senso della terra" (sense of the earth) and the relationship with nature developed by ancient agrarian civilizations. The coordinates of the writer's polemically anticapitalist thought come to the surface here as he traces the history of the loss of the sacred in modernity. Pasolini looks back nostalgically to the mythical relationship of ancient civilizations with nature and the earth from the extreme margins of this "*universo orrendo*" (horrendous universe) perceived, from a Marxist perspective, as the dominion of bourgeois homogenization and consumerism. Talking about his film *Teorema* (*Theorem, 1968*), which brings to the screen the bourgeois condition as the *tout court* human condition with the exception of a few significant historical niches, in *Il sogno del centauro* Pasolini states that

> the industrial civilization was formed in total contradiction with the previous one, the agrarian civilization ... which had its own sense of the sacred. Subsequently, this sense of the sacred was tied to ecclesiastical institutions and sometimes degenerated into savagery, especially when alienated by power. In any case, the sense of the sacred used to be rooted at the heart of human life. The bourgeois civilization has lost it. And what has it substituted for this sense of the sacred after its loss? An ideology of wealth and power. That's it. For the moment we live in a negative time whose outcome still escapes me. I can therefore propose only hypotheses and no solutions. (*SC, SPS,* 1483–4)[10]

The sacred thus represents a crucial juncture where the author's contradictions meet. It is a fragile, profaned fabric, wrenched by the rising tide of commodities and the market economy, the object of a regressive desire, but it is also an explosive survival, a subterranean fault that surfaces and cracks what Pasolini sees as the omnivorous impenetrability of the empty neo-capitalistic world. According to Pasolini, the sacred embodies the nemesis of modernity, the return of the uncanny archaic that shatters the apparent coherence of bourgeois existence, as shown by many of his late 1960s films, from *Teorema* (1968) to *Medea* (1969).

The director defines in detail the sense of the sacred in ancient agrarian civilizations in *Medea.* In this work, the sacred consists of the relationship between a "non-natural" vision and a "hierophanic" perception of nature, as outlined in the first lines spoken by the centaur, who initiates young Jason into myth and religion. The centaur aptly embodies the mystery of the sacred, for which he speaks in his own double nature – human and animal – and in his sublime and terrifying ambivalence:

> CENTAUR – Everything is holy; everything is holy; everything is holy. There is nothing natural in nature, my boy, keep that always in mind. When nature appears natural to you, everything is over – and something else will begin.

> Farewell sky, farewell sea! What a beautiful sky! Close, happy! Say, does it look to you like there's even a little bit of it that is not un-natural? That is not possessed by some God? And so also is the sea, on this day when you are thirteen, and you fish with your feet in the warm water. Look behind your shoulders! What do you see? Anything natural, by chance? No, it's an apparition that you see behind you, with the clouds mirrored in the still heavy water of this third hour in the afternoon!
>
> ... Look down there ... that black strip on a sea as shiny and pink as oil. And those tree shadows ... those reed thickets ... everywhere your eyes look, a God is hiding!
>
> And if by any chance there isn't one, they left there the signs of their sacred presence, either silence or the smell of grass, or the coolness of fresh water ...
>
> Ah yes, everything is holy, but holiness is also a curse. The Gods who love – at the same time – also hate. (*PPC1*, 1274–5)[11]

Pasolini's childhood, spent in the maternal peasant Friuli of his first collections of poems, was immersed in that same sense of the sacred and similar hierophanies. Later, Pasolini's sacred was theoretically validated by the ethnic-anthropological texts the writer discovered in the 1960s, from Frazer to Levy-Bruhl to the pages of historian Mircea Eliade's *Traité d'histoire des religions.*[12]

Mircea Eliade's words – with some minimal variation – are those Pasolini puts in the centaur's mouth when Jason, now an adult and about to leave for Iolcos and Aea to conquer the Golden Fleece, abandons a mythical view of nature and enters a historical rational dimension; he lets *ratio* (instrumental logic) prevail over magical thinking. It is the centaur himself who predicts the loss of the sacred symbolized by the Argonauts' conquest of the Fleece. As the *axis mundi* of Medea's world, the Fleece is the centre of a barbaric agrarian society founded upon the myth of eternal return and sowing cycles, which is destined to be vanquished by the "abulic technician" Jason (*SPS,* 1504), exclusively intent on reaching the immediate practical goals of success and power. "Give life to the seed and be reborn with the seed": these words of Medea who, back in the Colchis, celebrates a sacrificial rite for a propitious harvest, are juxtaposed with the centaur's disillusionment as he announces that Jason is destined to abuse his power in the name of the *logos* and to abandon the sense of the sacred he previously described – in Eliade's words, *verbatim*:

> CENTAUR: What man *saw* in grain, discovering agriculture, what man *learned* from this link, what he *understood* from the example of the seeds that

lose their form in the ground in order to be reborn, all this represented the definitive lesson.

Resurrection, my dear.

But now this final lesson is no longer useful. What you see in grain, what you understand of the rebirth of seed has no meaning for you, like a distant memory that no longer concerns you. There is actually no God. (*PPC1*, 1276)[13]

As we will see, Pasolini does not forget the lesson of the seed. By repeatedly and fetishistically probing bodies and objects in his search for its traces, the director attempts to recuperate this threatened, lost dimension of the sacred any way he can. As he writes in "Battute sul Cinema" (Quips on the cinema, 1966–67), Pasolini is pushed by his "hallucinated, infantile, and pragmatic love for reality" (*HE*, 225; *EE*, *SLA1*, 1544).[14] He is obsessed with trying to discover and capture on film the inner mechanisms of sacredness in human beings and the surrounding world, conceived as a sacred *machina*.[15] Pasolini's approach to the sacred is not purely thematic or functional; it is his language, both cinematic and not, that presents itself as an expression of the sacred. Speaking with Duflot about the sacrality of his first film, *Accattone* (1961), the writer clarifies his wish to return to the film the aura of objects, things, and images, the hierophanic dimension of the presence of the sacred. With his cinema of poetry, Pasolini would thus seem to suggest an alternative to Walter Benjamin's thesis regarding the disappearance of the aura in the age of the mechanical reproduction of the work of art. According to the director, for example, filmic technique does not necessarily destroy myth but, on the contrary, finds it in the humblest and most forgotten objects and bodies, those that do not correspond to the traditional aesthetic canons swallowed up by the society of spectacle and the culture industry. The sacred is found at the margins, and the aura survives precisely where poverty excludes consumerism. In Pasolini's words:

In *Accattone*, sacrality was in its pure state. It must be specified that when I talk about this presence of the sacred, I do not talk about the film in general, about its internal forms, about the events, about the sequences of cause and effect, about the inner qualities of a certain character. I talk about the sacred, one thing after the other, object after object, image after image. (*SC*, *SPS*, 1495)[16]

This fascination with the sacred and the archaic could appear to be a regressive escape from reality, but it is not so for Pasolini or for cinema, for which the director claims the definition "the written language of reality" (*HE*, 197–222). His mythical imagination does not exclude realism; on the contrary, "only he who believes in myth is a realist. The 'mythical' is but the other face of realism."[17] This sounds paradoxical, but it is actually a position that is theoretically justified by Mircea Eliade's thought. As the historian of religion states in *The Sacred and the Profane* (1956), the sacred is the real because it manifests being, while what we called the profane dimension is not true reality:

> Members of archaic societies tend to live as much as possible *in* the sacred or in close proximity to consecrated objects. The tendency is perfectly understandable, because, for primitive as well as all pre-modern societies, the *sacred* is equivalent to a *power*, and, in the last analysis, to *reality*. The sacred is saturated with *being*. Sacred power means reality and at the same time enduringness and efficacy. The polarity sacred–profane is often expressed as an opposition between *real* and *unreal* or pseudoreal ... Thus it is easy to understand that religious man deeply desires *to be*, to participate in *reality*, to be saturated with power. (1959, 13)

It is in this key that Pasolini's realism must be read, especially in the late 1960s, the years of the economic boom and of Pasolini's most cryptic works. It is a realism that, as we will see in this volume, is characterized by lack of transparency and readability, a realism that requires effort to be interpreted and that privileges formal constructions and citations, even as it aims at exalting the pro-filmic. It is a non-mimetic realism, in which a story does not advance in a linear fashion but in bursts, ellipses, and short circuits. Pasolini's vision is justified by its philosophical basis, since he does not believe in the Hegelian dialectic and grounds his thought in the *coincidentia oppositorum*, the rhetorical figure of antithesis pushed, as shown by Franco Fortini, all the way to the *synoeciosis* with which two opposites are attributed to the same subject (1993, 22). In Pasolini, the myth of nature is anti-Hegelian and anti-dialectic because, as he states in *Il sogno del centauro*, "nature does not know 'overcomings.' Everything in it is juxtaposed and coexists" (*SC, SPS*, 1461).[18] This is true also of the sacred, which is never erased but survives side by side with its desecration since, as Pasolini claims, "Being sacred is always juxtaposed to being desecrated. With this, I mean that, by living, I have carried out a series of overcomings, of desecrations, of evolutions. What I was, however, before these overcomings, desecrations, evolutions, has not disappeared" (*SC, SPS*, 1473).[19] He continues: "I am instead so metaphysical, mythical, so mythological ... that I cannot venture to say that a given thing that overcomes a previous one, dialectically, must incorporate it, assimilate it. I say that they are juxtaposed" (*SC*, *SPS*, 1474).[20]

During the shooting of *Medea*, Pasolini reasserts the conflict between the illusory linearity of history and the circularity of an indifferent flourishing nature, the civilization of the line and that of the circle borrowed from Eliade, in the verses of "Callas," a poem from the collection *Trasumanar e organizzar* (Transhumanize and organize, 1971):

> The overcomings, the syntheses! They are illusions ...
> thesis
> and antithesis coexist with synthesis: this
> is the true trinity of a humanity that is neither pre-logical nor logical
> but real ...
> History is not there, we could say, there is substance: which is apparition.
> (*TO*, *TP2*, 262)[21]

Hegelian synthesis makes no sense if it is laid out on an Eliadian nonlinear trajectory; it belongs to a circular one, sacred and meta-historical, where "overcoming" represents a phase that is juxtaposed to the preceding ones. The goal is to return to the origins, whence time always returns. Substance is apparition, which is another way to say "hierophany," the key concept, mutuated from Eliade, in defining the modality of existence of the sacred.

As noted by Conti Calabrese, Pasolini's main concern is finding and acknowledging what Eliade calls "archaic ontology" in every religious belief. The ontology at the foundation of premodern agrarian civilizations (with their immersion in circular time), as well as that of Christian liturgy (inscribed within the myth of eternal return),[22] makes possible the expressive turn to the auscultation of the traces of the sacred that emerge from the primogenial nuclei of sex, laughter, and death. As clearly evidenced by Duflot in his comments to Pasolini, the director's poetics thus condenses around these great themes:

> [Duflot]: *So that the sacred, myth, ancient civilizations, the peoples of the earth and of nature, prehistoric man, are buried ... without ever disappearing completely. In the heart of man, the child lives on. At the center of erotic rituals, wild Eros burns. All these presences define a profound ethics, as deep as, if not deeper than, the morality of progress and of production.*
>
> [Pasolini]: The tragic is exactly the definitive rupture of this continuity. *(SC, SPS*, 1506)[23]

The tragic is thus a quintessential part of the sacred: it is the break, the fissure that the sacred produces in the apparent progressive and linear trajectory of history. In this coexistence of primal states within humankind's modernity lies the perennial (and threatening) resurfacing of the sacred as tragedy. The sacred erupts and breaks the surface of history, exploding through the Pasolinian characters who cannot but be physically or spiritually dying.

Pasolini between Eliade and De Martino

If we follow Eliade's notion of archetypes and archaic ontology a bit further, we find that Pasolini, part *homo religiosus* and part historical man,[24] relives both sides of the relationship with the sacred in his imagination and in his work. Consequently, he brings to the screen "hierophanies" that he projects against the background of bourgeois civilization's desecrations. Eliade describes these two poles of human belief, the two fundamental existential attitudes of the sacred and the profane, as follows:

> Whatever the historical context in which he is placed, *homo religiosus* always believes that there is an absolute reality, *the sacred*, which transcends this world but manifests itself in this world, thereby sanctifying it and making it real. He further believes that life has a sacred origin and that human existence realizes all of its potentialities in proportion as it is religious – that is, participates in reality ... By reactualizing sacred history, by imitating the divine behavior, man puts and keeps himself close to the gods – that is, in the real and the significant. (Eliade 1959, 202)

Modern nonreligious man, according to Eliade, sees himself at the centre of history and refuses transcendence. He creates himself through desacralization: "He will not be truly free until he has killed the last god" (Eliade 1959, 203). Eliade's anti-historical vision is ill-adapted to the Marxist historicism that inspired Pasolini's rationalism, especially in his Roman works, with the contrasted adhesion to Marxist ideology in the poems of *Le ceneri di Gramsci* (*The Ashes of Gramsci*, 1957). In an even darker picture, Eliade sketches a portrait of modern man after Christianity introduced faith and history into the human dimension, leaving man in a condition of "being fallen" from the archetypically transcendent horizon. It is no longer possible to read the tragedies of history in a trans-historical key. We can only succumb to God or to despair over the meaninglessness of history and the terror it generates.

> In this respect, Christianity incontestably proves to be the religion of "fallen man": and this to the extent to which modern man is irremediably identified with history and progress, and to which history and progress are a fall, both implying the final abandonment of the paradise of archetypes and repetition. (Eliade 2005, 161–2)

In the late 1960s, Pasolini found in Eliade the perfect match for his anthropological pessimism or, better, apocalypticism, according to which we are living in the age of the end of the sacred, and we no longer can defeat history with myths and rites. The sacred world of the eternal return is pointing towards a never-ending fall. It is not by chance that this vision of the sacred will prevail in Pasolini's last works in cinema and literature, where apocalypticism takes over through the paradigms of the "anthropological mutation" of Pasolini's young characters and the "cultural genocide" of the subproletarians.

Another interpretive paradigm of the sacred – this time wholly historical and immanent, and therefore more suited to Pasolini's thought in its first, more Marxist and Gramscian stage – is found in the realm of historicist Italian ethnology and anthropology. It is the vision of the sacred elaborated by Ernesto De Martino (1908–1965), an anthropologist whose research in the history of religions was particularly concentrated between the late 1950s and early 1960s. De Martino studied rituals and myths of southern Italy and other Mediterranean civilizations, such as "tarantismo,"[25] as well as the funerary lamentation and wailing rooted in the deepest archaic and pagan layers of Catholic rural southern civilization.

Centred on the polarity of two terms – "crisis" and "presence" – De Martino's sacred is the immanent answer to the *Ganz Andere* – the Wholly Other – of Lutheran theologian Rudolf Otto, already at the foundation of the irrational and transcendent vision of the sacred proposed by Mircea Eliade. Unlike Eliade, however, De Martino grounds his activity as a historian of religion on a strictly rational and historicist basis rather than a phenomenological one. He elaborates on an interpretation of the human response to the sacred that is wholly immanent and strongly dependent on history – a history from which man apparently escapes at the precise moment at which he participates in it. According to De Martino, the sacred can appear as a rejection of history and an attempt to escape the world, but in every religious development there is "a technical mediation that returns to history from history and that, because of this dialectic, limits the merely technical moment of the mythical and ritual, opening up the mundane and profane to different levels of autonomy and self-awareness" (1995, 90).[26]

A fundamental notion in De Martino's theory of the sacred is that of "crisis of presence," to which the sacred represents a technical response, a strategic tool to reinstate the individual in his or her own presence. Presence is thus defined by De Martino as being beyond merely organic or animal existence, beyond the dimension of the body, but rather located in those human powers that make decisions and choices possible. Civilization finds its roots in what is precisely human, in this presence that presides over technical, artistic, ethical, and philosophical creation.

Presence means "being there" in history. It is the fundamental element of personal identity. It is what allows an individual to take action and confront the regimen of perpetual change to which history subjects all of us, every day. Angst is the sign of the terror history imposes on us, and it is a symptom of the possibility of getting lost and returning to a primal biological level, deprived of the self, no longer able to choose a trajectory in the context of the events taking place around us. The answer to this angst is human action, the development of human activities – in other words, culture. As De Martino explains, the crisis of presence can assume the aspect of something "wholly other," but this radical alterity is precisely the alienated presence that announces the catastrophe of the individual (1995, 61).

The mechanism that allows mankind to remain an active and integral part of history is a process of "de-historicization" through the mythical-ritual nexus. The de-historicization that religions set in motion helps us to overcome moments of crisis by feigning an arrest of history that, in fact, allows history to go on. This mechanism is analogous to the iterations and repetitions described by Eliade. However, whereas in Eliade's theory this process draws on a transcendent source of archetypes, for De Martino it iterates the identical metahistorical in order to allow change and cope with the distress caused by history. According to the Italian anthropologist:

> Through such de-historicization, first, a relationship is established with the alienated self (either naturalized or de-historicized); second, thanks to a vital *pia fraus* [pious fraud], we remain in history AS IF we were not in it: exactly because man's operational powers are not recognized in their quality as human initiatives, those powers are in fact allowed and disclosed, and culture as the TOTALITY of values is made possible. (1995, 62–3)[27]

Like Eliade, De Martino attributes the end of the sacred in modernity to the secularization brought on by Christianity itself. De Martino does not identify in the sacred a transcendent reality but rather a technical process that allowed humanity to develop civilization. Many millennia later, this technical process is in its last phase; modern man thus faces the challenge of finding a mechanism to substitute for the sacred in order to continue to be able to resist the crisis of presence. De Martino fully addresses this issue in his 1959 essay "Mito, scienze religiose e civiltà moderna," ("Myth, religious sciences and modern civilization"), in which he observes that the sacred is not a permanent human need and that it has entered a phase of agony:

> The sacred is agonizing and we are faced with the problem of surviving its death as human beings, without running the risk of losing – together with the sacred – our access to human cultural values or being terrorized by a history horizon and perspective that are no longer constituted by the mythical-ritual metahistory. The choice between human and divine, which has troubled the long history of religions and that, with Christianity, began a dramatic process of maturation, today presents itself in the terms of an actual choice we cannot avoid. What is "sacred" in the traditional modes of a metahistorical horizon, articulated into an organic nexus of myths and rituals, does not constitute a permanent exigence of human nature. It is rather a great historical era that, going back in the direction of the past, gets lost in the night of its origins, and that reaches out to us, heirs of Western civilization. However, no matter how long this era has been, it is clear that we are coming out of it, that its sun is setting within us. The risk of an existential crisis, the need for protective and restorative symbolisms certainly pertains to the human condition and therefore also to modern civilization. The technique of the metahistorical horizon, however, has become obsolete, so that modern civilization is busy organizing a society and a culture whose symbolism may express the sense of history and the humanistic consciousness without resorting to ambiguous double-faced politics. (De Martino 1959, 45–46)[28]

Here Pasolini departs from De Martino: whereas the anthropologist believes it is possible for modern man to invent new techniques to adapt to – and even overcome – the terror of history, Pasolini is closer to Eliade's more pessimistic view regarding modern man's capacity to replace the sacred without succumbing to fideism or despair.

Nevertheless, Pasolini's encounter with De Martino was undoubtedly fruitful. The director was involved with the anthropological and ethnographic circles in Rome, and he collaborated in the production of anthropological films by Cecilia Mangini, an ethnographer and documentarist of De Martino's school (Caminati 2010, 48–9). As Tommaso Subini notes, religion historian and anthropologist Angelo Brelich – a follower of the historicist Italian ethnological school – advised the director during the production of *Medea.* In addition, Pasolini incorporated several elements of De Martino's theory; for example, Subini suggests that Pasolini's analysis of the proletariat and his theorization of its anthropological difference – a foundational axis of his work – are based on De Martino (Subini 2008, 28). In a conversation with Bruno Voglino, Rolando Iotti, and Nino Ferrero, Pasolini explains:

> Remaining at the level of instrumental communication where we currently are, I would say that angst is a bourgeois fact ... The sub-proletariat feels a different kind of anguish, what De Martino studied in his research on popular poetry in Lucania, for example, that is, a pre-historic anguish compared to the bourgeois existentialistic angst, which is historically determined. In *Accattone,* I studied this kind of prehistoric anguish in relation to our own ... the anguish of a Lucanian peasant who sings a funerary lamentation over a dead relative is an anguish that has different historical components than those experienced by a bourgeois like the character in Moravia's *Boredom* ... It's a totally different thing! (*PPC2,* 2812)[29]

Pasolini's adherence to De Martino's theories is certainly not monolithic; the director adopts them or rejects them according to his own sensibility and purpose. As noted by Maggi (2009, 9), in the case of the conversation quoted here, for example, Pasolini in fact contradicts De Martino. For De Martino, the crisis of both the Lucanian peasant and contemporary man is a crisis of presence; even though today we face it with invalid, ineffective tools, that angst is the same. For Pasolini, the two forms of angst are radically different, and the prehistorical angst of the subproletariat is rooted in an anthropologically different realm. That anguish is not the existential and bourgeois malaise on the threshold of boredom, but rather is a primal crisis of survival in the face of death. De Martino does not trace an absolute difference between modernity and prehistory: humankind reacts to the same issues, the only problem being that the de-historicizing device of the sacred no longer functions in modern times, though the crisis of presence remains substantially the same.

Elsewhere, Pasolini contradicts De Martino's statement on the radically different "angst" of the peasant and of the bourgeois, and again refers to him and to the crisis of presence, applying it to himself and his own cinema. In a response to one of the readers of his column "Il Caos," for example, he writes about drug use:

> It is clear that people who use drugs do it to fill a void, an absence of something that gives a feeling of disorientation and angst. It is a substitute for magic. The primitive are always facing this terrifying void, on the inside. Ernesto De Martino calls it "fear of the loss of one's own presence"; and primitives fill this void by turning directly to magic, which explains it and fills it. In the modern world, the alienation due to conditioning by nature is replaced by the alienation due to conditioning by society: after the first moment of euphoria (Enlightenment, science, applied science, comfort, wealth, production, and consumption), the alienated start feeling all alone; then, like the primitive, they are terrorized by the idea of the loss of their own presence. In reality, we all do drugs. I do it (as far as I know) by making movies. (*DIAL*, 549–50)[30]

Pasolini here returns to De Martino's theory of the crisis of presence as a phenomenon that affects contemporary man no less than the man of archaic civilizations, even though in modernity the crisis of presence comes from society-induced alienation. What has changed, however, are the instruments used to overcome the crisis and fill the void. Pasolini gives existential and sacred dignity to cinema by turning it into a tool for survival at the same moment it is dismissed as a drug, as cultural diversion. Cinema replaces the sacred, magic, and miracles – the mythical-ritual devices that make de-historicization possible. In a certain sense, through films, cinema becomes an antidote to history and death, the extreme and ultimate form of the crisis of presence. As Pasolini explains:

> [A]s opposed to life or to cinema, an action in film – or figural sign, or expressive device, or reproduced living syntagma ... – has as its meaning the meaning of the analogous real action performed by those persons in flesh and blood, in that same social or natural milieu, but its meaning is already completed and decipherable, as if death had already occurred. This means that [in the film][31] time is complete, even if only through a pretense. Therefore one must necessarily accept the story. Time in this context is not that of life when it lives, but of life after death; as such it is real, it is not an illusion, and it very well can be that of the story of a film. (*HE*, 243)[32]

According to Pasolini, every film is inscribed in a moral configuration and describes a catalogue of human examples, of destinies expressed and constructed under the sign of death. The director thus acts upon the stories that develop in his films in the same way death intervenes in life, giving back to it a meaning that is, first of all, moral. Giuliana Bruno emphasizes Pasolini's "culture of death":

> A process of fragmentation, juxtaposition, and deconstruction, epitomized by montage, enacts historicity for cinema: montage interrupts the continuous present of cinema and life, and changes into the "historical present" of film and death ... Film, a devouring machine, a "reality eater," is positioned on the brink of death and history. (Bruno 1994, 95–6)

In fact, it is a culture of presence, mediated by the "mythical-ritual" device of cinema that, through films, enables the process of de-historicization once triggered by myth. We are in a film *as if* we were in real life, in history. In films, we live as full of meaning as if we were dead, but we are still alive. For directors and spectators, living cinema involves this game at the threshold of death and history. It represents a "sacred" device that makes de-historicizing death possible, remembering that, for Pasolini, expression is death: "Either be immortal and unexpressed, or express oneself and die"[33] (*HE*, 243).

As Pasolini wrote in 1967:

> Cinema ... is grounded in time, and it thus obeys the same rules as life: the rules of an illusion. It may seem strange but we must accept this illusion. Because those who ... do not accept it, rather than entering a phase of heightened reality, lose the presence of reality: which therefore consists only of this illusion. (*PPC1*, 1056)[34]

Temporality is essential to the establishment of a discourse on presence. In this sense, the time of the film must be framed within the more general discussion of the image of time delineated by Jean-Luc Nancy in *The Ground of the Image* (2005) on the basis of Kant's concept of time: namely, as the pure image of all sensory objects. In Nancy's words:

> This pure image is the image of images, the opening of unity as such. It violently folds together the dismembered exterior, but its tightened folds are also the slit that unity cuts in the continuity of extension. The pure image is the earthquake in being that opens the chasm or the fault of presence. There where being was in itself, presence will no longer return to itself: it is

thus that being is, or will be, for itself. One can understand how time is, in many respects, violence itself. (23–4).

The temporality-death-presence nexus thus established becomes central to the image of cinema. It appears to be the foundational connection among the mythical dimension of cinema, the sphere of the sacred, and the sacred techniques so clearly identified in De Martino's studies. Cinema, too, represents one of the mythical devices available to modern man to escape history; like myth before it, cinema allows us to remain within history as if we were outside of it. To both director and spectators, cinema reveals a more attentive comprehension of the mechanisms of reality; cinema is in fact the "written language of reality," and as such it can be studied and analysed.

The Archaic and the Christian Sacred

The crisis of presence brought on by mourning, for example, prompts the de-historicization process typical of the archaic sacred. Not surprisingly, this process changes with the rise of Christian thought centred on the irreversible event of the Incarnation. According to Ernesto De Martino in *Morte e pianto rituale del mondo antico* (*Death and Ritual Tears in the Ancient World*, 1958):

> The pagan dehistoricization oriented towards the ritual iteration of the meta-historical "origins," as well as the Judaic dehistoricization oriented towards waiting for the "end" of history, are now countered by the dehistoricization of a "central" event that shaped the course of history: an event through which salvation is given and the Reign that has made death only apparent already begins, until the second, definitive *parousia*. (De Martino 1958, 322)[35]

Pasolini's notion of the sacred is based primarily on the religious vision that was still alive in the Friulian countryside of his childhood, a vision that is typical of archaic agrarian cultures that have been influenced by the contradictory syncretism of the archaic and Christian sacred. In the age of the disappearance of the sacred, Pasolini preserves the violence of the archaic sacred while incorporating the lesson of the Incarnation and of the suffering Christ. According to Remo Cacitti, Pasolini's atheism expresses the tragic sense of God's distance from a humanity that cannot stop looking for the divine despite knowing that it cannot be reached (1997, 7). Cacitti argues that Pasolini is, in certain respects, close to the vision of the sacred proposed by the "theology of the death of God"[36] that animated the Protestant theological debate in texts such as Thomas Altizer's *The Gospel of Christian Atheism* (1966) in the 1960s. The movement had been anticipated in Continental philosophy by the thought of Lutheran pastor and anti-Nazi hero Dietrich Bonhoeffer, a proponent of a Christianity without religion.

Bonhoeffer writes at length about a vision of the Christian sacred based on a theology of the suffering Christ that abolishes the god of metaphysics. This view is described in the intense sequence of passages analysed by Paul Ricoeur in his essay "The Non-religious Interpretation of Christianity in Bonhoeffer" (2009). According to Bonhoeffer as cited by Ricoeur, the God who is with us is the God who forsakes us. Humankind lives without God, because God has allowed Himself to be pushed out of the world onto the cross. His powerlessness is His only way to be present for mankind. "This text," Ricoeur argues, "clearly indicates an orientation towards an atheism of the philosophical God and a theology of the suffering God, and it is this conjunction that we must try to intercept" (161).

Pasolini moves within an analogous horizon, where the lesson Christ imparts from the cross is none other than the disappearance of the omnipotent God and the Incarnation of a god who becomes man. It is an all-human god whose greatness, as Slovenian philosopher Slavoj Žižek says in *The Fragile Absolute* (2000), depends on the fact that "man directly is part of the divine Life, ... it is only in man, in human history, that God fully realizes Himself, that He becomes an actual living God" (107). Pasolini's "Christianity" thus anticipates in part the materialistic vision of the Incarnation elaborated by Žižek in his texts on radical theology. We will see in chapters 2 and 3 below how the kenotic dimension of Pasolini's Christ materializes in the crucifixion scenes that recur in the corpus of his cinematography.

Religiosity: *Caritas*

Within the range of different variants of the sacred in Pasolini – now embodied in the social otherness of the Friulan peasantry or urban subproletariat, now in the temporal otherness of classical myth or in the geographical otherness of the Third World – religious language takes on a privileged role. This language despises every ecclesiastical confessional form and favours the barbaric (i.e., what is pre-human) in an age in which the human has become synonymous with the bourgeois. In this sense, Pasolini's language of religiosity can be said to be paradoxically reanimated through the heretical filter of a *caritas* without faith or hope.

Pasolini's obsession with religious themes is incontrovertible; this fixation is frequently acknowledged by the author himself. The titles of his collections of verses (*L'usignolo della Chiesa Cattolica* [The nightingale of the Catholic Church, 1958], *La religione del mio tempo* [The religion of my time, 1961], *Trasumanar e organizzar* [Transhumanize and organize, 1971], and his script in verses *Bestemmia* [*Blasphemy*, 1962–67]) all seem to confirm beyond any reasonable doubt the poetic genealogy of this thematic constant. At the same time, Pasolini's religiosity, tied to a mystical contemplation of the world, an ongoing interrogation of the mystery of death, and the need to "admire nature and man, recognize the depth ... of things"[37] (*SC, SPS*, 1422), strongly rejects an affiliation with any church or creed and avoids any institutionalization of faith. Pasolini is religious in the sense that he partially embraces the condition of *homo religiosus*, notwithstanding his being *homo historicus*. It is not baptism that makes him religious: his religiosity is not inscribed in a Christian horizon in the institutional sense. He does not belong to a church although he is permeated by a culture that is deeply Christianized, surrounded by the churches and sacred art, music, and architecture of Italian civilization.

Pasolini is extremely clear in his vindication of a free religious spirit that goes beyond clerical institutions:

> I do not like Catholicism as an institution, not because of militant atheism but because my religion, or rather my religious spirit – which has nothing to do with an affiliation founded on baptism – is offended by it. Then there's this crypto-Christianity with which the most aggressive charge me, as if it were a mark of infamy. I will respond to them saying that it is rare for a Westerner not to be Christianized, if not a staunch Christian. Even more so for an Italian. (*SC, SPS*, 1421)[38]

Christianity is therefore seen as a cultural imprinting that Pasolini conflates with the obscure and confused sense of the divine rooted in his childhood, a psychological status that can never ripen into faith, as Pasolini reaffirms in an interview given to Aldo Bernardini:

> My sense of the divine is a shapeless psychological feeling that I found left in me from birth, in infancy, and probably because of this it is not very

> strong ... In reality, this ascetic openness, this sense of life seen from the point of view of eternity is always present in my work, but it never explodes and grows to an acceptance of the divine. (1969, 310)[39]

If for Pasolini the relationship with religion is never inscribed within the horizon of faith, by the same token neither does it contemplate the constellation of hope. The sense of the sacred in Pasolini is primarily tragic and centred particularly on the theme of death, which has been considered the defining feature of his religiosity. With regard to Pasolini's characters, Cacitti spoke of a "religion of suffering" (1997, 8).[40] The spirit of Greek tragedy presides over the stories of Pasolini's anti-heroes, but this tragedy is rendered from the (Christian) point of view of the victims who become the author's sole protagonists.

The constellation of hope is present in Pasolini only in the "perspectivist" phase of his Marxism *en poète*. In one of the "*interviste corsare*" from December 1964, "Marxismo e Cristianesimo" (Marxism and Christianity, *SPS*, 786–824), Pasolini reasserts the fundamental spiritualism of Marxist philosophy. In the heart of every bourgeois who has chosen to take the worker's side, "there is, at the basis, this mysterious, remote but irrepressible Christian humanitarian impulse" (*SPS*, 801).[41] Beyond this deep fundamental Christianity, the impulse of the *homo religiosus* still permeates contemporary humanity mostly in its Marxist evolution. Religion goes inward and deeper into the subconscious only to resurface later as religiosity. True compassion and true love come from this latent religious feeling:

> We are still children, direct heirs of men from two thousand years ago. And the religious moment that is in us is therefore still very much alive and very relevant. It is impossible to eliminate it. We still live in that cultural environment that produced Christianity and produced all religions. ... I mean to say that the religion we Marxists refuse *in toto* because we have chosen a different ideology, in part, disappears into our depth, into our subconscious, and there it lives a life that we can never determine, since we do not know what goes on in our innermost depth; and in part, it survives and floats around our consciousness, taking on the form of un-organized religion: it becomes religiosity ... None of us could ever deny a religious element in our relationship with our neighbor. This feeling of compassion, of love, has a profoundly religious root. (*SPS*, 802).[42]

We feel here the Eliadian and Jungian roots of Pasolini's religiosity, which is deeply indebted to the collective unconscious (Jung) or to the archaic ontology of archetypes (Eliade). Pasolini bridges the condition of *homo religiosus* with that of historical man on the basis of the value of the hope/perspective shared by both the Christian and the Marxist dimension. In the same lecture on Marxism and Christianity, the poet continues his analysis of the radical differences between a Marxist and a Catholic, between a fully human and an otherwordly dimension, finding therein an unexpected point of convergence, namely, the dimension of hope. In Marxist terms, hope becomes "perspective," pointing towards the end of history, that is, the triumph of social justice: a metahistorical moment when history ends with the victory of the poor. Pasolini explains:

> In their general concept of humanity, there's a great difference between a Marxist and a Catholic. The Marxist places man's life and future completely within the realm of time, in the sphere of earthly life, while a Catholic projects human life into the afterworld. And this is such a fundamental difference as to seem irreconcilable. However, I believe there is a point of contact. It is exactly that religion that, if it's thrown out the door, comes back in through the window. You know that Marxists ... hold as the basis of their being, of their action, the so-called "perspective": the perspective of the future, what in all these years has been called Hope, with a capital letter. Now, what is this perspective of the future, this Hope that holds up the faith, ideology, and action of a communist? It is, in my opinion, a profoundly religious vision. A communist conceives history as a history of class warfare ... If history is conceived as class warfare, then the perspective, the hope of the communists, implies, postulates, a moment of a-historicity, if only ideal. Beyond the future, there is a moment in which history ends and there is a moment of meta-historicity, of a-historicity, also in Marxist thought. Thus, the Marxist is essentially a religious man. If he founds all his action on strikes and struggle, and he does it in the name of a faith that has victory as its final result in the struggle of the poor against the rich, that is, the end of history, in this he is a religious man. It is in this that, in my opinion, we can see a deep, subtle possibility that the ideological position of a Catholic and that of a Marxist may coincide. (*SPS*, 803–4)[43]

In the late 1960s, with the end of modernity and the advent of what he calls the "Dopostoria"[44] (Post-history), the new prehistory generated by neo-capitalism, and the end of cyclical time, Pasolini will increasingly reject not only a transcendental Christian dimension but a Marxist revolutionary perspective on praxis. Consequently, the future aspires to a return to origins; progress, understood Marxistically in a linear sense, will be abolished and expressed as a "reflection of the past." The moment when the visible line is broken, folds back upon itself, and finds again all its points in a perfect circle, makes the past meaningful and turns life into destiny: this is precisely the sense of death. As a moment of extreme authenticity, death is the only possible narration in Pasolini's immanent world. It is a death that remembers other deaths and recalls civilizations stratified in the memory of cyclical disappearances in an epic of human frailty and suffering.

Asked about the validity of a comment by Mario Soldati on the presence of a historicist and Catholic element in his work (Catholic in the sense of a negative interpretation of history, as in the expression "from dust to dust"), Pasolini locates epic-religious greatness in the individual's trajectory towards death[45] and recognizes as his own this Catholic vein, but adds:

> If that is Catholicism, if Catholicism is the idea that everything will end, that is, if it is an element of tragedy in man ...: however, Catholicism does not say that everything ends, it says that this world ends but then there is another one ... and to me the difference seems substantial. I agree: inside me there is the tragic idea that always contradicts everything, the idea of death. The only thing that lends true greatness to man is the fact that we die ... man's only greatness is our tragedy: if it weren't there, we would still be in prehistoric times. I mean to say that I have accepted Soldati's definition only after he specified that Catholicism is pure sense of tragedy ... Unfortunately in fact Catholicism is not this. Catholicism is the promise that beyond these ruins there is another world, and this is not present in my movies, not at all! There is only death, but not the afterworld. (*PPC2*, 2833)[46]

Also, Pasolini inscribes in the same tragic dimension of existence what is unthinkable for the most orthodox Marxist thought – unable as it is to reclaim the irrational dimension beyond the use of the Enlightment *ratio.* When Pasolini takes on the theme of evangelism in *Il Vangelo secondo Matteo* (1964), for example, his Marxist reading of the sacred text belongs to a Marxism that can face "the charm of the irrational, of the divine that dominates the whole Gospel" (*RILL*, 104).[47]

In the 1965 interview with Ponzi, Pasolini explains how he could discredit everything – even Christ himself – but death, "The problem I cannot demystify is that something that's profoundly irrational, and thus in some ways religious, in the mystery of the world. That is not demystifiable" (*PPC2*, 2885).[48] Later, he repeats the same explanation in *Il sogno del centauro,* where he comments upon the possibility of building the figure of Christ as an agitprop, knowing that this choice would have met official Marxist approval: "Something I didn't do because desecrating things or people is contrary to my innermost nature. I tend instead to re-sacralize them as much as possible" (*SC*, *SPS*, 1423).[49]

The remaking of the evangelical text, however, does not imply conversion. Using a Pauline image, Pasolini describes his encounter: "A fall from the horse ... on the way to Damascus did not happen ...: I didn't fall because I had already fallen and had been dragged by this horse, let's say, of rationality, of the life of the world" (*RILL*, 103).[50] Plunged into this terrible situation, stunned by the sacred but carried away by rationality, Pasolini neither converts to Christianity nor rejects Marxism or atheism. It is the same visceral antinomy between Passion – the lesson of the cross – and ideology that we find in his writings since *Le ceneri di Gramsci*. The director traverses the sacred "without renouncing personal ideas, simply coagulating into images a confusedly religious personal experience,"[51] crystallizing the religious and irrational elements that punctuate his work and personality. The sacred, religiosity, and the adoption of Christian images are not intended to indicate adherence to confessional Catholicism, as the director never fails to emphasize.

In Pasolini's work, Christianity appears to be a cultural or psychological trait, or an element of a subconscious episteme, acquired as a sense of the sacred due to his roots – claimed and invoked – in the peasant and agrarian civilizations that survived until modernity (such as Pasolini's Friuli). For Pasolini, this element coincides with the myth of origins. According to Conti Calabrese, the agrarian universe understands Christianity "in a more cosmic than historical form" (1994, 28).[52] For millennia, the same universe fed the Catholic Church with a sacred that, as a cosmogonic vision of the world marked by the circularity of time or, in Eliade's terminology, as "ontologia arcaica" (archaic ontology), predates the foundation of Christianity. Pasolini stresses this point in a "scritto corsaro" (corsair writing), one of the articles written for the Italian newspaper *Corriere della Sera* in the early 1970s, and later published in a volume (*Scritti Corsari* [*Corsair Writings*, 1975], *SCOR*, *SPS*, 265–535):

> Until today, the Church has been the Church of a peasant universe that has stolen from Christianity its only original moment compared to other religions, namely Christ. In the peasant universe, Christ has been assimilated to one of the thousands of existing adonises and proserpinas who ignored real time, that is, history. The age of agrarian deities who were similar to Christ was a "sacred" or "liturgical" time in which cyclicity was what counted, the

> eternal return. The time of their birth, of their actions, of their death, of their descent to the underworld and their resurrection, was a paradigmatic time on which the time of living was periodically modeled, making it actual again. (*SCOR*, *SPS*, 359–60)[53]

At the same time, Pasolini clearly sees the binary dynamism between the Church and the peasant world, both of which present themselves as repositories of the sacred. The Catholic Church preserved a sort of religious syncretism that allowed it to consolidate and grow its relationship with its devout followers. For example, it adapted the Christian calendar to the pagan one, keeping the festivities for the solstices and fertility rites. Another example is found in the cult of saints. Denounced by Protestant criticism as a remnant of polytheism, saint worship represents one of the most popular forms of Catholic religiosity. The Catholic Church has always been careful to integrate the expressions of religiosity that preceded it; the archaic ontology to which these expressions belong has integrated Catholicism in turn, thus fashioning a new expression of the originary sense of the sacred as witnessed by Pasolini. In Jungian terms, it is the collective unconscious *sub specie religiosa* that Pasolini addresses in the following passage, tracing archetypes among different religions, and finding in Christianity the supreme syncretic form of all the religious beliefs of the archaic world:

> But speaking, discussing, thinking, even rather well educated people *never* keep in mind, for example, that, since time immemorial, the Jews had developed the idea of the scapegoat, to which they could transfer all social evils and erase them with its sacrifice; or that the Virgin Mary's and Isis' destiny is the same, like also that of Christ and Adonis; or even that, before sacrificing the goat, innumerable people used to hold a banquet (sometimes an orgy), a banquet that is reflected in the Last Supper; or also that transubstantiation was a common notion for dozens of peoples who therefore celebrated the sacrament of the holy communion ... In conclusion, if an anthropologist had tried syncretistically to condense all religious beliefs of peasant civilization, he could not have done a better job than what is done in the gospels. (*DIAL*, *SPS*, 1219)[54]

For this reason, even as he rejects the institutional aspect of Catholicism, Pasolini opens a dialogue with the Church insofar as it is heir to and matrix of an archaic sacrality. The dialogue is an "atto di solidarietà" (act of solidarity). Witnessing the disappearance of the sacred in the neo-capitalistic world, Pasolini is keenly aware of the fact that this phenomenon also implies the disappearance of the Church as an institution.[55] From the perspective of the end of history, the Church thus appears to Pasolini to be finally defeated by the blows of industrialism, "finally free from itself, that is, from power"[56] (*SCOR*, *SPS*, 358). The religion-power nexus is central in Pasolini. The dialogue with the Church passes through a "liberazione dal potere" (liberation from power) – that is, the liberation of the institution from itself, specifically the elimination of the Church hierarchy and its reconstruction as *Ecclesia*.

This new Church is destined to lose the countryside and to become urbanized, and as urban religion it must move on from "*pietas* rustica" (rustic piety) to "misticismo soteriologico" (soteriological mysticism). It is finally called to follow the true example of Christ, and "to embrace the culture it always hated, a culture whose nature is free, anti-authoritarian, always changing, contradictory, collective, scandalous" (*SCOR*, *SPS*, 360).[57]

Mentioning this defeat of the Church, Pasolini talks about a possible – and desirable – schism, which should accompany the separation of the Church from power. In his opinion, such a schism should take place in the name of the only Christian value he adopts as part of his religiosity: charity, or brotherly love. As he says in *Il sogno del centauro*, "What I most care about in institutions is the code that makes brotherly love possible. Any institution constitutes ground for possible exchanges" (*SPS*, 1453).[58] And charity is the platform on which such exchanges can be articulated. Pasolini writes:

> I will turn to Saint Paul. In the First Letter to the Corinthians we read this wonderful sentence ...: "these three things are left, faith, hope, and charity: the best of all is charity."
>
> Charity – this mysterious and neglected "thing" – unlike faith and hope, which are so clear and common, is indispensable precisely to faith and hope. While we can think of charity by itself, faith and hope are unthinkable without charity: not only are they unthinkable, they are *monstrous*. The hope and the faith of Nazism (and therefore of an entire people) were faith and hope without charity. The same can be said about the clerical Church.
>
> In conclusion, power – any power – needs the alibi of faith and hope. It doesn't need charity in the least. (*SPS*, 1122)[59]

Faith and hope without charity are nothing other than "amorphous and blind forces of power" (*SPS*, 1123)[60] – the possibility of exchange and dialogue is therefore wholly founded on charity. Consequently, the question is no longer whether to believe or not to believe, but whether to love or not to love. This is the lesson of Christian *agape*, that is, love for one's neighbour – a love that breaks down faith and ideological barriers, a love that is the ultimate lesson of both Christianity and Marxism, the love for the humble, the poor, and the wretched of the world. Pasolini explains that

> only through Charity can we avoid the atrocious inhumanity of discrimination and repression: of the artificial and monstrous creation of the "other" (with the consequent ghettos and the consequent holy lands). And only through Charity can the inhuman notion of the non-believers be defeated, insofar as Charity can recognize Charity also in them (even if it finds in them lack of Faith and Hope, or even if it finds in them another Faith and another Hope). (*SPS*, 1128)[61]

These are the words of the atheist Pasolini, who seems intent on building his own "evangelical-visceral"[62] religion – or, rather, his heretical fusion of class consciousness with the message of the Gospels and St Paul – founded on the Pauline precept of charity. On this precept, Pasolini can base new exchanges never imagined before. A comparison with the theology of the death of God comes to mind again, particularly with Ricoeur's interpretation of Bonhoeffer's idea that the Church is true to its own message only insofar as it embraces the other. As Ricoeur stresses:

> He [Bonhoeffer] likes to say that Christ is the man for others. The true church is the church for others. Often, he says, it has fought for its preservation. But it exists only in pronouncing a word of reconciliation for all human beings. Or again: "The measure of preaching is the non-religious human being. Attending to the non-religious human being measures the faith of the church." (2009, 169)

Thanks to his discussion of the sacred and his anti-capitalistic and anticlerical polemic, Pasolini establishes a correlation between Marxist and Catholic thought, a connection considered as pure heresy by the most orthodox on either side in the 1960s – even if it fell within the open horizon of Pope John XXIII and found favour with such a prominent exponent of Marxism as Jean-Paul Sartre (who strongly supported the Italian director's evangelical choice). As a catalyst of ideological tension, Pasolini was repeatedly "burned at the stake" by the press and in cultural debates, first charged with contempt of state religion – for *La Ricotta* (1963), for example – and then condemned by the *maîtres à penser* of French Marxism (with the aforementioned exception of Sartre) for his "Catholic" film *Il Vangelo secondo Matteo* (1964).

The dynamics of the debate between Marxists and Catholics as reflected in Pasolini's work are recorded by the Friulian author in his column "I dialoghi" in the weekly *Vie Nuove* (from 1960 to 1965), and in his column "Il Caos" in the weekly *Il Tempo* (from 1968 to 1970). The discussion was continued in *Scritti Corsari* (1975) and in the posthumous *Lettere luterane* (*Lutheran Letters*, 1976), a collection of Pasolini's articles published in *Corriere della Sera* in the early 1970s. Pasolini emerges from these pages as one of the most prominent participants in the debate, reflected also in several of his contemporary poetic and cinematographic efforts.

Three Popes

The criterion against which Pasolini evaluates institutional Catholicism – i.e., the Vatican – can be gleaned from his judgment of three contemporary popes: Pius XII, John XXIII, and Paul VI. In his 1958 poem "A un Papa" ("To a Pope"), Pasolini expresses his opinion on one of the most controversial papal figures of the twentieth century, the recently departed Pius XII, fiercely opposed to Marxism:

> It would have taken just a nod, a word from you
> For those children to have a home:
> You did not nod; you did not say a word.
> You were not asked to forgive Marx! A huge
> Wave breaking for thousands of years
> Separated you from him, from his religion:
> But doesn't your religion speak of pity?
> Thousands of men during your pontificate,
> Lived in stables and pigsties, in front of your eyes,
> And you knew it, sinning does not mean doing evil:
> Not doing good, this means to sin.
> How much good you could have done! You didn't do it:
> There has never been a greater sinner than you. (*RT*, *TP1*, 1009)[63]

Pius XII was for Pasolini a highly problematic figure, intent on invading the political sphere with his religious mandate and on incorporating the political action of the dominant Christian Democratic party into the papal agenda. However, his political involvement was not in the name of the poor. Pasolini writes the poem in memory of two people: one is the Pope, the other is the drunkard Zucchetto, who was run over by a trolley in Rome. Pius XII dies a few days later, completely unaware of Zucchetto's fate and the fate of the thousands of poor and homeless during his papacy. Pope Pius did not know *pietas*: Pasolini puns around his name and his betrayed vocation. "Not doing good, this means to sin" – no greater sinner, then, than a Pope who did not act politically with *pietas* for the wretched of the world.

In the same spirit of his epigram against Pius XII, in a 6 May 1961 piece for *I dialoghi*, "Lotta al fariseismo (che è dappertutto)" (Fight against the Pharisees [Who Are Everywhere])," Pasolini writes:

> Italian society appears to be completely invaded by that rot that is the corruption of Christianity. In every action, in every relationship, we always end up putting our hand on this pus, on this infectious relic of what originally was great and pure. In Italy, Christian observance and the small bourgeoisie constitute one single entity that generates the moral rot that mars every day, every action of our life. (*DIAL*, 118)[64]

Initially, Pasolini is extremely critical of the Church's pharisaical clerical positions. In a rather Dantesque manner, he whips the clergy and even the pope for their sins – not according to external, Marxist tenets but on the basis of internal values derived from the lessons of the gospels: "If I have to face a religious 'situation,' I'd rather do it, I repeat, within the sphere of that same religious spirit. I just have to pick up the Gospel in order to condemn without any doubt or exception that cold, arid, corrupt, and ignorant institution the Catholic Church is today" (*DIAL*, 134).[65]

The atmosphere changes radically with the ascent to the Papal See of Angelo Roncalli, Pope John XXIII. Though his papacy lasted only five years (1958–63), it brought revolutionary changes within the Catholic Church. Reflecting on the figure of the "Papa buono" ("the good Pope") after his death, Pasolini comments on the importance of the Johannine experience in "our history," underlining the novelty of the pope's self-ironic stance. John XXIII was trained in the highest forms of lay culture and thus ready to understand both forces of his time – the bourgeoisie and socialism. In 1964, Pasolini wrote:

> Pope John was not simply a good pope, an angelic apparition in our society and our history. He was something much deeper, definitive, in my opinion,

> because Pope John was the first man of the Church, at the supreme level ... who led the Church to live the lay and democratic experience of this last century at its fullest. To live, that is, the best the bourgeoisie has given us since the French Revolution.
>
> ... There is this basic simplicity, this humor à la Manzoni. And then there is a whole manner of expression, of speaking and being that is typical of the learned man, very learned, at the highest bourgeois level. Something new in the Church, humor, irony ... Pope John laughed at himself as pope ...
>
> Could you imagine anything more revolutionary in the Church, in the Church that has always stood as authoritarian, paternalistic, dogmatic, and as fundamentally anti-liberal and anti-democratic? ... For the first time within the Church, in the depth of its Christian spirit, Pope John lived the great lay and democratic experience of the bourgeoisie. He lived, that is, the true reality of his time, and in the true reality of his time, besides this fundamental lay and democratic experience of the bourgeoisie, there are new realities, there is the reality of socialism. (SPS, 794–5).[66]

What Pasolini liked in the saintly figure of Papa Roncalli was his lay and democratic core, "the best the bourgeoisie has given us since the French Revolution." In a sense, John XXIIII was a Pope with a secular vocation, which made him ready to understand the two political realities of his time (the bourgeois and the socialist) and to leave behind the most hierarchical and dogmatic aspects of his faith. It was in the name of Papa Roncalli that Pasolini participated in the dialogue between Marxists and Catholics with many of his works, dedicated to his "beloved" Pope John XXIII. *Il Vangelo secondo Matteo* would probably have been unthinkable outside the climate of the Second Vatican Council. At the time, Pasolini was in close contact with the Pro Civitate Christiana in Assisi, a lay organization that brought together lay believers and a few priests, in the form of a militant *Ecclesia* open to the dialogue between Marxists and Catholics. The special relationship Pasolini established with Pro Civitate deeply influenced his works, particularly *Sopralluoghi in Palestina* (*Location Hunting in Palestine*, 1963) and *Il Vangelo secondo Matteo.*[67] An important moment in the debate between Marxism and Catholicism, in the context of the Johannine climate, is Pasolini's reflection on what Marxists and Catholics share. As already seen with regard to perspectivism and hope, in a passage from a piece in *I dialoghi* entitled "Marxismo e società" ("Marxism and Society") Pasolini identifies in Marxists a stage of profound identification with the Christian message and recognizes three steps in the conversion to Marxism that take on decidedly religious characteristics. The first is a heretical moment, "a strengthening of evangelism as pure religion versus the official, conformist, state religion; or a strengthening of a 'Protestant' moralism" (*DIAL*, 206).[68] The second is an anarchic moment, "a general protest against the pre-established, institutionalized, unberably alienating and suffocating status quo" (206).[69] The third and final one is a humanitarian moment, the transformation of "the first two moments into some form of action,"[70] which makes Marxists "dynamic towards one's neighbor" (206).[71]

Before taking what Pasolini calls a qualitative leap – which leads to shedding irrationalism, individualism, and metaphysical perspectivism in order to embrace rationalism, sociality, and a lay perspective – the proto-Marxist lives in a phase influenced by more than two thousand years of *Imitatio Christi.* Pasolini comments about himself:

> Myself, I'm anti-clerical ... but I know that there are two thousand years of Christianity in me: my forebears and I have built Romanesque churches, and then Gothic churches, and then Baroque churches: they are my heritage, in content and style. I would be crazy if I denied such a powerful force that is in me: if I left to the priests the monopoly of Good. (*DIAL*, 206–7)[72]

Pasolini never underestimates the importance of his relationship with Christianity; he realizes that the upcoming challenge is that of building a new *Ecclesia.* This new organization must especially embrace non-believers in the name of the common objective of *agape,* a value that – as we will see in chapters 5 and 6 – unites the Franciscan and the Pauline matrices of Pasolini's subversive hagiographies, and that reverberates widely in contemporary materialist philosophy from Žižek to Negri and Hardt. Pasolini thus sets off to establish a schism, embodied in the figure of a crucified Pope: this is the powerful image Pasolini paints of the papacy of Paul VI, who succeeded John XXIII. Paul VI had to make a decision of capital importance: whether to follow in the steps of his predecessor or to return to the status quo of the pre-conciliar Church, which Pasolini saw as an ally of the bourgeoisie and fascism. The dilemma is expressed by Pasolini in a "dialogo" of 28 September 1968, "Ora il Papa si trova disarmato" ("The Pope is now defenseless"):

> So far, Paul VI has been a victim of a crisis of the Church that could not have exploded with greater violence or more suddenly: victim, I repeat, inasmuch as he himself was split in two, torn by a schism lived in his own self ... And he seems to understand that he is faced with only two real choices that can solve, once and for all, his anguished impotence: that

> is, either make the great refusal and leave the Papacy, like Pope Celestine V, who was possibly the greatest Pope (and certainly the saintliest); or unleash the schism by separating the Catholic Church, along with himself, from clerico-Fascism, that is, by re-establishing the primary function of charity according to the teachings of the Apostle whose name he chose. (*DIAL*, 495)[73]

The dialogue between the Catholic Church and Marxism is written on Pasolini's own body; institutions will always fight against those individuals who decide not to belong and express dissent. The debate between insiders and outsiders will take place regardless. Pasolini's enduring relevance consists in his offering himself as a scapegoat for the difficult but necessary historical process of conflict and dialogue between religious and political beliefs. It is something that has not lost its resonance, because charity – or brotherhood or solidarity or *agape* – does not look at church or party affiliation.

Tommaso Subini (2004) has identified *Teorema* (1968) as marking the moment when Pasolini breaks off his dialogue between Marxism and Catholicism. *Teorema* received the prize of the Office Catholique International du Cinéma (OCIC) at the Venice Film Festival. In a famous speech delivered at Castel Gandolfo on 18 September 1968, Pope Paul VI distanced himself from a series of events as well as a revolutionary opening of the Church to interfaith dialogue, and he specifically condemned "the approval of inadmissible films" (Moscati 1995, 164).[74] This speech marks the end of the dialogue between Pasolini and institutional Catholicism. Following what had been suggested in a letter by the Vatican Secretary of State, Cardinal Amleto Giovanni Cicognani, the board of directors of OCIC issued a press release in which it expressed its regret for the film award given to Pasolini by one of its committees. Pasolini retorted: "The International Catholic Office for Cinema can keep their award, and they can also take back the one they gave me for *Il Vangelo secondo Matteo* ... I'm preparing a film on the life of Saint Paul, so I will obviously continue my 'dialogue,' but only with independent learned priests and, one day perhaps, with separatist priests" (Moscati 1995, 155).[75] The season of the dialogue between Catholics and Marxists, inaugurated in Pasolini's work and in his own person, thus came to a close. The vicissitudes of the project on St Paul, which I will analyse in chapter 6, will reveal the changed ideological atmosphere and the closing of the channel of communication Pasolini opened during and immediately after the Johannine period.

Pasolini's lesson, unheeded by both the Left and the Right, consisted of his heretical stance, capable of denouncing the inner contradictions of both faiths, Catholic and communist, by placing them face to face with contemporary phenomena and tragedies. Pasolini's meditations were already centred on secularization, globalization (foreseen by Pasolini in the 1960s), and the catastrophic universalism of neo-capitalism – the common omnivorous enemy of both Catholicism and Marxism, whose first victim had been the archaic sacred, together with peasant civilizations. Pasolini fully realized the danger and answered with the courageous example of his solitude and of his intellectual independence, for which he paid the highest price:

> I'm *completely alone.* And on top of it, I'm at the mercy of anybody who may want to strike me. I'm vulnerable. I can be blackmailed. Maybe, it's true, I do find some solidarity: but it is purely ideal. It cannot bring me any practical help ... After all is said and done, I will be able to preserve my independence: *my defiant independence.* That's exactly what ... provokes such hostility against me. My independence, which is my strength, implies solitude, which is my weakness ... Mine is therefore a, let's say, human independence. An addiction. I couldn't do without it. I'm its slave. I couldn't even pride myself with it, brag a bit about it. I love solitude, instead. But it is dangerous. I could praise it highly ... Maybe it is nostalgia for the perfect solitude experienced in the maternal womb. In fact, I'm almost certain of it. (*DIAL*, 557–8)[76]

By targeting neo-capitalism as the common enemy, Pasolini finds himself facing the attacks of his critics on the Right (because he is considered a communist) and on the Left (because he is considered a clerical Catholic) – and he is ostracized by both sides. In the end, what prevails in Pasolini's thought is his disillusionment about the possibility of any kind of *eschaton,* be it a heavenly other-world (with the disappearance of heaven in his last cinematic treatment, *Porno-Teo-Kolossal*) or the possibility of a revolution (although after an apocalyptic voyage through Sodom, Gomorrah, and Numantia – that is, Rome, Milan, and Paris – in *Porno-Teo-Kolossal,* one can still hear in the empty sky the noise of a revolution on planet Earth). The last season of Pasolini's creations leaves no way out: in *Porno-Teo-Kolossal,* Christ comes unnoticed and dies unknown to the world, while the Earth lives its last season immersed in apocalyptic rituals that recall *Salò,* Pasolini's most extreme film, with its genocide of "la meglio gioventù" (the best of youth). As an expression of the demonic sacred, *Salò* brings to the screen the triumph of neo-capitalism, of the civilization of consumerism and entertainment, and leaves us dangling over the abyss. It is from its edges that we can best analyse Pasolini's interpretations of the sacred, which have often been read as prophetic, almost four decades after his still-mysterious assassins left on his mangled body the marks of the agony of a whole nation.

Chapter Two

The Passion and the Incarnation: *Ricotta* and *The Gospel according to Matthew*

A defining aspect of Pasolini's work is his focus on Christ and, in particular, on the crucified Christ – that is, on the Incarnation. It is a crucial theme throughout this volume, but I investigate it most literally in this chapter and the next one. Although later in the book I will examine Pasolini's other Christological or soteriological figures – incarnated in his criminal, mad, or heretical saints – here I analyse the Christ images that frequently recur in Pasolini's work, with a specific focus on the Italian director's treatment of scenes from Christ's life and the Crucifixion. I will thus begin to assess how the Christ figure haunted Pasolini's imagination throughout his life, beginning with his earliest literary endeavours, by exploring in detail a scene of the Passion from *La Ricotta* (*Ricotta,* 1963), and then comparing it with the Passion scenes in *Il Vangelo secondo Matteo* (*The Gospel according to Matthew,* 1964). These scenes also document the development of Pasolini's reflections on cinema as the "written language of reality" and exemplify his elaboration of a poetics centred on a theology of the image and on the production of presence.

La Ricotta

Initially conceived as a full-length movie, *La Ricotta* was realized as a short feature film included as one of four episodes in the movie *RoGoPag,* the title of which was derived from the initials of the directors of each episode (Rossellini, Godard, Pasolini, and Gregoretti). In his interview with Oswald Stack, Pasolini explains:

> I wrote the script of *La Ricotta* while I was still shooting *Mamma Roma,* but I thought of doing *The Gospel,* before I started shooting *La Ricotta* and when I

> actually shot *La Ricotta* I'd already written the treatment for *The Gospel*, and the initial ideas ... Anyway, I hadn't managed to get the film off the ground and so I found myself with a script ready when Bini[1] asked me if I'd do the film for him. But he'd already decided to make an episode film. So that was that. I didn't have any contact with Rossellini and the others at all, I just knew they were doing episodes as well. (Stack 1969, 59)

The protagonist of Pasolini's episode, shot in 1963, is the film extra Stracci (Mario Cipriani). Stracci is playing the good thief in a movie about Christ's Passion that a Marxist director (Orson Welles), an aesthete and a mannerist, is filming among ruins and caves in the Roman suburbs. The opening scene shows members of the cast, some of them still in their angel or saint costumes, as they dance a hell-raising twist. Stracci instead finds a quiet spot with his big family that has come to see him and share his lunch. As in a sacred "last supper," the family eats the small meal contained in Stracci's basket while he looks for a way to bum another one. He manages to do so by posing, however improbably, as a female saint, complete with wig and costume, and then he hides in a nearby cave.

Called to the set, Stracci leaves the basket and later finds out that his meal has been eaten by the Pomeranian dog of the film star (Laura Betti). Stracci becomes acutely aware of class differences when he realizes that the Pomeranian, which eats like a prince, has eaten even his poor meal. With tears in his eyes, he calls the dog "infame" (rotten) and accuses it of thinking it is better than him just because it belongs to a millionaire.

In the meantime, a journalist, a certain Pedote from Teglie Sera, arrives and wants to interview the director. The latter, closed in his isolation and surrounded by empty chairs and discarded jackets, receives him and answers his "naïve," run-of-the-mill questions with fierce sarcasm. He recites a poem by Pasolini ("Io sono una forza del passato" ["I'm a force of the past"]) and then cynically dismisses the journalist with cutting irony, asking him if he has heart problems, because if he were to die right there, on the set, it would be great publicity for the movie.

The journalist leaves and meets Stracci, who is holding the Pomeranian dog. He falls in love with the little animal and buys it from Stracci for a thousand lire, which Stracci, running in fast motion like Chaplin's Little Tramp to a nearby street vendor, immediately spends on some ricotta wheels. When he returns, he hides the basket with the ricotta but is interrupted when he is called to the set to be tied to a cross while the other members of the cast tease him with temptations to which, because he is a prisoner on the cross, he cannot respond: food, drink, and – finally – sex.[2]

Later in the film, the leading actress orders that the cross scene be changed, and Pontormo's *Deposition* is recreated in Technicolor. The *tableau vivant* represents a carnivalesque reversal of the sacred (notwithstanding some occasional sparks of sacrality and the fictional director's aestheticizing intentions), and Stracci's story shifts towards farce. In the cave, Stracci devours a giant loaf of bread and the ricotta wheels, and the repeatedly postponed meal suddenly becomes an entertaining show for the film crew and extras, who, dressed like saints, witness the Passion of Stracci – an authentic saint in Pasolini's view. Stracci is portrayed as an insatiable mouth: he devours in fast motion ricotta, eggs, watermelons, spaghetti, fish, and grapes. The entire Last Supper table is taken into the cave to satisfy Stracci's Pantagruelic hunger as the noisy, vulgar audience of film crew members and saints throws him food as if he were a dog.

The air fills with the notes of "Sempre libera degg'io" ("Always free I must") from Verdi's *La Traviata*, which a small orchestra plays to welcome the producer (the "Commendatore") and a parade of prigs, journalists, and guests from Roman high society. Against the tragic background of the three crosses, everyone chats as if at a cocktail party, complete with the large table set for the guests of honour. The Crucifixion thus becomes a great spectacle, with young extras pouring champagne and technicians showing off their special effects with the thunder and lightning of God's ire. The assistant director approaches Stracci and asks him to deliver his line, which Stracci, stuffed with food, repeats twice with great difficulty. Between hiccups, he utters: "When you are in the kingdom of heaven, remember me." The second time that Stracci exhales his line, there is a deep silence, as if his words were coming from elsewhere, far from the fanfare and chaos of the production party.

Finally, the director yells "action" – once, twice, three times. Stracci does not respond. Someone climbs up the cross to see what happened and announces that Stracci is dead. "Poor Stracci. Croaking … that was the only way he had to remind us he was alive …" the director comments laconically. The final scene focuses on a ricotta wheel seen from behind the credits, at the centre of the richly set Caravaggesque table with which the film opened, and accompanied by the same soundtrack of a devilish twist. Nothing is left of Stracci but the instrument of his passion (the ricotta) in a still life. As Pasolini explained to Jean Duflot in *Il sogno del centauro*:

> It may be my least calculated work, in which all the elements of a popular code that I was trying to define mix very simply: humor, the Roman popular spirit, cruelty and selfishness. It is also the movie I shot the quickest and with the least resources. Its length was so limited (30 minutes) it forced me to be concise. (*SC, SPS,* 1498–9)[3]

There are four protagonists in this Passion. Two are its heroes and two are the social horizons in which they move and that reflect them. First, there is Stracci, the comic subproletarian epic hero who will consummate his tragedy moving about like Charlie Chaplin, dying from the atavistic hunger he is finally able to feed. Second, there is the Marxist movie director – certainly not Gramscian in his isolation from the people and the rest of the film crew – who, above the fray, with detachment casts his gaze upon Stracci's tragicomical vicissitudes from the vantage point of his artistic vision, which contemplates aesthetically both the Passion and class dynamics. The two men are surrounded by the loud vulgar crowd of the film crew and extras, who are ready to camp on the set and sabotage the director's aestheticizing mannerist frames with giggles, falls, and coarse comical gestures – not to mention their proneness to breaking out in a frenzy of dance and cruel jokes at the expense of any victim at hand, including Stracci. This lowbrow crowd at once contrasts with and resembles the obscenely bourgeois spectators who visit the set, a presence that alludes to the mechanisms of production of the society of spectacle and to the dynamics of society at large. Though the visitors' vulgarity is that of a higher class, it is no less crass than that of the set hands and extras.

The term "stracci," which means "rags" in Italian, is both the protagonist's nickname and an iconic sign disseminated throughout the film – "stracci" as "clothes" and "costumes." Rags are the costumes abandoned on the set: simulacra of sanctity like *tableaux vivants* reduced to mere envelopes, empty wraps, and colours; simulacra of art, cinema, and faith. Both Stracci and these other "rags" signify the two antithetical meanings conveyed by this word: they represent either an actual visitation of the sacred or an escape from it.

Pasolini himself reveals this difference in one of his poems: authentic sanctity belongs to Stracci, the good thief, a thief of dogs and lunch baskets, no less "pictorial" than the extras in Pontormo's *Deposition*, or, rather, belonging to the contrast of light in the paintings of Giotto and Masaccio and – from a cinematic perspective – in the frames of Charlie Chaplin and Dreyer.

The Saint is Stracci. The face of an ancient peasant
that Giotto saw against tuff and castle ruins,
the round hips that Masaccio shaped in chiaroscuro
like a bread maker would a loaf of holy bread ...
If obscure is the goodness with which he takes out of his mouth
the basket, to give it to his family that they may chew on it
to the sound of the *Dies Irae*; if obscure is the naïveté
with which he cries for his meal stolen by the dog;
if obscure is the tenderness with which he then pets
the guilty animal; if obscure is the humble courage
with which he answers those who offend him singing a song
of his peasant elders; if obscure is the decisiveness
with which he takes on his destiny of underdog,
singing its philosophy in the thieves' jargon dear to him;
if obscure is the anxiety with which he signs himself with the cross
in front of one of your tabernacles for the poor,
running towards his meal; if obscure is the gratitude
with which, after a happy dance like Chaplin's Little Tramp,
he signs himself with the cross again at the same tabernacle
with which you consecrate his inferiority;
if obscure is the simplicity with which he dies. (*Pietro II, PFR, TP1*, 1150–1)[4]

Stracci embodies the excesses of natural instincts driven by atavistic poverty, particularly those of the most basic of these instincts: hunger. He is the subproletarian without awareness of class struggle, like Accattone. ("Compared to *Accattone*," Pasolini observes, "*La Ricotta* is a variation of the same *suite*. Just like an allegro can be, in comparison to an adagio" [*SC, SPS*, 1499].)[5]

Stracci is resigned to suffering hunger (he fatalistically claims he was born with the vocation to play someone starving to death), yet he shows great vitality as he actively tries every possible way to escape his destiny. He is incapable of reclaiming his dignity, with the only exception of a glimpse of class consciousness in the tears he shed in front of the dog who has stolen his food. With an acrobat's sudden leap, Stracci tries to reinvent his fate and seize the opportunity by selling the movie star's Pomeranian, without knowing that his own gorging, encouraged by the cruelty of the film crew and cast disguised as sympathy, will lead him to the end of his tragic parable as chosen victim.

In a 1965 interview with Bertolucci and Comolli for *Cahiers du Cinema*, Pasolini stated that he had been criticized for not judging objectively the world he brought to the screen in *Accattone* and for not showing the relation between Marxist or bourgeois universality and a certain proletarian particularity. He responded:

> On the contrary, in *Ricotta*, my personal judgment as critic intervenes: I did not get "lost" in Stracci. Stracci is a more mechanical character than Accattone, because it is I – and this is evident – who pulls his strings. And it is clearly noticeable in the constant self-irony. This is why Stracci is a less poetic character than Accattone. But he is more meaningful, more generalized. The crisis to which the movie bears witness is not my own, but it is the crisis of a certain way of looking at the problems of the Italian reality. Before *Accattone* I saw social issues as immersed exclusively in the particular and specific Italian situation, something that became impossible with *Ricotta*. Society has changed, it is changing. The only way to look at the Roman subproletariat is to consider it as one of the many Third World phenomena. Stracci is no longer a hero of the Roman subproletariat insofar as he presents a specific problem; rather he is the symbolic hero of the Third World: undoubtedly more abstract and less poetic but, for me, more important. (*PPC2*, 2901–2)[6]

We can think of a quotation from Marx in *The Eigtheenth Brumaire of Louis Bonaparte* (1852) as the epitome of the whole episode of *La Ricotta*: "Hegel remarks somewhere that all great world-historic facts and personages appear, so to speak, twice. He forgot to add: the first time as tragedy, the second time as farce." The tragedy of the Passion of Christ is thus farcically rendered as the Passion of Stracci – the real, authentic passion of the starving extra who dies of indigestion on the cross.

Like Accattone in Fabio Vighi's interpretation (2003), Stracci is a *homo sacer* as defined by Giorgio Agamben in his 1995 book that takes this term as its title. Agamben's definition comes from a quotation from the Latin author Pompeius Festus' *On the Significance of Words*, in which Festus explained that a *homo sacer* is a criminal who cannot be sacrificed by being put to death as sanctioned punishment but whose death, were someone to kill him, would not be considered murder (Agamben 1998, 71).

Embodying a double exclusion, from the human and from the divine, in his starving excess Stracci represents life at its barest. He is already the object of a *sacratio*, first as farce (when, tied on the cross on the ground, he is denied food, water, and sex); second as both farce and tragedy (in the fatal last supper in the underworld of the Roman caves, where he is condemned to death through neither sacrifice nor murder); and third as pure tragedy, when he dies of indigestion on the cross.

Stracci embraces his condition as the abject of history, "the point of inherent exception/exclusion ... the only point of true universality" in the global order (Žižek, 2000, 224). Like Accattone and all of Pasolini's heroes, he has only the "freedom to choose death" (*HE*, 267). Devoted to the infernal divinities of his own hunger, Stracci gorges himself to death and dies on the cross by fatally reversing his destiny of starvation. Between the sinister carnivalesque *sacratio* of the last supper and the epitaph pronounced by the director, the poor extra rips apart the narrative of the Passion, becoming what Vighi calls the subject "out of joint," representing "the traumatic encounter with the excluded other" (2003, 118). The *homo sacer* is the subproletarian flesh who represents bare life doomed to an abject fate and to a death that expresses the crisis of the false positivity of the bourgeois order. It "is precisely within the space of the (im)possible encounter with what throws the subject 'out of joint' that the true struggle for historical change takes place," claims Vighi (2003, 117–18). The sacred flesh is the site of this possibility.

Stracci jams the spectacular machine of cinema and neo-capitalism: "Croaking ... that was the only way he had to remind us he was alive ..." The Crucifixion is the spectacle par excellence for the prim bourgeois mingling and partying with journalists and the producer at the foot of the cross. Yet the final perspective from which we observe the scene is reversed – presented from the point of view of the crosses. Stracci, or God through him, looks down towards the director, a Marxist simulacrum among simulacra of saints-as-*cinematografari.* Pasolini's notion of immanent transcendence is all contained in this shot from above, in Stracci's blank stare, more alive than any in that host of characters who are nothing but dead masks. Stracci dies and the "twist" begins again; the hellish apparatus of the society of spectacle has no desire to stop and reflect. The only trace of the poor extra's martyrdom is a still-life-with-ricotta, the crumbs of cheese signalling a death that both denounces and realizes the evangelical message.

For the others, however, faith is dead. People dance and so does cinema, with Fellini at the head of the line just like Pasolini's Wellesian alter ego.[7] The still life alludes to the death of the sacred, the death of God, the death of the incarnated god – this time as the good thief. It is a death marked by class dynamics and immediately recomposed and erased in the precious set-up of a learned-yet-vulgar scenography of pictorial quotations and the modern "twist." The curtain falls, just as it opened, on a vortex of foods and brocade, a final exorcism of hoarding and excess in the face of the death from indigestion (but actually from hunger) of the subproletarian hero.

In addition to being the name of the poor extra, "stracci," or "rags," also refers to the jackets abandoned on the circle of chairs on the set, an image that highlights the isolation of the Marxist director in his ideological cage. The empty chairs are simulacra of an empty community that appears to be denouncing the crisis of the director's own organic Gramscian identity. With his cynicism and aesthetic passion, the director appears to conform completely to such a vacuous community, starting with his cynical invocation of the death of the journalist, Pedote, who interviews him. His wish will soon be fulfilled by another victim, one not from the middle class such as Pedote but from the people (the subproletarian Stracci, the very victim the Marxist director should presumably wish to protect). Such dynamics of conformity represent Pasolini's intellectual nightmare, one from which he tried to escape along the whole trajectory of his artistic life. The drama of his entrapment within bourgeois dynamics led Pasolini to the forefront of this battle: it pushed the director to reverse and abjure his poetics in a perennial attempt to escape the process of "normalization" enforced by those in power. Pasolini detailed the mechanisms of this enforcement as ranging from reactionary censorship to all-commodifying pretended tolerance, yet always remaining within the neo-capitalistic logic of control and profit.

Welles' character, the director, has no dialogue *with* the people: his interactions are limited to a vertical relationship of leadership and power and a horizontal relationship of detached and objectifying observation. Although he observes Stracci's Passion, he does nothing to put an end to it. Even more than in his mandate of leftist intellectual, he is trapped in his mannerist dreams and in his sarcasm towards the journalist. The journalist represents the same political and cultural power that produces the director's film; at the end of the movie, it is to this power that the director pays homage when he bows to the producer and his guests under the crosses. Turning his back to the cross, he addresses his profession of faith to the Commendatore. Pasolini thus satirizes the economic apparatus of the cinema and culture industry, an industry even a director who claims to be a Marxist finds too easy to venerate – and in the context of a supposedly spiritual film. Inevitably, it seems, the director will adore the icon of the producer (i.e., capital) more fervently than Christ. As Pasolini explained in 1974:

> Welles, a director who has moved beyond his old convictions and has turned cynical, is also an aesthete – cynicism and aestheticism, for an intellectual, are almost synonyms – and he thinks about his religious film precisely in

an aestheticizing formalistic key, through the exquisite reconstruction of some paintings. This, I think, is totally counterproductive and fundamentally insincere for a representation of the New Testament. Therefore, Welles does not represent me. He probably is a sort of caricature of me who's gone beyond certain limits and is viewed as if, through a process of inner withering, I had become an ex-communist ... This could explain his caustic and cynical answers that attack the world from all sides. (*SPS*, 758)[8]

The director represents an ironic exaggeration of Pasolini; though Welles' passion for citations is presented in a carnivalesque mode, his aesthetic choices reveal the anti-naturalistic taste of the Friulian director. His preference for some of the most tormented and problematic figures in mannerist painting (Pontormo and Rosso Fiorentino) as figural sources for his *tableaux vivants* belies that search for "brothers who are no more" evidenced in the fragment of "Io sono una forza del passato" ("I'm a force of the past"). Pasolini plays heavily against his own poetics – the Technicolor passion in *La Ricotta* is actually an enactment of that aesthetic passion for a past that makes him "more modern than any modern." This passion is delineated in the poem read to the journalist from *Tegliesera,* one of the "Poesie Mondane" in *Poesia in forma di rosa* (*Poetry in the shape of a rose*):

I'm a force of the past.
Only in tradition is my love.
I come from ruins, from churches,
from altarpieces, from the abandoned
villages in the Appennines or the Prealps,
where the brothers used to live.
I run around the Tuscolana like a madman,
around the Appia like a dog with no master.
Or I watch the sunsets, the mornings
above Roma, above Ciociaria, above the world,
like the first acts of Posthistory,
which I witness, as a privilege of my age,
from the farthest edge of some buried
era. Monstrous is he who is born
from the womb of a dead woman.
And I, adult fetus, wander
more modern than any modern
looking for brothers who are no more. (*PFR, TP1,* 1099)[9]

As articulated by Adelio Ferrero,[10] there are three Passions in the film: Stracci's authentic Passion, the director's citational and mannerist one, and the false and spectacular one of the film crew and cast. These three Passions are presented and superimposed one over the other, causing now comical, now tragic, now sacral conflagrations. Consider, for example, the crown scene: the sacred object is closed in a box of proletarian "pasta Federici" and held up by two anonymous hands against the Roman sky, at the apex of a farcical crescendo of close-ups of grotesque faces screaming "La corona!" (living, moving *tableaux vivants,* not pictorial but cinematic, whose final close-up is that of a dog barking "La corona!"). The sacred object emerges from its comical context in all its auratic reverentiality and, for a moment, freezes the film time in a pause outside history. *La ricotta* thus reveals its character as sacred film: although its sacrality is threatened and beaten, apparently only a remnant, if we dig beneath the chaos of the spectacular and ideological surface we will find it still intact. This is another movie within the movie, a film in which sacral paradigms are revealed through sudden fulgurations: the Crown; the cross lying abandoned on the ground; the suddenly inspired faces of some extras in the Deposition scene; the close-up of Stracci, prostrate and already visibly agonizing before he dies; the Gregorian *Dies Irae* that accompanies the sacred meal of Stracci's family as well as providing a counterpoint, during the fatal banquet that seals the extra's destiny, resounding in an unreal silence, mythical, belonging to a different time, a different story. These are all metaphysical flashes of a sacred story that manages to reverberate even beneath the ludicrous surface. Stracci's tragedy plays out here and in an "elsewhere" that suggests, thanks to the view from above, the illumination of the plane of immanence with a free indirect point of view on death itself, descending upon Stracci and lingering on the scene, echoing through this world of false simulacra.

The discourse on the sacred, however, finds no redemption or resurrection. The twist of indifference starts up again with no solution of continuity, and even the god postulated by the view from above seems to be condemned – like the Marxist director – to the status of a mere observer, an impotent witness to the scandal of his own death as it is reinterpreted and incarnated in the extra's story. He is a god who dies over and over again in Pasolini's subproletarian characters without bringing salvation. The show goes on, as does the tragedy of the incarnated god, with some other emblem of social injustice, and Pasolini leaves no room for hope. Neither revolution nor salvation is possible for Stracci and the subproletarian world he represents. Thus, the humble Masaccioesque neo-realist chiaroscuro of Pasolini's camerawork, full of Franciscan dignity and simplicity, is dramatically translated into the vibrant, glowing, and visibly false colours of the Technicolor twist. This shift marks the end of Rossellini's aura and of the auroral neo-realist world, replaced by a kind of cinema that is coarse and visionary, a postmodern pastiche that no longer believes in the possibility of palingenesis and merely recycles the simulacra of a past that will not return.

Already in 1963, the arc of development of the story presented in *La Ricotta* – hopeless but sacred, comical and tragic at the same time – exposes the dangers of some developments of postmodernism (Pasolini's "Post-history").[11] Quoting Jameson, we find ourselves facing a new historical situation "in which we are condemned to seek History by way of our own pop images and simulacra of that history, which itself remains forever out of reach" (1991, 25).

Il Vangelo secondo Matteo

Pasolini was already planning a film about the New Testament on 2 October 1962, when he was in Assisi as a guest of the local Pro Civitate Christiana association. The little Umbrian town was celebrating the visit of Pope John XXIII, but Pasolini could not decide whether to go meet the Pope or not. Finally, he chose to stay in his room and began to read the Gospel of Matthew:

> At the end, when I put the book down, I discovered that between the first muffled voices and the last bells pealing to salute the departing Pilgrim Pope, I had read all that hard yet tender text, so Jewish and hot-tempered, that is Matthew's gospel.
>
> The idea of a film on the New Testament had come to me before, but that film was born there, that day, in those hours. And I realized that, besides the double fascination – of the reading and of the musical score, of those voices and those bells – there already was in my mind also the actual nucleus and outline of the screenplay. The only person to whom I could dedicate my film was therefore he, Pope John. And it is to that dear "spirit" that I dedicated it. A spirit that is the regal poverty of faith, not its opposite. (*RILL*, 103)[12]

The movie was dedicated precisely "To the beloved, happy, familiar memory of Pope John XXIII." Pope John certainly had a great impact on Pasolini as the emblem of a Catholicism that was open to the original evangelical teachings and as a symbol of an important moment of inspiration in the dialogue between Catholics and Marxists. Pasolini goes on to say, "I was thinking about that sweet peasant Pope who had opened all hearts to a hope that then seemed to become ever more difficult, and for whom also the doors of Regina Coeli had been opened, where, armed only with an immense witty piety, he had gone to look at thieves and murderers in the eyes" (*RILL*, 103).[13] A peasant Pope who went to console thieves and murderers was a Pope imbued with the values of an archaic, century-old civilization; these values rendered him sensitive to the subproletariat's tragedy and therefore the most Pasolinian Pope imaginable. In her *Italian Location: Reinhabiting the Past in Postwar Cinema* (2008), Noa Steimatsky discussed the "intimate" style of the film's dedication to the Pope "on the part of a non-practicing, anticlerical Catholic" (121). We should not, however, disregard the absolute atheism Pasolini professed on numerous occasions; Pasolini was not so much a non-practicing and anticlerical Catholic as he was a spiritual non-believer. He did not believe in Christ as the son of God, he did not believe in the immortality of the soul, and he did not believe in the Christian afterlife. Nevertheless, the constellation of his religiosity is very complex, and it was instilled with a visceral evangelism expressed in his constant attention to the world's underprivileged.

Pasolini's reading of the Gospel according to Matthew confirmed his mystical sensitivity, which was apparent when he described his "fulguration" upon direct contact with the evangelical text. A most powerful illumination results, evoking in the writer and director a dizzying "increase of vitality," a strong "aesthetic emotion":

> As soon as I finished reading the Gospel of Matthew (a day of this October, in Assisi, surrounded by the muffled, alien, and somewhat hostile, celebration of the Pope's arrival), I immediately felt the need to "do something": a terrible energy, almost physical, almost tactile. It was the "increase of vitality" of which Berenson talked ... – the increase of vitality that generally finds concrete expression in an effort to understand critically a work of art, in its exegesis: in a work that may illustrate it and that may transform the initial pre-grammatical impetus of enthusiasm and commotion into a logical, historical contribution. What could I have done for Saint Matthew? Still, I had to do something; it was not possible to remain idle, inefficient, after so deep an aesthetic emotion as I had rarely experienced in my life. I said "aesthetic emotion." Truly so, because it is as such that the powerful, visionary, increase of vitality presented itself. (*PPC1*, 672)[14]

In a passage from *Sopralluoghi in Palestina* (*Location Hunting in Palestine*), the film that producer Alfredo Bini requests from Pasolini as preparation for the movie on the gospel and that Pasolini shoots in June 1963 with Father Andrea Carraro of Pro Civitate, Pasolini reiterates his spirituality without faith. This spirituality is entrusted to an aesthetic rather than a religious sensitivity, but it is no less a revelation:

> You see, Father Andrea, for the two of us the word spiritual has a somewhat different meaning. When you say spiritual, you mean to say primarily religious, intimate and religious. For me, spiritual corresponds to aesthetic. Now, even if coming here I found actual disappointment, it does not matter at all. This actual disappointment corresponds, in fact, to a profound aesthetic revelation ..., my idea that the smaller and humbler things are, the more profound and beautiful they are ... This is even truer that I imagined. Therefore, the idea of these four paltry hills of [Christ's] preaching has become an aesthetic idea and thus, spiritual. (*SP, PPC1,* 666)[15]

The evangelical ideal relived as an aesthetic and ethical formula states that "the smaller and humbler things are, the more profound and beautiful they are." As emphasized by one of Pasolini's theorizing guardian angels, Erich Auerbach, in *Mimesis: The Representation of Reality in Western Literature,* this is the lesson in realism that Pasolini draws from the Gospel and from the mystery of the Incarnation. Discussing the episode of Peter's denial of Christ in the Gospel of Mark, Auerbach underlines Peter's importance:

> Peter is no mere accessory figure ... He is the image of man in the highest and deepest and most tragic sense. Of course this mingling of styles ... was graphically and harshly dramatized through God's incarnation in a human being of the humblest social station, through his existence on earth amid humble everyday people and conditions, and through his Passion which, judged by earthly standards, was ignominious; and it naturally came to have – in view of the wide diffusion and strong effect on that literature in later ages – a most decisive bearing upon man's conception of the tragic and the sublime. (1953, 41)

This is the message of Christ's Incarnation, its unsublimated sublimity – that is, its subversive power to translate transcendence as the totally alien God of the Old Testament into the immanence of a totally human limit, marked by the Crucifixion and by the questioning of faith with the cry of *Eloi, Eloi, Lama Sabachtani?* ("Father, Father why hast thou forsaken me?"). This lamentation shows how God leaves Himself and lets Himself die in order to fulfil the Incarnation. It represents, in Pasolini, the paradigmatic configuration of the tragic and the sublime to which all Pasolini's subproletarian heroes conform. From the Pasolinian point of view – a perspective in line with the most recent developments of radical theology (Žižek 2009, 59) – the Incarnation teaches a lesson of absolute realism: namely that God is impotent and cannot even save Himself. Christ is cast into the human condition, and His sacrifice does not redeem the world but rather prompts it to reject transcendence and to embrace the commandment of love. Redemption is wholly immanent, and thus will not be brought on at the end of time by the Messiah's return, but instead here and now by *agape* within the community of believers. This community is Pasolinian, populated by outlaws who are marginalized and unhinged from the traditional social order, and is thus emblematic of a universal condition of exclusion. This exclusion is the fulcrum of Pasolini's challenge to the neo-capitalist socio-symbolic order: like Christ, Pasolini's subproletarians represent, according to Vighi, "the anthropological breaking-point ... that can cause the short-circuit of capitalist ideology" (2003, 116).

Thus, there was no conversion – not in Pasolini's *Il Vangelo* and not in his own spiritual trajectory. Although the director approached Christian religiosity in the name of charity and love, he remained alien to the idea of redemption in the afterlife. Pasolini reiterated:

> To those who were waiting with hope, that is, to the priests and to my friends in Assisi, and to those who helped me in my philological and historical research, I answer that there was no fall from a horse, as they wished, on the way to Damascus, for the simple reason that it's been a long time since I was thrown from a horse, and I was dragged, caught in the stirrup, hitting my head in the dust, on the rocks and in the mud on the way to Damascus! So nothing happened: I did not fall because I had already fallen and had been dragged by this horse, let's say, of rationality, of the life of the world. (*SPS*, 749–50)[16]

Pasolini sits in a liminal situation: on the ground, thrown from the horse, but unable to experience conversion because he is being dragged by "the life of the world." He is sucked in, pulled down by this life, by its reality: this is his calling, however painful his renunciation of conversion may be.

He was well aware that rationality was holding him down, as he testified in a broadcast by Switzerland Public Radio on 5 February 1964:

> My reading of the Gospel could not but be a Marxist reading but, at the same time, the allure of the irrational, of the divine that dominates throughout the gospel, snaked around within me. As a Marxist, I cannot explain it, and it cannot be explained by Marxism itself. Up to a certain conscious place, actually in full conscience, it is a Marxist work: I couldn't shoot those scenes without a moment of truth, understood as actual life. What could I make Herod's soldiers like? Could I portray them with big mustaches and gnashing teeth like an opera choir? No, I could not make them look like that. I dressed them a bit like Fascists and imagined them like Fascist gangs or like the Fascists who killed Slavonic children by throwing them in the air. How did I envision Joseph's and Mary's flight to Egypt? I imagined it remembering certain evacuations, certain marches of Spanish refugees across the Pyrenees. (*RILL*, 103–4)[17]

At the same time, however, the fulguration of the sacred persists, an obscure illumination in keeping with Pasolini's oxymoronic style. The call of the divine is an unsublimated call, rendered impotent by Pasolini's inability to believe. It is a yearning without conversion, a possession of nothing, an event Pasolini observes with fascination but from which he is distanced by his materialist mentality that makes him an objective witness, firmly planted in reality. His realism is as religiously evangelical as it is politically aware. It is the light of historical truth that shines in the darkened gaze of those who are fulgurated without faith. Referring to a poem titled "La domenica uliva" from his first collection of poetry, *Poesie a Casarsa*, Pasolini underlined two verses: "'Christ calls me, BUT WITH NO LIGHT.' These two verses could be an epigraph that I could place on my *Gospel* even today" (*SPS*, 750).[18]

Behind Pasolini's fall from the horse is the knot of that torsion between the subject and the world; this knot is exemplified by the *synoeciosis* that Fortini identified as Pasolini's favourite rhetorical figure. This coupling of binaries is also the foundation of the director's linguistic theory and his vision of the world. As Marco Bazzocchi emphasizes, "synoeciosis is a way to go back once more to the foundational word, a word that contains the co-presence of all opposites and can never find its geographical place, almost to the point of self-destruction."[19]

The supreme matrix of the *synoeciosis* is the figure of God emptying Himself into Man, who contemplates the coexistence of two opposite entities incarnated in Christ. As a consequence, nested in Christology we also find the aesthetic lesson that presides over the writer and director's stylistic choices in the name of contamination and of free indirect speech. These are phenomena that comprehend the co-presence of the sacred and profane and of two opposed subjectivities, two voices in one word, in one styleme. "Contamination" constitutes the main horizon of Pasolini's stylistic and linguistic interventions both in literature and film. In a seminal interview in *Bianco e nero*, Pasolini explained:

> The sign under which I work is always that of contamination. If you read a page from my books, you will actually see that contamination is the predominant stylistic element because I, coming from a bourgeois world, and not only bourgeois but, at least in my youth, from the most refined parts of that world, as reader of decadent writers among the most refined etcetera, etcetera, I have arrived at my own world. Consequently, it was inevitable for *pastiche* to be born. And so, in a page from my novels, there are at least three levels on which I move, that is, the dialogue of the characters who speak in the dialect, in a jargon, in the most vulgar, most physical jargon, I would say; then, the free indirect speech that is my characters' inner monologue, and finally, the narrative or didactic component, which is my own. Now, these three linguistic levels cannot live each in its separate sphere without ever meeting the others: they must continually cross and get confused. Thus, in the characters' lines, even those whose register seems to be the most physical and brutal, there is always a *cursus*, often a certain number, hendecasyllables, even, composed also with curse words. It is therefore my bourgeois education that enters the dialogue and transforms phrases from the real world, in a physical register, into hendecasyllables. In free indirect speech then, contamination takes place in a very clear manner, as the dialect, the jargon, get contaminated with the spoken language. This contamination happens also at a higher level that is the level of the descriptive and narrative text. (*PPC2*, 2871–2)[20]

The definition of free indirect speech in cinema is a free indirect point-of-view shot that documents two distinct realities – that of the subproletarian subject and that of the bourgeois director – which coexist side by side in the film shot. Thus, in the case of *Il Vangelo*, the director Pasolini's lay and atheist gaze is presented side by side with the devoted gaze of the believer, generating images in which Marxist and Catholic elements overlap in a magmatic flow. As Pasolini explained:

> *Il Vangelo* posed the following problem: I could not recount it in a classical narration because I am not a believer but an atheist. On the other hand, I really wanted to shoot the Gospel according to Matthew, that is, tell the story of Christ son of God. I had to tell a story in which I did not believe. Therefore, I couldn't be the one narrating it. Without really meaning to do it, I was thus brought to completely overhaul my cinematic technique and from this that *stylistic magma* that is characteristic of "cinema of poetry" was born. Because, in order to be able to narrate *Il Vangelo,* I had to immerse myself into the soul of a believer. This is what free indirect speech is: on one side the story is seen through my eyes; on the other, it is seen through the eyes of a believer. And it is the use of this kind of free indirect speech that causes stylistic contamination, the magma in question. (*PPC2,* 2899)[21]

This antinomic discursive structure that carries two opposite points of view allows for multivocality. It is a polysemy that feeds on its own semantic tension, always teetering on the brink of schizophrenia and yet holding on in this uneasy coexistence of opposites, which actually are nourished by the very contradictions that develop within their dialogue. Again, Pasolini intuitively turned to the figure of the God-Man as a symbolic matrix of such poetics of contamination and "magma," of a polarization that produces meaning. In a polemic against a certain Marxist fundamentalism, Pasolini underlined how he chose to dig deep inside the perspective of a believer:

> There is a scandalous relationship between myself and this man of the people who thinks about Christ. On my part, there are an attempt and an effort to understand that have nothing rationalistic in them, and they originate from the irrational elements that live within me, perhaps from a latent religious state within me: yet, I lived in osmosis with this man of the people who believes. Our two natures had melted. (*PPC2,* 2904–5)[22]

The sacred paradigm of the Incarnation and of the two opposite natures united in one and the same reality can again be seen in action. The process of mimetic immersion into the other's mentality – bourgeois writer into simple believer and vice versa – requires a superhuman effort of the director:

> *Il Vangelo* was for me such a frightening thing to do that, as I was doing it, I had to grab on to it and not think about anything. Reflection came later. To tell the truth, the beginning of contamination, of stylistic magma, of

> free indirect speech, all this came about without me realizing it. (*PPC2*, 2905–6)[23]

The figure of Christ plays an important role in Pasolini's effort to assimilate a religious perspective as an atheist. Almost certainly, this effort involved transferring the image of the Friulian writer and director onto Christ. Pasolini reveals his fascination since his early years with the link he perceived between the Crucified Christ and his own sacrificial vocation (contaminated with eroticism). For example, in the *Quaderni rossi* (*Red Notebooks*, 1946), he talks about a preadolescent fantasy:

> I had a fantasy similar to this one a few years later, but before puberty. It arose, I believe, from watching or imagining a representation of the crucified Christ. That naked body, barely covered by a strange white band at the hips (which I assumed was a discreet convention) invited thoughts that were not openly illicit, and even if I often looked at that silken band as if at a veil lying over a frightening abyss (this was the absolute gratuitousness of childhood), nevertheless, I immediately turned those feelings to piety and prayer. Then, in my fantasies, the desire to imitate Jesus in his sacrifice to be condemned and killed for other men even if completely innocent would come to the surface. I saw myself hung on the cross, nailed. My hips were scantily wrapped in that light cloth and an immense crowd was looking at me. That public martyrdom ended up becoming a sensuous image and a bit at a time I was nailed with my body entirely naked. High over the head of the present, intent in veneration, their eyes fixed upon me – I felt [*blank space*] in front of an immense turquoise sky. With my arms open, hands and feet nailed, I was perfectly defenseless, lost ... Sometimes [*illegible*] tight with my arms stretched out against a gate or a tree to imitate the Crucifix; but I could not resist the unsettling audacity of that pose. (1986, *Lettere 1940–1954*, xx–xxi)[24]

This powerful fantasy of being sacrificed on the cross in public martyrdom and full *Imitatio Christi* is reflected in Pasolini's youthful poetry. For example, this fantasy was apparent in several poems from *L'Usignolo della Chiesa Cattolica* (*The Nightingale of the Catholic Church*, 1958) that were dedicated to the figure of Christ, and – more specifically – to the scene of the Crucifixion. (I will discuss this confluence of *eros* and heresy later in this volume.)[25] The author's process of identification with representations of Christ in a self-sacrificial dynamic is expressed in *Il Vangelo secondo Matteo* by the character of the old Mary as played by Pasolini's own mother, Susanna Colussi, in the last scenes of her son's preaching, under the cross, and in the scene of the Resurrection. As discussed by Marcello Walter Bruno (2008), the feature that links these two figures – Pasolini and Christ – is *parrhesia*, which, according to Michel Foucault (1999), is a concept of Euripides that binds together elements such as frankness, danger, criticism (and self-criticism), freedom, and moral duty, relative to the verbalization of truth.

Foucault writes:

> Parrhesia is a kind of verbal activity where the speaker has a specific relation to truth through frankness, a certain relationship to his own life through danger, a certain type of relation to himself or other people through criticism (self-criticism or criticism of other people), and a specific relation to moral law through freedom and duty. More precisely, parrhesia is a verbal activity in which a speaker expresses his personal relationship to truth, and risks his life because he recognizes truth-telling as a duty to improve or help other people (as well as himself). In parrhesia, the speaker uses his freedom and chooses frankness instead of persuasion, truth instead of falsehood or silence, the risk of death instead of life and security, criticism instead of flattery, and moral duty instead of self-interest and moral apathy. (1999)

This quotation from Foucault contains Pasolini's entire existential and artistic developmental curve, from the narcissist poet of the Friulian poems to the Lutheran and "corsair" writer of his last years, as well as all the trajectories of the other Pasolinian alter egos, such as the Christ of *Il Vangelo secondo Matteo* and Paul of Tarsus from *San Paolo.* It is Pasolini himself who "sees" in Christ the coordinates of *parrhesia*, as we can infer from the following passage in which he again describes the fulguration of his faithless spirituality:

> But, I repeat it, this was the outer manifestation, fantastically visual, of the increase in vitality. At the bottom of it, there was something even more violent that was shaking me up.
>
> It was the figure of Christ as Matthew sees it. And here I should stop, with my aestheticizing journalistic vocabulary. I would like, however, to add that nothing seems to me to be farther away from the modern world than that figure: of that Christ, meek of heart but "never" in his mind, who doesn't back away for a moment from his own terrible freedom, as the will to prove continuously his own religion and express an enduring spite of contradiction and scandal. Following Matthew's "stylistic accelerations" to

> the letter – the barbaric and practical functionality of his tale, the abolition of a chronological time-line, the elliptical jumps within the story with its "disproportionate" didactic stases (the wonderful, endless Sermon on the Mount) – the figure of Christ should have, at the end, the same violence of a resistance: something that radically contradicts the life that is evolving for the modern man, its grey orgy of cynicism, irony, practical brutality, compromise, conformism, glorification of one's own identity with the features of the masses, hate for any form of diversity, theological anger without religion. (*PPC1*, 673–4)[26]

Matthew's Christ clearly represents for Pasolini the antithesis of the modern man (and especially of the bourgeois) in the age of late capitalism. This barbaric Christ, meek of heart but with an implacable will, takes on the autobiographical characteristics of the scandalous intellectual of the new pre-historic era. He is meek and violent at the same time, merciful but also radically resistant to the orgy of cynicism and conformism of his age. Pasolini often underlines that it is this quality of Christ's character that most struck him in Matthew's depiction of Jesus: "'*I did not come to bring peace but a sword.*' The key in which I produced the movie is this; it is this that led me to do it" (*SPS*, 767).[27]

Pasolini continues:

> Matthew's Christ doesn't speak with sweetness. He doesn't have a sweet disposition. Sweetness is a typically bourgeois characteristic and, in Matthew's text, this sweetness really doesn't come through. The first impression I got – very strong – was the absolute and lasting tension in Matthew's Christ. If this tension hadn't been there, he would no longer have been God but a man without any divine trait. Easing this tension would have been like denying Christ. (*RILL*, 106–7)[28]

Christ represents total "resistance" against the conformity of our time: a foreign body and a divine body, he uses the weapons of poetry to make the present explode in its spiritual squalor. Pasolini's Christ is above all a revolutionary and poetic saviour: Pasolini confirms that he wants to produce neither a religious nor an ideological work, but "a work of poetry" (press release no. 95, 1964, 4). He once again embraces his atheism, even though he speaks of Christ as a man of a superior and ideal humanity:

> In very simple and poor words: I do not believe that Christ is the son of God, because I'm not a believer – at least in my conscience. But I do believe

that Christ is divine: that is, I believe that, in him, humanity is so high, rigorous, ideal, that it goes beyond the common limits of humanity. For this reason I say, "poetry": irrational instrument to express my irrational feelings for Christ ... I wish that my expressive needs, my poetic inspiration, may never contradict your sensitivity as believers. Otherwise I could not reach my goal to re-propose to everybody a life that is a model – although unreachable – for everybody. (4)[29]

Pasolini stresses Christ's humanity, although he recognizes that it is "driven by such inner strength, by such an unquenchable thirst to gain and to verify knowledge, with no fear of any scandal or any contradiction, that through it the "divine" metaphor reaches the limits of metaphor to the point that ideally it is a reality" (5).[30] In this statement, the characteristics of *parrhesia* take shape as an ethical and epistemological paradigm pursued by Pasolini and incarnated in Christ at the highest level. Pasolini's Christ stands at the edge of the superhuman, as an unmatched example at the threshold of an immanence that, in its perfection, fulfils transcendence.

The second issue Pasolini underlines is the ethical value of beauty, the necessary link between ethos and beauty, which we generally encounter in mediated form. As he says: "The only case of 'moral beauty' that is not mediated but un-mediated, in its pure state, is what I have experienced in the gospel" (press release no. 95, 5).[31] For Pasolini, aesthetics always translates into ethics, and this is particularly true in the case of the exemplarity of the life and sacrifice of Christ, where spirituality, ethics, and aesthetics meet and become equivalent. As to the form in which such co-presence of elements should best be rendered in *Il Vangelo,* Pasolini envisions it as "the fruit of a furious irrationalistic wave. I want to create a work of pure poetry" (5).[32] Yet he is aware of the "dangers of aestheticism (Bach and in part also Mozart for the musical score; Piero della Francesca and in part also Duccio as figural inspiration; the essentially pre-historic and exotic reality of the Arab world as background and setting)" (5).[33] On the one hand, we find a formal stylistic irrationality; on the other, we see the rejection of what had been the private, individual line followed in Pasolini's previous religious works in favour of an objectifying process that transposes the religious element "into faith, myth, and mythology of the other." (6).[34] Pasolini writes:

Now, this film can truly be in the "national-popular" vein of which Gramsci spoke. There are some refined things; in the costumes, in the music, in the

> landscapes, there are elements that are, so to speak, "exquisite" and perhaps "decadent," in the common meaning of the word, with moments of great national popular afflatus. It is a story with a fabulous background, on the one hand, and ideological on the other, that does not look for historical accuracy, philological accuracy, reconstruction, the national Jewish world of the time ... The Saint Matthew I intend to do is somewhat of an exaltation of the elements that were already present in *Accattone*, in *Mamma Roma*, and in *Ricotta* ... That is, the liberation of religious inspiration in a Marxist ... In my opinion, *San Matteo* should be a violent wake-up call for the bourgeoisie that is stupidly projected towards a future that will bring the destruction of humanity, of man's anthropologically human, classical and religious elements ... I have not added or taken out a single line; I follow the narration in its sequence exactly as it is in St. Matthew, with some narrative cuts of the same almost magical violence and epic proportions present in the very text of the Gospel. (7)[35]

It is an objectifying reading that is nonetheless furiously mythical and irrationalistic; it translates stylistically into a "magma," something that is decisively different from the "technical sacrality" Pasolini employed in his previous movies and characterized by frontal shots, simple camera movements, and an alternation of pans and close-ups. Pasolini describes this kind of "sacrality" as "a frontal Christ filmed with a 50 or 75 [lens], accompanied by short intense pan shots," that turned into "pure emphasis: a reproduction" (*PPC2*, 2770).[36]

The scene of Christ's baptism in the Jordan (shot in the gorges of the Chia River in the province of Viterbo) marks for Pasolini a reverse fulguration. He zooms in and "all frontal views, all order, all symmetry was thus unsettled: the magmatic, the casual, the asymmetric rushed in: faces could no longer be seen from the front and at the center of the frame but showed themselves haphazardly, at all possible angles and always eccentric within the frame" (*PPC2*, 2771).[37]

Shot with a 300 lens, flattened and at the same time suffused with the aura of a documentary typical of a bike race finish, as Pasolini tells us, images become more and more expressionistic and in a certain sense excessive, as they give life to that expressive magma Pasolini announces as a new technical mythology, "less religious and more epic, less hieratic and more modern, less romantic and more impressionistic-expressionistic" (*PPC2*, 2772).[38] Yet the final result of this style, so openly extreme, is a smooth, level flow of images with "magmatic, expressionistic, casual, arbitrary, asymmetrical points, all ... editing freedoms, all ...

irregularities: even the quotations from Dreyer and Ejzenštejn or memories of Mizoguchi"[39] (*PPC2,* 2772) appear fused in a continuum with no interruption. Pasolini wonders why "evocation now strangely prevails on representation. Chaos has found an unforeseen technical and stylistic equilibrium" (*PPC2,* 2772).[40] To portray transgressive subjects as if they were images of Christ in primitive painting worked wonderfully in movies like *Accattone* or *Mamma Roma,* but to portray Christ Himself in the same style means producing a popular holy image. Pasolini does not give in to the visual perspective of the thousand-year-old traditional Christian iconography. Rather, he creates an expressionistic technique through his portrayal of Christ in the manner of a bike race or – as in the scenes of the Sermon on the Mount – as an inspired and revolutionary Lenin who moves from one close-up to the next against ever-changing atmospheric backgrounds. This movement is then combined with shots imbued with the earlier Pasolinian technical sacrality, thus giving birth to a coherent style. Just as the two points of view adopted by the director – the atheistic and the religious – fuse together, one contaminating the other in the camera's gaze without generating any stridency, so, too, Pasolini's opposite technical mythologies – modernist and primitive – produce an epic-sacral effect that makes his evangelical movie one of the most successful films with a religious theme, even according to the Vatican. He explains:

> I was looking for the scandal that always produces poetry, through the scandal that sincerity can cause; and instead, it is clear that through their common result, that is not, I repeat it, expressionistic or magmatic but, in its own way, extremely orderly and regular, I was using expressive scandal in order to find poetry. (*PPC2,* Autumn 1965, 2775–6)[41]

Pasolini's Christ is certainly a revolutionary Christ, but He is not transcendent. In fact, the omissions in the rewriting of *Il Vangelo secondo Matteo* as a screenplay reveal the writer's lay and immanent point of view. As highlighted by Morando Morandini in his introduction to the printed edition of the screenplay for *Il Vangelo,* the passages that refer to the otherworldly and supernatural dimensions are missing from Pasolini's film. There is no trace of the Transfiguration, of the prophecy of Christ's triumphal return at the end of time; all the apocalyptical visions of the Apostles in the screenplay are deleted in the film; miracles and parables are also limited. The Pasolinian gospel, according to Morandini, is "a gospel without hope. There is Heaven coming down to earth, yet no earth going to Heaven" (1991, iii). This is only partially true, since

Pasolini does present some miracles (although from the anthropological perspective of De Martino rather than as proof of Christ's supernatural essence) and, above all, he shows the final Resurrection. Nevertheless, these scenes do not play a central role in inspiring the movie, and Pasolini on purpose downplays their "supernatural" and divine quality.

In his thorough study of the texts of *Il Vangelo secondo Matteo*, Zygmunt G. Baranski investigates the relationship between the Gospel of Matthew, Pasolini's screenplay, and Pasolini's actual film, underlining the complexity of a vision that changed several times in its making and that generated a series of contradictory claims. Baranski underlines the "immanent," earthbound quality of the film on several occasions, particularly when he mentions the deletions. He claims that "the miraculous in *Il Vangelo secondo Matteo* is no longer the very stuff of Christ's mission, as it is in Matthew's Gospel, but it is presented as something illogical and arbitrary" (1999, 298). The screenplay contains a series of "miracles" – there are twenty in the Gospel, according to Baranski – but in the film Pasolini reduces them to only six. Later, in an interview with Oswald Stack published in 1969, Pasolini distanced himself from these episodes, defining them as "horrible moments ... The miracles of the loaves and the fishes and Christ walking on the water are disgusting pietism." The treatment of miracles in Pasolini's films varies from one film to the other: if they are contained, downplayed, and later dismissed in *Il Vangelo*, in subsequent movies they become a central feature of Pasolini's subversive hagiographies, and they are vindicated as a crucial characteristic of Pasolini's allegorical and parodic saints. In the 1969 interview with Stack, Pasolini pondered:

> Perhaps I should have tried to invent completely new miracles, miracles which are not miracles, like healing or walking on the water; perhaps I should have tried to convey the sense of miraculousness each of us can experience watching the dawn, for example: nothing happens, the sun rises, trees are lit up by the sun. Perhaps for us this is what a miracle is. (1969, 91)

This ambivalence towards the "religious," "divine" nature of Christ as expressed through miracles will generate in Pasolini "new miracles" such as the dawn in *Teorema*, an authentic hierophanic experience of Paolo, the industrialist father protagonist of the movie, as well as traditional miracles such as those of Brother Ciccillo in *Uccellacci e Uccellini* or of the maid Emilia in *Teorema*. It is important to notice how in *Il Vangelo* Pasolini subtracts the eschatological elements to instead add subplots or points of view that question the centrality of his Jesus. The relationship between Peter and Jesus, and especially that between Judas and Christ, acquire much more dramatic weight in Pasolini's narration, whereas the figure of Jesus himself and his words are progressively toned down. In the long sequence of the Sermon on the Mount, Pasolini begins by depicting a revolutionary Christ, always in close-ups with different backgrounds, as if He were a Soviet political leader in a Russian avant-garde film. Later, with the Jerusalem sermons against the scribes and the pharisees, Pasolini's Jesus almost disappears among the crowds and only His disembodied voice, a quasi voiceover, interrogates and shakes the mass of faces and bodies of the listeners assembled in the hills. The director appears to be more interested in investigating the image of the listening peasant body, the subproletarian flesh, from the children to the elderly, insisting on long shots of the crowds as well as on close-ups of revealing faces and gazes, permeated by the soundtrack of Jesus' voice. The film's trajectory goes from Jesus as the preaching leader, to Jesus as His words, to Jesus as silence in the trial scenes – where He speaks only a few words – to His final, inarticulate cry of death.

The trial scenes are long shots of *cinèma verité*, framed through the free indirect point-of-view shots of Peter first and then John, with details of the eyes of the apostles interspersed first with the scenes of Pilate's trial and then with Jesus' *via crucis.* The culmination of this progressive distancing of the cinematic gaze from the figure of Christ is in the Crucifixion scene, always taken from afar, with long shots in which, alternatively, either the ground or the sky occupies the main portion of the visual field. Groups of bystanders and pious women move about and then stand in convulsive movements of pain, with the focus more on the *planctus Mariae* than on the agony of Christ. "For Pasolini, the Virgin's final acts of witnessing Christ's death and resurgence means celebrating the poor, humble, and innocent at large" (Ryan-Scheutz 2007, 149). The whole crucifixion scene lasts only two minutes, with only a couple of close-ups of the suffering Christ: Pasolini is particularly reluctant to dwell on the details of the Passion. Among the long shots, with details of the Madonna, John, and the pious women, only the dying Christ's wrenching cry "Father, why hast thou forsaken me?" and the final, terrifying, exhaling cry of death are close-ups shot from below. This cinematography goes against the indications of the screenplay, where the director seems to emphasize much more the physicality of the Passion and the unsustainability of its vision of pain:

TOTAL with the three crosses, against the nocturnal sky.

PAN. At the feet of the usual small crowd: John, the Marys, Joseph of Arimathea, in pain, terrified, and mute.

CLOSE-UP of the three crucified, suffering the throes of death. (No crucifixion would have ever given the unsustainable physicality of pain, as this cinematic rendition of it: a terrifying naturalism, to make its sight unbearable.)

...

CLOSE-UP of a thief that suffers indescribable pains, lost in them, without any more voice or gaze ... Close up of the other thief, who, suffering what is sufferable, has still the strength to hate, and insults Christ:

THIEF (*insults?*)

CLOSE-UP of Christ, prey of a physical pain whose sight is unbearable. (*PC1*, 644–5)[42]

In the movie, all this physical emphasis is downplayed. The camera gaze points again onto the faces and movements of the followers, particularly Mary, as well as on the surroundings, much more than onto Christ. After the close-up on Jesus' last cry, the montage shows alternate shots of crumbling buildings following God's wrath, and, after a pan on Jerusalem, another close-up of the face of the dead Christ. Then comes the shot of the Deposition, taken again from afar. The Passion is thus summoned up in three close-ups: the *Eloi, Eloi Lama Sabachtani* moment, then death, and then the post-mortem frame. The context prevails over the lyrical climaxes of Christ's agony. Physicality is abandoned for the pursuitof emblematicity, and the wave of its effects.

Such sobriety will later give way to a much more articulated vision of sacrifice in the Crucifixion, which I explore in detail in the next chapter in an analysis of the Passion scene in the unfinished verse screenplay for *Bestemmia*, which Pasolini worked on between 1962 and 1967. My main focus, however, is on the passage dedicated to the Crucifixion – the only one the poet published in his lifetime – and on his "Christology of the Flesh," an attitude that suggests a different and even more kenotic interpretation of the death of Christ, as well as a possible abjuration of *Il Vangelo secondo Matteo.* In light of this passage, we will reread the semiotic analyses developed by Giuliana Bruno and Noa Steimatsky, modelling our reflections on the paradigm of the Incarnation.

Chapter Three

The Words of the Flesh: *Blasphemy*

Bestemmia (*Blasphemy*, 1962–7), a complex Pasolinian project with a very difficult production, was both a screenplay and a poetic text. Chapter 5 further discusses the plot details of this work as one of the best examples of Pasolini's subversive hagiographies. At the very moment in which the scoundrel and future saint Bestemmia, the protagonist of the screenplay, has his conversion through the vision of the Passion of Christ, Pasolini launches into a long digression on the Crucifixion. This digression then becomes a separate poetic fragment, which was included in the collection of poems also titled *Bestemmia* (1993) and forms the focus of this chapter.[1]

Bestemmia: Barbaric Christology

The Passion fragment of *Bestemmia* is foundational in Pasolini's poetics, since it constitutes one of the most self-evident passages in the director's polemic against representation. As seen in the previous chapter, the problem of representation for Pasolini is connected with the fundamental Western Christian *Weltanschauung* of the Passion of Christ, and he explicitly thematized it – after broad Christological references in *Accattone* and *Mamma Roma* – in *La Ricotta*. The Passion scene, which he would so starkly present at the end of *Il Vangelo secondo Matteo* in 1964, had been the object of a twofold metafilmic meditation in *La Ricotta* in 1963. In that film, it was represented as the passion of a poor wretch, the film extra Stracci, who played one of the thieves crucified with the Nazarene and who actually died of indigestion during the filming of a movie about the Passion.

As we have seen in the previous chapter, the enormous divide between a lived Passion, Stracci's own, and a merely represented one, orchestrated by the mannerist director in the movie, played by Orson Welles, is made explicit. It is the unfathomable distance between "a representation without suffering and the reality of suffering that no representation can present" (Micciché, *Il cinema italiano*, 1975, 162, cited by Greene 1990, 63). The movie-within-the-movie in *La Ricotta* is the work of a maniacally aestheticizing citationist director intent on recreating the episodes of the Passion as cinematic copies – *tableaux vivants* – of paintings by the great Italian mannerists, from Pontormo to Rosso Fiorentino. In the carnivalesque scene of the final hours of Christ's life, Pasolini inserts Stracci's agony on the cross as a tragic parody. The clash between real life and fiction could not be more brutal. Pasolini thus gives voice to his split vocation. On one side, with great self-deprecation, he apes himself and his own mannerism; on the other, he turns the *tableaux vivant* into a heart-rending, authentic Passion and death without resurrection. Pasolini's attraction to mannerism "with its implied distance from reality" represents, according to Naomi Greene, "the infernal mirror image of this intense desire to apprehend the real in a total and tangible way" (1990, 62). Once again, we have an example of oxymoronic poetics: a realism that captures reality through an excess of form. The staging of the death on the cross, the supreme image of the Incarnation of the son of God, the icon of two thousand years of Catholicism, turns into an actual death, with the bulky and burping body, the swollen full belly of poor Stracci, fictionally hanging from the cross but actually dying after a tragicomic last supper. Reality and representation alternate and are differentiated along the line of suffering and irony in an endless play of mirrors. How can we grasp the reality that, as shown quintessentially by pain and death, powerfully proves all representations wrong? This is the question the director has tried to answer since his early youth, as he himself expressed in a passage of his letters. Pasolini responds with anguish to the "gap between the real and the represented" (Greene 1990, 65):

> The kitchen was the scene of my unbridled adventures; I saw myself bent over the pages, tortured simply by the *pure* problem of the relationship between the real and the artificial. The fact of representation appeared to me then as something terrible and primordial, precisely because in a pure state the equivalent would have to be definitive. Faced with the problem of reproducing a meadow I went crazy. The question for me was: should I

draw all the blades of grass? I did not know then that, by filling up the whole space with a green crayon, I could have conveyed the *mass* of the meadow and ... neglected the blades of the grass, I was still far removed from such hypocrisies. (66)[2]

It is with this experience in mind – the oscillation between an extreme awareness of the imprinting of the images inherited from his culture and a fetishistic obsession for the real – that Pasolini composes this long fragment, a long digression on Bestemmia's vision:

At the beginning of an education, source of passions,
I could not have helped but to imagine
the Christ of a vision
in *some sort of style*;
imposing it
with the partisanship of youth ...
My Christology is now barbaric,
rather than beardless; it wants to be; it fears failure
if it cannot conjure up an idea of Christ
that precedes any style, any turn of history,
any fixation, any development; virgin;
reproduced by reality with reality
without any memory of poems and pictures;
with the tools of reality that represents itself.
Not only do I not want to know Masaccio,
(the Masaccio of Longhi,
who for so long has dominated my eyes, my heart,
my sex), I do not even
want
to know language or painting.
I want that Christ to present himself as reality.
Isn't this a good reason
for this to be a movie, not a poem?
In the movie I am thinking, and I make you think of,
reader,
I am an unrefined magician,
I no longer want to need the evocative
potions of language;
language is a rough tool, a childish
concert of bells the poet rings

to evoke reality by charming it.
But it is only that reality that, once evoked, *counts*!
It is the only beautiful thing and truly loved!
How many words, tools and style,
to evoke a real image of Christ on the cross!
But I, a man of flesh and blood,
with a real wooden cross,
with real nails,
and, I wish, with real blood and pain,
I reproduce reality with reality.
The new reality *looks like*,
only *looks like*, the true reality that is evoked;
but it is a reality in its own right.
The poor mime of Christ in flesh and blood
– paid little money –
Is as real as the true Christ is physically real.
Evoking that reality, I do not leave the world of the real.
I live always; I do not differentiate myself from life in order to bear witness to it.
I live on this side of my forest of things learnt and withered.
I cannot write, cannot read, cannot speak.
My great childhood dream has become real,
I stand before the muscles and veins of my Christ
who looks like none of those in the imagination
and in history;
two thousand years of art works have passed, luckily, in vain;
here are muscles, veins, wood, the ground where a real cross has been planted,
an actual breath, an agony,
all things that these words of mine cannot express,
but I don't care,
because here, in this screenplay, I evoke provisionally,
with the cheers of triumph,
a Christ I will then evoke, in the movie, really with reality,
and you will finally see him
real, physically real
speaking to you with the language of his own self,
older than any other form of speech:
with the words of the Flesh.
Thus Bestemmia saw Christ – and of course!

He saw him like he was: a body;
there is no physical difference between Bestemmia and what he sees.
It is only a question of turning around the camera.
...
Completely innocent,
like a dog,
like me. (*Bestemmia, TP2*, 1014–16)[3]

The first element one can notice about this digression is that, emerging from the experience of making *Il Vangelo* and *La Ricotta* (where the weight of cultural images is enormous), Pasolini in *Bestemmia* announces his program of stylistic and symbolic annihilation. His utopian goal is the representation – the re-presentation, we may say, in the sense of production of presence – of the archetypal event of the Crucifixion in all its factuality. The event is captured in its immediacy as a simple action that is repeated by spontaneous mimesis, just like the miracle of transubstantiation is repeated at every celebration of the Eucharist. It is precisely an effect of transubstantial presence that Pasolini wants to achieve. Cinema, the "*mangiarealtà*" (devourer of reality), is the tool that makes the abolition of linguistic mediation possible by duplicating and presentifying what it represents. A tension between presence and representation is thus established. As Jean-Luc Nancy puts it: "Presence does not come without effacing the presence that representation would like to designate (its fundaments, its origin, its subject)" (1993, 4). The result is a representation that tends to abolish itself as representation in order to establish itself as a phenomenon. The body is an actual body and, as for blood and pain, the director would like real blood and real pain (and here lies the intrinsic limit of representation, which can only be *similar* to the original event without truly producing it in itself).

In this regard, Noa Steimatsky comments:

> The cinematographic impression can be seen to bind, then, Pasolini's realism with a reverential perception. Pasolini's archaistic imagination aspires to a primal sense of the cinematic image as reality's direct emanation – one that carries the evidentiary force of an imprint but also the magical resonance of a temporal bridge to the past. As to an alternate state: a simultaneity of different temporalities, different orders of being ... this confronts us with the doctrine of the Incarnation and, more specifically, with the theology of the icon. (2008, 138)

Contrary to what happens in *Il Vangelo secondo Matteo* (to which Steimatsky refers, speaking of "the potency of the devotional image" in that work) and in Pasolini's creation in *La Ricotta* of a network of archaic iconographic references from Giotto to Masaccio to Piero della Francesca to the mannerists, in *Bestemmia*'s fragment on the Passion the iconographic tradition is abolished in an effort to approximate the form of the *Acheiropoietos*, the first, the original icon. Steimatsky affirms:

> The rhetoric of the icon – which, like the relic, claims to provide visual, material evidence for the incarnation of the sacred in the world – asserts Christianity's redemptive vision of God's materialization in Jesus. The iconic image is not simply "symbolic" or "allegorical" in relation to its divine referent ... Rather, it is grasped as participating in what it represents: it is an index of Christ's humanity; in partaking of his body it incarnates God ...
>
> It is, most forcefully, the *acheiropoietic* icon, the icon "made without hands," that proclaims an evidentiary, causal link in an original instance of contact or direct emanation, to reinforce the claim of resemblance between the sacred image and its referent. Following the Eastern Mandylion, the Veronica, or *vera icona*, is the Western rival to the status archetype of the sacred portrait of Christ from the early thirteenth century. The *acheiropoietic* icon, typically depicting the Holy Face on a cloth, is believed to have received the image by direct physical impression, sustaining the sacral presence, the original moment of contact, of identity, between represented and representation: whence its claim of causal, indexical link between the image and its referent. (2008, 138–9)

The indexical image of the Passion implies that the language of praxis, of Christ's action, be "edited" and acquire meaning from His death: this is reality according to Pasolini. The film would depict the agonizing body of Christ in a poem of tragic action (an action that is above all suffering) and pain. In *Bestemmia*, the creation of a frame of the Passion as *Acheiropoietos* demystifies two thousand years of Christian devotional iconography, proceeding in the opposite direction from that taken in *Il Vangelo secondo Matteo*, in which Pasolini was instead preoccupied with retracing a map of the archaic repertoire of devotional images in Christian religious art as copies of the "True Icon." In *Bestemmia*, Pasolini invokes the abolition of repetition to move instead towards the transubstantiation of film, so that there is a theology of the image but also a demystification of representation.

The reality that is made visible through Pasolini's production of presence is that of the humanity of the incarnated God. The mystery of the Incarnation is preserved in the body of each human being, evoked and created through the semiotic secretion of bodily fluids that testifies to a life that surfaces and then is lost, flowing into dryness and aridity, leaving on the film visible traces that are almost obscene and scatological in their physicality:

> [Nobody had ever written of that Christ *he was seeing*,
> nobody had ever painted him.
> Bestemmia thus saw him in front of him as someone else.
> He shared his same nature and, keeping silent, he talked to him.
> He was his neighbour; son of another mother; still young;
> but what was the language of his Flesh saying?
> That he was dying.
> The upturned eyes said it,
> the taut grey cheeks like a mummy's,
> the short hair and his sweat as dense as pus,
> the narrow, wise man's chest ripped open
> with the edges of the wound lined with rot,
> his arms desperately stretched,
> and the whole body weighed down by its own weight
> like a naked victim on the trough,
> his legs wet with urine
> trickling down like that of beasts
> to his feet, to mix with blood,
> feces sticking to his thighs and reeking,
> new feces on top of the old dried ones,
> lost through the poor anus with no will left.]
>
> (Appendix to *Bestemmia, TP2*, 1114)[4]

As in the Eucharist, the truth of the Passion is contained in flesh and blood. According to Pasolini, it is also contained in feces, sweat, urine, and in all the physical and material traces of human life, even the humblest and lowest. Pasolini's is a purposefully barbaric, primitive Christology: it highlights its inability to abstract meaning while intentionally not recreating meaning effects.

Pasolini tries to cast upon the Crucifixion a newly innocent gaze, where "innocent" means "originary": the gaze of whoever witnesses the event for the first time, unaware. What he captures is the presence – the letter – of a human body nailed to a cross. The revelation of the divinity passes through the "given" of this image: Christ's suffering captured in the immediacy and universality of "a brother's body covered in blood." Pasolini thus intends to repeat the miracle but, in order to do so, he chooses to humanize the passion. "God" becomes "god" when he dies like a man and, more importantly, the sacred surfaces exactly where the event is barbaric, uncodified, not filtered through interpretations. Rather, the sacred is given in its primitive phenomenology, in a completely human dimension that appears primal and ancestral every time. The miracle and heresy are those of a Christ without Christianity. As explained by Giuseppe Conti Calabrese,

> Here emerges the identification of the body of the poor, innocent, ignorant, and "barbaric" saint with the body of Christ, whose nature does not appear "en-godded" with the attribution of a transcendental character, as in a Christological theology. On the contrary, we could say that there is a decisive suppression of the dualism between the world of transcendence and that of reality. Pasolini's Christ is a man who dies according to a Christology that exhibits strongly heretic, radically kenotic features. (1994, 150)
>
> ... The teaching that results from this is that of a Christian heresy that, spread and "divulged" in a desacralized time, turns out to be even more unsettling and irreducible, as the holder of an ancient knowledge devoid of hope or "faith" but full of love for life. Within such an immanent religiosity, Pasolini is a Christian who finds the essence of Christianity in passion-redemption rather than in passion-resurrection. "A desperate vitality" leads him to suffer, that is, to recognize and to be grateful for the original gift of the sacred, life that always leads to new life. (155–6)[5]

This Christ in all his bodily, scatological presence becomes the ultimate remnant of humanity, one that is reduced to its agonizing fluids – pure humble *pathos* – which desublimate the Divine into the opposite polarity, the Abject, the impure evident presence of a corpse. The Way of the Cross is the affirmation of humanity over divinity, in the imperfection of a decaying body aflame with pure love. As Slavoj Žižek reminds us, it brings forth the crucial aspect of the Christian *agape* as incompleteness, and thus imperfection, positing it in the site of the Divine:

> Only a lacking, vulnerable being is capable of love: the ultimate mystery of love, therefore, is that incompleteness is, in a way, higher than completion. On the one hand, only an imperfect, lacking being loves: we love because

> we do not know all. On the other hand, even if we were to know everything, love would, inexplicably, still be higher than completed knowledge. Perhaps the true achievement of Christianity is to elevate a loving (imperfect) Being to the place of God, that is, of ultimate perfection. That is the kernel of the Christian experience. (2003, 115)

In his effort to return to this effect of presence, Pasolini intends to represent the event of the Passion without any interpretation, without any mediation of a linguistic, pictorial, or cultural kind. He distrusts language more than ever before, while his trust in cinema as the "written language of reality" has never been greater.[6] The writer wishes to abolish temporality and all its stratifications.

It is crucial to notice the difference between the version of Christ in *Bestemmia* – heretical in its being absolutely present and yet outside of history – and that portrayed in *Il Vangelo secondo Matteo,* where the emphasis is entirely on returning a historical dimension to the images. Pasolini clearly expressed his interpretative goal:

> I did not want to reconstruct the life of Christ as it really was … I wanted to do the story of Christ plus 2,000 years of Christian translation, because it is the 2,000 years of Christian history which has mythicized this biography, which would otherwise be almost an insignificant biography as such. My film is the life of Christ plus 2,000 years of storytelling about the life of Christ. That was my intention. (Stack 1969, 83)

Pasolini's vision in *Bestemmia* makes a *tabula rasa* of the historical dimension, suggesting once more that *Bestemmia* is one of Pasolini's many palinodes, his abjuration of *Il Vangelo.* There is no wish to establish a genealogy of sacred images, but rather a desire to ground the foundational nature of the event of the crucifixion in all its human, carnal reality.

As he uproots two thousand years of Christian iconography, Pasolini responds to the need expressed by Félix Guattari for a new, yet-to-be-invented semiotics. According to Guattari – cited by Renè Schérer and Giorgio Passerone in *Passage Pasoliniens* (2006) – all of society's problems and revolutionary changes are strictly dependent on a difference in the "regime of signs." Contemporary capitalism is given two options: either a system of significations that consists in the sciences and the dominant values or a system based on contesting those values, and on social and cultural change.

> People, writes Guattari, are mainly caught up in a signifying semiotic system which, he points out, makes futile any attempt to change the social order, as well as to create within the domain of art. These limiting significations ... throw a veil over thought and action[:] ... "the painter doesn't have to fill a white surface, he would rather have to empty it out, clear it out, and free it."[7] Since it is tied to signification, the impetus of desire is blocked.
>
> The "signifying images" act as a screen for decisive ruptures, for true desires. There is a prerequisite for every fight, for every work, which is to get rid of or break the "anti-production system"; and that first of all belongs to the order of semiotics ... To condense it into one word – more exactly, two words – this prerequisite is the passage, the leap from the signifying system to the system of expression, which is also a system of experimentation ... The problem, Félix Guattari sums up, is to distinguish radically a politics of signification from a politics of what I would not call information but expression."[8] (Schérer and Passerone 2006, 172)[9]

Schérer and Passerone place Pasolini's semiotic revolution within the framework of a Guattarian politics of expression, an expression that is physical and that connects the individual to the world and to the cosmos, underlining the "trans-substantial" valence of the cinematic image. They claim that the link between film image and reality is "something like an impression, a footprint, an emanation of a quasi-physical nature" (and mention the notion of photographical image in Barthes' *Camera Lucida*).

> Footprint or emanation? In either case, a certain immanence of reality has this idiom, or rather, this "langue," in order to distinguish it as an expression chosen, extracted, and composed, moving from a reality that fundamentally has no other idiom than itself, an idiom which is that of its own presence in itself for the duration of the continuous sequence shot it constitutes. (181)[10]

We return to the *acheiropoietic* nature of the film image Steimatsky referred to in her analysis of *Il Vangelo*, a footprint or emanation grounded in the body: for Schérer, the image is anchored to "the affective and ritual real." It is rooted "in the flesh of the living" (187). Similarly, in the never-produced project of *Bestemmia* – with the iconographic and semiotic resetting of the scope of signification – the palinode lives at the original time of the sacrifice. Pasolini inscribes his crucifixion as "the" Crucifixion: in the Passion scene of *Bestemmia*, the film image must capture the footprint of incarnated pain, the factuality of the Incarnation in the dying

Christ, the "corporeality" of the definitive event of God's death. It is not the eternal return of an archetypal Christological pattern, the multiple, stratified vision of the critical salvific event of mankind, but rather the unique manifestation of the cross, the *acheiropoietic* icon, its imprinting on the film by the agonizing bodily traces of Christ's corpse. Ground zero of the image, the Passion is action painting in film, pure expression, pure pathos stamped on the surface of the cinematic script; it is Christ's death as Everyman's death in its finitude and uniqueness. As we saw in the first chapter, the Christian values that Pasolini endorses are those of suffering, brotherhood, and charity: faith and hope do not matter, but charity does. The empathy Bestemmia feels, faced with the terrible spectacle of the Passion, wins him over and transforms him from villain into saint. It is the reality of the Passion that teaches the sacred to Bestemmia. There are no evangelical words, polyptychs, or depositions – only the most powerful lesson of sacrificial violence and pain. "Presence" is the key word.

In the Passion of Christ in *Bestemmia,* the passage on the "presence" of this vision is particularly crucial.There the emphasis on *kenosis* is heretical and extreme. It is in Christ's Passion and death that the supreme event of the Incarnation is realized. Pasolini does not need a resurrected Christ: he only needs a suffering Christ. As Slavoj Žižek pointed out in his "Only a Suffering God Can Save Us":

> A God who – like the suffering Christ on the Cross – is agonized, assumes the burden of suffering, in solidarity with the human misery ... It was already Schelling who wrote: "God is a life, not merely a being. But all life has a fate and is subject to suffering and becoming ... Without the concept of a humanly suffering God ... all of history remains incomprehensible" ... Why? Because God's suffering implies that He is involved in history, affected by it, not just a transcendent Master pulling the strings from above: God's suffering means that human history is not just a theater of shadows, but the place of the real struggle, the struggle in which the Absolute itself is involved and its fate is decided." (2013, 156–7)

History is the human struggle, the human confrontation with death, a confrontation to which the divinity submits itself, fulfilling itself through the acceptance of its humanness "because it is only in man, in human History that God fully realizes Himself, becomes an actual living God" (Žižek 2000, 107). As Michael Hardt noted in his analysis of another Pasolinian Crucifixion – that in *L'Usignolo della Chiesa Cattolica* – the moment of Incarnation, signalled by the dramatic event of the Crucifixion, marks the passage from a transcendent vision of divinity to an immanent one. It thus follows the formula of "immanent transcendence" made evident in the materiality of Christ's suffering body.

> What exactly did Christ abandon when he emptied himself? Certainly he did not abandon divinity as such; rather, he emptied the transcendental *form* and carried divinity into the material ... The self-emptying or *kenosis* of Christ, the evacuation of the transcendental, is the affirmation of the plenitude of the material, the fullness of the flesh. (2002, 78)

For Hardt, transcendence is the "in-dwelling potentiality" of the material, located at its surface:

> Incarnation is the claim that there is no opposition and no mediation necessary between the transcendent and the immanent, but an intimate complementariness. This immanent transcendence is the innermost exteriority of being, the potentiality of the flesh ... Divinity resides precisely in the boundaries or thresholds of things, at their limits, passionate and exposed, as if surrounding them with a halo. Incarnation abandons any notion of a hidden God, any transcendental notion of a divinity that remains "pure" outside the exposure of materiality. (79)

Pasolini stresses Christ's human nature in the exposure of presence realized in Bestemmia's vision, where "being there" becomes the central axis of Bestemmia's conversion. Bestemmia mirrors himself in this "fraternal body" of Christ: a suffering presence, a martyred flesh that speaks for itself:

> He saw Christ in his own nature.
> A nailed body etc.
> ...
> Almost as if nobody had ever talked about him,
> no one had painted him,
> reality that re-presents itself as reality in the vision.
> He recognized him – a friend, a man, himself;
> that is why he felt his pain,
> and he almost threw himself on top of him, to help him,
> to save him
> as any living being,
> wounded or fallen,

like when instinct tells us to help an unknown
martyr who burns in his house,
or bleeds pierced through by the torn metal of his truck;
that image,
that frame
that reproduced live, physically living,
a brother's body covered in blood
and had the same nature as Bestemmia's nature,
two realities both reproduced,
by merely "being there" told Bestemmia
everything entire poems cannot tell.
And Bestemmia was unable to say anything but that he "was there":
but this had immense meaning,
it was waiting to develop
with a radiant impatience ...[11]
He was there, what to do?
He was there, what to say?
He was there, what had life been?
Everything changed meaning under that stony moon,
And six whores and a little boy still dirty with sperm.
But I don't want to pervert Bestemmia.
Rightfully religion does not take poetry seriously!
And I would sin against my own theory
if I did not see Bestemmia as an object that speaks
even without speaking,
by his mere presence,
by his mere action,
by his mere being there.
He is the object!
I do not create him but entertain a dialogue with him,
a real dialogue,
like with the grass tuft on which his knees rest,
the grass of geese and gnats,
which talks to me itself,
to tell me what it is:
and if I can have a dialogue, as if among equals, with the grass,
I should also be able to have one with Bestemmia!
– and I will in the movie!
– I'm just laying down the blueprint.
But you, reader, must collaborate with me,

look at thing as present, images, sounds,
which talk about themselves. (*TP2*, 1016–18)[12]

Pasolini's quest for presence is revealed in this passage by its emphasis on "being there" (*era lì*), on its unveiling of the vision of the Passion. It is not by chance that this search is manifested in his medieval imagination, embodied in later films, such as *The Decameron* (1971) and *The Canterbury Tales* (1972), but also in his "medieval" focus on the flesh as presence. In his 2004 volume *Production of Presence*, Hans Ulrich Gumbrecht claims that the humanities can move beyond the current "age of the sign" as defined by Derrida, an age obsessed by interpretation and by a focus on meaning, on metaphysics intended as "a worldview that always wants to go 'beyond' (or 'below') that which is 'physical'" (2004, xiv) to embrace, instead, "a presence-based relationship to the world" (xv).

Gumbrecht welcomes the opening of new lines of investigation that, in the name of "production of presence," may go beyond interpretation by escaping the exclusive control of the Cartesian *res cogitans* and a hermeneutic paradigm that devalues any materiality in comparison with the subject's interiority. Even taking culture into consideration as a complex configuration that exhibits components of both presence and meaning, Gumbrecht nonetheless identifies some defining traits among those he characterizes as cultures of meaning and cultures of presence. He delineates the contemporary world as belonging to the sphere of meaning and the medieval to that of presence. He recognizes many traits as typical of the cultures of presence: the pre-eminence of the body over the mind; the predominance of cosmology over subjectivity; the supremacy of revealed knowledge over interpretive and conceptual knowledge; the eminence of a different concept of the sign, articulated on four levels as substance/form and content/expression, rather than signifier/signified, where the materialities of communication belong to the field of expression; the importance of immersion in a universal order over action construed as intentionality and transformation; the predominance of space over time; the supremacy of violence over power; the pre-eminence of the possibility of events independent of the values of innovation and surprise; the prominence of the function of Carnival over that of play; and, finally, the eminence of the Eucharist as ritual prototype over the parliamentary discussion typical of the cultures of meaning:

> The Eucharist ... is a ritual of magic because it makes God's body physically present as the central part of a past situation ... But what can be the point

> of a ritual that produces the real presence of God – if this real presence of God already is a generalized frame condition of human life? The only possible answer is that the celebration of the Eucharist, day after day, will not only maintain but intensify the already existing real presence of God. (85)

Pasolini's poetics focuses on "presence effects." The director searches for just such a transubstantiating effect of the film image – this intensified "production of presence" – by referring to the image of the Passion as the archetypal substratum both of the Eucharist and of cinematic representation, and by invoking Bestemmia's transformation into a saint. The paradigm of sanctity precisely suggests an analogous production of presence and a similar impasse of representation.

As Edith Wyschogrod emphasizes in her *Saints and Postmodernism*, the imperative of *Imitatio Christi* that guides the life of saints clashes with the unrepresentability of such a model:

> Human nature ... cannot conform itself to divine perfection. Thus *Imitatio Christi* is an unrealizable imperative because the life of Christ cannot be replicated.
>
> The saint's task is to undertake two intersecting lines of endeavour. The first strategy is to *construct* a content, necessarily extreme – self-mortification, voluntary poverty, and the like – to reach for what is inherently refractory to representation, a life like that of Jesus. The second strategy, parasitic on the first, is, paradoxically, to "*show*" unrepresentability itself, in this case to display how impossible it is to bring the divine life into plenary presence ... to *fully* re-present the divine life or to *fully* realize the divine will. (1990, 13)

Pasolini thus moves between the search for effects of presence and the search for effects of meaning, to the point of wishing to eliminate all interpretive strata from the vision of the Passion by transforming the representation into a re-presentation, a production of presence. The constant oscillation between the two paradigms results in the placing of the trans-substantial emphasis more on the humanity of Christ than on His divinity, exactly at the moment when the latter is manifested to Bestemmia. The oscillation between presence and meaning is thematized by the difficult path of Bestemmia's own sanctity, which is revealed and denied three times before its final liberation, when the *imitatio Christi* is definitively abandoned in the name of action. Pasolini's farewell to hagiography is fully realized in the rewriting of Bestemmia's destiny in the key of violence and abuse, as expressed in his final speech to his followers. The script advances through reversals and resettings. If the vision has restaged the life of the young man Bestemmia, if it really was the original manifestation of the presence of the sacred, through the *deus ex machina* of angelic intervention, it is reset in its own turn.

In *Bestemmia* we therefore have a saint who does not want to be a saint, a God who reveals himself and then abandons his followers, a representation that represents unrepresentability, and a resistance to linguistic mediation and semiosis that is reconfigured as a pan-semiosis. Reality opposes language – but is itself a language. In Pasolini's own words, presence is the first and last language: *the words of the Flesh.*

Bestemmia: The Words of the Flesh

Pasolini entrusts this formula to us: *the words of the Flesh.* It clearly alludes to corporeality meant as the first language of mankind, which, however, becomes the foundation of an ontological vision in which the body of any individual is an integral part of the Body of the Real. In an essay from *Empirismo eretico,* "Il codice dei codici" ("The Code of Codes," 1967), Pasolini responds to Umberto Eco's criticism of his semiological theories and Eco's accusations that he has traced "the facts of culture back to natural phenomena" (*HE,* 278).[13] Pasolini actually claims he had done the opposite, since his theories tend "*to bring Semiology to the definitive transformation of nature into culture*" (*HE,* 278)[14] through his proposal to identify a semiology of reality. By contrast, both the famous semiologist and contemporary semiology always stop at the threshold of the physicality of reality, leaving our sensorial relations with it buried deeply in an "abyss" (*HE,* 278).[15] It is an epistemological resistance that Pasolini's semiological approach wants to overcome.

> The hair of Jerry Malanga and the eyes of Umberto Eco therefore belong to the same Body, the physical manifestation of the Real, of the Existing, of Being; and if the hair of Jerry Malanga is an object that "reveals itself" as a "sign of itself" to the receptive eyes of Umberto Eco, it cannot be said that this is a dialogue; [it is] a monologue which the infinite Body of Reality has with itself. (*HE,* 279)[16]

> I [Pasolini] have already written and rewritten this. Reality doesn't do anything else but speak with itself using human experience as a vehicle. God, as all religions state, created man to speak with Himself. (*HE,* 247)[17]

The role of cinema thus appears to be central in establishing this general semiology of reality. Pasolini underscores how the language of reality once stood "outside of our consciousness" insofar as it was a natural attribute, but (thanks to the appearance of cinema and audiovisual technology in general) as the "written language of reality" it will become the object of a conscious reflection and will transform our "physical" relations with reality into cultural relations. In Pasolini there is a constant oscillation between culture and nature in a vision of an "acculturated nature" that, in turn, is ready to become a culture stripped of its layers, simply and totally assimilated into life.

This happens to whoever studies cinema: since cinema reproduces reality, it ends up bringing us back to the study of reality, but in a new and special way, as if reality had been discovered through its reproduction, and as if some of its expressive mechanisms had been revealed only through this new "reflected" situation.

> Cinema, in fact, by reproducing reality, gives testimony to its expressiveness, which could have escaped us. In short, it makes a natural semiology. (*HE*, 228)[18]

In addition, Pasolini's semiology of reality is foundational for a reading of cinema that privileges the materiality of communication. For him, the power of cinema thus consists in its returning physicality to the signs. Pasolini talks about the sign's reappropriation of an archaic ability to "*suggest eidetically*, through the physical violence of its reproduction of reality" (*HE*, 232).[19] In this regard, it is significant that he speaks of the movie camera as a "Reality-eater" or "Eye-mouth," in which the mouth has a double connotation, referring both to linguistic expression and to an almost cannibalistic assimilation of reality. It is a "moving" camera, chasing after and capturing images in an almost tactile way. Physicality and violence accompany the sensorial impact of cinema in its reproduction of reality, revealing, beneath the weaving of images, the pure presence of a being that is language that speaks, and that, in its indifference, expresses nothing else but pure life:

> In the world there is (!) a machine that not for nothing is said to shoot
> It is the "Reality eater," or the "Eye-mouth," as you like.
> It does not limit itself to looking at Joaquim with his father and mother, in the favela.
> It looks at him and reproduces him.
> It speaks of him through himself and through his parents.

In the reproduction – on screens large and small –
I interpret him ...
as in reality.
... On the laboratory of big and small screen, he is language.
... Then the language of the "Reality eater" is a brother to the language of Reality.
Illusion, yes, illusion, here and there: because
Who speaks through that language is a Being who [is there][20] and does not love. (*HE*, 255)[21]

And if, for Pasolini, cinema (which does not concretely exist as anything other than the *langue* of those *paroles* that are the movies) is none other than an infinite, hypothetical sequence shot, which image of reality would it return to us? It would return life pure and simple – that is, presence in all its "insignificance" as something that precedes the signified:

> The hypothetical pure sequence shot thus reveals, by representing it, the insignificance of life as life. But through this hypothetical pure sequence shot I also come to know – with the same precision of laboratory tests – that the fundamental proposition that something insignificant expresses is "I am," or "there is," or simply "to be."
>
> But is being natural? No, I don't think so, on the contrary, it seems to me miraculous, mysterious and – if anything – absolutely unnatural. (*HE*, 240)[22]

Pasolini moves in a Saussurian sphere, but he soon realizes that his vision of cinema leads him to force open and amplify the concept of language, "to expand the horizon of semiology and of linguistics to such an extent as to lose our heads at the very thought" (*HE*, 204).[23]

Cinema comes to coincide with life itself as the written language of action, of praxis, of that gigantic representation that is life, in which the subject is actor and spectator at once, present to the others and immersed in their presence. In Pasolini's words:

> In reality, we make cinema by living, that is, by existing practically, that is by acting. *All of life in the entirety of its actions is a natural, living [cinema]*[24]*: in this sense, it is the linguistic equivalent of oral language in its natural and biological aspect.*
>
> By living, therefore, we represent ourselves, and we observe the representation of others. The reality of the human world is nothing more than this double representation in which we are both actors and spectators: a gigantic *happening*, if you will. (*HE*, 204)[25]

Luca Caminati has pointed out how Pasolini's cinematic interpretation of life could be read through the lens of an *esthétique relationelle* as proposed by Nicolas Bourriaud. In this paradigm, the work of art becomes a shared epistemological experiment that engages all the participants, and its intentionality is disseminated and redirected onto all the spectators who are turned into actors, involved beyond their will (2010, 47). The happening, a trend in the art of the 1960s and 1970s, represents for Pasolini the ideal formula for mirroring in life cinema "the written language of reality" as compared with life as "natural, living cinema," which is linguistically affiliated to the oral strata of the language. Life is thus a random, collaborative, spontaneous performance, in which we are all engaged, both spectators and actors, in a collective epistemological laboratory. Cinema is the written transcription of that language of praxis which is life.

Thus, for Pasolini we make cinema by simply living our lives, but, as he contended in his essay "Il Cinema di Poesia" ("The Cinema of Poetry," 1965), the nature of visual communication at the basis of cinema stands at the limit of the human. He is aware of the semiological and linguistic prison, but, although he realizes that cinema brings on the crisis of the Saussurian model, he does not abandon its interpretive grid. The pre-grammatical and pre-morphological character of this "language," however, makes it foreign to the linguistic model, unless reality itself is identified as a system of signs that signify only their own presence. With its mix of absolute objectivity and absolute oneirism, cinema is able to capture the primeval and essential aspect of reality. In Pasolini's words:

> the visual communication which is the basis of [cinematic][26] language is, on the contrary, extremely crude, almost animal-like. As with gestures and brute reality, so dreams and the processes of our memory are almost pre-human events, or on the border of what is human. In any case, they are pre-grammatical and even pre-morphological … *The linguistic instrument on which [cinema][27] is predicated is, therefore, of an irrational type*: and this explains the deeply oneiric quality of the cinema, and also its concreteness as, let us say, object, which is both absolute and impossible to overlook. (*HE*, 168–9)[28]

Although Pasolini intuitively realized the need for a different frame of reference, after him Gilles Deleuze made a clean break from the Saussurian framework. As Naomi Greene noted, Deleuze took up some of Pasolini's key concepts and intuitions and developed them accordingly, pushing them beyond the definition of cinema as language:

> Echoing Pasolini's concept of a "semiology of reality," and his conviction that cinema "reveals" the world to us, Deleuze suggests that we "read" images as we "read" the world ... And, for Deleuze, the world thus revealed is not, or not necessarily, or not at first, a conceptual one; rather, to use Pasolini's terms, it is a world of "physical presence," a pregrammatical and preverbal world where the "non-said" may be more important than the said, a world where bodies themselves "speak." (Greene 1990, 108–9)[29]

According to Deleuze, we have lost faith in the world. For the subject, the link between humankind and the world has been broken, and it can be re-established only through belief, through faith. Belief needs to be addressed not towards a world of beyond, but towards the world we are in. We must believe in this connection, and cinema can help us do that. We need to believe in reality, and the reality of our experience of it. It is what Pasolini calls in *Bestemmia*'s screenplay the "being there." There is a "thereness," and we are in it with all our presence and our perceptions. Deleuze explains:

> The modern fact is that we no longer believe in this world ... The link between man and the world is broken. Henceforth this link must become an object of belief: it is the impossible which can only be restored within a faith. Belief is no longer addressed to a different or transformed world. Man is in the world as if in a pure optical and sound situation. The reaction of which man has been dispossessed can be replaced only by belief. Only belief in the world can reconnect man to what he sees and hears. The cinema must film, not the world, but belief in this world, our only link. Restoring our belief in the world – this is the power of modern cinema ... Whether we are Christians or atheists, in our universal schizophrenia, *we need reasons to believe in this world.* (1989, 171–2)

What does "believing in this world" mean for Deleuze? It means believing in this world just the way it is, and not in another world. To believe in the world means to believe in the body, in the flesh. These are, according to Deleuze, categories defined by Antonin Artaud, but they are not far from Pasolini's "Words of the Flesh" in *Bestemmia.* Deleuze writes:

> What is certain is that believing is no longer believing in another world, or in a transformed world. It is only, it is simply believing in the body. It is giving discourse to the body, and, for this purpose, reaching the body before discourses, before words, before things are named: the "first name,"

> and even before the first name. Artaud said the same thing, believe in the *flesh* ... Our belief can have no object but "the flesh" ... We must believe in the body, but as in the germ of life, the seed which splits open the paving-stones, which has been preserved and lives on in the holy shrouds or the mummy's bandages, and which bears witness to life, in this world as it is. We need an ethic or a faith, which makes fools laugh; it is not a need to believe in something else, but a need to believe in this world, of which fools are a part. (1989, 172–3)

Here Deleuze makes reference to the image of life as the rebirth of a seed, an Eliadian (but also evangelical) image already present in Pasolini, as noted in the first chapter, where I characterized his 1969 *Medea* as connected to the sacred, cyclical time of the harvest. Deleuze also speaks of the "holy shrouds," the *Vera Icona,* which testify to the transubstantiation of the body (the sacred corpse of Christ) into an icon, an image, via the essudation of bodily fluids onto an absorbing surface, like light on film. These, I believe, are exactly the "words of the Flesh" that Pasolini referred to in *Bestemmia,* "words" in the "language" of the agonizing Christ, made of blood, of urine, of excrement, of "sweat as thick as pus." This is the reality of the Incarnation, of *kenosis,* the extreme degree of the "corporeality" discussed by Giuliana Bruno in her essay on Pasolini's semiotics, a corporeality or "body-reality" in front of which, until now, the study of signs has always stopped but that now has become the hub of the articulation of a new semiotics that will trace the "semiotic interplay" (Bruno 1994, 98) of the body and the world of signs. Bruno points out that

> both [Pasolini's] cinematic and theoretical works are informed by "fisicità," a physical pregnancy, as Pasolini practices writing's visibility. In the dialogue between the subject and *res,* the position of the subject is defined in relation to the corporeal "'smell" – the imprint of sex, class, race and the geopolitics of physiognomy. This imprint is marked on the subject's body as well as on the body of things, on their system of use and exchange values. The pragmatic and proxemic relation between *res* and *nomina* (i.e., social practice and language), as mediated by the body, is the territory of definition of ideology. (98)
>
> His subject of language is not a transcendental, disembodied subject. Rather it is the body that is the "scene of writing." The body constitutes a reserve, an archive that informs the decoding of the images – the locus where signification makes its mark, embodying the social process and historicity.

> Such is, for Pasolini, the site of the sign's impact. Communication is ingrained in a social process where signs and object-signs are shaped by, and shape, the social geography. (99)

What Bruno defines as "fisicità" is "presence"; it is a different articulation of the sign, which finds further elaboration in Deleuze. Moving from the configuration proposed by Hjemslev, who articulates the sign in terms of the pair matter-form, rather than the binomial signifier-signified, Deleuze emphasizes how cinematic images represent "a plastic mass, an a-signifying and a-syntaxic material, a material not formed linguistically even though it is not amorphous and is formed semiotically, aesthetically and pragmatically" (1989, 29). It is a matter that is neither *langue* nor *parole* but precedes all linguistic and semantic articulation. It represents a step beyond Pasolini's: from the words of the flesh to the flesh *tout court.*

However, some of Pasolini's statements about cinema are not far from Deleuze's elaborations:

> [Cinema][30] is fundamentally oneiric because of the elementary nature of its archetypes (which I will list once again: habitual and thus unconscious observation of the environment, gestures, memory, dreams) and because of the fundamental prevalence of the pre-grammatical qualities of objects as symbols of the visual language. (*HE*, 171)
>
> For now, therefore, cinema is an artistic and not a philosophic language. It may be parable, but never a directly conceptual expression. This, then, is a third way of restating the dominant artistic nature of cinema, its expressive violence, its oneiric physical quality. (*HE*, 172)[31]

It is in violence – the fruit of a sacrificial archaic sacred and of the very gesture of the Incarnation that abolishes it – that Pasolini deposits the sacrality of his cinema.

The expressive violence of cinema is the violence of the image in and of itself. As Jean-Luc Nancy observes in *The Ground of the Image*:

> Violence and truth have in common a self-showing act; both the core of this act and its realization take place in the image. The image is the imitation of a thing only in the sense in which imitation *emulates* the thing: that is, it rivals the thing, and this rivalry implies not so much reproduction as competition, and, in relation to what concerns us here, competition for presence. The image disputes the presence of the thing. In the image, the

> thing is not content simply to be; the image shows *that* the thing is and *how* it is. The image is what takes the thing out of its simple presence and brings it to pres-ence, to *pres-entia*, to being-out-in-front-of-itself, turned toward the outside … This is not a presence "for a subject" (it is not a "representation" in the ordinary, mimetic sense of the word). It is, on the contrary, if one can put it in this way, "presence as subject." In the image, or as image, and only in this way, the thing – whether it is an inert thing or a person – is posited as subject. The thing *presents itself.* (2005, 21)
>
> Consequently, the phrase "the image of" signifies, not that the image comes after that of which is the image, but that "the image of" is, above all, that within which what is presents itself – and nothing presents itself otherwise. (24)

Nancy fully enunciates in this text the theory of the production of presence in the image, and how the revelation of the image – its opening up – is necessarily linked to a form of violence that bears its identifying mark. The image presents (elsewhere I have said "presentifies") the thing that gathers up, shapes, and pulls itself together while at the same time it pulls itself apart from the ground of being, revealing the violent surface of its presentation. Nancy continues:

> Therefore being is torn away from being; and it is the image that tears itself away. It bears within itself the mark of this tearing away: its ground monstrously opened to its very bottom, that is, to the depthless underside of its presentation. (24).

The image therefore incubates violence within itself as an essential part of its formation. Not only can violence be *pre-sentia*, it can also be expressed through violent images in the content of the representation. In the Pasolinian constellation of artistry, violence, and physicality – in the filmic project of *Bestemmia* as well as in the movies that were produced – the director's fascination with violent images, those Viano defines as "pathological images," plays a special role (Viano 1993, 246). According to Viano, the space Pasolini gives to these images has three explanations. First, the author makes clear his intention to *èpater le bourgeois*, to scandalize and provoke his audience by forcing them to watch the "horrendous universe" of the director as well as their own obscure and repressed shadow. Second, the violent images of torture are linked to Pasolini's realistic imperative; he aims to show the reality of those aspects of life that are normally censured, such as sex and poverty. Finally, every image of torture shifts the focus of representation to corporeality and to vulnerability, emphasizing the unrepresentable, which is, in fact, expressed by pain and suffering. In conclusion, Viano emphasizes how the matrix of Pasolini's obsession with pathological images is precisely the Christian setting of the Passion:

> Pasolini's fascination with pathology is most readily explained by the meaning that passion (pathos) has in Catholic culture, where it is first and foremost the image of a suffering Christ. As the tremendous image of a crucified Christ dominates the Catholic imagination, there is a sense in which Pasolini is not doing anything new, but is simply bringing out a certain pathology already present in our culture. From the fifth century on, religious art indulged in the portrayal of Christ on the cross, wounded, nails through his flesh, pierced by lance and thorns; of martyred saints and women's *pietas*. Such images were meant to have a curative, energized effect on those exposed to them. Such art was meant to cure believers' souls by exposing them to the inevitability of suffering and its redemptive potential, by encouraging them to regard pain as a noble means to achieve a superior stance. At once open wound and cure, Catholicism has been the most prolific purveyor of psychopathological imagery in Western history.
>
> ... But mythology, too, is an inexhaustible source of pathological imagery which can have curative powers, as in Jungian psychotherapy. Greek myth, or the Christian myth for that matter, provided Pasolini with a culturally legitimate outlet for his "pedagogical" desire to pathologize the cinema as a private and public experience of soul-making. (1993, 247–9)

Physicality, corporeality, the flesh, materiality, the Passion: they constitute the knot of themes that tie together Pasolini and Deleuze's film theories, as well as Pasolini's heresy and his vision of the sacred as immanent. This "presence," which Michael Hardt, pushing the concept even further, defines as "exposure," finds its paradigm in the Incarnation as the expression of the immanent transcendence at the centre of the director's vision. In Hardt's words:

> Finally, incarnation is an ethical injunction: empty yourself, become flesh! ... Incarnation is an option of joy and love. And the ultimate form of love is precisely the belief in *this* world, as it is. (2002, 79)
>
> Flesh is the vital materiality of existence. Flesh certainly refers to matter, a passionately charged, intense matter, but it is always equally intellectual. It is not opposed to or excluded from thought or consciousness. Rather, the

> paths of thought and existence are all traced on the flesh. Flesh subtends existence: it is its very potentiality. (82)
>
> Flesh is the condition of possibility of the qualities of the world, but it is never contained within or defined by those qualities. In this sense, it is both a superficial foundation and an immanent transcendence – alien to any dialectic of reality and appearance, or depth and surface. It confounds all of these antinomies. Flesh is the superficial depth, the real appearance of existence. That the world is, how the world is, precisely such as it is, is exposed perfectly and irremediably in the flesh ... The exposure of the flesh is indeed the mystery of life, or rather the miracle of the world. (83)

We can relate Michael Hardt's immanent horizon to Gilles Deleuze's belief in modernity's need to believe in this world just the way it is and in our connection to it. The link between humanity and the world is expressed in the highest degree in the *kenosis,* in the exposition and paradigmatic presence of the Flesh in Christ's Crucifixion. This is the mystery of life, the miracle of the world, the sacred, the immanent transcendence that stirs at the bottom of existence and is inscribed in the divine horizon of the flesh.

The debate over the hereticality of the filmic image found in *Empirismo eretico* and in the fragment of *Bestemmia* about barbaric Christology is intertwined with the iconoclastic polemic of the criminal saint in the subsequent parts of the verse script. Bestemmia's heresy targets images in particular: their insufficiency and fundamental betrayal of any representation of the real. Life becomes the substitute for representation, a body thrown into a fight that takes the place of a staged scene: not paintings, banners, or representations, not the genealogy of sacred images, but rather the true *Imitatio Christi,* the true example: martyrdom. One can consider Bestemmia's speech at the moment in which he tears down the banners and the images of Christ and the Virgin:

> How else do God's witnesses speak if not through examples?
> The words I now pronounce
> are but a part, the last one, of the example
> I give you, as God's witness, with my actions
> that is, with my life.
> Do not throw your spirit into the fight!
> Throw your body into the fight!
> It is through it that your spirit, what you are, speaks.

How much Christ has spoken!
And yet nothing has spoken more than his body
nailed silently to the cross.
Do not use words, do not use images,
do not use symbols.
Be what you are!
Do not pass through any symbol!
Always be what you are.
Tear up with your hands, stomp with your feet
all symbols: throw crosses away.
Let Christ speak with his self,
not with his words, nor with words about him.
And where is Christ? He's within us.
…
But unlike richness that without gold *is not*
Christ *is* without the gold of words
Christ *is* in reality.
Why then are we not with him alone?
Why do we exchange symbols?
What use is the Christ you sell
to me with your word or your image,
that is, with your symbols,
which are necessities of life
and therefore its alteration,
the accepted loss of its reality?
Life is the site of un-reality,
and yet I tell you that there is only life;
because living means only living,
and reality means only reality,
and life can be lived only with itself
and reality can be re-presented only with reality.
… But don't you listen to my words,
follow my example!
And every one of you will live in Christ
not in his words. (*TP2*, 1045–6)[32]

Every linguistic or iconographic mediation represents, for Bestemmia-Pasolini, a fundamental betrayal of life, a life that does not want to be represented but, rather, wants to be simply lived and can only be expressed by the body. "Throw your body into the fight," a slogan of the

American Black Power movement, thus becomes Bestemmia's motto, his *raison d'être*, the narrative thread of his hagiography that also will lead to his end as a saint abandoned by God, intent to answer the human call to class warfare.

In his anti-semiological polemic, Bestemmia will swing from the iconoclasticism of this passage, delivered at the apex of his sanctity, to the acceptance of linguistic and artistic mediation marked by the "invention" of the *Cantico delle creature* (*Canticle of Creatures*). The rewriting of the *Canticle*, with its anti-representational and anti-cultural fury, is an infratextual palinodic gesture not only of Bestemmia but also of Pasolini himself, if we may judge from what is programmatically stated in this long fragment on barbaric Christology. Nevertheless, the quotation of *Cantico* (with an effect *à la* Pierre Menard, although we can hardly imagine two characters farther apart than Borges' citationist and Pasolini's uncouth saint) appears to embrace semiotics: creation is read as divine code, and creatures are read as signs:

> Bless You, my Lord, with all Your creatures,
> especially my bro the sun,
> which is day, and with it You brighten us,
> and it's a beauty and radiant with great splendour:
> it bears Your sign. (*Bestemmia, TP2,* 1065).[33]

Pasolini thematizes in this way, at the textual level, the entire debate on the semiotics of representation, and particularly of cinema, shifting back and forth between a pre-grammatical and pre-morphological paradigm of presence and a linguistic point of view. Pasolini is impatient with Saussurian fetters and is ready to switch the ontological foundation of reality into an absolute pan-semiotics, where language is not the site of being but being itself.

Pasolini is a child of his time in his grammatical and semiological obsession; he approaches cinema bearing in mind the categories established by Metz and other theorists who were attempting to establish a semiological approach to and a linguistic codification of the cinematic medium. At the heart of Pasolini's theory of cinema, however, we always find the intuition, later developed by Deleuze, that what is crucial in cinema is precisely its placement within the "pre-human," its "oneiric, barbaric, irregular, aggressive, visionary quality" (*EE, SLA1,* 1477; *HE,* 178). In reality, for Pasolini, cinema belongs to the origins of humanity; it belongs to life, and it therefore rebels against any sort of systematization, institutionalization, and grammaticalization. As anarchic a *medium* as life itself, cinema gives voice to the flesh before words, to the body as the horizon within which the sacred is inscribed.

In conclusion, however, at least one word points directly to this complementarity of human and divine, of transcendent and immanent, which is also the target of the semiotic status of the cinematic image. It is the name of the protagonist of yet another of Pasolini's subversive hagiographies and the title of the screenplay, "Bestemmia." The explosive contact between animal and divine that Conti Calabrese identified in the name "Bestemmia" (Blasphemy), so dear to Pasolini, points to an immanent vision of the Pasolinian sacred in which "the sacrality of the body and that of the cosmos end up coinciding" in a sacred "contamination":

> The name "Bestemmia" should likely be interpreted as a metaphor used by the author in order to postulate a heretical concept of Christ, denied by the official church but corresponding to that mythical-cosmogonic vision of the redeemer elaborated and assimilated by archaic peasant civilizations …
>
> The use of blasphemy then offers the possibility of affirming that the human body in its integrity is just as sacred as that of the cosmogonic deity to which one refers in invoking it. The sanctity of the body and of the cosmos is brought to coincide in a unity sealed by blasphemy, through which it is possible to regain a mythical anthropocosmic identity. By demoting god to animal and promoting animal to god (as it is done with blasphemy), humanity acknowledges that it stands in a relation of continuity with the cosmos (such as that signalled by the condition of the animal), partaking of an immanent religion that consequently entails an attitude of perennial consecration. (Conti Calabrese 1994, 150–1)[34]

The hybridization between animality and divinity locates the human in a circularity of sacredness. In its structural configuration, the realm of the curse alludes to a cosmic unity that makes the divine closer to the human. It is an immanent circle centred in humanity. The whole emphasis of Pasolini is on the human dimension, from the divine self-emptying of the Incarnation to the elevation of animality to divine status. Blasphemy is the cypher (the reversed prayer) that connects full circle the world of the sacred, from animality to divinity, into its human configuration. The body is the sacred middle ground where the processes of ascent and Incarnation, as the sacred paradigms of the animal and the god, happen. The body is the site of this sacred encounter of high and low, pure and impure, holy and abject, and these manifestations are vocalized in blasphemy or prayer. *Bestemmia* is all about learning – through a troubled saintliness – the lesson of full humanity: to throw one's body into the fight.

Ethical Constellations: Example and Martyrdom

Pasolini also elaborates a new interpretive level that associates metalinguistic reflection on cinema with a hagiographic and sacrificial theme. As seen in *Bestemmia*, the making of the cinematic project – never concretely produced by the director – becomes a laboratory that parallels *Empirismo eretico*'s contemporary meditations on film theory. As previously discussed, Pasolini identifies language with reality. In a human being, language is configured as a language of action, of praxis, that is, of a series of languages socially and historically determined – synthetically summed up in an example – in the moral sense of *exemplum*. Pasolini claims:

> Accordingly, the only language that could be defined as LANGUAGE and only that is that of natural reality. And that of human reality in the moment in which it is not simply natural, but historical? That is: while a poplar speaks a pure language, do I, Pier Paolo Pasolini, speak (while remaining silent, with my being, my face, my action(s) spread out over all the instants, the days, the years, and the decades of my life), do I speak a pure language? Obviously not. This pure language is contaminated in the first place by the first social contract, that is, by language, first in its spoken, then in its written form; and then, by all the infinite non-arbitrary languages which I experience as a result of my birth, my economic condition, my education – society and the historical moment in which I live.
>
> A synthesis of all these integrating languages united with the PURE LANGUAGE of my natural presence as living being (like a poplar) is the language of my human reality, which is therefore primarily an EXAMPLE. (*HE*, 247)[35]

There is always an ethical constellation in which human action is inscribed – first ambiguously, in life, and then redefined and expressed clearly and ineluctably, starting from the moment of death – that changes moral action into a defined, describable, and irrevocable example. Death thus appears to be an essential agent of the moral realization of a destiny, that which makes it necessary. It is death that makes presence meaningful again at the exact moment when it ceases to be. In Pasolini's own words:

> By living, every one of us (willing or not) performs a moral action whose meaning is suspended.
>
> Hence the reason for death. If we were immortal, we would be immoral, because our example would never have an end; therefore, it would be undecipherable, eternally suspended and ambiguous. (*HE*, 247–8)
>
> Either express oneself and die, or remain unexpressed and immortal, I said. (*HE*, 247)
>
> But my idea of death, then, was a behavioral and moral idea: it was not concerned with the aftermath of death, but with the premise of it – not with the beyond, but with life. With life, then, understood as a fulfillment, as a desperate, uncertain search for its expressive perfection, constantly seeking supports, opportunities, and relationships. (*HE*, 248)[36]

Life is thus the continuous search for meaning and fulfilment, which is inscribed in an ethical horizon as well as in an aesthetic one as our own form of expression. Death is thus the signifying agency; it is what makes us intelligible and expressed. Every single existence is reoriented towards meaning by death, and whence it becomes legible. In fact, death acts upon human life in a way analogous to montage in cinema. We can thus remember that, for Pasolini, dying is absolutely necessary. He writes:

> *So long as we live we have no meaning*, and the language of our lives … is untranslatable: a chaos of possibilities, a search for relations and meanings without resolution. *Death effects an instantaneous montage of our lives*: that is, it chooses the truly meaningful moments (which are no longer modifiable by other possible contrary or incoherent moments) and puts them in a sequence, transforming an infinite, unstable, and uncertain – and therefore linguistically not describable – present into a clear, stable, certain and therefore easily describable past (exactly in the context of a General Semiology). *It is only thanks to death that our life serves us to express ourselves.*
>
> Editing, therefore, performs on the material of the film … the operations that death performs on life. (*HE*, 236–7)[37]

There is, therefore, a deep similarity between the stories told in films and human destiny "edited" by death. If cinema is life captured in an endless shot sequence, films, intervening as material filtered through montage, are realized under the sign of death, writing in a tense that presents life from the perspective of its end, as we have seen in chapter 1. Thus, Pasolini establishes a conflation of meaning and senseless life, ethical paradigms and expression around the editing tool of death: obviously the constellation of the ethical example as well as the narrative meaning of a life are thought to be for the "readers," the "spectators," the "witnesses," to whom the dying author of a life entrusts the ultimate deciphering of his or her own fate. They become agents of signification, enabled by death to extract meaning and form from what up to that point was a collection of contingencies and ambiguities. Death is the key to a signifying presence, which acquires meaning in the moment in which it disappears in the corpse.

Pasolini, however, does not choose death only and solely as a privileged point of view on human destiny. According to him, the relation between author and work of art and between author and audience is also always structured under the sign of the death drive. If the exemplum is the ethical constellation to which human life belongs thanks to death, the work of art is always inscribed in the ethical constellation of scandal, inasmuch as it is an infraction of the law and of the survival instinct. As Pasolini writes, "every infraction of the code … is an infraction of self-preservation: it is the exhibition of an autolesionistic act: through which something tragic and unknown is chosen in the place of something quotidian and known (life)" (*HE*, 268).[38] The author embodies the conflict between the instinct of survival and the death drive; he is the individual who digs into this dichotomy, expresses it, and thematizes it. In so doing, as the champion of a freedom that is none other than "freedom to choose death" (*HE*, 267),[39] "*an autolesionistic assault on self-preservation*" (*HE*, 267, italics in original),[40] he consciously challenges life and society, appearing necessarily to be a martyr. The relationship with his audience thus becomes a sadomasochistic phenomenon in a ritual in which *pathos* and *eros* overlap, amplified by the spectacularization and mass-mediatization of the relationship between author and audience in movie theatres. Pasolini continues:

> I must repeat the refrain; the spectators are wounded by the filmmaker "aware of his language," and in turn they wound the filmmaker (with the exception of the privileged spectators who share with him the idea that extremist scandal is necessary), so that the filmmaker can enjoy equally the pleasure and the pain of martyrdom equally testifying to his own "freedom from repression," as suicidal intoxication, defeatist vitality, didactic self-exclusion, exhibition of meaningful sores. Are these virtually hagiographic "examples" loci of a reactionary writing? No; I myself, when working with the moviola (or earlier, when shooting), feel the almost sexual effect of the infraction of the code as the exhibitionism of something violated (a feeling

> that one also experiences when writing verses, but which cinema multiplies ad infinitum; it is one thing to be martyred in private, and something else altogether to be martyred in the public square, in a "spectacular death"). (*HE*, 273)
>
> Only the death of the hero is a show, and only it is useful.
>
> By their own decision, therefore, the martyr-filmmakers always find themselves, stylistically, on the firing line; that is, on the front line of linguistic transgressions. (*HE*, 273)[41]

In the years when Pasolini was writing his heretical crucifixions and subversive hagiographies, the importance of the hagiographic model and of a martyrological modality in his vision of life and art emerges very clearly in his metafilmic reflections. In "Progetto di Opere Future" ("Project for Future Works," 1964), Pasolini writes: "It is necessary to disillusion. To jump on the embers always / like roasted ridiculous martyrs" (*PFR, TP1*, 1248). The motives of the Passion and the Crucifixion thus work as fundamental matrices in the poet's imagination, at once archetypes of the urgency of representation and of all that representation cannot represent. *Imitatio Christi*, pain, suffering, and the unrepresentable act within representation as destabilizing elements, denouncing and pushing its limits to the extreme. At the same time, the same pain and the same suffering respond to the ethical constellation of the choice expressed in breaking the law of self-preservation, the choice of the death drive against life. The artistic choice is also so configured as conflict and scandal, aiming at inhabiting the uninhabitable, at choosing to represent and express the unrepresentable. The character Bestemmia is therefore a martyr in the description of the crazed trajectory of his cursed sanctity, in his holding on to a faith suspended over the void of a God who calls to him and then abandons him, in his offering himself as the extreme example of a constant oscillation between life and death, sanctity and crime, sacred vision and orgy, self-sacrifice and death armed to one's teeth. Bestemmia's director is also a martyr, one who continuously violates the audience's expectations and the moralistic and vital horizon of the society to which he belongs, ready to climb onto the gallows of censorship and scandal. In his "being for" death, Pasolini violates the self-perpetuating surface of society in order to respond to a deeper, more "desperate" vitality. We return full circle to the theme of *kenosis* and sacrifice as the central nerve of Pasolini's thought. As Conti Calabrese has pointed out:

> Death allows us to dive into the depth of the sacred donation that is the reservoir from which to continue to donate. Only one who has a passion for life can truly die, because one sees redemption in death: freedom from new life. Pasolini's Christian heresy is all here: a Christ-Man suffers and dies; thus, by sacrificing himself, he gives humanity the awareness that the sacred in sacrifice consists in giving oneself in leaving, and to recognize this means to partake of the mystery the Redeemer reveals in dying. (Conti Calabrese 1994, 155–6)[42]

Finally, in writing his subversive hagiographies, as we will see in the following chapters, Pasolini does not do anything other than bring onto the scene his own scandal of being a martyr-filmmaker "on the firing line," "testifying to his own 'freedom from repression,'as suicidal intoxication, defeatist vitality, didactic self-exclusion, exhibition of meaningful sores" (*HE*, 273). Pasolini will give voice to the anthropological mutations of his society, between the impasse of the omnivorous bourgeoisie and the disappearance of the innocent bodies of the subproletarians, in the context of the irrelevant but crucial presence of a vanishing and *tremendum* sacred.

Chapter Four

The Mad Saint and the Anchorite: *Theorem*

What do you mean exactly by allegorical film?
A work in which everything signifies something else, it refers to another reality. In *Teorema*, for example, the young visitor is not only a visitor who has come to spend some time at some friends' family home in Milan; he is an allegory of God.

Pier Paolo Pasolini, *Il sogno del centauro*[1]

As we have seen, the theme of the sacred is central for Pasolini; particularly at the end of the 1960s. We have also noted the "heretical" perspective with which the atheist Marxist writer and director viewed his relationship with the Catholic Church, through his lens of the Incarnation. I now examine one of the specific aspects of the sacred – "saintliness" – as well as the "medieval" genre of "hagiography." These elements often recur in Pasolini's films as well as in his texts that stand between cinema and literature (i.e., screenplays in prose and verse, movie projects, and narrative reworkings of films). In the world of show business, it is simply a given that the cinematic medium lends itself to a hagiographic perspective; the Hollywood star system has fully embraced this function – albeit in secular terms – and serves as the presenter of behavioural *exempla* in the same way hagiographies did in the Middle Ages.

An exemplary hagiography is Pasolini's presentation of Marilyn Monroe in the visual cinematic poem *La rabbia* (*Rage*, 1963). This piece of cinematic poetry is one of the first "found footage" masterpieces in the history of Italian cinema. In *La rabbia*, Pasolini elegizes a disappearing mythical world, and includes nightmarish, apocalyptic images of contemporary history – a history doomed to end in the all-pervasive atomic mushroom cloud of the nuclear holocaust. Monroe symbolizes the world's beauty, a beauty threatened by the prospect of atomic catastrophe. Pasolini presents her both as an innocent little girl and as a Christ-like figure, juxtaposing images of the mature Monroe with images of the Savior in a popular Passion play. According to Sandro Bernardi (2010), Monroe's portrayal implies two myths: the Christian myth of Christ's Passion and the classical myth of the disappearance of Astrea (Justice) from the human sphere.

Apart from *La rabbia*, Pasolini rejects these hagiographies of stardom. Instead, he presents examples of archaic or heretical sanctity from the bottom up: behavioural *exempla* grounded in socio-economic reality, parables of impossible conversions, and representations of total dissent and anonymous or aberrant sacrifice.

Pasolini's *Teorema*

Within the range of these heretical models of sanctity, we find also a specifically feminine variant exemplified by the "mad saint" in *Teorema*, a work in which Pasolini's obsession with the sacred and with sanctity reverberates in another form of hagiographic subject – that of the anchorite.

The movie begins with a prologue in which a journalist is interviewing workers about the factory owner's recent decision to donate his industrial plant to them. Through the cut of a desert landscape, the five protagonists of the movie then appear, caught by the camera in their environment. They are Paolo, the industrialist, driving back home from his factory in a chauffeured car; his son Pietro, joking with his classmates outside of his school; his daughter Odetta, shyly talking to a boy on the way home from her religious college; and Paolo's wife Lucia, reading a book and conversing with her maid Emilia, the final central character. These sequences, presented without any dialogue and accompanied by an avant-garde jazz soundtrack, share a decidedly eerie quality.

As the film's action begins, Angelo, the postman, brings a telegram to the family announcing the arrival of a Visitor, who in fact arrives the following day. He is a handsome young man, probably an engineering student, who reads Rimbaud. Every family member seems irresistibly attracted to the young Visitor; Emilia tries to commit suicide for fear of not being loved by him, but he saves her and they make love. Pietro discovers his homosexuality through his relationship with the young man. Lucia seduces him, renouncing her identity as a chaste bourgeois wife. Odetta lets the visitor make love to her, and she overcomes her Oedipal fixation on her father. After an illness, the father, Paolo, also begins to question his identity as an upper-class *pater familias* and embraces his sexual desire for the young guest.

Eventually, a telegram arrives calling the guest away. Since he is to leave the next day, each member of the household must confront his or her self-revelations. After their sexual encounters with the visitor, each confesses his or her angst over the upcoming separation and the new direction life will take. In the aftermath of his departure, each attempts to cope with a new reality. Odetta entrusts herself to her clenched fist, becoming catatonic and ending up in a psychiatric clinic. Pietro becomes an artist, leaving his family and trying to convey in his art the loss of his beloved, although his artistic efforts prove disappointing. Lucia has casual sex with other young men who remind her of the visitor, yet she is unable to relive that first miraculous sexual encounter.

Emilia leaves the house to go back to her family in the countryside. She lives in the courtyard of her farm, nurtured and venerated as a saint by her people, and at the film's end she even performs miracles and achieves levitation. She gives herself to her community, burying herself alive at a construction site and giving birth, through her self-sacrifice, to a miraculous fountain of tears. Finally, Paolo removes his clothes in the Milan train station, like a new Saint Francis, and walks away from the crowd until he reaches the desert glimpsed intermittently throughout the movie. He thus submits himself to a fate of social death and total annihilation of his previous identity, transfixed in a cry that seems destined to last forever.

Teorema, which was conceived as both a film and a book between 1968 and 1969, had a troubled gestation. It was born, as the author tells us, as a "tragedy" or a "verse play." Functioning as a mythical device, it was the seventh work conceived in the course of the intense 1966 "theatrical" season when Pasolini, who was recovering from an ulcer, created six dramatic texts that he would fully develop over the next two years.[2] Pasolini imagined *Teorema* as a film, sensing that the story he wanted to tell, "the love between the divine visitor and the bourgeois characters[,] was more beautiful if silent" (*PPC2*, 2934).[3] He initially deemed the movie project impossible to realize, instead opting for the form of a story, a treatment that progressively acquired literary autonomy. But this anti-novel would eventually be developed into a screenplay and made into a film. On the jacket of the book, published in March 1968, the author states, "*Teorema* was created, as if on a gold background, painted with my right hand, while with my left hand I painted a fresco on a large wall (the eponymous film). Given its amphibolous nature, I honestly cannot say which element prevails, the literary or the filmic" (Garboli 1969, 264).[4]

As Pasolini's comment indicates, the allegorical character of the text appears to position it along archaic medieval coordinates. In his analysis, Cesare Garboli introduced the categories of "sacred example," "mirror," or "miracle play" – three standard medieval genres based on the narration of exemplary stories with a didactic, moral, and educational purpose.

> The brief parables that neatly comprise the whole of the "sacred example" that is *Teorema* often recall the varied bourgeois polychromy of Trecento and Quattrocento predellas: scenes with moments of sacred or country life, stories of the saints, miracles, legends, rich interiors, landscapes, episodes painted with a taste for the real, with a precision that results in a sharp, fantastic realism ... As we said, *Teorema* is a treatment, a "written film." ... As in fables, everything has already been written. There is an implicit movie in *Teorema* that is certainly not the one we will watch. This movie is a sacred story, an exemplum, a medieval "mirror" (the gold background), against which the stupid story of bourgeois impotence that the poet gradually tells us disappears. In candid, naive language, indeed, the language of a devout narrator – as befits the poor human story – but also in luxurious language – as befits the ineffable theme – Pasolini explains, comments on and illustrates in a series of panels the essence of a miracle play. (Garboli 1969, 265–6)[5]

A polyptych on a gold background, a didactic poem, or a *prosimetrum* from medieval origins, the novel *Teorema* is a modern, abased, and – albeit with one important exception – an unredeemed *Vita Nova.* Rather than a story of redemption, the novel tells the story of different ways in which the duplicity of bourgeois existence is destroyed by the sacred. The hypothesis that informs this cinematic and literary parable is "a hypothesis that is mathematically demonstrated *per absurdum.* The question is this: if a bourgeois family were visited by a young god, whether Dionysus or Jehovah, what would happen?" (*SC, SPS,* 1483).[6]

If we follow the development of the plot, the movie is a series of hypotheses and corollaries. In the *cinèma verité* opening – which, we will eventually discover, is in fact the end of the movie – we see a television crew filming the journalist Cesare Garboli as he interviews several factory workers. Garboli asks them what they think of the owner's recent decision to give the factory to them. Pasolini immediately places us face to face with the sociological hypothesis in relation to the sacred theorem: "no matter how he acts, even if he donates his factory, a bourgeois is wrong. Isn't he?" (*PPC1*, 1081–2).[7] The interview, like the movie itself, remains open-ended. The workers have been deprived of the revolution by this incomprehensible gesture of their employer and are unable to understand the new dynamics. These "new demands" of the bourgeoisie are tied to a very different kind of revolution, one that sweeps the proletariat by assimilating it into the bourgeoisie itself. They will thus counter the journalist's persistent "Can you answer these questions? Can you answer these questions?" (*PPC1*, 1081–2)[8] with a meaningful disconcerted silence.

Maurizio Viano identifies a fundamental aspect of the film in this first scene: its representation of a crisis of signs on the horizon of the post-modern – or, in Pasolini's own terminology, of Post-history (*Dopostoria*). The crisis is one of grand narratives, including the fundamental tenets of Marxist philosophy:

> Since such fundamental signifiers as "bourgeoisie," "factory," and "class struggle" can no longer go unquestioned, the text postulates a crisis of the signs following the disintegration of History as the ultimate signified. Thus, the film's first sequence positions the viewer within the uncertainty of postmodernity, the end of teleological master-narratives, the crisis of signs. (Viano 1993, 200)

As the opening credits roll, the images of a desert – the red, volcanic slopes of Mount Etna – appear to visually correlate with such a crisis. The images are followed by a quotation from the Old Testament, "But God led the people about, through the way of the wilderness" (Exodus 13:18), and recur as a leitmotif throughout the film. For example, the desert appears in the scenes that immediately follow, as a reverse shot of the faces of a series of characters filmed without sound recording. Scenes of daily life are set to a dissonant soundtrack: a chauffeured private car leaves the prison-like grounds of a factory; students in coats and ties come out of their high school; girls exit a religious school; an elegant bourgeois lady converses (without sound) with her maid; and the interior of a luxurious villa sits still, the action of the story yet to begin. The oppressive feeling of homogenization and assimilation, the visible mark of bourgeois pretense, is heightened by the livid hue of the images and by the soundless dialogue of the characters, as in a silent movie. Though the images of the family and those of the desert are in many ways antithetical, at the same time they function as true mirrors for one another, as the desert hints forebodingly of events destined for emblematic and revelatory dialectic integration. The scenes continuously slip back into the livid images of the desert, thus anticipating the impetuous entrance of the sacred – that is, the tragic and mythic – into the colourless, silent daily life of the hypocritical bourgeoisie.

We will later recognize the faces and bodies shown in the initial sequences as those of the protagonists of the story. We are in the northern Po Valley, with its poplar groves and its factories, at the home of a family of the high industrial bourgeoisie, who welcome the arrival of a mysterious and very handsome visitor. One after the other, the inhabitants of this *hortus conclusus* fall in love with this Rimbaudian guest, who, during his short visit, reveals each of them to him- or herself. Then, as mysteriously as he has come, he vanishes.

The conflict Pasolini stages through the metaphor of a silent apocalyptic *eros* is that between authenticity and deceit or, in Girardian terms, between the lie of bourgeois life and the even deeper lie of mimetic desire projected beyond the threshold of the "metaphysical."[9] After seeing themselves reflected in the gaze and wrapped in the embrace of a mysterious being who enlightens them and then leaves, each character falls into a personal abyss. In the apotheosis of mimetic desire aroused in this bourgeois family, where the Visitor is at the same time the object of desire and its model, everything comes crashing down.

> In short, desire relieves its subject of an intolerable knowledge... . In effect, desire is responsible for its own evolution ... Desire is always using for its own ends the knowledge it has acquired of itself; it places the truth in the service of its own untruth, so to speak, and it is always becoming better equipped to reject everything that surrenders to its embrace ... seeking always to entrap itself in the cul-de-sac that is its very *raison d'être*.
>
> The idea of the demon who bears light is more far-reaching than any notion in psychoanalysis. Desire brings light but puts that light in the service of its own darkness. (Girard 1987, 303–4)

The revelation prompted by this Old Testament *eros* is destined to make each household member a potential victim, ready to be sacrificed or expelled from the community. They become, in the end, a madwoman (Odetta), a prostitute (Lucia), an artist (Pietro), an anchorite (Paolo), and a saint (Emilia). *Teorema* therefore functions as a mythical device configured to tell the tale of a series of rites of expulsion. The family explodes, or rather, it silently implodes. Each character leaves on a personal exodus, each an empty body off to forty years in the desert to face a God who has prompted a self-revelation that includes an awareness of their frightening aloneness.

Normal parameters are pulverized: Lucia, Odetta, and Pietro experience a subjective revolution only in bouts, one that leads nowhere. Pasolini himself confirms this intuition in the book, when he explores their personal corollaries and tells how each of them "ends up losing and betraying God."[10] They have undergone a conversion, but there is no redemption for them, no resurrection or revolution. One could quote David Maria Turoldo's poetry, caught in the moment of revelation and despair:

> Prophecy is extinguished / poetry is mute / music is a cry ... / God is not there in the new Chaos: no more the Spirit lifts over these abysses / to conduce the exodus / towards new Forms: // Beauty has been defeated! (*Nel Segno del Tau: E ridiamo,* quoted in Finotti 1993, 100)

There is something deeply Christian in the crisis of the family of *Teorema,* in the way they suffer the "ontological paradox" of the Christian faith, a paradox that Turoldo experienced within a different sacred framework:

> The fullest revelation corresponded to the most absolute despair, the dismay of a God ... If the supreme revelation and the supreme creation consisted in the incarnation of the Word and in our possibility to relive the experience of it via *imitatio Christi,* then one needed to be ready to re-experience not only the suffering, but also the desperate upheaval of Christ and his detachment from the foundation. (Finotti 1993, 102)[11]

The difference between Turoldo and Pasolini is in the possibility of redemption, which does not appear in Pasolini's vision. Pasolini frames his characters like imploded monads: Lucia gives in to a compulsive sexual repetition, Pietro to a frenetic and impotent artistic frustration, Odetta to full-fledged schizophrenia. In this parable, the bodies are arranged in an arc: at one end, there is Odetta's catatonic immobility, represented by her tightly closed fist, brought on by her failure to grasp God's incommensurable absence. Then there is Pietro's gesticulation during a creative bout of desperate and casual action painting, in which he urinates over his artwork as he tries to banish the control of the gaze over artistic expression. Finally, at the other end of the arc, there is Lucia's serial intercourse with young simulacra of God and her angry, enigmatic escape to an (aptly) abandoned church.

In that church, Lucia finds herself in the presence of a different simulacrum of the Divine – the opposite of the bodies, gazes, and clothes she fetishizes. She is not the only one to seek substitutes: Odetta has a photograph, Pietro has the portrait that cannot be painted. But God has departed, and no simulacrum seems sufficient to return His presence; this presence-absence emerges in all of them, like the trace of an unfillable void.[12] One turns inward, one turns to artistic frenzy, one turns to repeated sex acts, and finally turns to an encounter with an altar and a crucifix looming up behind it. They all confront what Mark Taylor defines as "altarity," and they all go through "disfiguring":

> To disfigure is to de-sign by removing figures, symbols, designs, and ornaments. Second, to disfigure is to mar, deform, or deface and thus destroy the beauty of a person or object. Finally, disfiguring is an unfiguring that (impossibly) "figures" the unfigurable.
>
> ... In this interstitial site, figure is neither erased nor absolutized but it is used with and against itself to figure that which eludes figuring. Torn figures mark the trace of something else, something other that *almost* emerges in the crack of faulty images. This other neither is nor is not – it is neither being nor nonbeing, fullness nor void, immanent nor transcendent. It is more radically other than the other that is the other *of* the same. I improperly "name" this unnamable other "altarity." Never present without being absent, altarity approaches by withdrawing and withdraws by approaching. (1992, 8–9)

Odetta's closed fist, the biting of Lucia's hand after casual intercourse, the stream of urine on Pietro's canvas and his uncertain steps with blindfolded eyes as he attempts to recapture in paint the traces of the lost visitor – all of these actions are existential gestures. They are all extreme, final acts, distorted syntagms of the language of the characters' actions, marked by the disfiguration of memory and the impossibility of stopping, grasping, and transubstantiating the Visitor's presence, which has become an irreversible absence, his "altarity."

The father (Paolo) tries to give up his role of master as described by the axiom of the Pasolinian theorem: "No matter how he acts, a bourgeois [or should we perhaps say desire?] is wrong" (*RR2*, 1081). This axiom, invoked as a hypothesis at the movie's beginning, manifests itself as the film progresses. According to Pasolini, a bourgeois no longer has a soul, only a conscience. For the ailing bourgeoisie, truth is a void: it is the desert in which Paolo finds himself at the point where the two narrative frames collapse into one: like a modern-day Saint Francis, he takes off his clothes at the Milan railway station and walks naked into the desert. The desert is something that simply is; it holds us without giving us direction, answers, resources, or a horizon. There, we are only bodies without social masks, without death and therefore, according to Pasolini, without destiny (even if we consider symbolic suicide),[13] and no longer with God. Contrary to any messianic perspective, that God – like Rimbaud's "Adorable" cited in the film – "had already come, did not come back, and will never return."[14] The road of return, of advent, is barred. As Jean-Luc Nancy writes in *The Inoperative Community*, "Eyes filled and deserted by divinity, that is our condition" (1991, 126).

"The irrupting of the sacred into everyday life," which for Pasolini is the essence of tragedy, is represented in *Teorema* through two elements: the body of the Visitor and the desert. Pasolini leaves ample room for speculation on the Visitor's identity, making him the latest manifestation of his taste for contamination and religious syncretism. He also underlines the dual nature of the sacred, which is divine and demonic at the same time – as we will see, for example, in *San Paolo* or in *Appunto 34 bis* of the posthumous novel *Petrolio* (1992). According to Viano, the Visitor is a catalyst, an authentic reflecting device, a mirror (like the edifying literary genre with which Garboli identified the novel *Teorema*). He is, in Viano's interpretation,

> a sort of provocative mirror held up to the faces of the spectators in order to reflect the reality of their readings … He embodies an exceptional force capable of driving the signs in the text to a passionate (pathological) self-revelation. Hence, it is less a question of defining him than of understanding his effects. (1993, 202)

Before we examine these effects, it is important to identify the syncretistic aspects of the sacred in Pasolini. On several occasions, the author insists on the archaic nature of this ambiguous divinity, an ambiguity that results from the combination of the Old Testament God with both the Eurypidean Dionysus (especially in his undifferentiated seductive modality)[15] and the mystery of Christ's Incarnation. The Visitor is a young father with a maternal side who, in his uniqueness, constitutes a sort of transgenerational, transgendered trinity of father, son, and mother.

Massimo Fusillo provides a Dionysian interpretation of *Teorema* in his book *Il Dio Ibrido* (*The Hybrid God*):

> The sacred Dionysian dimension of the film emerges especially in the fetishistic attention to detail and in the poetics of the body and the gaze typical of Pasolini. The body thus becomes the figure of a primitive, subversive sexuality, which unhinges the societal control of the family. (2006, 215)[16]

However, in an interview, Pasolini declared that the Visitor represents the *ingham* [*sic*], the Sanskrit word for "penis" (Magrelli 1977, 93). Beyond this strictly sexual interpretation, it is useful to follow the trail delineated by Pasolini's statements about the identity of this loving Visitor, who is changed into exterminating angel of the bourgeoisie by the devastating effects his apocalyptic presence has on those he meets. In several interviews and articles, Pasolini explained:

> Originally, I would have liked to make this visitor a god of fertility, the typical god of the pre-industrial religion, the sun god, the biblical god, God the Father. Obviously, once I faced reality, I had to abandon my first idea and turned Terence Stamp into a generically otherworldly metaphysical apparition. He could be the Devil or a mix of God and the Devil. What matters is just the fact that the result is authentic and unstoppable. (*SPS*, 1392–3)[17]

> I don't court scandal. God is scandal, in this world. If Christ came back, he would again cause scandal. He did it in his time, and he would do it again today. My stranger ... is not Christ presented in a contemporary setting, and he is not Eros in absolute terms. He is the message of the unmerciful god, of Jehovah who, through a concrete sign, a mysterious presence, draws the mortals out of their false safety.
>
> He is a god who destroys the good conscience dearly paid for by the prim bourgeois who live, or vegetate, in its safety, wrapped up in a false idea of self. [18]
>
> This character cannot be identified with Christ. If anything, he is God, God the Father (or a messenger representing God the Father). He is the biblical visitor of the Old Testament, not the visitor of the New Testament. (*PPC2*, 2933)[19]

According to Millicent Marcus, however, among the different sacred or religious characteristics that syncretistically bring the figure of the Visitor to life, there is also a New Testament component connected to the motif of the Incarnation, which is brought to its extreme development in the image of a god who carnally possesses those he calls to himself in "the ultimate act of *caritas.*" The paradox of this parable is that it is interrupted:

> Yet the analogy between the visitor and Christ remains incomplete, for the visitor is Christ unresurrected, the savior who remains on the cross and whose death is not followed by rebirth into eternal life. This half-realized *imitatio Christi* explains the destructive effect of the visitor on the members of the household. While he motivates conversions, urging his disciples to abandon the old way and follow him, these conversions are partial. The visitor completes only the first half of the conversion process: that of the *askesis,* and departs before indicating how his converts can remake themselves in his image. He leaves them without a prescription for change, without anything to replace their discarded selves. Lacking a guide, suddenly bereft of sanctifying grace, the family flounders and fails.
>
> Pasolini has used both Old Testament and New Testament typology to demonstrate the sorrow of incomplete conversion. (1986, 258–9)

Although it is not by chance that Pasolini makes reference to the image of the Exodus and of the Jews wandering in the desert, I believe that Pasolini diverts *Teorema* – with its Christ *sans* crucifixion or resurrection, its Incarnation *sans* redemption – to a space beyond the Old and the New Testament. Post-history[20] has undone the work of the *verbum,* issuing a call that essentially becomes a condemnation of a hopeless desire for a lost Other. For those who have lost the path of the sacred or have relied exclusively on the resources of their own monadic identity, the world of Revelation has returned to an Old Testament relationship with the absolute. The call has been issued and the road to Revelation has been opened, but he who came has taken away his secret and those who answered his call do not understand its code. The Messiah came but deserted us, and he left no Gospel or prescriptions, no Church of followers, no guidance, no institution. The figure of the Visitor seems to refer to a sudden voluntary defection of the absolute – as expressed also in "Il poeta delle ceneri" ("The Poet of the Ashes," 1966) – rather than to God's death:

> And everyone, in waiting, in reminiscing,
> as apostle of a Christ who was not crucified but lost,
> finds his destiny.
> It is a theorem:
> and every destiny is a consequence. (*TP2,* 1281)[21]

We could actually agree with Pasolini about the Old Testament identity of the Visitor, "the God of beyond" of whom Žižek speaks. The God of the Old Testament establishes a new model of incarnation: not Christ's agonizing body but the erotic body of the Canticle of Canticles. This erotic body is combined with a new form of incarnation based on physical possession to form a different theology of the flesh. God does not become man. He only possesses man physically, and this allows Him to undo the covenant of the cross and establish a relationship that humanity is largely condemned to misunderstand. Neither Emilia nor Paolo, however, will suffer this misunderstanding. They will both reclaim their path to a God who has abandoned them by setting their actions within the horizon of a community inspired by the presence of the Spirit. Emilia's farmhands and Paolo's factory workers will thus be the true beneficiaries of this covenant. Emilia will sacrifice herself as a *trait d'union* between the archaic rural world and working-class modernity. Paolo will give his labourers control of their own tools, committing a symbolic suicide and ending up in the sublime realm of the real, where God no longer exists and is forever out of the reach of the bourgeois.

We are thus dealing with an archaic biblical God, a unique God – different in what He reflects and unique in His essence in the pure passion He arouses in those who see themselves mirrored in His gaze. He has a singular power to strip to the core those who heed His call; the image of the desert, almost subliminally disseminated throughout the film and in some key passages of the book, reflects the uniqueness of this God. The book reflects on this aspect of the desert in the chapter "The Jews set forth towards the desert":

> The Jews set forth towards the desert.
>
> All day long, from the moment the horizon was outlined against the red of dawn, in flat dunes dark with rocks and in rounder ones, made of sand but also dark, until the moment when it was again outlined against the red of the sunset, *the desert was always the same.*
>
> Its inhospitality had only one form. It went on always the same wherever the Jews may be, whether walking or not.
>
> With every mile, the horizon appeared to be a mile further, so that the distance between the eyes and the horizon never changed. The desert changed like a desert ... The landscape of the opposite of life went on and on without ever being obstructed or interrupted by anything. It was born of itself, went on as itself, and ended in itself, but it did not reject man. On the contrary, it took him in. It was inhospitable but not hostile, contrary to

> his nature but profoundly similar to his reality ... The Jews began to understand Oneness. *The Oneness of the desert was like a dream that doesn't let us rest but from which we cannot awake.*
>
> The desert was One, and it was One a step further; One two steps further; One no matter how many steps the Jews might take.
>
> ... It was the endless pain of the sick who turn from one side to the other, languishing in bed. On one side, they feel the desert; on the other, they again feel the desert, and while they are turning they feel together *the desire to forget it and the desire to find it again.* (*RR2*, 961–3, italics mine)[22]

The sense of the passing of time is marked by an inexorable cyclicity; the day eternally returns, the immutable landscape obsessively crushes infinity to a point. The subject loses direction and any sense of perspective or distance – the loss of history that entails the lack of any term of comparison, the nullification of the concepts of progress, origin, and end (in the sense of purpose and of conclusion); and the disappearance of any sign to grab on to that is not the eternal return to the desert. Such loss is soothed by the feeling of uniqueness and of the absolute, of a substance that permeates everything we see, of a noumenon that subtends every phenomenon.[23]

At one point, there is a reference to Paul the Apostle in the desert at the moment of his conversion, which is identified with a return not to the womb of the mother but to the loins of the father. Again subjectivity is simultaneously lost and defined under an absolute gaze.[24]

> The desert began to appear again in all it was, and to see it like it was – a desert and nothing other than a desert – one only had to *be there.* Paolo walked and walked, and every step he took confirmed it. Once the last feathery palm trees gathered in picturesque groups had disappeared, the obsession returned, that is, the walking without going anywhere.
>
> ... Whatever Paolo might be thinking was contaminated or dominated by that presence. Everything in his life, which now appeared very clearly not to be the simple life of the oasis, was unified by that Thing, which he experienced always in the same way because it was always the same.
>
> He couldn't go crazy because, after all, as something unique insofar as only itself, the desert gave him a profound sense of peace. It was as if he had returned, no, *not to his mother's, but to his father's loins.*
>
> And precisely like a father, the desert watched him from every part of its boundless open horizon. There was nothing that could shield Paolo from that gaze. Wherever he may be – that is, always in the same place – that gaze

> found him across the vast dark expanse of sand and stones without any difficulty, with the same deep peace, naturalness and violence with which the sun shone immutably ...
>
> Paolo travelled on that road without history, in the complete identification of the light of the sun with the consciousness that he was living. (*RR2*, 964–5)[25]

In his moment of conversion, Paolo finds himself living in a primeval Eden, preceding the creation of the world. In a poem dedicated to Odetta and titled "The First Paradise," Pasolini tells the myth of the loss of Paradise, "of the departure from a maternal happy Eden."[26] He later introduces a variant in what he calls the "theory of the two paradises"; this alternative paradise, one that precedes that of tradition, is dominated by the Father and by the uniqueness of the desert.

> The first Paradise, Odetta, was that of the father.
> There was an alliance of the senses in the son
> – male and female –
> derived from the adoration of something unique.
> And the world, all around,
> had only one trait: that of the desert.
> In that dim endless light,
> in the circle of the desert like on a powerful lap,
> the child enjoyed Paradise.
> Remember: there was only a Father (no mother).
> He smiled his protection
> with an adult smile, but young
> and slightly ironic, like that of those who protect the weak,
> the tender-hearted – male or little girl – always is. (*RR2*, 951)[27]

What, then, is this desert obsessively associated with the paths walked by the characters in *Teorema*, who are diverted without any hope of return? The answer comes from Paolo – not the apostle, but the father in the family "visited" by God – in the last pages of the book when, as in the film, he wanders in the desert. "I'M FILLED WITH A QUESTION," he says, "TO WHICH I HAVE NO ANSWER."[28]

> Like to the people of Israel or to Paul the apostle before me,
> the desert is revealed to me like that
> which alone, in reality, is indispensable.
> Or, better said, like reality

stripped of everything but its essence,
just like it is seen by those who live it and, sometimes,
think about it even without being philosophers.
There is nothing more around here
than what is really necessary:
the earth, the sky, and the body of a man.
...
But what will prevail? *The mundane barrenness*
of reason or religion, the despicable
fertility of those who live left behind by history? (*RR2*, 1053–4, italics mine)[29]

Paolo's answer is an inarticulate cry, "a cry let out to call someone's attention / or his help, but maybe also to curse him" (*RR2*, 1055).[30] Prayer or curse, sound of hope or cry of utter despair, "destined to last beyond any possible end" (*RR2*, 1056),[31] Paolo's cry expresses the position of humankind in Post-history or, better, in the new Pre-history, an era without any horizon of hope or revolution in view, stuck in a moment of transition that does not seem to lead anywhere. The totality that supports us is a desert with no answer: this is reality behind the phantasmagoria of appearances.

The desert is the place of God's desertion. As Jean-Luc Nancy argues, "Our experience of the divine is our experience of its desertion. It is no longer a question of meeting God in the desert: but of this – and *this* is the desert – we do not encounter God, God has deserted all encounters" (1991, 148).

In the closing pages of the book, Pasolini talks about "the mundane barrenness / of reason or religion, the despicable / fertility of those who live left behind by history" as being the two alternatives between which the body is suspended. He presents them as two solutions. The first is represented by Paolo, the father, who is forever confined in the desert of a conversion closed in on itself (although the gift of the factory announces a new equilibrium for the lower classes). The second is embodied by Emilia, the maid who follows instead the millenarian path of the sacred and carries out her *Imitatio Christi* to the very end, offering a sacrificial and salvific answer to the impossible mourning of metaphysical mimetic desire.

Emilia and Paolo

Someone is saved, then: Emilia the maid. Pasolini introduces her in the novel *Teorema* with a few meaningful strokes:

> Emilia is an ageless woman who could be eight just as well as thirty-eight, a poor northern Italian, excluded from the white race. (She very likely comes from some poor town of the Po Valley, not far from Milan but still completely rural; possibly from the Lodi province, from the area that gave birth to a saint who probably looked like her, Saint Maria Cabrini.) (*RR2,* 903)[32]

The constellation of Emilia's humble qualities given in part 1 returns in the appendix in the middle of the book, in the series of poems that precedes the novel's second part. In contrast with all the previous poetic texts, which offer a heartfelt appeal to the Visitor who is about to leave the bourgeois family he seduced, "Complicity between the subproletariat and God" ("Complicità tra il sottoproletariato e Dio") is the first-person song of the departing God who addresses only Emilia. Echoing evangelical and Franciscan tones, the Visitor compares Emilia to the birds in the sky and the lilies in the fields while, in an almost parodic manner, he rejects all idyllic images and any possible aesthetic and lyrical sweetening of the verse portrait he sketches.

Emilia does not talk. She does not even try to articulate her pain. She is a silent suffering body. She is not a beautiful soul, she has no language, she has been dispossessed by the world, she has only one dimension, and yet she touches God's heart. After He abandons the family he has destroyed and all its members, notwithstanding his apparent indifference and carelessness, He chooses her:

> I say goodbye to you last, and quickly,
> because I know that your sorrow is inconsolable
> and does not even need to ask for consolation.
> You live fully in the present.
> Like the birds in the sky and the lilies in the fields,
> you don't think about tomorrow. But then,
> have we ever talked? We have never
> exchanged a word, as if the others
> had a conscience, and you had none.
> Instead, evidently, you too,
> poor Emilia, low-cost woman,
> left out, dispossessed by the world,
> you do have a conscience.
> A conscience without words.
> You don't have a beautiful soul, you. For all this,
> our quick goodbyes, devoid of any solemnity,

are nothing other than the proof
of the mysterious complicity between the two of us.
The taxi is here …
You will be the only one to know, once I'm gone,
that I will never come back, and you will look for me
wherever you must look. (*RR2*, 978)[33]

Emilia goes looking for God where she feels she must look for Him. She leaves the villa and returns to the cloistered space of the farmhouse of her childhood in the Po Valley. Rapt in her passion for origins, like the Pasolini of *Poesia in forma di rosa*, "a force of the past," Emilia returns to ruins, churches, altarpieces. Before becoming a hagiography, Emilia's story is the story of a *nostos*, a homecoming to a community dominated by the sense of the sacred. Emilia does not leave the family in order to convert; rather, she returns to be converted. A servant, she returns to be served; lost, she returns to be redeemed. The roles are inverted: it is now the community that takes care of her and feeds her. The archaic, instinctive religiosity of the farming community to which Emilia belongs is, in addition to her own heart, the source of the sacred.

Although it follows the typical outline of feminine hagiography, Emilia's spiritual itinerary is delineated in terms of poverty and peasant life. Along the way, the transcendent and the institutional dimensions of religion are both mediated by minimal, essential symbologies. Emilia's Eucharist is not the Host of the mystics but, rather, nettle soup.[34] Her dialogue with the Divine is not captured on film. The only dialogues – short, practical, in dialect – are the utterances of the old women and the children who take care of her: "Emilia, eat, eat, it's good … c'mon, eat something."[35] Emilia becomes rarefied. She loses her old identity and assimilates into the dusty, crumbling space of a civilization in danger of extinction. The sacred is all here, in a universe typical of Pascoli: candles, kneeling old women, bells, and children.

The tone, however, is somewhat parodic. "She is a mad saint," Pasolini writes. "In the novelistic text, she is 'a mad woman who carries her suitcase like an infanticide'" (*SC, SPS*, 1502).[36] Emilia's hagiography, developed in purposeful contrast to Odetta's catatonia, is thus layered and complex, as such accounts always are in Pasolini. Whereas Emilia's silence becomes a presence, first welcome, then fed, and finally venerated by the rural community that saves her from madness and donates her to the sacred, Odetta's silence is instead an odyssey among objects that no longer communicate with her, and it ends with her implosion, her self-removal from the world, and the schizophrenic closing of her fist. In an iconic reversal, the closed fist of bourgeois youth no longer points to revolution but to a psychiatric clinic.

Although Emilia does not speak, her silence is not an indicator of catatonia but of saintliness. She stands against the farmhouse wall as still as an altarpiece, her eyes looking straight out at the camera like a sphinx. If the first part of the film is completely focused on the fascination of the visitor's erotic gaze, the second follows Emilia's gaze as she silently scans the surrounding space. The close-up of Laura Betti – the actress chosen because "deep down she holds something of the Apocalypse; her core is biblical; she can cast powerful curses as well as overwhelming blessings" (De Giusti 1983, 94)[37] – is absolutely hermetic. It lets nothing through. Hers is a gaze that mirrors and sees without letting others read it, without signifying anything more than its own disturbing presence. It is a look that expresses madness or maybe infinite wisdom: the fully inaccessible gaze of the sacred. It is the free indirect point-of-view shot[38] of Padan peasants, who watch Emilia with great expectation. It is also Pasolini's own point-of-view shot, as a lay bourgeois intellectual who rapturously contemplates this strange primitive "saint" and her slow progress along the inscrutable paths of the sacred. Emilia's sainthood is free indirect silence, almost an autistic ascesis, which although it has none of the gesticulation of traditional hagiographies nonetheless communicates what is otherwise impossible to communicate: the ineffable contact with the sacred.

As Colleen Ryan-Scheutz points out:

> The other family members verbalize their feelings to the guest, and these monologues represent the symbolic outpouring of subjectivity, [and] thus constitute their quasi-spiritual/social awakenings. However, Emilia, who has been endowed with purity from the start, will not need to access spoken language in order to cleanse her conscience or become clear on who she is. For, through the guest, she has simply renewed the profoundly spiritual character that was really part of her all along. (2007, 153)

The waiting of the community, which searches Emilia's silence and distills sanctity from madness, bears its fruit: her miracles. Emilia's first miracle, the healing of a child covered in pustules, marks a reversal in the relationship between the woman and her people. Now it is she who takes care of them. The second miracle, Emilia's levitation, represents a step further in this process of distillation. In this scene, we witness her transfiguration, and Pasolini's pictorial sensitivity, although mannerist as usual, simultaneously reproduces, parodies, and celebrates the Raphaelesque iconography essential to the popular tradition of devotional holy cards. Pasolini describes the scene in *Teorema* the novel as painted with the right hand "as if on a gold background"; it is a cheap Raphael of this kind:

> Some stand still to watch, some fall to their knees, some are quiet, some pray; there are those who are stunned and those who are moved to tears. The stupefying presence of that small black figure suspended over the edge of the roof, against a dizzying sky full of melancholic clouds bordered by the light of the setting sun, is a vision that cannot satisfy and sate the maddening happiness it gives. (*RR2*, 1033–4)[39]

Pasolini inserts these miracles for different purposes. On the one hand, they are necessitated by his decision to mimic the fundamental stages of traditional hagiographies; on the other hand, they are a response to the ambiguous desire to parody the scene and the character for an audience for whom allegory is largely an alien concept. In addition, we cannot dismiss an anthropological angle, such as that of De Martino,[40] which would find in this scene a survival of the sacred among the peasantry. Such a survival was guaranteed in a historical niche that exemplifies the religious choice Pasolini defined with Paolo's words, "the despicable / fertility of those who live left behind by history." Pasolini affirms about miracles that they

> upset our so-called objective and scientific vision of reality. But the "subjective" reality of miracles does exist. It exists for the peasants of Southern Italy like it existed for those in Palestine. A miracle is the innocent and naïve explanation of the real mystery that lives in humanity, of the power that hides in man ... Regardless of its theological side, the revelation of the miracle participates also in magic.
>
> In any case, I chose to stand at a technical distance from the reality of miracles in order to place in full relief the fact that they really belong to a certain mindset, to a culture that is no longer totally ours. (*SPS*, 1423)[41]

The last miracle performed by Emilia – by now an *alter Christus* – is the generous gift of herself and her tears. She leaves her community at sunset, headed towards Milan with an old woman (Susanna Colussi, the poet's mother and Pasolinian icon of the Virgin Mary, whom she portrayed in *Il Vangelo secondo Matteo*). On the first fringes of the city outskirts, the two women stop in front of an uncovered excavation site. They climb down a dirt path into the hole and, in tears, Emilia asks to be buried. It is almost a solitary miracle, witnessed only by the old woman and by the looming mechanical presence of an excavator. Emilia disappears under the dirt. Only her eyes remain visible as she delivers her longest line in the whole movie, a goodbye to the old woman who has buried her alive: "Don't be afraid, I didn't come here to die but to cry ... and mine are not tears of sorrow, no, they will be a source ... that will not be a source of sorrow."[42]

We are reminded of Derrida's words on tears, the "essence of the eye":

> The blindness that opens the eye is not the one that darkens the vision. The revelatory or apocalyptic blindness, the blindness that reveals the very truth of the eyes, would be the gaze veiled by tears. It neither sees nor does not see: it is indifferent to its blurred vision. It implores: first of all in order to know from where these tears stream down and from whose eyes they come to well up. From where and from whom this mourning or these tears of joy? This essence of the eye, this eye water? (1993, 126–7)

A quick rereading of Emilia's story as told in the long autobiographical poem "Il poeta delle Ceneri" by Pasolini reveals a series of crypto-paradigms at work in the character, notwithstanding the parodic tone of the narration:

> But the servant becomes instead a mad saint;
> she goes into the courtyard of her sub-proletarian house,
> doesn't speak but prays and performs miracles;
> she heals the sick,
> eats only nettles till her hair turns green,
> and finally, to die,
> she asks to be buried by an excavator,
> and her tears bubble up from the mud
> to become a miraculous spring. (*TP2*, 1282)[43]

A fundamental archetype of Christian spirituality emerges here – that of Mary Magdalen, a saint who enjoyed great popularity in the Middle Ages, when she was referred to with the oxymora of "*beata peccatrix*" and "*castissima meretrix.*" She was a symbol of concupiscence but also of penance, because of her life as "privileged witness of the humanity, of the sensitivity of the God-man" (Nagy 2000, 262)[44] and because of her ascetic practices and fasts that, according to Jacobus de Varagine's *Legenda Aurea*, culminated in miracles and repeated levitations. For these reasons, Mary Magdalen represented an undeniable point of reference for medieval female mystics. As the protagonist of medieval sermons on the themes of conversion and penance, she always appears crying. She is depicted this way also in the scenes most commonly celebrated by Christian iconography, as when she washes Christ's feet with her tears at Simon's house or when she meets the resurrected Christ by the sepulchre and he asks her, "Woman, why are you crying?" (John 20:15).

In *The Making of the Magdalen* (2000), Katherine Ludwig Jansen described Mary Magdalen's character particularly in the sermons of the Franciscan and Dominican preachers who popularized her cult in the Middle Ages. With regard to Emilia, Jansen's discussion of the theme of liquefaction, as opposed to that of petrifaction, is especially interesting; this contrast corresponds to the visual counterpoint of water/desert found at the end of *Teorema*. Tears are symbols of contrition but also of baptism and rebirth, and they pertain archetypically to the feminine sphere. As Jansen writes,

> The preachers contrasted the image of liquefaction, representing the state of contrition, to the condition of sin, characterized by frigidity, sterility and obduracy ... Spiritual hardness or frigidity, however, could be overcome by heat, the divine infusion of *caritas*, ardent love. Through the application of *caritas*, hardness dissolves into liquid. Just as the Magdalen transformed her vices to virtues through the tears of sorrow, she converted frigidity to ardor, barrenness to fertility, obduracy to liquid tears. (2000, 209)

The connection between Mary Magdalen, tears, and the image of the spring is further discussed by Piroska Nagy in her book on the gift of tears in the Middle Ages. She emphasizes the symbolic aspect of fluidity, of transformation and rebirth tied to the symbol of the spring as a source of tears and of grace:

> The image of the *spring* is a central metaphor of the Magdalenian progress and of the path proposed to the faithful. The pairing *spring of grace/spring of tears*, representing Christ and the woman, was found in most texts. It's the spring of tears that allows Magdalen to get to the spring of mercy that is Christ; conversely, it's the spring of mercy that gives her the spring of tears ... The *spring of mercy* has all the characteristics of some sort of spiritual

water: it washes off sins and, like spring water, quenches thirst and irrigates the arid soul. Finally, thanks to its power to cleanse sins and convert, the fluid of mercy and its main material form – the water of tears – becomes one and the same with the water of baptism. (2000, 262–3)[45]

The same concept of rebirth and transformation, which is cryptically expressed by Pasolini through the recovery of Christian iconography, is linked to an internal reference to his own poetry. The verses of revolution and hope in "Il pianto della scavatrice" ("The cry of the excavator"), from *Le ceneri di Gramsci*, resurface through their visual correlative.[46] Pasolini appears almost to literalize the metaphor from the poem in *Le ceneri* by introducing a human presence buried in the "stunned, dug up earth." In this memorable text from *Le ceneri*, the word "hope" shines, rather than being dismissed by Pasolini as it often is elsewhere in his works as referring to something that is no longer relevant. The revelation of the roots of the working class, which take their nourishment from the peasants' sacred ground, already constitutes a revolution.

For Pasolini, the ground is always a palimpsest,[47] and this is the meaning of Emilia's burial, as the writer stated in an interview with Duflot:

[Duflot]: *What is the meaning of the moment when the servant has herself buried in the construction site?*

[Pasolini]: Also here, the reference is rather simple. I want to remind the audience that civilizations that came before ours have not vanished but they're simply buried, so that peasant culture survives beneath the world of the industrial working class. Actually, we could say that this may be the only optimistic moment in the film. (*SC*, *SPS*, 1502)[48]

In 2003, drawing on Giambattista Vico's philosophy, Robert Harrison described the humic, foundational relation tombs establish between the dead and the living by allowing the residential, social, national, and institutional spaces of the living to take root in the ground in which their dead are buried:

It is as if we the living can stand (culturally, institutionally, economically, in other words humanly), only because the dead underlie the ground on which we build our homes, world and commonwealths.

... As the primordial sign of human mortality, the grave domesticates the inhuman transcendence of space and marks human time off from the timelessness of the gods and the eternal returns of nature. That is why gods are not the original founders of place – mortals are. An immortal god may bless

> a place that has already been founded, but such a god cannot introduce the mark of finite time necessary to ground it. (2003, 22–3)

Unlike in the cult of heroes, however, Emilia's tomb is completely anonymous and unmarked by anything other than the spring, a sign meant to reveal the relation of continuity and contiguity between nature and the sacred in humanity, as it is defined in agrarian and archaic civilizations. The space of the excavation where Emilia has herself buried is thus a natural, human, and sacred space at one and the same time. Emilia becomes its *genius loci.* Through Emilia's sacrifice, Pasolini roots in death the suburban Milan of the working class but also sanctifies it, thanks to the miracle of the spring. Furthermore, saints' burial places were traditionally located outside city walls, far from the centre, and their tombs became nuclei of urban aggregation and requalification.[49]

Emilia and her tears are therefore the *trait-d'union* between the archaic roots – anonymous and "oral" – of the rural world and the industrial working class. In the movie, this link is only implicit, not visible. Pasolini elides the metaphor and sums it up in the mute emblem of the excavator. The situation is different in the novel, where, at the end of chapter 16, we find that the miracle that links Emilia to the workers is presented explicitly. Pasolini describes the workers at the construction site as they transform the excavation into an embankment, while the excavator screeches without interruption. An accident occurs, and the workers run, carrying a man with a wounded arm. When they arrive at the pool of tears, an old worker

> washes his companion's wounded hand and arm ... The water begins to cleanse the flesh from the blood, and it also begins to heal the wound: in a few instants the cut closes and the blood stops running.
>
> ... Before the workers begin, as is natural, to raise their astonished cries – allowing themselves to express their feelings with the naive and rather silly gestures men cannot avoid when facing things they have never experienced before – there is a moment of profound silence. Their poor faces, emaciated, hard and kind are turned toward that little pool that shines, inconceivable, in the sun. (*RR2,* 1043–4)[50]

In the novel, the miracle is recounted in every detail; in contrast, in the movie Emilia's story ends with the camera aimed at her half-buried face, with a tight close-up of her eyes full of tears.

The story of the post-mortem miracle that would offer crucial proof of Emilia's sainthood is thus left out of the film, and it is only hinted at in the enigmatic promise of her final words. To use a formula dear to Pasolini, the movie is left "a canone sospeso," unresolved. Whether suicide or Christological sacrifice, madness or sainthood, the knot of the "corollary" in the filmic theorem is not undone. In passing from the pen to the camera, Emilia's hagiography loses the Gramscian illusion. Pasolini has abandoned the epic lower-class perspective that had characterized his poetics since *Le ceneri di Gramsci*:

> This Gramscian illusion has now objectively fallen, I no longer have it. Because the world has objectively changed in front of me. While in Gramsci's time and at the time I was thinking of my first works and elaborating my first ideology, a sharp classical distinction between the working class and the bourgeoisie was still possible, nowadays it is no longer objectively so. That is, what Gramsci was saying forty years ago and what I thought ten years ago is no longer licit, no longer plausible, because Italy has entered a new historical phase. The result is that the distinction between popular, in the Gramscian sense of the term, and bourgeois is no longer possible ... it would be wrong for me to have in mind an ideal people to whom I could address my works ... Later on ... instead of attempting to create epic popular works, which would have risked becoming synchronous with a work typical of mass culture (since the notion of people has come to coincide with the notion of mass), I tried to find films that countered this, that were difficult and therefore inconsumable ..., now I aim at inconsumability.
>
> And therefore at difficulty, impenetrability, stylistic complexity, etc. It is a first awkward, individualistic and somewhat anarchoid attempt to fight against the determinations of mass culture. (Bernardini 1969, 313–14)[51]

Facing a working class that has been transformed into a colony of the bourgeoisie, the director opts for "élite cinema," aimed not at a social but rather at an intellectual élite, "a group of intelligent individuals ready to fight against mass culture"[52] (Bernardini 1969, 318).

Pasolini, the bourgeois intellectual filled with an idea of the sacred that his community does not share, tries somehow to assign to his audience a supporting and caring role similar to that played by the peasants for Emilia. The task of the lower classes is not that of consuming but of understanding. In 1969, Pasolini said:

> If I were writing verses with the specific purpose to be understood by a Calabrian peasant, I would be mouthing rhetoric, pedagogism, propaganda – perhaps with noble intentions, in good faith – but I would be betraying

> myself as a writer. That is, I would be countering the injustice of the Calabrian peasant who cannot understand with that of the writer who betrays himself. ("Incontro con Pasolini," *PPC2*, 2967)[53]

Serafino Murri underlines how the loss of the Gramscian illusion and of the concept of "people" in a Western world crushed by the triumph of the masses goes hand in hand with the recovery, in a mythical key, of the role of the Third World and of the sense of the sacred experienced thanks to the reclamation of the dimension of irrationality (1994, 69–70). At the end of the 1960s, Pasolini's films were thoroughly marked by the revealing presence of the Third World,[54] invoked as a possible alternative to the West. The first takes for *Appunti per un'Orestiade Africana* were shot at the end of 1968, and those for *Medea* were shot between 1968 and 1969.

As noted earlier, *Medea* provides a great point of entrance for an analysis of Pasolini's relationship with the sacred. *Medea* was shot a year after *Teorema*. In these films, Medea and Emilia, the high priestess and the maid, appear at once similar and very different in their "sacredness." Medea embodies the archaic sacred in its violent and sacrificial turn; Emilia gives voice to a different kind of sacred vocation, one devoted to *caritas* for the community of believers, in a progressive offering of her miracles and her body to them. If sex is the sacred trigger of both these characters' fates, Emilia turns it into saintliness, Medea into what Pasolini called a "negative revelation."

Shot in Anatolia, Cappadocia, Syria, and Italy, *Medea* resembles an anthropological documentary, framing the mythical character of the Euripidean tragedy within a conflict of cultures.[55] As Massimo Fusillo commented,

> Medea and Jason are really two symbolic characters who, on one hand, represent a primitive, magic and sacral culture and, on the other, a modern, rationalistic and bourgeois culture (seen however in its development). This cultural bipolarity is added to a psychoanalytic one between Id and Ego (Pasolini claimed, among other things, that he had conceived Jason and Medea as a single character), and to a political one between the West and the Third World (as it will become even more evident in *Appunti per un'Orestiade africana*). (1996, 134)[56]

Also, in the case of Medea, as for Emilia or the Visitor in *Teorema*, the choice of the actress, of that body, of those eyes, is dictated by the director's poetic sensibilities, and at the same time it determines the development of the screenplay. Regarding Medea, impersonated by Maria Callas, Pasolini reveals:

> At times, I write the screenplay without knowing who the interpreter will be. In this case, I knew the actress would be Callas and therefore, I calibrated the script as a function of her performance all along. She meant a great deal in the creation of the character ... The barbarity that has taken root inside and comes out in her eyes, in her features, is not openly manifest, on the contrary. She belongs in a peasant, Greek, agrarian world, but was then educated for a bourgeois society. In a certain sense, I have therefore tried to concentrate in her character Medea's complex totality.[57]

Callas interprets the role in a hieratic and solemn acting style in which her voice is given little space while a great deal is granted to her long, dark, sideways gaze, a "barbaric" gaze *par excellence*, appropriate to the chthonic and demonic dimension of the character.[58] Medea, great priestess of the Colchis, is another feminine character emblematically tied to the sacred but, contrary to what happens to Emilia in *Teorema*, her coming in contact with *eros* implies the loss of the sacred rather than access to it. It is the Centaur, Jason's childhood pedagogue, who diagnoses Medea's alienated condition, appearing to him in double form when he is about to marry Glauce, King Creon's daughter. What ensues is one of the most significant dialogues for our analysis of the relationship between Pasolini and the sacred:

> JASON –Is this a vision?
>
> *(It is the human, rational Centaur who answers him while the mythical one keeps silent and looks at him, laughing.)*
>
> CENTAUR –If it is, it is you who creates it. The two of us, we are actually inside of you.
>
> JASON –But I knew only *one* Centaur ...
>
> CENTAUR –No, you knew two: a sacred one when you were a child and a profane one when you became an adult. But what is sacred is preserved next to its new profane form. And here we are, one next to the other!
>
> JASON –But what is the function of the old Centaur, the one I knew as a child and that you, New Centaur, have replaced, if I understand well, not by making him vanish but joining with him?
>
> CENTAUR –He does not talk, obviously, because his logic is so different from ours that we could not understand ... But I can speak also for him. It is under his influence that you – outside your planning and your understanding – in reality love Medea.

JASON –I love Medea?
CENTAUR –Yes. And you also pity her, and you understand her ... spiritual catastrophe ... her disorientation as an ancient woman in a world that no longer believes in anything she has always believed in ... The poor soul has had a backward conversion, and she has never recovered. (*PPC1*, 1245–6)[59]

In this passage, referring to Medea, the author talks about a "spiritual catastrophe" and a "backward conversion." Similarly, in one of the poems written at the time of the shooting of the film, Pasolini describes its narrative arc, making reference to Jason's "backward religious education" – on a path that, as we saw in the first chapter, leads from "everything is sacred!" to "There is no God." Concerning Medea, in the same poem he writes again of "a backward conversion – or negative revelation – / a believing female Saul who falls from the horse and no longer believes" (*Endoxa*, in Pasolini 1991, 576).[60] The loss of the sacred occurs at the moment in which the bond between Medea and her community is broken. Inside the temple, in the instant when Medea loses her powers (which in the movie are symbolically returned to her through the use of a strongly rhythmical and obsessive music), the silence of the priestess becomes louder, and a different, almost alien, gaze is cast upon the sacred furnishings and the Fleece. Then, Jason appears and *eros* takes hold of Medea.

In reality, *Medea*'s story perfectly mirrors and complements that of *Teorema*: in both cases, it is an erupting sexuality that upsets the community. In the same way that the natural sensuality of the Visitor destroys bourgeois civilization in *Teorema*, in Medea's case it is the bourgeois sexuality of Jason, "aboulic technician," that robs the high priestess of her powers, pushing her to steal the *axis mundi* from her people. What takes place is the "violation of an archaic universe at the hands of a modern pragmatic universe" (Fusillo 2006, 163).[61] Immediately after her escape with Jason, however, Medea realizes, when the Argonauts pitch their tents without establishing a centre for the camp, that she has caused the greatest of rifts. As if in a raptus, Medea launches into a monologue invoking the trees, the Earth, the Sun, and the Moon that no longer speak to her:

You can't pitch your tents like that, without rhyme or reason. You must first turn to the Gods, pray to them, bless the place because every place where men pitch their tents is sacred. It repeats the creation of the cosmos, it becomes a *center*, and this center must be marked by a stone, a tree, by some

> sort of sign, a *sacred* sign. This is all Medea knows and, to her, not knowing it, not observing it seems sacrilegious. And she says so in broken sentences, incomprehensible ... At first, the Argonauts listen to her and watch her in amazement. But their eyes are immediately veiled by irony (also, and especially, Jason's eyes) and they listen with mocking patience ...
>
> Medea then leaves them to their own folly, and she tries to keep to herself (like a wounded animal etc.).
>
> What is she looking for in this foreign land? She is looking for the "sacred." Which she abandoned in the Colchis and whose sense suddenly vanished with Jason's "carnal" apparition in the very Center, in the Omphalos in which the golden fleece was kept.
>
> ... In the light of the atrociously sweet sunset, among the longest shadows, Medea looks for a tree that might be a *sacred tree.* There are many trees all around: poplars, elderberry, blackberry bushes, fig trees, but none of them is the tree she is looking for. They are all poor, common, humble trees in their summer glory.
>
> As if in a crazed monologue – to overcome the deafness of all things – Medea whispers to herself a Hymn to vegetation (to be invented mixing fragments of Hymns from different ancient religions etc.) ...
>
> Now, Medea desperately looks for a rock. A *sacred stone.* They abound around there, on that Mediterranean coast. But like the trees, they do not answer Medea's imploration: they remain what they are, meaningless and very beautiful rocks. Monologuing, Medea sings a hymn also to them. (*PPC1,* 1234–6)[62]

The dimension of the sacred has disappeared. Medea is still invoking a cosmic sense of time, addressing at the end the sun and the moon, composing a third hymn to them ... the celestial bodies remain inert and silent. They do not speak to her anymore.

Pasolini describes Medea's reaction:

> Medea sits on a rock without speaking: just like the world around her does not speak but is purely physical, like an atrocious yet wonderful unreal apparition ... She is dumbfounded: she is expressionless but with the grandiosity of a giant grasshopper, or of a stone divinity. She does not know what to do with herself, and she shuts herself off from the world as if in a display case. (*PPC1,* 1236)[63]

We recognize Medea's final stance. It is the same one that Emilia assumed when she returned to the farmhouse, to her origins, and sat in the courtyard: "She does not know what to do with herself, and she shuts herself off from the world as if in a display case." In Medea's story, the person who comes to save her is Jason, who arrives to take her to his tent and makes love to her. Medea then loses "her atonia of disoriented animal: in love, she suddenly finds a substitute for her lost religiosity (becoming more human). In sexual experience, she finds again the lost sacral relationship with reality ... possessing with [Jason], in her own turn, the regeneration of life" (*PPC1*, 1238).[64] In Emilia's story, it is, instead, the community of peasants that succeeds in helping the mad maid find again the lost path to the sacred that she had glimpsed thanks to her sexual relationship with the Visitor.

The trajectory covered by Medea is therefore reversed in comparison with Emilia's. Medea's erotic passion, which takes her away from sacrality, is finally revealed to be destructive – even if it initially seemed compensatory. Temporarily blind, Medea places her lust above any other sacred duty. She will regain her own identity and her own ties with her original world only when she loses the fruit of her love – in a violent sacrifice, fatal, desacralized, and against nature. The conflict between Medea and Jason – between the culture of the circle and that of the line, between magic and rational thought – appears irreconcilable.

Quite to the contrary, after the initial erotic impetus Emilia enters a completely different sacrificial dimension. Hers is a Christological sacrifice that does not sever bonds. Instead, thanks to chthonic cyclicity and her salvific vocation for atonement and Christian sacrifice, Emilia's self-immolation presents itself as a sacralizing foundation of the popular space. Her self-burial represents a mythical peasant root of the industrial working class and of the subproletariat who inhabited the outskirts of Italian cities in the 1960s. At this point, Pasolini grafts Christian *agape*, love for the victims, upon erotic mimetic desire. Walter Siti has clearly identified this typology:

> In broad terms, we could say that Eros is love as desire; it directs man to the heavens; it pushes him to become divine; it loves what is beautiful and recognizes that only what is valuable is lovable. *Agape* is sacrifice; it gives itself for what is inferior; it loves especially what is worthless, and therefore it has no ulterior motive and is humanly inconceivable. Eros is the love of man who recognizes divinity in man; *Agape* is the love that comes from God ...
>
> Love as sacrifice whispers a different truth: "peccatores sunt pulchri, quia diluguntur, non diliguntur, quia sunt pulchri," Luther says. Nothing can be inferred from beauty. The poor must be loved without ulterior motive or motivated by reasons that are independent from the individual subject.

> I believe we can say that, for Pasolini, the discovery of historical objectivity coincides with the superimposition of the motive of Agape onto the original Eros. (1984, 144–5)[65]

Agape or *caritas* thus seems to constitute for Pasolini one of the possible ways to heal the laceration the world has suffered and overcome the impasse into which it has fallen due to its rejection of the sacred.

According to Fusillo, "In the conflict between archaic culture and modern culture, Pasolini does not intend to make the first triumph, since it is inevitably the loser, nor does he want to demonize the second. He only intends to show the unilateral naiveté of a society that believes it has moved beyond the sacred, has learned to control passions" (1996, 179).[66] In the movie, Medea's female body, which she defines as a "vessel of a knowledge" that is not her own, becomes the bearer of a victimized and alienated sacred that is inevitably pushed to violence and conflict. As she utters her last sentence ("Nothing is possible any more") among the flames in which the sons she killed are burning, the element of fire is clearly predominant. In contrast, in *Teorema*, Emilia's sacrifice evokes images of liquidity and a paradigm of fertility. Buried in the soil, she is like a seed that will germinate and regenerate. The paradigm of seeding announced by Eliade returns and so does the hope for salvation, as underlined by the poet Andrea Zanzotto in his commentary to the movie:

> When we see Emilia buried, or about to bury herself, with those tears that flow from her whole face like some sort of "Christian" bloody sweat that has transformed into something clearer and also more acceptable – due to the sense of beauty and of a starry nature that is present throughout the movie – we go back to the idea of a live spring issuing forth from that part of human reality that may yet be uncontaminated, that might have never been contaminated, and that possibly, perhaps in vitro or on another planet, will manage to save itself and save others. In the end, that pool of water, that pool of pure tears that flows from Emilia's obliterated gaze is perhaps worth more than the cry in the desert with which the movie ends, that cry that goes on forever and is so full of meanings and symbols, of a humanity that, unable to transhumanize (a verb that Pasolini was to make more and more his own), finds itself to be feral and ever more unrecognizable. (1994, 164)[67]

At the end of *Teorema*, Paolo encounters Emilia's Christological sacrifice, which is characterized by images of fluidity and liquefaction such as her sinking in the wet soil of the excavation. Her body seems almost to ooze from the soil and immediately turns into a soteriological emblem, a place of stratification and of rumination on death. Through tears, this body is metabolized by the earth into life and becomes a sort of baptismal font for the uprooted urbanized masses of the metropolis. Although Paolo, too, throws himself to the ground, his action is fruitless. Inscribed as the desert is in a petrified horizon, he cannot find a haven: the desert is absolutely horizontal, and its unchanging depth is unwelcoming. It is a land with no forebears and no seed, a land that knows no death or season, with Paolo standing before an impenetrable god. It is what Bataille calls the rupturing "inner experience," as Janice Tong has pointed out in her reading of *Teorema* through Bataille:

> This eye which, to contemplate the sun, face to face in its nudity, opens up to it in all its glory, does not arise from my reason: it is a cry which escapes me. For at the moment when the lighting stroke blinds me, I am the flash of a broken life, and this life – anguish and vertigo – opening itself up to an infinite void, is ruptured and spends itself all at once in this void. (Bataille 1988, 77, quoted in Tong 2001, 84)

It is the impossibility of transhumanizing that, according to Pasolini, appears possible only when inscribed in the cryptic dimension of the "sense of the earth," in the sacred paradigm of seeding, in the religion of the eternal return to the origins that constitutes the director's central myth. Paolo belongs to a different reality of post-history. He is unable to become a seed and germinate, to die and be transhumanized, and he remains frozen in an inarticulate cry that, in Pasolini's words, can be either a prayer or a curse. Filled with *agape*, however, he has donated his factory and now, after changing his relationship with the working class like a new Saint Francis, he wanders like Pasolini, "an adult fetus ... more modern than any modern / looking for brothers who are no more" (*TP1*, 1099).[68] His horizon is deserted: impenetrable, undecipherable, the expression of a reality that is suspended over the void of a non-existent answer.

Given its connection with the theme of resurrection, it is not at all surprising that the image of the seed that dies and is reborn also has a source in John 12:24: "If a kernel of grain that has fallen to the ground does not die, it will be alone; but if it dies, it will bear many seeds." Pasolini quotes this same evangelical passage from Dostoevski, as an *exergo* to the poem "Il dì da la me muàrt" ("The Day of My Death," *NG*, *TP2*, 480) in *La nuova gioventù*, his last collection of poems (published in the year of his death, 1975). These poems were styled as an apocalyptic rewriting of his first book of Friulian verses, *La meglio gioventù* (1954). In the apparent circularity of the act of rewriting, which, as Zanzotto noted, is a trampling of the earlier poems more than simply a revisiting, Pasolini states, "I do not cry because that world no longer returns but because its returning is over,"[69] bitterly underlining the victory of the straight line over the circle in a clash of cultures already emblematically emphasized in *Medea.* In "Il dì da la me muàrt," Pasolini links the theme of sacrifice to that of the seed, to sainthood, and to the the fruitlessness of a life of poetry:

> Then, out of love for those who were young like him – until shortly before the light of the stars on his head changed – he would have liked to give his life for the entire unknown world – he, an unknown small saint, a little grain lost in a field.
>
> And instead, he wrote poems full of sanctity, thinking that then his heart would grow. The days went by lost in work that ruined the sanctity of his heart: the little grain didn't die, and he was left alone. (*NG, TP2,* 480–1)[70]

The poet's mission seems doomed to failure precisely because his attempt to sublimate in poetry his vocation to sacrifice makes such a vocation vain. In *Teorema,* by contrast, thanks to her sacrifice, Emilia is destined to germinate into a miracle of rooting. She blossoms into an epiphany of the sacred for the new urban proletarian and subproletarian audience. This audience is the heir to what survives of the rural world in modernity, even though it is deaf and threatened by an imminent transformation into the new bourgeoisie, and even though it moves in a context rich in ambiguity and parody as well as in lyricism.

Emilia dies. In fact, she is the only character who dies in *Teorema.* She is the only character who expresses herself and gains a meaning and a destiny, according to Pasolini's interpretation of death as a cinematic "montage" of the life we have lived, the only possible narrative, and the necessary and unavoidable condition for humans to become legible (*HE,* 236).

In Pasolini's work, however, death is much more than this: *thanatos* is, according to Lino Micciché, "the leitmotif, the dominant theme, the 'Todestriebe' that, explicitly or implicitly, characterizes all of Pasolini's works" ("La morte e la storia," 1975, 9).[71] Micciché claims that

> in Pasolini, death is not only, or not so much, the biochemical dissolution of biological life. It is rather the law that characterizes existence, its main pulsion, the necessary and definitive conclusion (the only definitive one and therefore the only one truly needed) of every discourse and of every existence, and it is therefore the only dominant tension of reality. ("La morte e la storia," 1975, 12)[72]

If on an individual level we need death in order to express ourselves and to make our human adventure legible, on a meta-individual level Pasolini inserts it into class dynamics. He makes death a protagonist in his films as the photographed death of the beloved working classes on the verge of disappearing, of being devoured by the universal bourgeoisie. For Pasolini, death is the death of the classes for which, as underlined by Micciché, "the jump from Pre-history to Post-history cannot be other than a present, History, made up of unavoidable death" ("La morte e la storia," 1975, 19).[73] Significantly, death is configured according to a typically Christian sacrificial model, although in the immanent context of the cult of the forefathers and of an eternal return to nature rather than of the advent of an otherworldly reign. Such a configuration constitutes a particularly meaningful facet of the religious syncretism that is constantly at work in Pasolini's writing and that finds in the Christian element a sort of unconscious *episteme.* Pasolini's perspective is therefore inscribed within a Christian horizon, which, however, belongs to a tragically heretical Christianity, without salvation: a sacrificial narrative from which the possibility of redemption in the other world has been subtracted. Once again, the model of a purely human *agape* shines as a crucifixion that, nailed into the immanent, remains as an interrupted revelation suspended and lost like a revolution.

If *Uccellacci e uccellini* (1966) was the movie that the Friulian director dedicated to the crisis of ideology, *Teorema* (1968) is the film in which he denounces the contemporary loss of the sacred. Although *Teorema* is considered by some "the film of Pasolini's Christian maturity" (Caruso 1988),[74] it indeed condemns this loss with ambiguous irony, identifying it with the universalization of the spiritually mutilated existential condition of the bourgeoisie and with the tragic survival of the religious spirit in a threatened historical niche. Only Emilia, poor and filled with *agape*, can germinate when she is planted in the soil of her forefathers. Paolo, "apostle of a Christ not crucified but lost" (*TP2*, 1281),[75] ends up the prisoner of a revelation without redemption, because it is without the sacrifice of life. Renouncing ownership of his factory is a necessary condition for redemption, but it is not sufficient. Destined to social but not to biological death, having performed a gesture that is rife with consequences for the working class to which it was addressed, Paolo seems to be a wild monad whose cry of desperation and frenetic self-doubt goes unanswered in a world that has lost touch with its origin and its established semantic horizon. The donation of the factory does not lead to sainthood, but it does lead, as we have said, to a crisis of signs. Paolo's desert and Emilia's spring converge to mark the entrance of the working class into a condition of fluidity that is open to different possible futures. The tears of the miracle in the working-class neighbourhood and the unanswered questions in the interview with the factory workers ideally constitute the inaugural, auroral, baptismal moment of a social subject in transition. As Janice Tong, in her reading of *Teorema* under the sign of Bataille, has pointed out, Emilia's eyes "are no longer needed for seeing, she does not need them to gain vision for she is already a visionary. Instead, her eyes are given over to weeping, and their openness will give rise to a new life and a new ideology" (2001, 87).

In transition, but with a darker future, is also where the bourgeois subject appears to be, divested of its status unanchored in the sacred. In *Teorema* the novel, Pasolini devotes an entire chapter to the analysis of the loss of the soul of the bourgeoisie, structured as a television report on sainthood. It is an interview with the crowd that witnesses the miracle of levitation, an interview dotted by unanswered questions in which the peasants' voices are once again silent, a free indirect silence. Through dialogue without actual interlocutors or answers, in the parodic hagiographic trial of the mad saint, the interview turns into the moment of her canonization. The role of inquisitor, traditionally assigned to the Church in the post-mortem canonization of saints, is now taken on by television *in medias res* with every display of vulgarity that, according to Pasolini, such intervention of the mass media entails. Nevertheless, with the writer's typical ambiguity, in the same way that parody and poetry blend together in the story of the mad saint, so vulgarity and theological/sociological analysis flow together in the densely entwined and "theorematic" series of unanswered interview questions. The trial to establish Emilia's sainthood actually becomes the building of the prosecution's case against a class that no longer possesses "*a real sense of the sacred*" (*RR2*, 1036).[76]

> "In your opinion, what's the reason God has chosen a poor woman of the lower classes to manifest Himself through a miracle?"
>
> ...

"Is it because the bourgeois cannot really be religious?"

…

"Is moralism the religion of the bourgeois (when he has one)?"

…

"Has then the bourgeois *exchanged his soul for his conscience?*"

…

"Does every old religious situation automatically change into a simple *case of conscience*, for him?"

…

"Is it then metaphysical religion that has been lost, that has changed into a sort of *religion of behavior?*"

…

"The soul had salvation as its purpose: but conscience?"

…

"The God … in whose name this daughter of peasants who has returned from the city after being a maid … performs miracle … isn't this an ancient God … peasant, we may say … Biblical and somewhat crazy?"

…

"And what does it mean that his miracles take place here, in this surviving corner of a peasant world?"

…

"Does then religion now survive as something authentic only in the rural world, that is … in the Third World?"

…

"Isn't this what this mad saint means, just outside Milan, in view of the first factories?"

…

"Isn't she a terrible walking accusation leveled against the bourgeoisie who (in the best of cases) has reduced religion to a code of behavior?"

…

"So, while this peasant saint *can save herself*, even in a historical niche, the bourgeois cannot save themselves, either individually or collectively? Individually, because they no longer have a soul but only a conscience – noble, perhaps, but for its very nature petty and limited –; collectively, because their history is ending without leaving any trace, transforming from history of the first industries to history of the industrialization of the whole world?"

…

"But the new kind of religion that will be born (and we can already see its first signs in the most advanced nations), will it have nothing to do with this shit (excuse the word) that is the bourgeois world, capitalistic or socialist, in which we live?" (*RR2*, 1036–8)[77]

As in the post-mortem miracle, the traces of this canonization and sociological and religious disquisition, problematized in the form of an interview, are also lost in the film. Pasolini prefers to leave the cinematic work open, "a canone sospeso," the emblematic trace of individual or collective itineraries that do not lead anywhere in this transitional age.

The bourgeoisie is pushed out of the cycle of the archaic sacred as well as out of the teleology of Christian history. With its loss of identity and of its social, civic, and economic role, it experiences an expulsion taken to its highest exaltation. Its exile will last as long as the cry of its mourning. The liberation of the masks of the symbolic order is also the condemnation of an unforgiving reality. Pasolini thus leaves the movie open-ended in a time that no is longer *kronos* but, rather, a *kairos* without *parousia* that requires all cards to be put on the table. This is what all the characters in *Teorema* do, all of them offering answers via victimization in forms that range from schizophrenia to exile. They hopelessly wait for a God who is not dead but who has left them, a God of whom Paolo's cry announces the invoked and yet definitively revoked return.

On the one hand, there is the moralizing and spiritually impoverished horizon of the bourgeoisie, trapped in the desert of the loss of identity without sacrificial death. On the other hand, there are Emilia's tears at the construction site, the liquidity that alludes to a developing fluid identity that is not easy to define, notwithstanding the solid foundational element of her burial and of the excavation (the peasant roots). In contrast with the scatological homogenization of the bourgeois world, a gesture of hope, a purgatorial motion rises from pockets of resistance around the world.

The Franciscan Model

As the humble and rebellious saint *par excellence*, the figure of Saint Francis and the model of sanctity he provided play an important role in Pasolini's work. Francis was the saint who challenged the traditional Church and the established powers with the weapons of love, choosing to be poor and a model of spirituality. He rejected his bourgeois status, founded a revolutionary community, and lived religion in the flesh. He established a visceral bond with the natural world, creature to creature, and challenged the limits of communication, preaching to birds and animals. As Antonio Attisani has stressed, it is not by chance that Francis became "an icon of heterodoxy and of rebellion" (2003, 116).

Tragic and Comic Franciscanism in Pasolini's Work

In his essay on Francis' inimitable revolution, Attisani highlights the performative aspect of Franciscan preaching. This emphasis in Francis's message on action powerfully influenced Pasolini, who himself insisted on the performative and ethical character of human existence: "By living every one of us (willing or not) performs a moral action whose meaning is suspended" (*HE*, 248).[1] Cinema is the written language of human praxis. It collects catalogues of examples of this praxis and composes them into films that follow a narrative line *sub specie mortis* – that is, it does what death does with our life, giving a finite sense to its "suspended" example. Performance is therefore central to our lives. According to Pasolini, "By living, therefore, we represent ourselves and we observe the representations of others ...: a gigantic *happening*, if you will" (*HE, 204)*.[2] This was even more true for Francis; as shown in Pasolini's meditations on cinema and on *Bestemmia*, the saint's desire to make Christ *present* prevails over the notion of simple representation. In Attisani's words:

> Francis placed himself *outside the text* and conceived his own life, as well as that of every good Christian, first of all of his brothers, as a "revolutionary performance," an action that changes the life of all those who take part in it and changes it from mere reaction to contingencies to an event capable of becoming similar to the divine. Its declared objective was to re-actualize and to re-incarnate Jesus' behaviors, and to concretize a certain idea of Christian community but, as it is typical of all re-actualizations, the issue went well beyond producing or re-producing a text. It was a matter of interpreting the sense of Christ's actions so that his own may be effective in the present. (2003, 124)[3]

This urgent need for "presence" in Franciscan teaching deeply resonated with Pasolini in the 1960s, when he thematized the production of presence in *Bestemmia* and he inherited the Franciscan icon from other, widely different, cinematic texts.

The first film to which Pasolini refers in *Uccellacci e uccellini* (*The Hawks and the Sparrows*, 1966) is Roberto Rossellini's *Francesco Giullare di Dio* (*The Flowers of St. Francis*, 1950), which, through its emphasis on the reality of the humble, the outcast, the poor, and the simple, brings to the fore the resonance between Franciscanism and neo-realism. At the time, Rossellini's staging of Francis' story scandalized the Catholic world. "Arcadia, infantilism, evasiveness, equivocity," was the verdict of Father Camillo de Piaz of the Corsia dei Servi Cultural Centre in Milan.[4] In addition, it appalled lay critics because of – in Pio Baldelli's words – its "historical falsification" (1951, 37). In his essay on Rossellini's film, Tommaso Subini describes the director's emphasis on the paradigmatic diversity of his Franciscan characters and on the choral and communal nature of the events he retells (2007, 23–50). Peter Brunette remembers the didactic value of Rossellini's Franciscan choice, about which, together with Fellini, he wrote a screenplay in which the centrality of the marginalized was also rendered at the narrative level. Rossellini's take appears in the collective dimension of the Franciscan phenomenon he chooses to represent that seems to push the main figure of the saint into the background and to concentrate instead on minor characters such as Friar Ginepro.

Related to this question is Rossellini's clear didactic purpose in making the film. As in his other works of this period, he was concerned with the despair and cynicism facing post-war Europe, and unashamedly offered Saint Francis and his philosophy as an answer, as a way back to an essential wholeness. The "message" of *The Flowers of St. Francis* is stubbornly old-fashioned, as Rossellini told students at the Centro Sperimentale di Cinematografia, in the early 1960s, as reported by Brunette:

> It was important for me then to affirm everything that stood against slyness and cunning. In other words, I believed then and still believe that simplicity is a very powerful weapon ... The innocent one will always defeat the evil one. I am absolutely convinced of this. And in our own era we have a vivid example in Gandhism ... Then, if we want to go back to the historical moment, we must remember that these were cruel and violent centuries, and yet in those centuries of violence appeared Saint Francis of Assisi and Saint Catherine of Siena.

Obviously, it took courage for Rossellini to offer such transparently "retrograde" values to a modern audience, and part of the film's radicalism lies in its fearless exposure of the director's vulnerable idealism.[5]

Rather than idealism, perhaps, Rossellini's approach is a different kind of realism that, as Fabio Finotti emphasizes, expresses "the rejection of critical rationalism" (2007, 28)[6] in dealing with the Franciscan theme. Andrè Bazin, the famous French cinema critic of the 1950s, identified in Rossellini "a realism that illuminated and documented a spiritual rather than objective reality" (Finotti 2007, 29),[7] close to the mystical realism of the original Franciscan thought. It is therefore necessary to reconstruct reality with absolutely realistic methods – the use of non-professional actors, of actual friars, of documentary filming techniques – in order to recreate a mystical adhesion to the dimension of the real, an enchanted spiritual environment almost fable-like in its simplicity and immediacy, a religiosity that is lived and incarnated rather than faithfully historically reconstructed. Rossellini recreated cinematically the atmosphere of his source, *Little Flowers of Saint Francis*, a collection in the vernacular of the miracles and pious episodes of the life of Francis from the last quarter of the fourteenth century (Frugoni 1998, 25). According to the *Catholic Encyclopedia*, the *Fioretti* show "the delicious fragrance of the early Franciscan spirit. Nowhere can there be found a more childlike faith, a livelier sense of the supernatural, or a simple literalness in ... following Christ."[8] Thus, the story progresses through a constellation of narrative fragments, breaking the hagiographic narration into a series of episodes and creating a lyrical and surreal climate – even though within the structure of a solid screenplay (a rare occurrence for Rossellini). Pasolini will remember this episodic framework when he organizes and edits the narrative segments of *Vangelo*. Above all, he will be inspired by

Rossellini's relationship with his sources to reconstruct Christ's life in a realistic but not rationalistic key: "*A non-realistic notion of realism* thus coincided with the anthropological ability to renounce the positivistic scientific categories in order to keep poetically faithful to the spiritual reality of a different era" (Finotti 2007, 30–1).[9] Pasolini, as Rossellini and Fellini in the script of their film, will be an evangelist (for *Il Vangelo*) and a hagiographer (for *Uccellacci*) *en poète*, recreating a lyrical rendition of the sacred texts rather than reconstructing a story as a historian, as an antiquarian, or as a theologian, and privileging, as we have seen, subplots with secondary characters (Peter, Judas, Mary) who do not occupy the same narrative space in the Gospel of Matthew.

The lesson of Rossellini is evident. Given the choice of *I Fioretti,* his source, the anonymous and popular booklet of late tradition , Rossellini's hagiography of Francis is already unconventional and subversive, focusing on the literature that presents the Franciscan holy madness in a lyrical neo-realistic key, and giving voice to yet another rewriting of the Franciscan message. In his essay "Il Messaggio di San Francesco," the neo-realist director wrote about his film:

> Approaching the figure of Francis, I did not presume to produce a life of the Saint. In *Francesco giullare di Dio,* I did not tell of his birth or his death, nor did I presume to explain fully the Franciscan message and spirit or to aim directly at Francis' formidable complex personality. Instead, I thought it necessary to show his effect on his followers so that, among them, Friar Ginepro and the simple Friar Giovanni acquired great relevance, for they reveal the spirit of simplicity, of innocence, of happiness that emanate from Francis' spirit, to the point of paradox.
>
> In essence, as the title already suggests, my film intends to be an exposition of the jester-like character of Franciscanism, of its playfulness, its "perfect happiness," of the freedom the spirit finds in poverty, in the total detachment from material things.
>
> And I decided to render this special aspect of the great Franciscan spirit along the lines of the *Fioretti* where, in my opinion, the flavour of primitive Franciscanism is preserved intact.
>
> ... Re-proposing some aspects of primitive Franciscanism today seems to me the action that can best answer the deepest aspirations and needs of a humanity that, because it has forgotten the lesson of the Poor of Assisi and is a slave to the desire for riches, has lost even its taste for life. (Rossellini 1987, 76–7)[10]

So many of the elements of this film serve as important lessons for Pasolini: the simple tools; the grainy images; the placing of the characters in their natural setting, in a fully human dimension; the episodic character of the narration that reflects the matrix of the *Fioretti di San Francesco*, from which the movie is freely adapted; and the exaltation of humility, simplicity, and innocence, as well as of the "cheerful" aspect of the Franciscan message. Pasolini will not forget them in *Uccellacci e Uccellini*: one need only think of the poetic tone of the scenes of evangelization of the hawks and the sparrows by Totò-Friar Ciccillo and Ninetto-Friar Ninetto, or of the violent joke the medieval loafers play at the expense of Ninetto, reminiscent of the abuses suffered by Rossellini's Friar Ginepro in the military camp of the tyrant Nicolaio. So close to the pictorial style of primitive painters, with its figures delineated against the two-dimensional background of a non-perspectival nature similar to the symbolic space of medieval art,[11] Rossellini's Franciscanism will suggest to Pasolini an analogous relation to the pictorial matrices of his films. One example is the figure of the Pasolinian Christ, portrayed as a Byzantine icon, or the proto-Renaissance echoes of works by Piero della Francesca in *Il Vangelo*.

Although inspired by a Franciscanism that is completely different from Rossellini's, Liliana Cavani's first movie, *Francesco D'Assisi* (*Francis of Assisi*, 1966), constitutes another significant referent in its differences from and similarities to Pasolini's works. Produced for Italian Public Television, *Francesco* was released in 1966, the same year in which *Uccellacci e uccellini* appeared, and also a year in which Pasolini was still busy writing *Bestemmia*.

Francesco, interpreted by Lou Castel, the iconic protester and matricide protagonist of Marco Bellocchio's *I pugni in tasca* (*Fists in the Pocket*, 1965), is presented by Liliana Cavani in the key of an *ante litteram* 1968. Marrone (2000), writing on Cavani's cinema, notes that the figure of Francis is humanized by following the example of Christ – that is, not by walking a path leading to a sanctification but rather by engaging in a simple human search for truth.

> In representing a classical subject that had inspired such different artists as Giulio Antamoro and Roberto Rossellini, Cavani opts to make of Francesco's *paupertas* the analogical principle of the biographical and visual narrative: she divests the figure of Francesco of all oleographic and legendary inscriptions, and portrays him as a "normal," "natural" individual who is

> "not particularly cheerful nor taken by a saintly madness as the legends based on an excess of piety have presented.
>
> ...
>
> After a quarter of a century, *Francesco di Assisi* retains its messianic appeal intact. It is a film about the present, as Cavani claimed, where the accent falls on the apostolic *agere* (to act) of the new man; but it is above all a film about the future, a symbol of the interpenetration of the historical and the spiritual, between the secular and the religious. Cavani transposes the exceptional life of a saint into a factual historical milieu. Francesco's exemplary human experience is enhanced by his relationship to quotidian reality. (17–18)

The movie became an emblem of the growing dissent among progressive Catholics at the end of the 1960s. It also provoked numerous polemics, both in Catholic circles and on the left because, as indicated by Marrone, it insists on a different mode of revolution, on the figure of a rebel "who does not actually oppose the *auctoritates* of his time but accepts them in order to transcend their imposing structures" (18). Cavani claims:

> Francesco did not want to be the leader of a movement, nor did he wish to found a religious order. His was a creative act, which escapes any codification, and therefore it was revolutionary. (18)[12]

On 5 June 1966, the journal *Orizzonti* published a debate on Cavani's film that included, besides the director's contribution, the opinions of theologian Adriana Zarri, critic Ludovico Alessandrini (editor of the Monday cultural page for the Vatican newspaper *Osservatore romano),* and Pier Paolo Pasolini. On the Franciscan episode in *Uccellacci e uccellini,* in reference to his encounter with the character of Francis, Pasolini writes:

> I must say that, in my case, it happened just by chance. I had never thought about Francis before and then I made a movie about him. I thought about the birds and, since Francis preached to the birds, I then brought in the saint from Assisi. While I was shooting my last film, the figure of Saint Francis did not particularly interest me. Sure, it may have happened for a series of internal coincidences. A couple of years ago I planned a movie on a sort of Saint Francis. The title was *Bestemmia.* The protagonist was a sort of Saint Francis but really poor, not the son of a bourgeois or of a small industry owner, but truly a son of the working masses, nicknamed Bestemmia

> because he is "sacrilegious." From here I developed a story analogous to that of the saint of Assisi. It could be that things then got mixed up inside me. In any case, my Francis is a symbolic character, fairytale-like, who represents the Church at a time of great progress. The words he pronounces are the same ones Pope Paul VI pronounced at the UN. (*Orizzonti* 1966, 29)[13]

Pasolini then expresses his opinion on Cavani's *Francesco*. Although he appreciates the aesthetic qualities of the film, he accuses the director of having attempted "to frame Catholicism in a low bourgeois mentality"[14] (29) and of having deliberately rejected the miraculous element present in the story. He comments:

> I would say that a non-believer may better like a Saint Francis who speaks to the birds and performs miracles. Western religion, which is impregnated with a secularism it mistakenly believes to be revolutionary in comparison to its own clerical spirit, tends to show itself skeptical and ironic towards miracles. But miracles are religion. A saint who does not fly, who cannot vanish, who cannot magically influence natural phenomena, is not a saint; or he is a Western saint.
>
> Sure, sometimes also I am skeptical about some miracles. But I do not exclude the possibility that they may happen. Christ's own have actually happened. Returning to the image of the saint portrayed by Cavani, it seems to me that the director carefully avoided making Francis perform miracles, thus following the rules and not courting scandal. She has "Westernized" Francis as much as possible ... She broke off the Eastern elements (hunger, death, dirt, lack of hope, cruelty) that existed in Francis' world, and she introduced low bourgeois elements ...
>
> No matter how hard he may try, Cavani's Francis cannot be different, different and therefore a saint ... we cannot say he has much to do with the crazy and sublime aristocratic nature of a religion: "Many are called but few are chosen." ... Such reduction in *Francesco* has, in my opinion, a character of religious irrationalism and of social pauperism and, more than representing a saint, it describes a beautiful soul. (29–30)[15]

It is clear that, for Pasolini, sanctity is connected to the typical Pasolinian theme of a radical diversity, which essentially means the rejection of the bourgeois condition and, in the narration, the refusal of a rationalist approach. His saints are absolutely human but at the same time exceptional, and they manifest their uniqueness and importance as examples of a revolution against the dominant bourgeois homogenization of the times through a sacred and sanctifying tool – namely, the miracle. It is a controversial tool for Pasolini, but nevertheless it represents a constant feature of his heretical saints. This is true of Bestemmia, who heals a young cripple, and of the comedic pair Friar Ciccillo and Friar Ninetto, when they preach to the birds, as it is of the maid Emilia in *Teorema.*[16]

Cavani's Francis is therefore a Western revolutionary; Pasolini's Francis, although irrational, can be viewed as almost having certain Marxist leanings. Beyond the difference in their "Franciscan" vision at the dawn of 1968, in Francis' figure both Pasolini and Cavani exalt the revolutionary message of rejection of the logic of private property and social class, the "insane" choice of extreme poverty, the peaceful struggle against repressive institutions, and the creation of alternative communities founded on basic, simple lifestyles in opposition to the consumerist logic of the economic boom years. The subversive example of Franciscan hagiography is still current in contemporary political theory; for instance, in the final pages of *Empire* (2000), Toni Negri and Michael Hardt invite readers to reflect upon the Franciscan example as a model for the new communist militancy in the postmodern era. It is a militancy that transforms "resistance into counterpower" and transforms "rebellion into a project of love":

> There is an ancient legend that might serve to illuminate the future life of communist militancy: that of Saint Francis of Assisi. Consider his work. To denounce the poverty of the multitude he adopted that common condition and discovered there the ontological power of a new society. The communist militant does the same, identifying in the common condition of the multitude its enormous wealth. Francis in opposition to nascent capitalism refused every instrumental discipline, and in opposition to the mortification of the flesh (in poverty and in the constituted order) he posed a joyous life, including all of being and nature, the animals, sister moon, brother sun, the birds of the field, the poor and exploited humans, together against the will of power and corruption. Once again in postmodernity we find ourselves in Francis' situation, posing against the misery of power the joy of being. This is a revolution that no power will control – because biopower and communism, cooperation and revolution remain together, in love, simplicity, and also innocence. This is the irrepressible lightness and joy of being communist. (Hardt and Negri 2001, 413)

Hardt and Negri thus propose a "politics of joy," the simple joy of being and the joy of being communist. Like other theorists,they retrace within the Christian legacy political models that can still speak to the postmodern world. As we will see for St Paul and his *agape*, reinterpreted as a politics of love (Žižek) and of poverty (Pasolini, via Chiesa and Toscano 2007), the political lesson of Saint Francis, reiterated throughout its cinematic trajectory from Rossellini to Cavani and Pasolini, espouses joyous poverty and richness of being and in so doing is the key to a new communist militancy.

Pasolini thus takes in both Rossellini's lesson of humble Franciscanism and radical simplicity and the revolutionary bent of Cavani's Francis. Seasoning it with an abundant dose of sacrality, Pasolini develops his own rendition of Francis, a figure who stands between comedy and tragedy, heresy and orthodoxy.

In *Uccellacci e Uccellini*, Pasolini chooses a passage from Pope Paul VI's speech to the United Nations[17] in order to introduce Francis in the context of Pope John XXIII's post-Conciliar Church. The speech is an explicit reference to the revolutionary message that emerged after Vatican Council II and to a Church that, with Pope John XXIII, was becoming more and more caring towards the world's forgotten and more aware of the unjust differences among men. Pasolini puts a particularly significant sentence in Francis' mouth as he tries to comfort the doubting Friar Ciccillo and Friar Ninetto: "The world must be changed," he has Francis say, a clear allusion to the revolutionary appeal of the Franciscan message.

At the same time, the character of Bestemmia in the eponymous verse screenplay represents the tragic incarnation of a failed Franciscan experiment that was defeated by the rich Roman Church of the twelfth century. Here, too, we have a saint who reinvents the *Canticle of Creatures* and who – rising to sainthood from a context of brazen orgiastic criminality after a crucified Christ speaks to him in a vision with "the words of the flesh" – invites his followers "to throw [their] body into the fight," thus making his own the memorable slogan of the 1960s American Black Power movement. Pasolini's *Bestemmia* draws inspiration from Rossellini's *Francesco Giullare di Dio* to insist on the suspicion towards semiosis, pointing out, like the Francis of the neo-realist director before him, that "it is more useful to preach by example than with words." It is only a small step from this kind of praxis to the heresy of Pasolini's saint –that is, the destruction of the sacred images and crosses.

Bestemmia mirrors Pasolini's reflections on cinema and its intrinsic mechanisms for the production of presence as opposed to the traditional mechanism of representation, the director's aforementioned difficult relation with representation and semiosis, his stylistic use of *pastiche* and contamination, and, finally, his poetics of the primitive and the barbaric and its connection to the sacred. In all of these aspects, Pasolini invokes a Franciscan model. In contrast, in *Uccellacci e uccellini*, the director evokes Francis in his meditation on the dialogue between Marxism and Catholicism – which shaped the period of *Il Vangelo secondo Matteo* (1964) – and on the late-1960s crisis of Marxism and of the leftist intellectuals' mandate. Pasolinian Franciscanism thus touches upon some of the most important themes of the Friulian director, and the subversive hagiography of Franciscan origin represents an important opening through which Pasolini's reflections on the 1960s as a whole are framed.

As discussed above, the modes of such hagiography in Pasolini range from the tragic in *Bestemmia* to the comic in *Uccellacci e Uccellini*. The cinematic poem *Bestemmia* can be taken as a particularly apt starting point for a detailed analysis of this trajectory. It remained unpublished as a whole for many years (with the exception of the long fragment published in 1967 on the Crucifixion and the "words of the flesh," which we examined in chapter 3); only in 2003 was it included in the writer's *opera omnia*. The Franciscan theme is here entwined with Christological motifs and therefore intersects the trajectory of two other movies, *La Ricotta* (1963) and *Il Vangelo secondo Matteo* (1964), both of which were contemporary with the composition of *Bestemmia*.

Bestemmia

Pasolini's original plan to produce a film about Saint Francis envisioned a saint adapted to the director's poetics and to the themes that obsessed him. In a 1962 interview, Pasolini mentions for the first time the project that would then become the core of *Bestemmia*:

> The film on Saint Francis is still a distant project and I do not know whether I will realize it or not ... And then, it's not really about Saint Francis, it deals with a made-up saint who vaguely looks like the saint from Assisi – even mentioning his name is totally pointless. If anything, we can do it after I finish the film, because this saint will invent the *Canticle of Creatures* – although in an even rougher language – he will become a heretic and will be even killed by the Pope's soldiers, as often happened in the Middle Ages ... But, I repeat, this project is so far into the future that it's useless to talk about it. (*PPC2*, 2834)[18]

From a chronological point of view, the project was born in the period between *Accattone* and *La Ricotta.* Composed as a verse treatment, it followed – in Walter Siti's opinion[19] – stylistic modes that also characterized Pasolini's poems from the same period, from *La religione del mio tempo* to the first poems in *Poesia in forma di rosa.* This project surfaces here and there in several statements by the poet. "*Bestemmia*" was originally supposed to be the title of what later became the collection of stories published as *Alì dagli occhi azzurri* (*Ali' with Blue Eyes*) in 1965. Pasolini was already planning to publish it in 1964, according to an interview with him published in the *Corriere* of December 1963:

> I then intend to collect all the stories I have been creating in the last decade, either as "stories to be written" (from '50, '51) or as screenplays. The last one I've been writing, under the curious legend of *verse treatment,* is titled "Bestemmia." And "Bestemmia" will in fact be the title of this volume that I hope to publish within the year.[20]

Bestemmia is mentioned also in the poem "Progetto di opere future" ("Project of Future Works"), later included in *Poesia in forma di rosa* ("I reinvent myself as a Catholic, a Romanesque / nationalist, in my search for 'BESTEMMIA' /or 'DIVINE MIMESIS'")[21] (*TP1,* 1246), and in a passage in *Poesie Mondane*:

> Medieval spring. A heretical Saint
> (called Bestemmia, by his mates.
> He'll be a pimp, as usual. Ask
> the plaintive leonetti consultation
> on prostitution [in the] Middle Ages).
> Then a vision. The popular passion
> (an endless tracking shot with Mary
> who advances asking, in Umbrian,
> about her son, singing her agony in Umbrian).
> Spring brings a blanket
> of hard yet soft grass, of primroses …
> and the atonia of the senses mixed in with libido.
> After the vision (mortuary
> debauchery, impious – of whores),
> a "prayer" in the glowing fields.
> Whores, pimps, thieves, peasants
> with hands joined under their chins

(everything in 50 against the light).
I will film the sunniest Apennines. (*PFR, TP1*, 1093)[22]

The project, however, suffered several setbacks due to Pasolini's simultaneous work on *Il Vangelo Secondo Matteo.* The beloved title (with which Pasolini is truly obsessed due to its perfect incarnation of the presence of the sacred that it simultaneously violently affirms and negates) and the uncertainty of the genre (which shifts from script to poem to cinematic treatment to narrative-in-verse) both made for a difficult gestation. Pasolini discussed the project at greater length in an interview on Swiss Television in February 1964:

> *Bestemmia* is a story in verse set in an ideal Middle Ages in central Italy – I would say during the time of the Norman invasions, in Salerno and in Apulia – which tells the story of someone profoundly similar to Accattone, a pimp who lives among prostitutes at the outskirts of that amazing thing Rome must have been in those years. And like Accattone Bestemmia has a mystical vein that, given the times, can offer some solutions. And the first solution is a vision. This sort of Accattone of the year 1100 imagines the Passion, a popular Passion with the Maries who follow Christs, etc. From that moment, from pimp and the despicable individual he is, he becomes a saint. But at the same time, he becomes also a revolutionary. That is, he founds a heretical order that I will invent, though on a rather precise historical basis. And from this the struggle against the papacy of the time will ensue. Bestemmia is killed after having preached the New Testament according to his rediscovery, which then will become the Franciscan rediscovery, of the holy texts. This story was born with the idea that it would be a film, but I didn't feel like writing it like that, normally, and so I wrote it, that is, I'm writing it, in verse. (*TP2*, 1724)[23]

Traces of *Bestemmia* also surface in letters exchanged with Garzanti (Pasolini, 1988, *Lettere 1955–1975*, 624) and in later interviews, including a document from August 1967 in which Pasolini refers to the unfinished state of a five-year work-in-progress that follows the parallel evolution of his reflection on the cinematic medium:

> I keep working on an odd thing I began four or five years ago that is called "Bestemmia": a screenplay I wrote in verse and carried inside me transforming it a bit at a time as my ideas on cinema changed.[24]

Again in a letter to Garzanti, we find the final reference to the broken path of *Bestemmia*'s composition. In 1970, mentioning the possibility of a complete collection of his poems, the author mentions "Bestemmia" as a probable title. Alluding to the aborted project for the film as a fragment, he states that "the title of this tome could be Bestemmia because it would include also a long fragment that bears that title."[25] In fact, the text published in the poetry collection titled *Bestemmia*[26] is a long fragment dedicated to his vision of the crucifix. The complete text of the film project was published only in 2003 by Walter Siti. Derived from a 158-page typed manuscript of a rather fragmentary and uneven nature, it contains several interesting bits that are particularly valuable for an analysis of the tragic-to-comic evolution of Pasolini's Franciscanism.

The screenplay begins with a long walk along the aqueduct. The places are the same as those in *Accattone*: the poor neighbourhoods at the outskirts of Rome, a Rome defined as "Shanghai a century / after the year One Thousand" (*TP2*, 997).[27] It is a suburban landscape traversed "in slow panoramic shots," a collection of precarious shelters inhabited by characters who are just as precarious and marginal, dotted with "masses of huts leaning against the aqueduct" (*TP2*, 997)[28] and with "herds of children / with extended bellies and trachoma – among groups of women as black as <corpses>" (*TP2*, 998).[29] The setting is Pasolini's typical view of the suburbs, with a postmodern touch that makes the Rome of the twelfth century completely undistinguishable from any city of the contemporary Third World, besieged as it is by caravans of refugees escaping from the Norman invaders – just like the Rome of *Ragazzi di Vita* is besieged by refugees and peasant masses uprooted from the land and forcibly urbanized.

Bestemmia's portrait is that of a medieval "Accattone" (protagonist of the eponymous film) marked by a criminal destiny, a "brother of Stracci"[30] (the protagonist of *Ricotta*), similar to Masaccio's figures in his chiaroscuro, in the strong thick features denoting his bastard race:

> Bestemmia seems made with steam
> from lentils and beans, with grapevine branches:
> a bunch of crushed grey leaves on each cheekbone,
> and above, the brownish eye, which feeds
> anger with tears; and his hair
> is that of a petty criminal, water seller
> or robber, grown from the grace

of a young boy, an orphaned bastard son,
to that of a young man. His strength, his height
do not take from his body the round curves
of the southern servant: and he is,
for his strength and height, a tiger, a bandit:
Musolino and an innocent Giuliano,
who only dream for now
of a life outside the law:
born to realize that dream. (*TP2*,1000)[31]

The typology is that of the petty criminal, and the portrait seems to emerge from a page of *Ragazzi di Vita.* Like Riccetto, the protagonist of Pasolini's picaresque novel from the 1950s, Bestemmia also sings Roman *stornelli.* One of them is particularly noteworthy for its hagiographic perspective, an ironic anticipation of what will later happen, completely unforeseen given the character. In this *stornello,* we find the same pairing of Passion and Carnival that incarnates the ambivalence of the sacred in Bestemmia's story. As we shall see, the criminal will become a saint; the debauchery of an orgy will be transformed into a vision of the Passion in a continuous cycle of reversals and carnivalizations, dominated (according to Pasolini's philosophy) by the ideas of *coincidentia oppositorum* and *tertium non datur.*

Lemon flower
– now that it is in the solitary plains –
lemon flower,
mommy made me during carnival:
she made me out of joy, not out of passion!
But everything is passion
in her grey colour full of health.
"Raising my eyes to the heaven I saw it starry,
and I saw my Jesus all wounded:
and I wounded him with my sin."
He has never thought
not once about Jesus and sin, bent
only on being cool among the cool. (TP2, 1000–1)[32]

As it once focused on the children at the aqueduct, filmed as they walked towards Rome or leaned like bullies against house walls, Pasolini's gaze now lingers on the description of Bestemmia's phallus, which the author describes as "a black, stinking beast / that knows no master nor God, / but glories itself only in a brother, Bestemmia" (*TP2*, 1001).[33] Sex and crime, along with indifference to religion, appear to be the distinctive features of this character. On his way to Rome with his partner in adventures and crime, Agonia, he is ready for anything: in the heat of the attempted rape of a young girl, Bestemmia causes her to jump in a river and drown (another typical motif of the Roman Pasolini); then he beats up her little brother, who had tried to defend her. This is Bestemmia. As if this were not enough, Pasolini then makes him arrive at the "place of whores," an alley full of rags, children, soldiers, and carts leaning against the Roman walls, carts that serve as the prostitutes' precarious shelters. The smell of "acacias," "of urine and human feces," is everywhere. Bestemmia is welcomed by six sisters who are described as "evil" and "dressed like brides." And so the orgy begins among the women, vulgar but also almost anthropologically sacred, with the explosion of laughter that in popular culture constitutes one of the possible manifestations of the sacred. Pasolini lingers on the details of "unmentionable things" and, immediately after a scene of homosexual fellatio (set against the background of the disorderly choir of impure mouths), the vision suddenly appears:

> The open mouths were left long open.
> But the poor are always ready to accept folly.
> The six sister whores and little boy whore Nicolino
> soon got used to that which
> was happening right in front of their open eyes.
> And like the crazy immediately know how to be crazy,
> the poor immediately know what to do with the crazy.
> Bestemmia, crazy, crying,
> with eyes like two sad water-filled fountains,
> lifted his big heavy head onto Nicolino's small shoulder
> and, with the assurance of the crazy, went to the door.
> Beyond that, the moon shone as blue as the sea. (*TP2*, 1013)[34]

The community of the poor can recognize madness and channel it into the paths of the sacred. Pasolini imports this ability into *Teorema*, a story of madness reclaimed to sanctity thanks to the welcoming and grateful gesture made by the community. In this tear in the heavy fabric of events, a hierophanic dimension opens in relation to which the moral and social given ("the six whores and the little boy whore"; *TP2*, 1013)[35] is reduced to a pure paradigm of the simple: "the poor immediately know what to do with the crazy" (*TP2*, 1013).[36]

At this point, Pasolini introduces into the screenplay a digression that focuses on the vision of the Crucifixion in *Bestemmia* and on the dynamic of such a vision; this digression was analysed in chapter 3. One has only to look around to realize that, against the background of the pimp struck by the vision of the Passion of Christ, a community is forming that welcomes the sacred and lets it shine in the eyes of its members, in their gestures, and over their bodies, which immediately recognize it. In Pasolini's primitive Christianity, there is no notion of conversion. True, a conversion is at work, but it does not change the souls of prostitutes and petty criminals. It leaves them intact, as innocent as ever, because they are as unaware of their violence as they are ignorant of their new goodness. Divine grace is an inscrutable mystery that transforms without transforming. The prostitutes' transformation into saints is immediate, natural, and inevitable:

> And look little by little at those faces,
> feared by the good bourgeois,
> reveal their sacred strength:
> the big animal eyes of the evil masses,
> the noble cheekbones, the uncontaminated skin,
> mouths and chins barely sketched with a sublime
> stroke of the thumb:
> look, look and tell me
> if Bestemmia hasn't found right away the perfect following for his sanctity.
> And nothing has changed in them, don't be fooled!
> Miracles don't happen inside of souls!
> They are always the same,
> the same whores who held tight as sisters,
> the belly of a bitch against the belly of another bitch,
> who lay together in an orgy they did not know was an orgy,
> who gave Nicolino to Bestemmia as if a filly to a stallion, they are the same:
> the same who laughed with their peasant mouths,
> missing some teeth between the red cheeks,
> with the same liquid light eyes of those girls
> who pass by in the street at night, already sinners
> and profoundly innocent.
> It is this innocence that is the same. God's beloved
> can even sin: if they are His beloved, they will be His beloved.

It's determined only by some design of His,
as mysterious as fire in fire,
that something in the life of his beloved
may change – *but without changing them!*
The saintly whores become saints, nothing other than saints;
they begin to pray around Bestemmia,
and they sing the rosary,
their voices in unison,
joined by the rougher voice of Nicolino.
And more people come out of their homes,
in the heart of the night. (*TP2*, 1019–20)[37]

The choice of the sacred welcomes grace without hesitation. The effects of Bestemmia's sanctity spread like oil throughout his surroundings, helped and fed by the environment itself. His ecstasy lasts three days and three nights. Bestemmia, with wide open eyes, kneeling, is surrounded by those who

imitated him as they could,
kneeling next to him.
They imitated the miracle, poor apes
in that summer of the world, as generous as children
...
Through him they adored what he adored. (*TP2*, 1021)[38]

Imitation of the miracle; sanctity as a process to be approached from the outside, repeating its gestures, the position of the bodies, feeling the ineffable in the mere repetition of the effects of a vision; sanctity as contagion – these radical choices are embraced just like that, like tossing a coin, with the same lightheartedness, the same irresponsibility with which we accept the rising of the sun, the changing of the seasons, and the inevitable facts of life. The choices are personal and, thanks to the times that allowed for it (as Pasolini points out), have resulted in the propagation of a mystical echo from body to body that gives birth to a community of rejects founded precisely in the sacred.

The priests arrive with their soldiers. Bestemmia is taken to a deserted place, where he can no longer cause scandal. His followers are beaten and kicked away. The violence of the institutions pours over these people who imitate saints; it is greeted with cries and smiles and the useless protestations of the prostitutes, "bitches angered for the love of God"

(*TP2*, 1023).[39] Bestemmia awakens from his mystical experience and, in a country landscape on the outskirts of Rome, begins to build a rudimentary chapel made of branches, with a big cross inside. Around that little church "in which the betrayal of God began anew" (*TP2*, 1026)[40] (since in Pasolini's notion of the sacred every form of institutionalization constitutes a betrayal, the rejection of the strength of the sacred, a tool of social domestication), a city is born.

The community thus establishes its presence in the landscape and is consolidated by the sanctity of its founding saint, who performs prodigious healings. A procession of desperate people leaves Rome for the village, hoping for a miracle. The community grows, day after day. The sick arrive with their families and, like at a small town fair, as around Friar Ciccillo in *Uccellacci e Uccellini*, they are joined by onlookers, nuns, friars, hawkers of candy and watermelon, male and female prostitutes looking for clients. Finally, surrounded by the Roman Curia, even the Pope arrives. In his features, we can recognize the portrait of Pope John XXIII, to whom *Bestemmia* is dedicated (as later *Il Vangelo secondo Matteo* will be): an old man from the north with a childish air, "with his big nose / and his head like an old peasant's" (*TP2*, 1036).[41] The meeting between Bestemmia and the Pope is characterized by the greatest sweetness. The Pope blesses Bestemmia and kneels to pray with him, "puppet of God / created to be used / in that fruitless work / that is communal prayer" (*TP2*, 1039).[42]

Immediately after his encounter with Bestemmia, on his way back to Rome, the Pope dies.[43] In the village, while the Curia are electing the new Pope, who is an emissary of the well-fed priests of that body, Bestemmia's iconoclastic adventure begins. The saint tears down the banners with the portraits of the Madonna and Christ from the flagpoles carried by the gathering faithful, and treads on them, launching into a fiercely anti-symbolic speech. Bestemmia's homily, which invites the people "to live in Christ, not in his words" (*TP2*, 1046)[44] and to make "Christ speak through himself, / not through his own words or words about him" (*TP2*, 1044–5),[45] would appear to be a veiled abjuration by Pasolini the screenwriter of Pasolini the director of *Il Vangelo secondo Matteo*, the film about Christ's life that was shot at the same time he was writing the verse script of *Bestemmia*. It is yet another palinode by Pasolini, a document illustrating the continual shifting of his thought: in a process of joining binary oppositions, he experiments in a certain direction only to swing back like a pendulum and end up in the opposite position.

Bestemmia's sermon has disconcerting effects on the nuns who are listening and ecstatically begin to invoke "God," cry, and tear their robes. Carried away by other women, they sing psalms all night long and then put on, like Francis, robes made of sack cloth. Bestemmia then gathers their discarded vestments and takes them to a minuscule Romanesque chapel, ravished by time and sacked. On its altar of bare stone, in front of the shadow of a cross and a "suffering Crucifix," he consecrates them to God with a prayer. This is clearly an episode reminiscent of the Saint Damian Crucifix of Saint Francis's life.

Meanwhile, in the Vatican, Bestemmia's fate is decided. The new Pope, whom Pasolini nicknames Pope Stork ("Papa Cicogna"), has been told that Bestemmia has destroyed "the symbols: / the images of the Madonna, of Christ, / and the Crosses" (*TP2*, 1052).[46] The Curia of the masters (literally masters of all there was in the land) deliberate whether to exile Bestemmia from Rome or kill him. The guards leave for the village "where Bestemmia and his faithful *adored God by living Him*" (*TP2*, 1055),[47] and their leader[48] warns these heretics to disperse by evening if they want to avoid being hung, impaled, or buried alive: "in conclusion, they were banished / from the city *where God is represented and invoked / and where his praise is sung* (*TP2*, 1055)."[49] Bestemmia, God's captive, naturally thinks about martyrdom: "What did the light in his eyes say / if not that death was a question / and a wounded body the answer?" (*TP2*, 1057)[50]

Cruel in his holiness, Bestemmia does not think about the others until an angel descends upon him to announce with unfriendly eyes but friendly intention that God is leaving him alone, free to decide for himself. "The world was world again" in a "devastating and wonderful disillusion" (*TP2*, 1059).[51] The crowd patiently waits "like dogs around a table" (*TP2*, 1059)[52] for Bestemmia to decide what to do. In the following scene, we see him walking away along a field towards the river, a typical Pasolinian setting that associates the empty expanse of fields with sex and death – all the way to the final scene of his own assassination. In the light of the moon, Bestemmia finds the body of the little boy whore, Nicolino. He picks him up like "a little bunch / of rags" (*TP2*, 1061)[53] and carries him into the woods where he digs him a grave. After he buries the young boy, he prays on his tomb, reinventing the *Canticle of Creatures*. The Franciscan model here becomes even stronger. This Bestemmia is a rougher Saint Francis, a poor Francis who has no literary education and composes his *Canticle of Creatures* in a tragic setting of death and desperation as a funerary ode on the grave of his old companion in orgy while, in the moonlit night, a nightingale's song rises as in a Provençal intermezzo:

> "Most high, all mighty, good Lord,
> Yours the praise, glory, honor and all blessings!" ...
> "To You alone, most high, they are due,
> and no man is worthy of naming You." ...
> "Bless You, my Lord, with all Your creatures,
> especially my bro the sun,
> which is day, and with it You brighten us,
> and it's a beauty and radiant with great splendour:
> it bears Your mark."
> Then, the peasant who cannot say anything
> if not naming things, like a child, realizes
> that there's the moon, in the sky above the woods. (*TP2*, 1063–4)[54]

At this point, with a break, Pasolini takes us back to a scene of a great religious procession, a miserable crowd, accompanying the new Pope. Bestemmia's fate is discussed once again. And if there were innocent people among the Christian rebels? "We will kill them all," the Pope confirms, "then God will separate / the souls of the innocent from those of the guilty" (*TP2*, 1071).[55] Another break follows, this time to the Roman countryside, closing in on Maria, a little blond girl who offers herself to Bestemmia. The saint loves her carnally but almost in a state of grace: now again God has left him alone. Bestemmia thus sees their future in a vision. He is "tied to a tree trunk at the bottom of a valley ... / dead of hunger and wounds, his flesh blackened by the ropes" (*TP2*, 1075);[56] she is dead "at the bottom of the ditch, wounded in her bare breast, with her head / buried in water and mud. / It was a source of holy water, / which went on calmly pouring forth / and flowing among the dead" (*TP2*, 1075).[57] Here is the suggestive image that will resurface in *Teorema* to characterize Emilia's death and her miraculous tears. After his vision, Bestemmia leaves, as even something as human and almost animal as an erection is redeemed and sanctified:

> but in God's grace, what is not grace?
> Even a swollen member that smells like an acacia.
> Thus the saint, with the weight of his youth
> that had belonged to evil and innocent evil and now was God's,
> got up to look for peace under the acacias. (*TP2*, 1077)[58]

With the arrival of a gold-clad bishop in the Roman countryside, Pasolini's lens moves again to the refugees' camp, "the theater of death" (*TP2*, 1082).[59] The script here depicts the parting moment when "who must leave, leaves; who must stay, stays … / Who leaves is guilty; who stays is lost" (*TP2*, 1085).[60] Maria, the little girl Bestemmia loved, also leaves. Bestemmia breaks down in tears, tears that take over the whole camp while the refugees load their poor carts, "carts like poor wooden altars" (*TP2*, 1085).[61] And Bestemmia's crying catches on "among the poor guilty who leave, / the poor lost who stay: yet nothing / changes in the acts, the gestures, the silence of departure" (*TP2*, 1087).[62] Pasolini's gaze then rests upon another camp, that of the soldiers who are approaching to destroy the community of the rebels "like Fascists in '22," as Pasolini describes their peasant traits that are similar to the faces of Herod's troops, whom he portrayed in *Il Vangelo* as wearing fezzes, or of the young Fascists in *Salò:*

Here and there, the brothers, one ready
to kill, one to be killed,
by mere chance victim or assassin,
by mere chance angelic or infernal. (*TP2*, 1088)[63]

They advance against backgrounds that recall Paolo Uccello and his battle frescoes ("on their crazy little horses with their thick black neck, / their shining rump, their eyes picked in orange groves" [*TP2*, 1087]).[64] And, as in the opening verses of *La ricchezza* in *La religione del mio tempo*, there are references to Piero della Francesca's *Cycle of the True Cross* in the troop leader, Monnezza:

Piero has not yet painted for him
his dark brown or lilac bowled helmet
or the vest in green earth …
Nor has Giotto cut his cloak
or his shoes – and in other lands, as far as Asias,
there are starry warriors, on golden backgrounds:
as uncouth as a beast
(the millennium since the death
of his imperial homeland has been lasting
as short as a decade, or ten months, and he
bears its Alexandrine delicacy intact)
he lives on life only,
unimaginably,

just like a beast,
that can beg for nothing
but life itself. (*TP2*, 1090)[65]

Meanwhile, in the refugees' camp, the crowd questions Bestemmia about their fate and future martyrdom. Bestemmia gives paradoxical answers that offer no consolation. While in "the camp of those dear to God" (the Pope's mercenaries), the soldiers ready themselves for battle, on the dawn of the day of his martyrdom Bestemmia is visited by an angel.

This is the angel's third visit to Bestemmia, as Pasolini suggests in the notes published in the appendix to the complete edition of the poem:

> The work is divided into three parts each of which ends with the apparition of the angel that announces to Bestemmia that God leaves him alone and free (and he is therefore immersed in reality and in facts – the world's empiricism, pragmatism): the first time, as soon as he pronounces his first heretical sentence and has some followers (the nuns who throw away their veil), so that he finds himself having to reorganize the life of the persecuted in a communistic no man's land, etc.; the second time, in the peace of his organization (his philosophical meditations etc.), when he finds himself carnally, humanly loving the girl and having to face Agonia's death; the third time at the end, when he is ready for death and therefore finds himself having to fight. (*TP2*, 1728)[66]

The angel again descends upon Bestemmia and announces his liberation from sainthood, since God once again leaves him alone. The angel thus does not come to announce Bestemmia's election by the Divine but rather his abandonment, his return to the human, to the univocal material dimension of existence, of pure life:

Bestemmia, the angel said – you pray and listen,
and you know that you die with the flesh.
God sent me.
His saints, like you wanted to be,
He has them elsewhere. Soldiers are coming to kill you.
But not to kill you alone. These are the facts of the world.
You are free, Bestemmia. The road of your sanctity,
is another, says the Lord.
How close He has been to you!

He touched you while the whores
loved carnally their sisters
and raped, innocently, a child.
He stayed close to help you fake miracles.
He stayed close as you tried to perform real ones.
He stayed close when you had to take care of men
instead of Him. To each man his heart,
to each saint his sanctity. You are free!
The Lord is now moving away from you. He is leaving you alone.
With the same high and unexpected love
With which he approached you, he now leaves.
...
The roosters are crowing, and you can only count on yourself.
God, by abandoning you, is leaving you the ultimate truth
very clear – it is here, with the light, but has no words. (*TP2*, 1102–3)[67]

Like a *deus ex machina*, the angel's apparition puts an end to Bestemmia's sacred voyage; completely turning it around, the angel makes it into a fully human story. Bestemmia goes back to being himself, a boy like any other, as Pasolini says, so that, paradoxically, "Bestemmia was now truly a saint. He no longer had by his side / God's presence. He was free; he was a youth with his whole life ahead of him!" (*TP2*, 1103). The epic dimension of "youth," so central in the author's poetics, returns. Bestemmia is reset to zero, he returns to the beginning, to his origins, to the untouched vitality of his "best youth," even if his life may be destined to last only a day.

Bestemmia wakes up from the dream of his sainthood ready to take up arms. He picks up a scythe and holds it in his hand. He rouses his companions, inviting them to pray and to arm themselves. Bestemmia's speech is the prelude to an armed conflict between factions of equals, between brothers of the same hungry people; it is the prelude to the fight against the Fascists, those who sided with the power of the predators. Sanctity gives way to class war and to a desperate claim to life, at the threshold of the end. Bestemmia addresses his followers, embraces the arms of the peasants' struggle (the scythes), and decides not to abdicate his very human destiny of "loser" but rather to vindicate it with violence:

"I wake up, I am again a youth from a poor mother, gone bad,
ferocious: with his viper eyes, a dog's teeth,
in the moment when Christ stripped me

like a man condemned to death. Enough. I'm here.
We only have a few hours of life.
Tomorrow's dawn will see us old corpses.
Young men like us are coming to kill us:
why isn't our place among them?
What chance made us martyrs instead of assassins?
I was born at the bottom of the West:
and so I found in my hand, during the sanctity
granted me by God, a hoe: and now a weapon.
I am one of the martyrs. As long as the Lord wanted it,
I was as much a saint as I could be. Now He has left me.
I have a bandit's words to tell you… .
Let's wait for them like men: we were born from the same people,
hungry, we are brothers and cousins,
it is by chance that we are not brothers in arms… .
Do whatever you want:
you can run away. I no longer ask you,
like the saints ask, for martyrdom. Smiling
they are much more evil than the devil!
I don't want to humiliate like this, with such a smile,
my assassins.
On the other hand, it is right, since my death
Can no longer teach anything,
that my life teach them something: I mean
the last actions of my life… .
I will teach them that it is possible to fight for God,
against the Fascists that call themselves His servants;
the servants of power, with their accursed strength,
they can always justly brag about! For if
they were weak, our victory would not carry pain!
…
This morning I want our life.
If you decide to stay and to fight,
you must truly want to live, to live
even by killing them, the mercenaries,
the masters of a world that doesn't want anything:
… We instead must really want to kill them.
Thousands and thousands of dead like them for many centuries,
and finally life will be safe. Let's start!"
Bestemmia's companions said that they wanted

to stay there and to fight:
"I – Bestemmia went on to say – no longer know anything.
God left with my sanctity:
He left me here naked. I repeat it because I still cannot believe it.
And yet sanctity has left me its light.
Who abandons you like this?
I'm unsure. Before I die, or make die,
I might not even pray. I'm unsure, unsure ...
No one can ever write the word End to our story." (*TP2*, 1104–7)[68]

The screenplay ends like this, another film "a canone sospeso" as *Teorema* will be. We do not know the outcome of the battle or whether Bestemmia survives. Only his act of rebellion remains; we do not know whether it is the beginning of a revolution. In his notes at the margins of the poem, Pasolini comments:

> At the end, Bestemmia – with the departure of Maria and his followers destined to return to normal life etc. With no hope, to plunge again in a history that's their enemy (that of a superior class) that wants them alive and nothing more etc., resigned, defeated etc. servants, happy servants, generations of animals that pass through the world, inferior, innocent, and evil, all with their evenings, their days, their migrations, their plagues, etc. Their religion with no truth, just simple obedience and conformity, etc. Of humble people etc. etc. – at the end, Bestemmia returns to the world and, rather than consigning his death to the memory of the people that would soon turn him into a myth, exorcise him turning him into saint, part of a querulous hagiography etc. alienated from himself by superstitious and extraneous adoration etc., he decides to offer his struggle. To counter vitality with life, mercenary anger with the anger of faith, the arrogance of the rich with the rights of the poor. He takes up arms – the weapons of popular uprisings, scythes and pitchforks, and with a few of his followers he waits and takes on the Fascists. The poem ends with this struggle, as yet un-ended, with this pure struggle, the eternal struggle. (*TP2*, 1728)[69]

Abandoned by God, the man responds simply to the call of life: the martyr dies fighting. The heretic slogan inviting adherents "to throw your body into the fight" is now literally lived as a moment of radical humanization of Bestemmia's historical destiny. Now freed from sainthood and immersed in revolution, he finds his own identity and path in the class struggle that characterizes the human race. God withdraws. The game has yet to be played: at stake is a life that is more than merely innocent, unconscious animality – a life that is that of neither an animal nor a saint, but of a man. The subversive hagiography in *Bestemmia* thus closes with the rejection of sainthood – a rejection allowed by God – and on the protagonist's decisive claim to his own destiny as a man marginalized by history. At the threshold of death, life becomes action and finds new meaning, as God leaves to the poor the freedom to carve their own destiny in revolution. The Franciscan matrix thus gives way to a heretic and violent *jacquerie* without solution. Spiritual rebirth is nullified three times by returning to the human dimension. Bestemmia's attempt at sanctity unsuccessfully folds in on itself, although it does give the dignity of class consciousness to this man destined for defeat. In moving from sanctity to its loss, Bestemmia becomes a man of action. The spiritual dimension is lost, but the political one remains. Preaching based on the primacy of action and on examples now becomes action performed in defence of the marginalized – until it turns into murderous violence, which is in fact a struggle for survival, a struggle historically aware of the predetermined fate against which life rebels.

Uccellacci e Uccellini

Bestemmia's tragic elaboration of the Franciscan hagiographic model and related theoretical considerations – encompassing Pasolini's meditation on the sacred (focused on a barbaric Christology) and on the cinematic language (parallel to his contemporary reflections in *Empirismo eretico*) – is countered by the "comical" Franciscan parenthesis of *Uccellacci e uccellini* (*The Hawks and the Sparrows*, 1966). Beyond Rossellini's and Cavani's neo-realist and dissenting intertexts, and beyond Pasolini's own explanations of his choice of the Franciscan theme, *Uccellacci e uccellini* clearly constitutes a cornerstone in the development of Pasolini's filmography. First of all, in it Pasolini deals with the usual subproletarian "matter" in a completely different way than in previous films. The tone and register are no longer those of a national-popular epic, and the film's narrative is far from clearly delineated. Pasolini has left behind the Gramscian illusion and has embraced a new way to make movies that he will define as "*elite* cinema," a form of cinema in which meaning is not clearly and explicitly presented but is rather encrypted, requiring an intelligent audience to search for it.

Starting with this work of interpretation, Pasolini creates his audience and shapes it as a privileged interlocutor. This interlocutor is no longer the amorphous mass of the traditional commercial movie audience that with neo-capitalism has replaced the ideal target of old Marxism, the people. Pasolini's answer to a blind mass audience, completely dependent on the traditional recognition mechanisms of commercial movies, is the creation of an "ambiguous, problematic, difficult" cinema. It is a cinema with just enough poetic and enigmatic features to cause a shift in meaning to new and original positions and open a dialogue with an audience of critical and informed viewers.

In this regard, Serafino Murri writes:

> With *Uccellacci e uccellini*, the dream from which Pasolini's cinematic adventure had begun, that of elaborating a language with which to talk to anybody, addressed to a people understood in the Gramscian sense of the term as "other" than the bourgeoisie, comes to its definitive conclusion. Having realized that that people had been substituted from above with an *ad hoc* mass built by the bourgeoisie, a mass whose apparent simplicity is actually desire for disengagement and vulgarization, Pasolini gradually strips his films of what, till then, could be considered their "cipher": their popular character.
>
> ... The receiver of the filmic message is no longer taken for granted; on the contrary, the receiver must be constructed (Just like the antagonist-mass is constructed). (1994, 69–70)[70]

Gone is the illusion of a cinema for everybody, if "everybody" means "for the masses." What is pursued is instead a difficult cinema, "for the few," if those few can realize the construction of their selves as critical subjects through the effort to interpret the cinematic text.

Uccellacci e uccellini is an expressly difficult and allegorical film, one that voices both the author's personal autobiographical crisis as well as the crisis of his time. In Moravia's words,

> Pier Paolo Pasolini's *Uccellacci e uccellini* belongs, with special features characteristic of its author, to the category of "crisis" films. What this crisis may be is by now well known: the end of the Fifties, Suez and Budapest, the reflux of engagement and the victory of disengagement, the loss of ideologies, the dawn of a consumerist civilization, in the East like in the West, made up of consuming and producing masses and of technological powers. As far as Italy is concerned, another explanation must be added: the neo-capitalist advance has included among the countries that "have" also a country like ours where many still "don't have." Hence a contradiction that cannot but be reflected also in literature. (1966)[71]

The two main characters in this movie, significantly named Innocenti Totò and Innocenti Ninetto, father and son, walk in a Post-history landscape, in a suburban area where large highways under construction advance alongside cornfields and shabby, illegally built houses. One has a Neapolitan accent, the other a Roman accent. We do not know where they are coming from or where they are going, as they walk on strange roads with Zavattinian[72] names where the only geographic coordinates appearing on road signs are those of very far places (Istanbul, Cuba) that evoke a Third World dimension. The movie's epigraph is an exchange inspired by Edgar Snow's 1965 interview with Mao Tse-tung: "Where is mankind going?" "Dunno." In this sort of road movie, in this picaresque itinerary, we do not discover where the protagonists are going until the very end. Not even the crow, which at some point shows up on their way and starts talking to them, manages to obtain this piece of information.

It is very clear, however, where the crow is coming from: it comes from the country of Ideology and is the child of Doubt and Conscience. Pasolini makes it the emblem of old Marxist intellectuals called to verify the role of the established powers (the *verifica di poteri*, to use Fortini's expression) at the moment of the loss of their mandate. The crow is the leftist intellectual of the 1950s who comes face to face with the missed integration with the people (*popolo*), a category that, at this time of crisis, is also on the wane. A father, a son, and a strange Holy Spirit: as noted by Guido Fink (1966, 422–3) and Maurizio Viano (1993, 147), this symbolic triadic structure so dear to Christianity and Marxism is reformulated upside down. It is not a dove but a crow that will end up devoured by the father and the son. Its devouring means extermination but also assimilation, cannibalistic absorption of the ideological message, interiorization of Marxist ideals that are destined never to die; as the crow says, "You shouldn't think however, Mr. Totò, that I'm crying for the end of what I believe in. I'm convinced that someone else will come and will pick up my flag to carry it on. I only cry for myself. It is human, isn't it, for one who feels he no longer counts."[73]

The story functions on several hagiographic levels. First, we have the sacrificial and Christological figure of the crow who is eucharistically immolated precisely because the seed of his ideas may germinate in a new context (i.e., among the new challenges of modernity). Also in evidence is the confluence of the revolutionary and the saint in the figure of Palmiro Togliatti, the famous leader of the Italian Communist Party from 1927 until his death in 1964, evoked in the film in the scenes from his funeral. This commemoration constitutes the poetic and political apex of the movie: we see the crowd as an ocean of closed fists and signs of the cross, in which the two great cultural axes of Catholicism and Marxism – supposed enemies – mix and become confused. As Morandini observed,

> Togliatti's funeral is a fragment of a few minutes set into the film: "politics and death, united by a solemn, deep, infinite violence." They are images from newsreels of current events edited with the hieratic rhythm of a Passion by Bach. Closed fists, the sign of the cross of mourning people who pay the final homage – that is, funeral obsequies – to a revolutionary leader "considered also a saint." It is another double-edged sequence with a complex meaning, at once moving and embarrassing for its turgid rhetoric alien to the characters' story: commemoration and detachment from an event that, poetically, marks the end of an era and the beginning of a different season with an "open" morality, rich in imbalances, uncertainty, confusion, of which *Uccellacci e uccellini*, a modern day fable, constitutes a testimony and a confession. (1966)[74]

Something similar happens in the third and most famous hagiographic episode. As the crow tells the story, Friar Ciccillo and Friar Ninetto are invited by Saint Francis to evangelize hawks and sparrows. The two friars spend a long time searching for the right way to communicate their evangelical message to the two bird species and, after many failed attempts, find it in screeching for the hawks and in hopping for the sparrows. After their miraculous discovery, however, as they return to tell Saint Francis about their mission, they witness the horrible sight of a hawk diving upon a sparrow to kill it. Immensely saddened and desperate, the two report to the saint:

> FRIAR CICCILLO: Well, Friar Francis, the hawks, we convinced them, and now the hawks, as hawks, they adore the Lord. And also the sparrows, we convinced them, and, as sparrows, they do fine, they adore the Lord. But the thing is that between them ... they break one another's face (*with great pain*) they kill one another, Friar Frank ... What can I do if there's a class of hawks and a class of sparrows, and they can't get along with one another? What can I do?
>
> SAINT FRANCIS: What can you do? Of course, you can do anything with the Lord's help!
>
> FRIAR CICCILLO: Whaddya mean?
>
> SAINT FRANCIS: I mean you gotta teach the hawks and the sparrows all they didn't get and you had to make them get!

FRIAR CICCILLO: How?
SAINT FRANCIS: Come on, brothers. You gotta start it all over again …
…
FRIAR CICCILLO: But the hawks are hawks, and the sparrows are sparrows … There's nothing to do, the world's like that …
SAINT FRANCIS: We gotta change the world, Friar Ciccillo. That's what you didn't get! Go and start all over, praise the Lord! (*PPC1*, 745)[75]

What is presented here is the figure of a saint that recalls the "Leninist" Christ of *Il Vangelo*, although – as noted also by Adelio Ferrero – without the polemical charge of Christian indignation that characterized the Christological film.[76] Francis appears to be closer to the model of Pope John XXIII's "revolutionary"; Pasolini intertwines the primitive Franciscan church and the advanced message of the contemporary church by placing in the saint's mouth Paul VI's words from his speech to the United Nations. In the comparison between Marxism and Catholicism, Pasolini seems to be trying to fit the first into the matrix of the second, at least in its new post-conciliar configuration. As he says in "La trama secondo l'autore" ("The Plot According to the Author," 1966), "the crow, the author tells us, is ideological rationalism outdone by Pope John's message" (*PPC1*, 834).[77]

As evidenced by Maurizio Viano, the dialogue between Catholicism and Marxism that characterizes the post-conciliar era has enlivened the critical debate on *Il Vangelo secondo Matteo* with sweeping polemics. Indeed, the message of *Uccellacci e uccellini* seems to confirm the opinions already advanced by Pasolini in his 1964 film, which foreshadowed the "Christian" turn of many contemporary radical thinkers from Žižek to Negri, mostly in terms of enmity towards global capitalism. Viano writes:

> [For Pasolini] Marxism is not "Christ's greatest enemy" but that in fact it "comprehends religion's highest moments." If it wants to survive, ideology must seek allies against "bourgeois materialism" which "opposes any religious occurrence as well as any movement aimed at knowing the real." Ideological thinking should open up to the sacred and should enhance peace and love rather than just class struggle. Marxism, Pasolini noted while discussing the ideology in *Uccellacci e uccellini*, "is not over insofar as it is able to accept many new realities hinted at in the film (the scandal of the Third World, the Chinese, and, above all, the immensity of human history and the end of the world, with the religiosity which this implies – and which constitutes the *other* theme of the film)." (Viano 1993, 152)

Pasolini also confirms this vision in an interview in Cannes on the occasion of the premiere of the movie, where he is asked about his position regarding the presence of religion in his films:

> By birth, education, and culture, I am a bourgeois, actually a petit bourgeois. So, I am on one side a rationalist – lay, liberal, rationalist – according to tradition, and on the other, I am an irrationalist. My religious sense is grafted onto my bourgeois irrationalism, of an anguished bourgeois that's a figure typical of European culture, I believe also in Northern Europe. Consequently, when I chose Marxist ideology to interpret reality, to understand what's around me, it's clear that my Marxism has been soaked through with irrationalism and therefore with religiosity. In fact, since I think that, after all, the petit bourgeoisie is exactly the opposite of the religious spirit, that it is incapable of experiencing a sense of the sacred in the highest and most sublime sense of the word, I believe that religion is a formidable weapon against the petit bourgeois spirit, narrow-minded, petty, backward, egotistic, hypocritical, etc. And so, in me Marxism and religion become natural allies in my polemic against the bourgeoisie.[78]

Torn between primitive Christianity and advanced rationalism (Casiraghi 1966, n.p.), Pasolini indicates the trace of what Ferdinando Taviani defines as "a road untraveled although open" (1966, 104).[79] This is precisely the religious and poetic dimension of love, as Mario Verdone has also pointed out. In Verdone's review, he finds the meaning of the movie "in this extreme comparison, in this extreme 'scandal': from the 'scandal' of such sincerity (politics is mortal) to the 'scandal' of poetry (love is eternal)" (1966, 76).[80]

On the jacket of the volume with the film screenplay, Pasolini appropriates some comments by Goldmann[81] on the genre of the novel and uses them to his own ends. He therefore claims that he has created

> two "real characters," *directly and explicitly* occupied in a "degraded search for authentic values in a degraded world."[82] *This is the very subject of my film.* And it is not by chance that the speaking crow, towards the end, cites a sentence by Lukàcs: "the road begins, and the voyage is over." In short, I refuse to surrender to echolalia, to the imitation of "reality" (the disappearance of problematic individuals, due to the conclusive prevailing of the exchange values over those of usage). My Marxism from the 1950s makes me go on believing, again paraphrasing Goldmann, in a "progressing search." Naturally without any optimism; in the darkest pessimism, in fact. In the allegory of these

> three fables, the basic theme is crisis and the need to renew Marxism … Many other motifs are grafted onto this fundamental theme: first of all, the condemnation of the tendency of bourgeois thought to "deny any sacrality, whether the celestial sacred of transcendental religions or the immanent sacred of the historical future" … (*PPC1*, 828–9)[83]

As we discussed in chapter 3 on barbaric Christology, on the basis of the long digression on the Passion of the visionary Bestemmia, the celestial sacred of transcendental religions and the immanent sacred of the historical future blend, for Pasolini, into a concept of immanent transcendence that lies at the heart of his vision of the sacred. Christ's *kenosis* is its central motif. It is with the dimension of the sacred, the irrational, and the mysterious that Marxism must learn to dialogue. That is the horizon within which its trajectory acquires meaning, even if in the transitional phase represented by the endless road of *Uccellacci e uccellini*, and later by the desert of *Teorema*. The former film's landscapes are important, be they post-historical such as the highways under construction or vertiginous "Romanesque" spaces such as the striking frames of Tuscania in the scenes of the medieval apologue. Suffice it simply to mention the scenes of the miracle of the preaching to the birds, of the towers, the ravines, and the Romanesque churches so bare in their simplicity, shot in Pasolini's luminous and melancholy black and white. This is the light and pensive atmosphere of the ideological comic fable with its both joyous and funereal Franciscan Marxism, with its religious revolutionary drive imbued with Fellinesque and Chaplinesque overtones, allegorically announcing the approaching year of 1968.

To return to a Franciscan motif *par excellence*, we might also consider the scene in which the *Canticle of the Creatures* is recited by Friar Ciccillo as an expression of joy and thanks for the miracle of the evangelization of the birds he had just performed:

> FRIAR CICCILLO (*euphoric*)
> Most high, all mighty, good Lord,
> how happy I am for the sun!
> And how happy I am there's also water,
> so who's dirty can wash their face.
> Bless you, my Lord, for this ass
> and all these sheep and this shepherd.
> The donkey's braying over there; and the shepherd with his animals, with his old face full of bumps.

And Ninetto, who every now and then, all happy, says amen.
FRIAR NINETTO Amen … amen …
FRIAR CICCILLO (*irresistible in his holy joy*)
Bless you my Lord for this holy world
Where everybody can live, even those who don't have any means …
Here comes a cripple, and one has to wonder how he can walk.
FRIAR CICCILLO
Blessed be the fresh grass, the nettle and chicory,
and may who eats them stand in God's Glory.
An old lady, poor thing, is just picking chicory.
FRIAR CICCILLO
Woe onto those who die in mortal sin
'cause I really don't like to see their sorry funerals!
Bless you my Lord for the joy that fills the heart,
'cause all around you is roses and flowers … (*PPC1*, 743–4)[84]

The euphoria of the two friars over the miracles that have just taken place gives voice to a sense of happy participation in the life of creation that recalls, in some respects, two important chapters in Pasolini's life: the Resistance and neo-realism. The Resistance is evoked by the euphoria, the sense of liberation and communion with the world, the auroral moment when something miraculous has just happened and from which the nightmare of history does not seem able to awaken us, so typical of the Marxism of the Resistance. Neo-realism informs the gaze on reality, which here, in these frames, in these pages of the script, is strongly reminiscent of the images and the atmosphere in Rossellini's *Francesco giullare di Dio.* In their immediacy and simple existence, Friar Ciccillo's words gather inspiration from the humble reality that surrounds him, faithfully observing and recording its events "with love."

We can compare this euphoric faith with Andrè Bazin's comments on De Sica:

> As for the technique, properly so called, *Ladri di biciclette*, like a lot of other films, was shot in the street with nonprofessional actors but its true merit lies elsewhere; in not betraying the essence of things, in allowing them first of all to exist for their own sakes, freely; it is in loving them in their singular individuality. "My little sister reality," says De Sica, and she circles about him like the birds around Saint Francis. Others put her in a cage or teach her to talk, but De Sica talks with her and it is the true language of reality that we hear, the word that cannot be denied, that only love can utter. (2005, "De Sica," 69)

In an interview released in Cannes for the presentation of the film, Pasolini claims that his movie is totally outside of neo-realism, but it has a nostalgia for it. This is clearly evident in the Franciscan apologue, where Pasolini questions the "perfect happiness" of the Rossellinian matrix through a brutal confrontation with the principle of reality. It is true that in Rossellini's film there also was a moment in which Francis clearly fell into a crisis, notwithstanding the character's general calling to holy madness. The episode of the meeting with the leper ended with Francis' tears as he turned his eyes to the ground, crying inconsolably, and the camera turned to frame a disconcerting empty sky. Pasolini then, in *Uccellacci e uccellini,* simply makes explicit the doubt that Francis, as Rossellini's "jester," had already foreshadowed, but he pushes it in a much more explicit political direction, although tempered by the post-conciliar atmosphere.

Sam Rohdie (1999) has outlined the factors that make Pasolini both the most obedient and most disobedient heir to neo-realism. On the one hand, a series of common themes and ideological perspectives demonstrates his similar perception of cinema as a reproduction of reality, as social engagement and political vocation; on the other, his anti-naturalism, the emphasis on the framing and on a fragmented time and space, as well as the predominance of artifice over the documentary and of the script over improvisation and casualness, take Pasolini's cinema far from the masters of neo-realism. According to Rohdie, Pasolini's reality is not the object of a discovery, an encounter, or a revelation: it is the object of a creation (1999, 167). Pasolini constructs his reality through a very elaborate pastiche of quotations:

> Pasolini's real was ... always removed from the thing or the event, always a quotation of them, not so much the object as its consciousness. (168)
>
> The function of Pasolinian language then, and of culture, was to lead one through consciousness to a self-effacement of consciousness, towards a pre-consciousness, a pre-symbolic, a pre-history, towards an irrationality and non-language, to dream and myth, which for Pasolini cinema perfectly embodied. Culture, for Pasolini, was an instrument for its own erasure. (172)

The objective of Pasolini's linguistic and cultural construction is therefore self-destruction and the demolition, through film, of one's own structures. In a sort of explosion that wipes out artifice with its opposite, the primitive, the barbaric, and the pro-filmic are reached through the proliferation of style, artifice, study, and technique. The video camera is felt, in contrast to the naturalistic perspective of the neo-realist long take. Poetic cinema is barbaric just like mannerist painting is barbaric, with its emphasis on citation, on anatomy, on the pathos of the composition, and on the strident colours, which reach reality through an excess of technique. This is Pasolini's challenge, as he embraces neo-realism's political theses but on an opposite trajectory, weaving elements of the "words of the flesh" (of a subproletarian and radical pro-filmic) into the fabric of the symbolic order. The distance of language from culture is established through a fulguration, a short circuit within technique itself (173). This game of abolition of cultural instruments represents, however, a tension that is never fully realized. The desire to create a reality – one that, as discussed in chapter 3, precedes conscience, the symbolic, history, and cultural stratifications – finds a structural limit in the linguistic and textual nature of reality that Pasolini himself recognizes as inevitable. Rohdie introduces the configuration of desiring machines for Pasolini works:

> His works were like self-perpetuating machines. Reality, for him, had all the intensity of a desire, but it was constructed in such a way as to maintain the desire infinitely. Desire was tempted but never satisfied. It was always turned away at the gates of reality by the discursive formations that had brought it there. His films were instruments for the production of the desire for reality, but his reality was produced in such a way as to make the desire insatiable. (177)

The insatiable desire for reality identified by Rohdie is the matrix of Pasolini's cinema as a whole. It represents the need to capture life corporally, to incarnate it in film: hence the centrality of the Passion and of the moment of Christ's Incarnation expressed in his Crucifixion.[85] Cinema represents reality according to a process that creates presence by fundamentally abolishing representation itself, and Pasolini's cinematic experiments stop at the threshold of untranslatability. The difference between representation and life is exemplified by the impossibility of incarnating pain; the original event, in its explosiveness as the extreme moment between life and death, cannot be reproduced through a process that pushes representation to dissolve the represented individual into the pain of torture and of life itself, into an emblem of incarnated presence. It is impossible to break free of the trap of representation, of linguistic mediation and mediated reproduction, imitated but not lived. Pasolini insists on action, the praxis, and the event, but he also recognizes the checkmate suffered when reproduction ends at the threshold of its opposite, death. It is not by chance that *La Ricotta* represented exactly the abolition of meta-cinema, of the reflection on representation in the terrible circuit of an actual death on the set, a real and unrepeatable event emblematic of the passage from the portrayal of death to the character's real demise. In this sense, death is the ultimate meaning of the words of the flesh – even if Pasolini tried (in *Trilogia della vita*) to inscribe the body according to the coordinates of *eros* and not only those of *thanatos*. However, it is only *thanatos* (and therefore the reality of the Passion) that leads semiosis to explode in a short circuit without any mediation. The sadomasochistic turn of Pasolini's late cinema is an attempt to push the limits of representation with the production of presence through pain, a pain that can also take on the form of the pleasure of pain. The term "Passion" thus assumes a different value in Pasolini as the *Totentanz* of his cinema as a whole.

Viano has identified the Passion as the keystone of Pasolini's poetics, where *pathos* is the mark left by the real on the individual, who is altered by it in mind and body. It is the imprimatur suffered by the individual who reacts with praxis. Pasolini cannot escape the language trap: the outside world is a world of signs asking to be deciphered, but it is also a world of objects that surround us, that penetrate our space, and that interact with our bodies, arousing desire or rejection. We interpret the world (a linguistic and intellectual operation) but, as we are affected by the world, we either embrace or reject its objects with our passions. In Viano's words:

> Physical reality, the world "out there," speaks a language, it is a language whose constant flow of messages constitutes ... an empire of signs. Everywhere we turn we find signs. This omnipresent sign-system performs a double operation on us, the addressees. In the first place, the presence of things/signs around us "demands to be deciphered" ...
>
> In the second place, not only does reality push the subject on the semiotic path but also speaks a language of its own ... the dialogic relationship between subject and object is a continuum of semiotic strata "synthesized by the language of action." The language of physical presence is part of the language of action, because things, by the mere fact of being there, *act* upon the subject.
>
> ... The empire of signs is the empire of passion because signs act on the body which, in turn, reacts to and reads them. The empire of signs is the empire of passion because the subject is at once the somewhat passive

> construct of primal semiotic encounters and the passionate reader of subsequent signifying situations. (1993, 33–4)

The empire of signs identified by Viano and confirmed by Pasolini's pan-semiotic vision is, however, also an empire of "things," real objects that precede the sign and strongly affect our corporeality. The Passion corresponds to this process of apprehension of the world and reaction to it. It is the direct encounter with its objects that results in the primary impulses of *eros* and *thanatos*, or in a mixture of both, where the penetration of things into our being is turned into the consciousness of those things and into their redistribution around our body at a distance determined by our praxis, our passion, and our attraction or repulsion to them. Again, Pasolini does not escape the semiotic trap. Semiosis consists exactly in this hand-to-hand combat with the real, in the attempt to erase the distance between the perceiving subject and the perceived object that become one and the same in the process of attribution of meaning. Pasolini wishes they could become one also in the corporeal sense, as a body that devours reality or is devoured by it, or as a landscape in which subject and object tend towards self-effacement in a reality constituted by the interpenetration of bodies and things. This is what happens in the Passion: God, incarnated into a body, becomes the immanent transcendence of matter that is manifested exactly at the moment of death in a dying god, in a subject that gets lost in his own body and, in so doing, transcends it. This is the Passion for Pasolini, according to Viano:

> The concept of passion according to Pasolini, then, alludes to the subject's bodily semiotic history, to the active memory in the flesh, which overdetermines our readings to some degree ... I would like to suggest that "passion" modifies the traditional conception of subjectivities and inaugurates the domain of subj*ac*tivity, the subject as activity, the subject as a compelling action. (1993, 43)
>
> Decoding, then, is not the discovery of a meaning that is already there, but an activity whereby the subject modifies the real in accordance with his/her passions: subjactivity. The external world, however, does act on the subject: first by branding his/her flesh in the course of primal scenes which demand semiotic intervention, and later by attempting to force its own meanings on him/her ... Both the subject and the object, "the decoder" and "the decodable," are territorialized within a larger picture, the language of reality, a linguistic totality in which they rank as living signs. Seen

> in this light, ideological pragmatism would seem the best definition of Pasolini's semiotics. (1993, 45)

Following Viano's interpretation, the true definition of Passion is the encounter between the subject and the world and the trace they leave on one another: *subjactivity*, that is, the action of a subject, his or her reaction to the world, but also his or her Passion (*eros* and *thanatos*, desire or rejection), that mute dialogue between the body and reality. This passion precedes the sign; it is the Incarnation that determines the event, the direct encounter that is translated and layered in the history of these meetings or confrontations, and that gradually settles into a meaning. According to Viano, this is how a sign is born as the semiotic corporeal story of the subject.

What, then, is Pasolini's realism? In an interview with Oswald Stack, Pasolini reflects on the meaning of the word "realism" and defines the difference between his film and those of Italian Neo-realism in these terms:

> Realism is such an ambiguous and loaded word that it is hard to agree on its meaning. I consider my own films realist compared with neorealist films. In neorealist films day-to-day reality is seen from a crepuscular, intimistic, credulous, and above all naturalistic point of view ... Compared with neorealism I think I have introduced a certain realism, but it would be hard to define it exactly. (1969, 129)

Undoubtedly, the crepuscular, credulous, intimistic, and naturalistic dimension seems to apply to the neo–*Canticle of the Creatures* in *Uccellacci e uccellini*, composed as it was in a moment of happy Franciscan madness – the interpretation of the visual stimuli in this joyful mystical sequence with Friar Ciccillo. Pasolini nonetheless demystifies the naturalistic reading of the world and the transparency of the real claimed by the Neo-realists and – although he misses it – replaces it with a more articulated, contradictory, and complex vision that requires, as a response, an intervention in the sphere of praxis.

Granting the subject the possibility of interacting and reacting variously with the real, of leaving on it different traces, Pasolini integrates the revolutionary message of Marxism with an agonistic vision of the relation between subject and reality in which the outcome of the confrontation between the subject and the world is left unresolved and open. This openness persists notwithstanding the awareness of the weight of a semiotic history that almost exclusively assigns the mode of self-immolation and sacrifice to Pasolini's outcasts. In the neo-capitalist world, it is *thanatos* that prevails and it is reality that devours the subject, particularly the subproletarian and marginalized subjects whose authenticity consists in making their own bodies into an arena that bears testimony to the harsh conditions of lives waiting for an unattainable remission-revolution that death can only further exalt. Realism and *Totentanz* thus coincide. Both attempt to tell the destiny of a special category of subjects, that of the drowned (to use Primo Levi's terminology) who inscribe their trajectory of rebellion in the ultimate event of their self-immolation/death, just like the incarnated Christ. At the same time, they reassert their destiny as defeated, as mortal human beings overpowered by history (a semiotic history of class conflicts), and as tokens of a revolutionary future and of a resurrection in which Pasolini will never really believe.

Viano, in tracing a history of the concept of realism and its possible configurations, locates Pasolini's experiment in realism as an example of "semiotic realism":

> Nearly all realist theories and practices before Pasolini can be grouped under the heading of *mimetic realism* ... Pasolini consistently called naturalism the style seeking to represent things the way they are as well as the accurate rendition of minute details: and he abhorred such a style, devising a film form as distant from naturalism as possible.
>
> ...
>
> The "classic realist text" ... treats the sign as transparent, privileges representation instead of signification, reinforces the passivity of the spectator, and fails to portray the real as contradictory and articulated.
>
> ... *Semiotic realism* was thus born of the attempt to combine Marxist commitment with the poststructuralist shift from representation to signification ... truly subversive films were supposed to make the spectator work. (55–7)

Pasolini's relationship with semiosis and referentiality is thus extremely complex. Because he detested the transparent sign of mimetic realism, Pasolini moves beyond mimesis in the direction of the production of presence. Fundamentally, this means producing an event in all its uniqueness and definitiveness; for example, reproducing pain with pain, death with death, cannibalizing the cinematic sign in the direction of an absolute referentiality that is, in fact, impossible. It is not a question of producing cinema but of producing life. The Pasolini of *Bestemmia* is nostalgic for a relationship with the real based on identity, on "presentification," on the incarnation of the event, a relationship in which distance is erased – as is the sign *qua* sign – through the production of an event. In the name of this impossible relationship with referentiality, Pasolini denounces all instances of simplification as a mystification of semiosis. Consequently, in order to approach the event through its creation, he amplifies the elements of artifice as opposed to those of mimesis and naturalism. Not only is his mannerism a stylistic factor; it is the key to access the real through the implosion of the rhetorical instrumentation of his cinema, the praxis that produces presence. Caught between a hermeneutics of suspicion (the lesson taught to the audience) and the production of presence (i.e., the fundamental desire to be devoured by the event and by reality), Pasolini adopts both the ideological perspective that produces the audience's critical awareness and the mystical one that expresses the irreproducibility of life as incarnated by the artist's creativity: the theorem and the mystery.[86]

In this return to Friar Ciccillo's *Canticle of Creatures*, the dimension of history as nightmare re-emerges and mystical enthusiasm is brought crashing down with the image of the hawk killing the sparrow. In a certain sense, the (neo-realist) Franciscan praise to creation flows into the acknowledgment (quoted by Francis) expressed by Paul VI's "realist" words on inequality and the imperfect composition – not of creation but of human and civil society.[87]

Lino Miccichè may be right in emphasizing how the message in *Uccellacci e uccellini* takes its distance from "the false myths of rational or mystical optimism" (1966)[88] and how it gives origin to a new conscience of the fact that "it will be only with his own hands that man may be able to break his chains."[89] There is an evident nostalgia for Rossellini's Francesco, but there is also a tireless denunciation of the crisis of the world of the 1950s and of all its auroral and euphoric elements, as well as the acknowledgment of the doubts inherited from that decade. History is no longer palingenesis but rather a story of inequalities that must be faced with the awareness of the new contexts, namely the transitional phase of the 1960s.

It is time for a new praxis – one more aware, one better able to change the world – not in the name of Christ's indignation in *Vangelo* ("I did not come to bring peace but a sword" [Matthew 10:34]), but in the name of Francis' love. Pasolini's Marxism here really seems to foreshadow the speculative developments of radical thought. *Agape, caritas*: love, Negri and Hardt's final frontier, will be the crucial political formula also for Žižek and Badiou. It is in the name of love that the Franciscan and the Pauline models meet in Pasolini's subversive hagiographies.

Chapter Six

The Pauline Model

The progression of Pasolini's subversive hagiographies that we have traced in the "Theorematic" variant of the "mad saint" and the anchorite, as well as in the Franciscan modalities of *Bestemmia* and *Uccellacci e Uccellini*, finds another fundamental incarnation in the Pauline model, one that intersects with the complex web of relationships that ties Pasolini to the Catholic institutions already examined in the first chapter.

San Paolo: 1966 to 1974

In 1966, Pasolini drafts a sketch for a film about St Paul, and sends it in March of that year to the head of Sampaolo Film, Don Emilio Cordero – this outline of a few pages is known as the *Progetto per un film su San Paolo* (*Project for a film on St. Paul*). The lines of communication between Pasolini and Catholics are still open: we are still in the post-Johannine climate, and Pasolini – after the test of *Il Vangelo secondo Matteo*, has gained the trust of the Vatican. The idea of a Catholic production of a film on the life of Paul seems therefore conceivable; although Don Cordero replies negatively to Pasolini's first proposal, he does not definitively close the door on possible future developments – for the project or for the director himself. In short, the Vatican is not ruling anything out.

Pasolini writes in a letter to Cordero:

> I suspect that this project will cause an unprepared reader's head to spin: but actually, for now, it is written for the reader's use. As for myself, I'm beginning to feel toward this project that exclusive and consuming love that ties me to my works at the point where making them becomes engrossing. (1988, *Lettere 1955–1975*, 615)[1]

In August of the same year, Pasolini travels to New York, where he discovers the great metropolis and comes face to face with the contemporary developments in – and revolutionary possibilities of – the American left. It is this contact that gives him the idea to set part of the film on St Paul in New York:

> My entire youth I was fascinated by American films, that is to say, by a violent, brutal America. But this is not the America that I found: I found a young, idealist, desperate America. Americans have a great pragmatism and at the same time an equal idealism. They are never cynical or skeptical as we are. They are never conformist, they are never realists: they live always in a dream and must idealize everything … I came to America and discovered the most beautiful left a Marxist could ever, today, discover. I meet the young people involved in the Student Nonviolent Coordinating Committee – you know, the students who go to the South to organize the blacks. They bring to mind the early Christians … they exude the same absoluteness that made Christ say to the wealthy young man: "To come with me you have to abandon everything; he who loves his mother and father hates me." They are neither communists nor anti-communists – they are mystics of democracy: their revolution consists in bringing democracy to its extreme, almost insane, consequences. In meeting them, I had the idea to set my film on St. Paul in America. I want to transfer the entire action from Rome to New York, setting it in our time but without changing anything. Am I clear? Remaining entirely faithful to his letters. New York has many analogies to the ancient Rome of which St. Paul speaks: corruption, clientelism, the racial problem, the drug problem. And to all this St. Paul gave a holy response, that is, a scandalous one, just like the SNCC. (*SPS*, 1600–1)[2]

Two years later, on 9 June 1968, Pasolini sends the *Abbozzo di sceneggiatura per un film su San Paolo (sotto forma di appunti per un direttore di produzione)* (*Draft of a screenplay for a film on St. Paul* [*in the form of notes to a production director*]) to Don Cordero. This document is essentially the screenplay of the project. Pasolini had written it in May of that year (contemporaneously with the crucial events in France that month),[3] full of hope regarding the possibilities of Pope Paul VI's pontificate. As we have seen in the first chapter, Pasolini believed that the pontiff intended to follow the lead of Pope John XXIII and distance himself from the most reactionary clerical positions. In his letter to Don Cordero, Pasolini tentatively characterizes the project as a "Film Teologico" (theological film) and indicates his need to review the passages selected from the Pauline letters, especially with other translations:

> Dear Don Cordero, ...
>
> I am sure that both you and Don Lamera will be shocked by this draft. In fact this text narrates the history of two Pauls: the saint and the priest. And there is an obvious contradiction in this: I am entirely on the side of the saint, while I am not very gentle with the priest. But I believe that the Church, precisely with Pope Paul VI, has reached the point of having the courage to condemn all clericalism, and thus to condemn even itself as much as it is such – I mean, in temporal and practical terms.
>
> I emphasize in this introductory letter, for the sake of honesty, this one point: in the screenplay, as you will see, this issue [of the two Pauls] is treated with less rigidity and schematicism, leaving the spectator free to choose and to resolve the contradictions: and to decide whether this THEOLOGICAL FILM is a hymn to Saintliness or to the Church. (1988, *Lettere 1955–1975*, 639)[4]

In 1968, in conversation with Jon Halliday, Pasolini mentions the *Bestemmia* project, which he has already transformed into a screenplay in verse. He adds, however, that he has abandoned his projects on other saints in order to concentrate exclusively on the life of Paul.

> I have decided to scrap that idea and all the other saint ideas I have had and do a life of Paul, which I am going to start in the spring of 1969. It will be completely transported into modern times: New York will be Rome, Paris will be Jerusalem and Rome will be Athens. I've tried to find a series of analogies between the capitals of the world today and the capitals of the ancient world, and I've done the same thing for the actual events – e.g. the opening episode where Paul, who is a Pharisee, a collaborator and a reactionary, is standing by at the murder of St. Stephen, along with the executioners, is going to be done in the film with an analogous episode during the Nazi occupation of Paris, where Paul will be a reactionary Parisian who kills a Resistance fighter. The whole film is going to be transpositions like that. But I am going to be extremely faithful to the text of Saint Paul and his words will be exactly the words he uses in his letters. (Stack 1969, 139–40)

We see here several Pasolinian constants: the use of analogy; the transposition of the past into the present (think of *Edipo re* [*Oedipus Rex*, 1967]), which will find a further outlet in *Salò* (1975); the faithful following of a sacred text as in *Il Vangelo secondo Matteo* – the text being in this case the Pauline letters.

In *Abbozzo di Sceneggiatura* (1968–74), the story, based on the *Acts of the Apostles* for its narrative and on Paul's letters for his speeches, starts in Paris (Jerusalem) during the years of the Nazi occupation. The Christians are depicted as gathering members of the clandestine Resistance. Among them is Stephen, who is arrested by the SS during a partisan action. A trial follows, in which Stephen proclaims his faith. Captured and insulted, he is later executed. The execution is framed through Paul's gaze, according to Pasolini the gaze of a Fascist.

> In Paul's face one can read something worse than malice: one could read cowardice, ferocity, the decision to be mean, a hypocrisy that operates to make it appear that everything that happens does so in the name of the Law, or of Tradition – or of God. All these features cannot but make that face also seem a desperate one (*PPC2*, 1888).[5]

After Stephen's execution, the life of Paul is changed forever. He becomes one of the fiercest participants in the ferocious persecution of the Christians throughout the city. In 36 AD, he takes his activities to Barcelona (Damascus). While crossing the Pyrenees in a car, he faints only to be awakened by God's voice asking him why he is persecuting Him. Blinded as a result of God's wrath, Paul regains his sight only after he is baptized by Ananias. Receiving the Holy Spirit, Paul, the erstwhile prosecutor, now flees from city to city, caught between suspicion of his new Christian companions and the threat of his old fascist allies. After meeting Peter, he is forced to leave Paris (Jerusalem) on the run. In another European city (Tarsus) he experiences his "ascent to the Third Heaven," a vision of a childhood earthly paradise. He leaves for Antiochia (Geneva), and then for Piedmont and Lombardy, preaching the scandal of the cross. He has a dream in which a beautiful Macedonian boy calls him to his land, while being progressively transformed during the vision into a victim of the extermination camps. Paul then follows his dream and actually travels to Macedonia (Germany), where he is beaten up and arrested by the German police. In prison he miraculously liberates himself from his chains by singing; the jailer too is converted by the miracle. Still in jail, Paul continues to suffer from his chronic disease and has a dream about the onset of his convulsions in childhood, connected with a sight of naked young boys in a stadium's locker room. The dream is openly revealing of his homosexual desire and his disease as the result of his sexual difference.

He moves then to Bonn (Philippi), where his preaching among the high bourgeoisie and intelligentsia is met with curiosity and scepticism.

The intellectual crowd frames his death-drive, his "thirst for death," within a Jungian interpretation as a "collective apocalyptic will." Forced to flee by a fascist mob that attacks the house of the political assembly, he goes to Rome (Athens). In the screenplay this is one of the greatest moments of Paul's preaching, in a sort of delirious state. He is attacked by a sudden mob of hooligans and his face becomes a bloody mask. The Aeropagus speech is set in a press room, where the intellectual audience listens incredulously to Paul's inflamed words. He walks along the streets of Rome and, seeing a group of soldiers from afar, he vomits while weeping. Later, he is interviewed by public television, presented as the star of the day, while being psychoanalized as a victim of a return to an infantile state, entrusted to the "transcendent" power – or grace – of his parents.

In Genoa (Corinth) he preaches again (from the Letters to the Corinthians), and the screenplay highlights Paul's impact on his audience: at first they are curious and admiring but later become suspicious, and finally are alienated by Paul's sexual politics. However, the listeners are fascinated by his account of his ascent to the Third Heaven, and by his explanation of how Christian grace is perfected through weakness, weakness in fact being the real power, the power of Christ.

In 54–57 AD Paul is in Naples (Ephesus), where he preaches as well as performing a miracle without even knowing it: his stolen shoelace revives a poor child in a Neapolitan slum. The screenplay presents at this point a slapstick scene, with three Neapolitan scoundrels pretending to do miracles like Paul. The rascals are later exposed as pretenders and reproached by Paul and his followers.

In 58 AD in Paris (Jerusalem) there is a decisive meeting of the Apostles on the foundation of the church as "a promise of redemption." Caught in a mob and almost lynched, Paul is arrested and runs the risk of being assassinated. He is brought to Vichy (Cesarea), where the prosecutor, Felix, interrogates him. From Vichy he asks to have a trial as a citizen of the Urbs in New York (Rome). He preaches again (with the words of the Letter to the Hebrews), meeting again hostility and indifference, with the exception of the crowd gathered in his little hotel, a crowd of almost all black people. In New York at the trial he counsels compliance with the authorities, thereby alienating the New York intelligentsia.

The last sequence in the screenplay is a sort of interlude with Paul passing again through the sites of his teaching, from Naples to Genoa, until he is arrested again and brought back to New York. After some time in prison, he is released and returns to a modest hotel in the city. Here he writes to his disciple Thimothy in Naples. The script draws a stark contrast between the parallel scenes of a baroque Christian rite celebrated in Naples and the gathering at the little hotel in New York, where, surrounded by a crowd of blacks, servants, intellectuals, and youth, Paul preaches in a sort of trance. In the final scene, while he is writing a second letter to Thimothy, he decides to step out on the balcony. There, he is shot twice and dies.

The previous version of *Progetto* (1966) was articulated in a series of key moments, partially reused in the final elaboration of the screenplay: from the martyrdom of Saint Stephen, to Paul's conversion (or, as Roberto Longhi would have called it, his "fulguration"), then to his decision to preach to the Gentiles, to his preaching in various locations, to the dream of the Macedonian boy, to his religious Passion in Paris and Vichy (Jerusalem and Cesarea), and finally to Paul's last days in Rome. Particularly interesting in this former version of the cinematic treatment is the Macedonian episode, with St Paul caught – in response to the call of the beautiful and monstrous young Macedonian – walking along an immense highway. Walking along the *autobahn* captures visually the contrast between the "actual" request to Paul and his answer as a "saint" (*PPC2*, 2029).[6]

In 1969, during the famous interview with Jean Duflot, Pasolini alludes to the Pauline project, underlining his fascination with the double nature of mysticism that is at the same time an absolute pragmatism, and thus part of the idealism mixed with pragmatism that Pasolini perceived in both the American New Left and the young revolutionaries of the Italian political group of Potere Operaio (Worker Power).[7] In fact, as Subini demonstrated in his essay "La caduta impossibile: San Paolo secondo Pasolini" (2004, 253), which traces the figure of the saint in Pasolini's oeuvre, Pasolini does not rule out linking on another level Marxist materialism and irrationalism – this time under the banner of St Paul. This attitude also signals a fundamental break with regard to the Student Movement (Movimento Studentesco) – think of Pasolini's infamous "Il PCI ai giovani!" ("The PCI to the youth!," 1968) of the previous year, with its attack on the rebelling youth and his polemic in favour of the police officers as "children of the people." Pasolini has now changed his opinion about the students and seems to perceive the political proposal of the youth of Potere Operaio as similar, in its idealism and pragmatism, to the founding acts of a revolutionary community to come.

How can the spirit of an upheaval be connected with the existing institutions? How can the revolutionary impulse be maintained without succumbing to the compromises that every type of institution necessitates? How can revolution and the dimension of the sacred be linked? How can one's own political action be rooted in this dimension? How can faith and *praxis*, sacredness and ideology, be assimilated? The figure of St Paul becomes an essential point of reference for Pasolini: he represents both the knot and the suture between the sacred dimension and the foundation of an institution. On the one hand, at the moment he ascends to the Third Heaven and issues the sacred word, Paul acts as the initiator of a process that over the long term will dismantle the classical world and its institutions, including slavery. On the other hand, it is also Paul who establishes the Church and its rules, rules that determine its relationship to institutional power.

Doing (*il fare*) and action become the perspective from which to look at saintliness: at heart, we are not so far removed from the Franciscanism of *Bestemmia* and its invitation to throw one's own body into the fight. We recall how *Bestemmia* ended with the protagonist's renunciation of saintliness and with the invitation to take up arms and rebel against the masses of papal troops who had intervened to violently repress the heretical revolt of the community. Now Pasolini moves even further back in time, no longer in the twelfth century but in the era of the early Christians, in order to describe the seeds of a nascent community, capturing the ambiguity between movement and institution, an ambivalence incarnate in the figure of Paul himself, both mystic and organizer. With his illness and proselytizing weakness, Paul also demonstrates the strengths and the haughtiness of his institutional involvement; it is he who dictates the policies and the norms that both nourish and compromise the growth of the nascent Christian community.

We thus witness an evolution from the Franciscan model to the Pauline model, from the Johannine holy heretic to the saint who has the potential to exceed and explode the institution in the very moment in which he founds it and establishes the basis of its development. Pasolini announces to Duflot:

> You know that I am preparing a film on St. Paul, on the religious ideology of his time, i.e., generally on the *Gnosis* through the different trends in thought in the Hellenistic period. The more I study the mystics, the more I discover that the other face of mysticism is precisely "doing," "acting," action.
>
> For the rest, the next collection of poetry that I will publish will be entitled *Trasumanar e organizzar* (*Transhumanize and Organize*). With this expression I want to claim that the other face of "transhumanizing" (the word is from Dante, in this apocopated form), or rather, of spiritual ascent, is precisely organization. In the case of St. Paul, the other face of saintliness, his abduction into the "third heaven," is the organization of Church. There

> will be much to say about the people who, according to us, act only on the pragmatic, practical level: they are always ascetics and profoundly religious. (*SC, SPS*, 1462)[8]

The model of saintliness changes and adapts to a new era. The project is started and abandoned multiple times until 1974, when Pasolini speaks of it in an interview with Gideon Bachmann as a current project, re-elaborated under the banner of a confluence between Johannine saintliness and Pauline "*demonicità*" (demonic-ness). The project has matured since the great disappointment of the "historical little discourse of Castle Gandolfo" (Moscati 1995, 164) of Pope Paul VI; Pasolini has revived the old, obsessive title of *Bestemmia* and applied it to the project of *San Paolo.* When asked what projects he is working on, Pasolini replies:

> One is called *Bestemmia,* and it is the life of St. Paul, which I wrote five or six years ago but now have rethought, in the sense that I made it more radical and violently anticlerical. While before it was political, now the sense of the film is a never-before-seen extremely violent attack against the Church and the Vatican. I made a double St. Paul, that is, schizophrenic, cleanly divided in two: one is the saint (from the letters it is clear that St. Paul had an authentic mystical experience); the other is the ex-Pharisee priest who recovers his former cultural positions and who will become the founder of the Church. As such, I condemn him; as a mystic it's okay, he has a typical mystical experience, respectable, and I don't judge it. But I violently condemn him as the founder of the Church, with all the negative elements of the Church already in place: its sex phobia, its sexism, its organization, its collections, its triumphalism, its morality. In short, all the things that have made the Church bad are already present in him.[9]

The trajectory Pasolini followed with regard to the Church is apparent in this 1974 comment. We see his general disenchantment towards the potential schism, which, in 1968, in the name of charity, could have re-established the Church of Pope Paul VI. On the contrary, according to Pasolini Pope Paul VI reconsigned the Church to a lethal alliance with its true adversary – neo-capitalist power. At this point, Pasolini does not nurture any hope of a palingenesis, of a rebirth of an *Ecclesia* like the original Pauline one; instead he unleashes his rage against the clerical and crypto-fascist dimension of the Vatican, staging a Paul as powerfully sacralized in his mystical dimension as he is powerfully used in the satanic project of the Church's founding. The ambiguity of the sacred, with its demonic dimension, is incarnated politically and allegorically in the figure of a Mephistophelean Pauline alter ego: Luke. Luke, already the author of the Gospel and now demonically possessed, is the scribe of satanic will in the *Acts of the Apostles.* The 1974 rewriting of the Pauline project, with the insertion of various scenes of demons, indeed veers in a decidedly anticlerical direction. Such scenes culminate in scene number 93, which stages the celebration of Satan and Luke for having founded the church. Here Pasolini introduces the list of the misdeeds and abuses perpetrated by Popes throughout history – a completely satanic Vatican genealogy. Paul's destiny becomes irrelevant: his beatification becomes a matter of course, and removes no cornerstone from the edifice of power.

The Poetic Idea between Relevance to the Present (*Attualità*) and Sanctity

At the heart of the St Paul project is the typical Pasolinian process of transposition. Above all, however, the project contains a poetic idea founded on a radical opposition. In the pages of the *Progetto per un film su San Paolo* (dated 1966), Pasolini describes the project in broad strokes, including its central dichotomy:

> The poetic idea of the film, and also its innovation – which together should become the film's main thread – is the transposition of the entire story of St. Paul to the present time ... Why would I want to transport his whole earthly life into the present? The reason is simple: to give cinematically, in the most direct and violent way, the impression and the conviction of his relevance to the present [*attualità*]. To say explicitly, so that the spectator doesn't even need to think, that "St. Paul is *here, today, among us*" and that he is so almost physically and materially. [To say] that it is our society that he addresses: it is our society, which he bemoans and loves, threatens and pardons, attacks and tenderly embraces. (*PPC2*, 2023)[10]

The term *attualità* assumes a central importance, here with the meaning of contemporaneity (*contemporaneità*), but also – as Armando Maggi (2009, 42) has emphasized in his *Resurrection of the Body* – relevance and conformism. This relevance and conformism allude to an auroral, nascent moment, a moment Pasolini identifies not only with the post-Johannine Church but also with the political crisis that the late 1960s, after the advent of the economic boom, seems to signal. Pasolini confirms the centrality of *attualità* and the short circuit it establishes with sanctity:

> The film uses this process to reveal its deep thematics, namely, the juxtaposition of "*attualità*" and "saintliness" The former refers to the historical world that tends, in its excess of presence and of urgency, to escape into mystery, into abstraction, into the pure interrogative. The latter is the divine world, that, in its religious abstraction, on the contrary, comes down among men, where it is made concrete and operative. (*PPC2*, 2025)[11]

The contrast between historical linearity and sacred atemporality could not be greater. On the one hand, the profane contemporary world remains closed in its enigmatic modernity; on the other, the divine world, through the sacred word, opens up from its traditional transcendence into an incarnated dimension. Here Pasolini is completely Eliadian, establishing an antagonism between history and the sacred, based on the opposite of the crisis of presence in De Martino:[12] instead of a lack, Pasolini articulates an excess of presence that borders on indecipherability.

At the heart of Pasolini's production in these years is the opposition between the historical and divine dimension, between *attualità* and sanctity, between politics and religion, and between institutions and revolutionary movements. What Francesca Parmeggiani has defined as "the desire to live within History" (citing the interview with Duflot)[13] plays a very strong role. In other words, *attualità* is imperative: the presence that makes itself a choice, and a political choice – the kind that Parmeggiani defines as "the anguish of contaminating oneself … [with History], of accepting its compromises" (1996, 205).

In *San Paolo*, the profane conceals itself as transcendence, and the sacred is revealed as immanent. Pasolini is a politician and a theologian *en poète*: the short circuit between the sacred word and the profane word reverses their positions. The conflict between ideology and contemporaneity on the one hand and religion and ahistoricity on the other could not be more productive than this. Pasolini gives the following indications in the *Progetto*:

> The things, the characters, and the settings will speak for themselves. And from here will be born the newest and perhaps most poetic part of the film: the "questions" that the evangelized will pose to St. Paul will be the questions of modern men; they will be specific, circumstantial, problematic, and

> political, formulated in the typical language of our time; the "answers" of St. Paul, however, will be such as they are: that is, exclusively religious, and moreover, formulated in St. Paul's typical language, that is, universal and eternal but *inattuale* [obsolete] (in the strict sense). (*PPC2*, 2025)[14]

The theories of the sacred that Pasolini follows are animated by a discomfort towards History and the willingness to remain inside it. This discomfort is expressed in *San Paolo* through the staging of the "misunderstanding of the sacred word": Pasolini evidences not only the intact fragment of the sacred word (element of saintliness), but also the difficulty of the reception of this word in *attualità*. The *inattualità* (obsoleteness) of the sacred reveals its disappearance in contemporaneity and at the same time leaves evocative traces, a symptom of an absence and of a crisis at the heart of modernity. It is in this distance between sacred and profane word that the entire drama of our time is articulated, and it is in this dichotomy that the duplicity of the figure of Paul – saint and pharisee, mystic and priest, believer and organizer of a church that, in the final 1974 version, is a criminal institution – is inscribed. In the aforementioned interview with Gideon Bachmann, Pasolini says: "This violence of mine against the Church is profoundly religious, in as much as I accuse St. Paul of having founded a church instead of a religion" (De Giusti 1979; cf. Subini 2004, 258).[15] Anti-clericalism reaches its maximum: Pasolini affirms that he will not reanimate the myth of St Paul but will instead destroy it.

The staging of the diffraction of the political and technical word and of the sacred word is accentuated in the 1974 version by the presence of Luke as a demonic scribe. Pasolini writes in a stage direction added to the end of scene 30: "Add an infernal scene in which Satan charges his principal to incarnate himself in Luke, who has finished writing the Gospel and is getting ready to write the *Acts* (and Satan advises him to write them in a false, euphemistic, and official style)" (*PPC2*, 1912).[16] This duplicity in the sacred word – on the one hand, the Letters, recognized as prophetic, and on the other hand, the Acts of the Apostles, identified by Pasolini as falsely sacred, as the founding discourse of Catholic clericalism – breaks the ranks of fidelity to the traditional sacred texts and reincarnates Paul's schizophrenia at the textual level.

This split installs a conflicted – and not confessional – dynamic in regard to the sacred word when that word becomes political. This is the knot that profoundly fascinates Pasolini: we recall the "*fare*" and "*pensare*" of his article on the activists of Potere Operaio, how belief (*il credere*) and doing (*il fare*]) were interdependent factors, as well as the *trasumanar e organizzar* of Pasolinian memory, the title of his 1971 poetry collection.

The incarnations of that technical, communicative language – a language that Pasolini had abhorred since the time of *Empirismo eretico* – are Luke on the one hand and Paul the pharisee and church founder on the other. This language is that of contemporaneity; it is the historically contaminated language of our time. As Anna Panicali has observed of Paul:

> His political word is constructed according to a precise nexus of cause and effect. It proceeds securely, acts on the sense of guilt, discriminates reason from irrationality, opens into "serious discussions," is organized in debates and demands obedience to its models ... Pasolini's critique here is radical: directed not only at the political language, but at all technical and rigidly communicative language ... The technical-political word is "hard," decisive, "almost authoritarian," or it is characterized by a "euphemistic sweetness," by triumphalism and by irony. On the contrary, the sacred or poetic word is pronounced as if in a delirium; it causes mind and body to suffer and is a monologue without an addressee. (1995, 81)[17]

The political word of Paul is identified by its authoritarianism as the language of the institution. And with institutions, compromises are born – with others and with ourselves – as well as fears. Indeed, scene 39 in *San Paolo* proves to be a central sequence in the staging of this schizophrenic drama of the word: a quasi-Rossellinian opening on the heavens is immediately and disturbingly turned on its head, transformed into the space of an infernal interlocutor, described as Luke, who prophesizes the institution:

39. Against the Sky

Outside. Daytime.

Against a profoundly blue sky, the distinguished face, sweet and elusive, of the author of the *Acts fades in.* The face lets the following words fall onto the spectator, abstractly and from far away, improvising:

> "With every institution, diplomatic actions and euphemistic words are born.
> With every institution, a pact with one's conscience is born.
> With every institution, fear of one's fellow is born.
> The institution of the Church was *only* a necessity."
>
> Devils (*PPC2*, 1919)[18]

It should be noted that this scene dates from the draft from 1968, in which Luke has not yet assumed the silent, satanic configuration that he will have in the 1974 variations, where he will no longer speak but instead write (Marchi 2006, 93). The insertion of a scene of devils occurs later, in 1974, where Luke, though still "sweet and elusive," nevertheless gives voice to the drama of the pragmatic word contaminated by the institution.

Armando Maggi has linked the words of the author of the Acts in *San Paolo* to those of hagiographies, precisely on the basis of a style that is purposefully "false, euphemistic and official": hagiographies are indeed, according to Maggi, falsified narratives. It is not a matter of inventing a history, but of adapting biographical data of a "saintly" person following a devotional model of biography, constructed according to the dictates of a specific genre. The Acts, analogously to hagiographies, follow this process of "falsification" or stylization in an official tone, recounting the "sacred" history of the institution of the Church (Maggi 2009).[19] There exists therefore an opposition between the "oral" and poetic word of Paul and the written word of Luke. While the former is always represented as a declaimed word, as the fruit of a public enunciation, accompanied by the reaction of diverse interlocutors, from the subproletariat of Ephesus-Naples to the exponents of the intelligentsia of Athens-Rome, the latter is, as Parmeggiani underscores, "narrative, history, discourse" (1996, 208). Paul's sacred word is part of Pasolini's attempts to recreate what Zanzotto has defined as "a Pentecostal language" (1983, 239) that Pasolini puts in relation to both historical language and to that of our own time, compromised by power. Pasolini wagers on leaving these two languages to interact: the language of the Sacred against that of History, the poetic and mystical language *par excellence* against the pragmatic and communicative dimension of prose. He thus creates a space in the "open" text, in the screenplay *in fieri* – and in the never-made film to come – in order to activate the spark between these two dimensions and to see the effects of this eruption and the laceration of the sacred in the dense fabric of prose.[20] The central fulcrum of the dynamic of the word in *San Paolo* is the *mise-en-scène* of a possibility, of a passage, an opening, and of the continual setback of this potentiality. The temporary nature of the stage-text, "structure that wants to be another structure,"[21] represents the ideal horizon where history and meta-history can encounter one another. They would meet in this indefinite space, between the impotence of the written word and the potentiality of an image evoked in the text but not yet incarnated, where the representation appears linked to a virtual dimension that constitutes the unique perspective in which the sacred and *attualità* can encounter one another and be mirrored in one another. Yet they are juxtaposed in a *coincidentia oppositorum* that does not, cannot, and will not know synthesis.

As Silvestra Mariniello (1999) has underlined,[22] the monologic and absolute nature of the sacred word comes face to face as much with interdiegetic interlocutors as with the reader, singling out the historical and experiential event in the transposition process of the "episodic tragedy." The sacred word thus becomes a dialogic, almost theatrical word, creating a temporal rewriting that includes both the absoluteness of the revealed word as well as the temporality of the historical one. This juxtaposition is captured in the film's two central temporal and geographic transpositions: 1930s Nazi-occupied Paris is aligned with 36 CE Jerusalem, and 1967 Rome/New York is aligned with 67 CE Jerusalem.

There exists a structural analogy between the revealed word of *San Paolo* and the word of the stage-text: Paul's sacred word likewise expresses in Pasolini's words "a will of the form to become another," to transform itself into a "form in movement." It is a sign that belongs to two different structures: that of the sacred and that of *attualità*, structures that are reconstructed in an absolute form in both the writing of the stage-text and in its reading by complicit and empathetic readers. The Pauline word belongs as much to the atemporality of the absolute as it does to the urgency of the announced *parousia* and the condition of the apocalyptic announcement. Indeed, it transfixes – lacerates and crucifies, we can say – the fabric of the present with the announcement of a liberated future that appears obsolete (*inattuale*) but is invoked in our present time. Pasolini writes about the screenplay:

> We must now complete this initial observation, pointing out that the kineme thus accentuated and functionalized, as we were saying, is not a mere, albeit dilated, element of the sign, but is the sign of another linguistic system. The sign of the screenplay therefore not only expresses "*a will of the form to become another" above and beyond the form; that is, it captures "the form in movement"* – a movement that finishes freely and in various manners in the fantasy of the writer and in the cooperating and friendly fantasy of the reader, the two coinciding freely and in different ways. All of this happens normally in the context of writing, and it presupposes only nominally another language [in which form finds fulfilment]. It is, in other words, an issue which establishes a rapport between metalanguages and their reciprocal form.

> What is most important to observe is that the word of the screenplay *is thus, contemporaneously, the sign of two different structures,* inasmuch as the meaning that it denotes is double: *and it belongs to two languages characterized by different structures.* (*HE*, 192–3)[23]

Thus Pasolini's sacred word belongs – in its eternity – to two chronological stages, the *attualità* of the contemporary world and the historic past of imperial Rome. These temporal transpositions reveal the "will of the form ... to become another": it is the reader/spectator who recreates with the contribution of his/her own imagination the ideal scenario of the sacred word that is both revealed and still waited for.

The text of the finale of the *Progetto per un film su San Paolo* – one of the two different finales in the two textual variants, namely of the *Progetto* and of the *Abbozzo di sceneggiatura* – ends with the pronouncement of the word "God." This word marks the culmination of the confrontation between the paroxysmal modernity of the American metropolis and the atemporality of the Origin. The outline reads:

> St. Paul will be martyred in the middle of traffic, in the suburbs of a large city, a painfully modern city, with all its suspension bridges, its skyscrapers, its crushing, immense crowds that pass by the spectacle of death without stopping, and continue to whirl around him, along their enormous streets – indifferent, hostile, senseless. But in that world of cement and steel the word "God" has resounded (or has returned to be resound again). (*PPC2*, 2030)[24]

Pasolini speaks of a death that "will have the mythical characters and symbols of a recall, like the earlier fall in the desert" (*PPC2*, 1900–1).[25] The death of the saint is invisible in this heavily "visible" city of steel and cement, with its extreme modernist architecture, overpopulated with heedless and obtuse people like in an ant farm, without sense.

But the sacred word – the divine name – resounds dreadfully with its inordinate and obsolete message: the "vertical" (Parmeggiani 1996, 211) word that nails the surface of immanence like a crucifixion. It is the first word, dating from the time before time; and it is the last word, spoken in the end times. It is a scream (like the one that ends *Teorema*) but an articulated scream, one that does not rise feral from below, but falls upon the enemy city like a revelation. We are still in a film "a canone sospeso," that is, still undetermined: it asks rather than answers questions.

Thus God signifies presence, but also abandonment in these end times. It is the word of origin, but of an origin of which one has lost track; it is a memento of the sacred in the moment of its disappearance. It is an explosion of history in the sacrificial, cruciform gesture that re-establishes the sacred in the moment in which power cancels it. The dynamic is one of sublime defeat, in Christian logic: "a scandal to Jews and foolishness to Gentiles" (1 Cor. 1:23). Paul, as saint, is "abandoned."

As Robert Escobar has observed:

> "Everyone has abandoned me ...," Paul writes, assailed by illness and bent over the prison cot; but immediately after, he adds: "... they have brought me to chains ... but the word of God is not chained." The sense of abandonment mutates into the opposite feeling of the closeness of God: this, which is at the heart of the psychology of the *theologia crucis*, is as typical for German mysticism as it is for the Lutheran experience, and is also the dominant aspect of the "religiosity" particular to Pasolini. (1978, 24)[26]

God is the lost utopia: but is the voice that resounds at the end of the project (or that returns to resound) the opening to the end times, or merely the missing symptom of the end of time? The second finale, that of the screenplay, substitutes the violent atmosphere of the metropolis with a "New York motel," similar to the one where Martin Luther King, Jr was killed. There is peace, sun. This time what "resounds" – Pasolini uses the same verb – is not the word "God" but rather "two gunshots, violent, piercing":

> *The door* to the toilet is still moving back and forth: the man who fired the shot has just disappeared.
>
> Paul falls down on the balcony, immobile in a pool of his own blood. He has a small fit of agony. Shortly all sign of life is gone. The balcony floor is broken up. His blood coagulates in a crack, and starts to drip down the pavement of the courtyard. It is a small rosy puddle, into which drops of Paul's blood continue to fall. (*PPC2*, 2020)[27]

This time the visual aspect of the death of the saint prevails over the auditory one. This city where Paul's martyrdom slips into indifference, where the threatening or merciful *parousia* that follows the abandonment is announced, or where one hears only the echo of the lost utopia – this apocalyptic city is no longer the focus of the finale. Rather, the camera focuses on the martyred body of the apostle: the martyrdom takes the form of traditional Christian mysticism.[28] From the perch on the pavement, Paul bleeds from his side, just like Christ.

In her book *Wonderful Blood* (2007), Caroline Walker Bynum examines the tradition of the cult of Christ's blood in the late German Middle Ages, summarizing the positions on the theology of blood within Catholic and Protestant mystical traditions. Two interesting positions arise from within these different traditions. The first is from Catherine of Siena, where Christ's blood and the fire of charity (a quintessential Pauline virtue) are metaphorically equated, and where blood is considered the seat of the soul.[29] The other theological image of the blood – this time a Protestant one – comes from Luther. In this case, the blood of Christ is connected both to baptism (the baptismal font) and to the Eucharist, and also to the word and preaching of the Evangelist.[30]

There is no doubt that the second death of Paul converges with traditional Christian martyrological iconology; the blood of the cross is reflected onto the blood spilled by Paul that bathes the pavement of an anonymous New York motel, blazing with charity. Blood is the material sign of the Incarnation and the Passion, and the "small rosy puddle" of Paul's blood represents the sacrificial moment of greatest closeness to Christ.

If this death, where the blood of Paul converges with the blood of Christ, represents the orthodox moment of the apostle's sanctification – in medieval etymology, *sanctus* meant *sanguine unctus* (Bynum 2007, 191) – the life of Paul, for Pasolini, scandalously incarnates the drama of the cross.

The Scandal of the Cross, the Scandal of Sickness: Homosexuality and *Caritas*

As we saw in chapter 2, the drama of the crucifixion is at the centre of Pasolini's meditations on the Incarnation and represents a crucial element in the creation of his characters. Christ is the director's alter ego, just as the anti-heroes of his films and novels are Christological. Pasolini's "Christology of the flesh" dates back to the early years of his poetic activity: we recall the dissemination of Christological themes in the collection *L'Usignolo della Chiesa Cattolica* (*The Nightingale of the Catholic Church,* 1958). His fascination with the crucifixion appears in a poem from this early volume, appropriately entitled *Crocifissione* (*Crucifixion*). The poem, which we examined in chapter 3, takes as its epigraph a verse from 1 Corinthians: "But we preach Christ crucified: a scandal for the Jews and folly for the Gentiles" (1 *Cor.* 1:23, cited in Hardt 2002, 77). Based on this poem,

Michael Hardt explains his theory of immanent transcendence, bringing together Pasolini's vision with that of Deleuze. The scandal of the cross is, according to Hardt, the abandonment of the transcendent form in order to fulfil the fullness of matter and flesh.[31] This abandonment is also an exposure: "What is exposed is naked flesh, absolute immanence, a pure affirmation" (Hardt 2002, 80) – that represents in itself an explosion of erotic intensity: "Eroticism," as George Bataille writes, "is assenting to life up to the point of death. Christ's incarnation is this pure affirmation of life, even to the point of death on the cross" (quoted by Hardt 2002, 80).[32] This association between abandonment and exposure constitutes not transgression but scandal: the scandal consists not so much in the violation of the law as in its operation in ignorance thereof, in its Pauline acting *as if* the law didn't exist.[33] Scandal is the horizon within which all of Pasolini's works will be inscribed: this horizon is a categorical imperative, as we have seen, for *parrhesia*[34] – a "gentle" and "ridicolous" *parrhesia* – and for desire, "trembling / with intellect and passion in the play / of the heart burning from its fire / testifying to the scandal."

> You must expose yourself (is this what the
> poor nailed-up Christ teaches?),
> the clarity of the heart is worthy
> of every sneer, every sin
> every more naked passion ...
> (is this what the Crucifix means?
> sacrifice every day the gift
> renounce every day forgiveness
> cast yourself ingenuous over the abyss).
> We will be offered on the cross
> on the pillory, among the pupils
> limpid with ferocious joy,
> leaving open to irony the drops
> of blood from the breast to the knees,
> gentle and ridicolous, trembling
> with intellect and passion in the play
> of the heart burning from its fire,
> testifying to the scandal. (Hardt 2002, 77–8)[35]

Bearing witness, exposing oneself through intellect and passion, offering one's own martyred body in sacrifice ... Hardt identifies the erotic component in this offering, in this extreme form of testimony. Pasolini has actually spoken about this "exposure" – pushing the term's meaning even further towards "exhibition" – in a crucial passage in *Empirismo eretico,* in the essay "Il cinema impopolare" ("The Unpopular Cinema," 1970), in which both the self-wounding valence of each artistic gesture and the masochistic pleasure the director takes in the affirmation of the death drive emerge. For Pasolini, being an author means being at the centre of a conflict: he underlines the authorial estrangement with his social horizon, that inhabiting of death rather than life, and the fierce reaction of "odio razziale" (race hate) that non-involvement provokes in those who surround him (*EE, SLA1,* 1602).

> I would like to stress the word "exhibition." The author's dedication of himself to the wounds of martyrdom in the very moment in which he transgresses against the instinct of self-preservation, substituting for it that of self-destruction, does not make sense if it is not made as explicit as possible; if, as I was saying, it isn't exhibited. In every author, in the act of invention, freedom presents itself as a masochistic loss of something certain. In the necessarily scandalous act of inventing he exposes himself, literally, to others; precisely to scandal, to ridicule, to reproach, to the feeling of difference, and – why not? – to admiration, even if it is somewhat questionable. There is, in short, the "pleasure" that one has in every fulfilment of the desire for pain and death. (*HE,* 268)[36]

As we saw at the end of chapter 3, Pasolini advances a vision of the director's and spectator's role as that of the martyr: the only freedom possible is that of going against the diktat of preservation (of the species, of law, of life). It is the "freedom to choose death" (*HE,* 267),[37] and its only manifestation can be "a great or small martyrdom" (*HE,* 267).[38] The director-martyr implies a scandalized and scandalous spectator, the former turned towards martyring the transgressive director, the other complicit and free to enjoy "the freedom of others" (*HE,* 269).[39] Pasolini continues:

> The spectator, as such, enjoys the example of this freedom, and as such objectifies it, she reinserts it into the speakable. But this happens outside all "integration"; in a certain sense outside of society (which integrates not only the scandal of the author but also the scandalous comprehension of the spectator). It is a relationship between individuals, which happens under the ambiguous sign of the instincts and under the religious (not confessional) sign of charity. (*HE,* 269–70)[40]

The ambiguous sign of instincts and the religious sign of charity: *eros* and *agape* are united in an unequivocal *coincidentia oppositorum* (Just like pleasure and pain) and represent an intensification of vitality in the horizon of one's being for death. In the Crucifixion poem, in that gentle and ridicolous self-offering to the "pupils limpid with ferocious joy" and to the "irony" of the crowd and the public, prevails a mystical component that melts the desire-inflamed heart with the fire of charity. This is precisely Pasolini's scandal, this fusion of the archaic sacred with the Christian sacred, of pagan love with the love preached in the Gospels and by Paul himself, this desire of the flesh – immanent transcendence – a flesh imbued with *caritas* and *parrhesia*, with love for the underprivileged and for the truth.

The scandal of the cross is thus close to the scandal of desire; for Pasolini, charity has a very strong erotic component. It is not the case, as Tomaso Subini argues, that for Pasolini "the cross, through Paul, will become the metaphor to justify his own weaknesses" (2004, 232)[41] and that "the scandal is none other than the ostentation of his own weaknesses" (233).[42] Though it is intrinsically rooted in the ignition of the senses, Pasolini lives the evangelical message of *agape* in his own flesh, and in the flesh of his characters: love for the meek, for the marginalized and forgotten, for all those who bear the shameful mark of difference.

Pasolini declares his love for the subproletariat – as well as his hate for the bourgeoisie – in *Quasi un testamento* (*Almost a Will*), published by the English journalist Peter Dragadze on 17 November 1975 in the Italian magazine *Gente* (*People*), just a few days following Pasolini's murder in Ostia. The director-poet confirms his attraction to the subproletarian with these words:

> The face of the subproletarian appeals to me, because it is clean (while the face of the bourgeois is dirty); because it is innocent (while the face of the bourgeois is guilty), because it is pure (while the face of the bourgeois is vulgar), because it is religious (while the face of the bourgeois is hypocritical), because it is crazy (while the face of the bourgeois is prudent), because it is sensual (while the face of the bourgeois is cold), because it is immediate (while the face of the bourgeois is calculating), because it is kind (while the face of the bourgeois is insolent), because it is unguarded (while the face of the bourgeois is dignified), because it is incomplete (while the face of the bourgeois is refined), because it is trusting (while the face of the bourgeois is hard), because it is tender (while the face of the bourgeois is ironic), because it is dangerous (while the face of the bourgeois is soft), because it is fierce (while the face of the bourgeois is blackmailing), because it is coloured (while the face of the bourgeois is white). (*SPS*, 868)[43]

Pasolini sublimates to a great degree this visceral passion for the world's least and underprivileged; it is a passion of the senses and of the intellect, a communist gospel of revolution and charity. This is the great myth of Pasolini's cinematic and literary poetics: the myth of *la meglio gioventù* (the best of youth), emblem of a millenarian past and rooted in the sacred and in the return of this past.

In the mid-1970s, however, time stops returning: this is evidenced throughout the final phase of Pasolini's film and literary production, a period that embraces works such as the incomplete novel *Petrolio* (*Petrolio: A Novel*, 1992), *Divina Mimesis* (*Divine Mimesis*, 1975, his magmatic rewriting of Dante's *Divine Comedy*), the outline for the movie *Porno-teo-kolossal* (1975), the second version of *San Paolo* (1974), or his last film, *Salò* (*Salò, or the 120 Days of Sodom*, 1975). *La nuova gioventù* (*The New Youth*, 1974), a poetic trampling of the myths of his early Friulian poems, already foreshadows what will come in *Salò*. And it is atrocious, the disenchantment Pasolini expresses with the subproletariat in "Abiura della *Trilogia della vita*" ("Repudiation of *The Trilogy of Life*"), written in June 1975 and published posthumously by the *Corriere della sera* on 9 November 1975. The subproletariat has mutated because power and the regime of sexual tolerance have produced monsters: the consumerist system has embraced the sexual revolution, integrating it with its "concession of a great (however false) tolerance" (*SPS*, 600). Pasolini continues:

> Second: also the "reality" of the innocent bodies has been violated, manipulated, tampered with by consumerist establishment: in fact, this violence on the bodies has become the most macroscopic element in the new human era.
>
> Third: private sexual lives (such as mine) have undergone the trauma of both false tolerance and also physical degradation, and that which in sexual fantasies was pain and joy, has become suicidal disappointment, shapeless sloth. ("Repudiation," *HE*, xviii)[44]

The past has stopped returning: what had been lost but still used to survive in historical niches of resistance has now been destroyed. Pasolini's tragedy is that the present collapse of the beloved object implies the collapse of the past: the love for those bodies evaporates and cancels even its memory. Nostalgia is a lie. The anthropological mutation is irreversible: Pasolini of the disavowal prefigures the apocalypse of *Salò*, that torture laboratory for the Pasolinian myth of youth set in the absolute and terrible present of omnivorous (and coprophagous) consumerism.

"Repudiation" continues:

> But today the degeneration of the bodies and of the sexual organs has assumed a retroactive value.
>
> If those who were *then* thus and so, have been able to become *now* thus, it means that they were potentially such already then: therefore also their way of being *then* is devalued by the present.
>
> The youths and boys of the Roman subproletariat ..., *if now* they are human garbage, it means that potentially they were such also *then*; they were, therefore, imbeciles compelled to be adorable, squalid criminals compelled to be likeable rascals, vile good-for-nothings compelled to be saintly innocents, etc. The collapse of the present implies the collapse of the past. Life is a pile of insignificant and ironic ruins. (*HE*, xviii–xix)[45]

San Paolo represents the threshold between the Pasolini who still loves and the later Pasolini intent on the fierce profanation of his own myths, the one who splits apart his earlier fusion of *eros* and *agape*, disdainfully transmuting them into an empty, repeated act of sexual copulation.

The complexity of *San Paolo*'s presentation of homosexuality serves as the starting point of Armando Maggi's analysis of Pasolini's later works in *The Resurrection of the Body* (2009). On one hand, Paul's homosexuality (which Pasolini deduces from the most radical and transgressive avant-garde Pauline theological studies) functions for the director as an autobiographical projection and reflection. On the other hand, it represents perfectly the knot between *eros* and *agape* that has characterized Pasolini's work up to that point. Now Paul would seem to embody the Christian paradox: just as Christ is crucified in the manner of slaves, as the least of the least, so too Paul, the chosen apostle, is positioned at the margins by his difficult and denied homosexuality, which he experiences as a chronic illness. Pasolini's St Paul is saintly in his homosexuality, in his difference, in his "illness" – convulsions, fevers, the contortion of the body – that seizes him intermittently and that accompanies the most sublime words of his apostolate. Paul incarnates *caritas* in his very body. If it is true, as Maggi has underlined, that for Pasolini homosexuality is a condition against nature and something to be resisted,[46] in this sense the apostle lives his saintliness through his troubled homosexuality. The saint is homosexual, the priest is homophobic and sex-phobic. Perhaps, as Maggi argues, this is a sign of the corruption of the times. But maybe in *San Paolo,* sin constitutes the very root of saintliness. It is the institution that is satanic, made so by the demonic behaviour of Luke, the author of the Acts of the Apostles. The Paul who institutes a new Law is the pharisee, the priest, the demonic device of the institution. The sick, homosexual Paul is the saint; he is the one who openly confesses the "sting of the flesh," given to him by God to increase his weakness, because it is in his weakness that Christ triumphs – a fact that represents the Christian paradox, the scandal of the cross.

In this sense, Pasolini's homosexuality is a kenotic and divine passion, it is an incarnate passion, just as it appears in the character of Paul in the *Appunti per un film su San Paolo.* Thus we share only in part Maggi's vision, which frames the character of the sodomite as the turnkey to the interpretation of Pasolini's later works:

> In *Saint Paul,* the apostle Paul lives a "difference" that makes him the spokesman for God's revelation. However, his persistent and painful illness also clarifies that Paul himself is the battlefield of the war between the "world" and God's message. Paul's "convulsions," which began when he first saw some young men naked in a locker room, testify to the tension between revelation and social conformity, between God's salvation and the perversion of the world (Paul's own homosexual tendency). In *Saint Paul,* Paul vehemently speaks against the "world" because he himself embodies the world and its division. (Maggi 2009, 85)

The most important element of Pasolini's *San Paolo,* expressed through Paul's homosexuality, is charity towards the human condition. The scandal of the cross teaches the lessons of the suffering Christ and of the charity extended towards the forgotten ones, towards the different, towards the marginalized. Desire is St Paul's cross, which provokes the response of *agape. Agape* is love of the least ones, while *eros* is the sting of the flesh: in Pasolini's *San Paolo* one comes with the other. Paul carries the stigmata of his desire as a perpetual lesson of love and humility. It is this suffering that opens him to the words of God.

Through his gloss of a passage from the Second Letter to the Corinthians,[47] Maggi reveals Pasolini's use of certain terms that force the translation of the Pauline text towards an emphasis on the elements of degradation and shame:

> The expression "*datus est mihi stimulus carni*" is usually translated as "I was given a thorn (or sting) in the flesh" (*una spina nella carne*). Pasolini's choice of *dolore* (pain) makes the apostle's suffering much less physical than intellectual. "Pain" alludes to an inner torment that comes from the flesh but

> reverberates through the apostle's identity, body and soul alike. Similarly, *"ut me colephizet"* (to buffet me; *per schiaffeggiarmi*) becomes *"per degradarmi"* (to debase me) in Pasolini's rendition. Again, "to debase" is much stronger than "to buffet" and involves a shameful humiliation of the victim. "To debase" has a negative, malicious connotation foreign to the Christian God. "Debasement" (*degradazione*) returns two sentences later. In the epistle, the apostle only says *"Dominum rogavi ut discederet a me"* (I begged the Lord that it might depart from me). There is no reference to degradation and shame. (2009, 92–3)

Pasolini's emphasis on degradation and shame is twofold: on the one hand it refers to the primal scene of debasement, the Incarnation, and in this way the whole constellation of shame assumes a distinct, very much Pauline, meaning. On the other hand it reconnects with Pasolini's masochistic pleasure in exhibition, abandonment, and difference. We recall the words of "Il cinema impopolare": "There is in short the 'pleasure' that one has in every fulfilment of the desire for pain and death" (*HE*, 268).[48] The paradigm of the Crucifixion represents the expression of this radical death-drive that characterizes all of Pasolini's characters. God abases himself in human form, and incarnates to the highest degree that "freedom to choose death" that, for Pasolini, epitomizes his concept of freedom. For him freedom means making a conscious choice of self-expression that entails removing oneself from actions designed to conserve the species, from actions taken to maintain life: either die and express oneself or live and remain unexpressed. This self-wounding action carries a strong erotic charge and a paradoxical vitality. It is death that assembles the inconclusive series of our lives' gestures, acts, and choices into an unequivocal destiny: God makes himself a man dying on the cross, and only thus does he fulfill his destiny. Only in this way does he transform the vocation to truth and charity to the point of martyrdom into the paradigm of the "freedom to choose death." That freedom is for Pasolini the true destiny of the director-spectator relationship – but it is also emblematic of the relationship between the artist and the public, between the intellectual and the body of the nation, between the martyr and the crowd, between God and humanity.

Illness is thus the mark of difference as well as the element that etches that mark onto the body: Paul's homosexuality appears as an "illness" in that it substitutes cultural relationships for natural ones. Pasolini believed that heterosexuality and reproduction were natural law, and thus that homosexuality represented a self-withdrawal from this law – the freedom to withdraw from the conservation instinct and to choose death.

For Maggi the question of the "sodomite flesh" is central to Pasolini's Pauline project:[49] it functions as an "apocalyptical flesh" that speaks the idiom of death, which as we know constitutes for Pasolini the other side of *eros*. As Maggi puts it: "Paul's blood has the luminosity of a beyond-time condition" (2009, 106). Like Saint Francis' stigmata – *como rosa vermeglia* in Jacopone da Todi's Laud – "this bleeding rose is the sign of Francis' sanctification, his mutation into an apocalyptic body announcing Christ's victory over death" (106). Here again my reading diverges from Maggi's: for him the resurrection of the body as the sodomitical flesh presents a transformative component that my reading does not contemplate: the sacred flesh, in my interpretation, is immanent. There is no resurrection, it is not a utopian flesh. It is death without resurrection, not even as a resurrected "flesh that dies." It is pure finitude, consigned in its presence, with God as the lost utopia (like the missing Heaven in *Porno-teo-kolossal*). There are, however, other possible readings of *San Paolo*, and Maggi's is certainly fascinating and appears well suited to make sense of the last years of Pasolini's cinematic and literary production. The theme of *agape* is nevertheless, I believe, the Pauline constant that intertwines both the 1960s and the 1970s within Pasolini's *corpus*.

Another reading is provided by Ward Blanton, who, in his essay on Foucault's biopolitics and the political significance of Pasolini's St Paul, notes how Paul's homosexuality makes him "a body not seamlessly incorporated into the healthy, docile economies of neo-capitalist life" (2010, 71), and how this body is presented *a latere*, that is, anamorphically:

> Rather, the unavowable trauma of the desire traverses the film and all its narrative structures without ever becoming a central structure itself. In casting Paul's desire this way, laterally, anamorphically, I think Pasolini uncovers a mode of remaining faithful to a thought of Paulinist scandal worthy of the name. A streak of opacity crossing and distending the screen of the visible, Paul's desire remains withdrawn from – and therefore perpetually mysterious to – the diegetic reality of Pasolini's constructions. Unnamed, unengaged, and therefore without any pre-established hope for future incorporation, it is in the aleatory sequences of "Paul, sick" " that the film stumbles on what may be most alive in the Pauline legacy. (2010, 72–3)

The unconfessing trauma of desire is circumnavigated and hinted at through the drama of sickness. Paul's illness originated in childhood, as evidenced by the dream he has immediately following the conversion of the jailor in the prison of Munich or Cologne, where he has been imprisoned with his disciple, Silas.

Dream of Paul. Tarsus.

> Paul dreams fragments of his childhood.
> Being nursed.
> A day when his father in the garden holds him up to the sky.
> An escape from school (which we have seen in his trip to Tarsus). With several companions he roams the outskirts of the city and arrives in an enchanted rustic place (that we have seen appear to him during his rapture into the Third Heaven).
> At last he and his companions arrive at the stadium. Older boys are competing. Then inside the locker room they undress and are naked in front of the eyes of the younger boys and Paul.
> Back at home, Paul feels sick. He is stricken with convulsions. The same ones that will plague him all his life. (*SP, PPC2*, 1934)[50]

In this passage we may notice the Oedipal scene, with the father holding Paul up to the sky, which textually brings us back to the images from *Edipo re* and to the autobiographical traces of Pasolini. In addition, the sequence of *San Paolo* recalls an analogous scenery, taken from the childhood memories cited by Pasolini in *Empirismo eretico*, where the director refers to his first encounter with the "pangs of sexual love": the physical, visceral impact of desire. In the life of Pasolini this first encounter with sexual (and homosexual) love has a mythopoetical effect: because there are no words to express this intense longing, Pasolini invents them: "teta veleta."

> In that period at Belluno, precisely between three and three and a half years, I experienced the first pangs of sexual love: identical to those that I would then have up to now (atrociously acute from sixteen to thirty) – that terrible and anxious sweetness that seizes the viscera and consumes them, burns them, twists them like a hot melting gust of wind in the presence of the love object. I believe I remember only the legs of this love object – and exactly the hollow behind the knee with its taut tendons – and the synthesis of the features of the inattentive creature – strong, happy, and protective (but a traitor, always called elsewhere), so much that one day I went to find that object of my tender-terrible heartache at [its][51] house ... Naturally I did not know what it was about; I knew only the physical nature of the presence of that feeling, so dense and burning that it twisted my viscera. I therefore found myself with the physical necessity of "naming" that sentiment, and, in my condition as only an oral speaker, not a writer, I invented a word. This term was, I remember perfectly, TETA VELETA. (*HE*, 66)[52]

The encounter with homosexuality thus produces a new, separate, essentially poetic idiom, in rhyme: homosexuality and poetry merge together, in what Schérer and Passerone have defined as a "hermeneutic maxim, an almost magical formula, gnostic '*abraxas*' of the Pasolinian body" (2006, 83).[53] "Teta veleta" represents the fusion of the homosexual body and poetic creation, and it thus describes the subject's state of physical and lyrical convulsion: a state analogous to that described in *San Paolo*. The "illness" is homosexuality that coincides with mystic exultation: the state of abandonment and prostration produces the "sublime" words of the apostle.

Maggi has underlined the apocalyptic and deathly element of the "sodomite flesh," but Pasolini's sacred flesh contains an enormous vitality, expressed in the strength of desire (even when it is against those very laws that the "priest" St Paul in part establishes and founds), even in the very moment in which this drive is revealed as a death drive.[54] Once again, *synoeciosis* – which is the *coincidentia oppositorum* at the foundation of Pasolini's entire poetics – merges the sacred and the cursed, sex and death drives, *eros* and *agape*: it is precisely the centrality of *caritas* in the framing of the theme of homosexuality that escapes Maggi's apocalyptic interpretation. Nevertheless, it does not escape the interpretation that contemporary (mostly materialist) philosophy has given of Pasolini's inheritance, from Žižek (2003) to Badiou (2003) and Agamben (2005).

"Christian charity is rare and fragile," Žižek writes in *The Fragile Absolute* (2000, 117), "something to be fought for and regained again and again," while Badiou underlines how Pasolini renders St Paul a revolutionary and makes the screenplay a meditation on the militant's condition. If on the one hand, Paul wants to destroy a social model based on inequality, imperialism, and slavery (Badiou 2003, 37), on the other hand, his trajectory is that of a betrayal: Paul is a man of institutions. He is at the same time defeated and victorious; it is true that he pronounces "the truth of the world" (Badiou 2003, 37), but he transforms his transgressive and revolutionary saintliness into something party- and institution-based.

> What Paul creates (the Church, the Organization, the Party) turns against his own inner saintliness. Here, Pasolini find support in a major tradition ... that sees in Paul not so much a theoretician of the Christian event as the tireless creator of the Church ... For Pasolini, reflecting on communism through Paul, the Party is what, little by little, inverts saintliness into priesthood through the narrow requirements of militantism ... the film script allows us to understand the truth behind this deception: in Paul, the immanent dialectic of saintliness and actuality construct a subjective figure of the

> priest. Paul also dies to the extent that saintliness has darkened within him. (Badiou 2003, 38–9).

A man of paradox, he incarnates not only the scandal of the cross, but also the scandal of power that goes from revolutionary to organized and authoritarian. In a meditation on both communism and Christianity, Badiou reads Pasolini's Paul in the direction of *caritas.* As Lorenzo Chiesa underscores in his essay "Pasolini, Badiou, Žižek and the Legacy of Christian Love," for Badiou and Žižek

> the leftist militant politics that recuperates the Pauline political legacy must at the same time be identified with a *politics of love* to be opposed to the politics of *jouissance* – or rather its *administrative regulation* – enacted by the hedonistic ruling power. Their common anti-ideological motto could thus be condensed in one of the beautiful verses with which Pasolini concludes his *Lutheran Letter:* "Father, enough with Hedone, we want Agape!" (2005, 5)

The unbridled hedonism of the "tolerant" regime of new Power must make way for a new Pauline, militant universalism. "Paul says to us: it is always possible for a nonconformist thought to think in the century. This is what a subject is. It is he who maintains the universal, not conformity" (Badiou 2003, 111). Pasolini has thus foreshadowed these debates in a modality that is not philosophical or systematic, but rather poetic and creative, signalling nonetheless the centrality of the sacred in thinking about politics, above all in the configuration of old and new power relations. The lesson of *caritas,* central to contemporary materialist thought, constitutes for Pasolini the fundamental link in the dialogue between Marxism and Catholicism in the 1960s, and it remains a fundamental aspect of his thought, functioning as an underlying matrix of his poetics even into the 1970s in the *Scritti Corsari* (*Corsair Writings*). Chiesa writes:

> For Pasolini post-Christian *agape* should definitely be translated as "charity" and its principal concern must unreservedly be "the question of the poor" [Pasolini, *SC, SPS,* 351] ... Thus, the politics of *agape* is a politics of poverty in two overlapping senses: it certainly defends the rights of the poor but it does so only in order to refound poverty as a (post-Christian) ethical value; "it is clear that superfluous goods make life superfluous" and the (concretely impossible) universalisation of the bourgeoisie is not worthy of being lived [Pasolini, *SC, SPS,* 321]. For this reason the politics of

> *agape* cannot be limited to Third Worldism ... or to the indiscriminate aestheticisation of the Western lumpenproletariat – which so strongly marks Pasolini's own early work and which he lucidly disowns in his "Abiura della *Trilogia della vita*." (2005, 11)

Pasolini has thus poetically opened a debate on Pauline *agape* that is ongoing in contemporary materialist thought, into which he inserts the problematic issue of sexual identity. The aestheticization of the subproletariat will be demystified in the director's final literary and cinematographic output; the visceral myth of the "best of youth" will succumb to the risk not only of transforming itself from an object of *eros/agape* to one of *hedone*, but also of losing the evangelical dimension of the Pasolinian passion of the senses. *Salò* will not allow replies and will give the public an unconsumable image of the holocaust of that myth. The cruel, sadistic practices of the four libertines of the *120 giornate di Sodoma* (*120 Days of Sodom*) represent the extreme level of profanation: as we have said, the coercive instances of repetition of the copulative action (which the sadist will try to stop through the martyrdoms of the circle of blood, extinguishing the object of sexual possession) and the disdain for the serial bodies of the victims will replace veneration for the auraticity of the sacred body of the peasant and subproletarian. *Petrolio* will stage, in the stroll of a young gentrified subproletarian meaningfully named "Shit" ("Il Merda") through the typical places of Pasolini's Roman peripheries, the hallucinatory vision of the disappearance of those bodies and those places in the bourgeois universalization. *Porno-Teo-Kolossal*, with its apocalyptic cities of aberrant rituals, once again represents neo-capitalist society's violence and abuse of power. The world is no longer redeemable; Christ is born and dies in vain, and the sky is an empty expanse, without Paradise. The pathway to *agape* appears ever more invoked and ever more apocalyptically perceived as unattainable. It is on such heretical sacrificial altars that, in Pasolini's final works, the sacred flesh of the passions is obliterated. The desecration is, at this point, complete.

Parodies of Saintliness: From *Sant'Infame* to *Petrolio*'s "Prima Fiaba sul Potere"

The theme of saintliness has always fascinated Pasolini. In an interview on this subject with Jean Duflot about *Teorema*, Pasolini responds with this definition of saintliness:

> It is an ontological fact; grace, the gift of the sublime, one has it or one acquires it. At the beginning it is a merely moral fact, the oneself-transmutation in an idealistic sense, in other words, it is the goodness, the sincerity, all moral qualities brought to the highest level of exultation.
>
> Next, saintliness can take on, in time, the sense of a rejection of the world, of ascesis, of the exercise of cruelty towards oneself, of the search for an unreachable deepening of oneself. (*SC*, in *SPS*, 1444)[55]

The definition contains the entire drama of St Paul and of the parrhesiastes intellectual that Pasolini intends to be: to delineate saintliness as the exultation of the moral qualities and the ascetic, self-wounding process of the rejection of the world, of the negation of the present, the choice to be *inattuali* (obsolete), to reach the unattainable bottom of oneself, facing one's darkest sides. Saintliness is acquired, Pasolini states ... and in a movie outline from 1967 to 1968 we encounter a perverse evolution of this saintliness in the oxymoronic declination of *Sant'Infame* (*St. Wicked*). Pasolini's treatment centres entirely on the staging, on the fiction of saintliness: a parodic *Imitatio Christi* that nevertheless ends with "saintly" outcomes. The protagonist Sant'Infame is a boy from a working-class suburb, led astray by his experience of the seminary, who in the end decides to return there simply out of cynical opportunism:

> Sent by his parents to the seminary against his will, with a strategy (told in a restaurant among thieves). He escapes from the seminary, and returns to the environment whence he came: an environment of poverty and perversion (a working-class suburb of a big city). The seminary has corrupted him, has made him vulgar, in as much as it has caused him to lose the innocence of his relationship to evil. Vice and criminality are therefore truly dirty: he falls all the way down. He makes a bit of money, then he's poor. Prospects of a future of poverty. He pretends to repent: he pretends to renew his religious vocation. He gets the seminary to take him back. He comes out a priest. He attains his ambitions for success and economic improvement under the absurd notion of becoming a saint or something similar. With the patience of a saint, he successfully organizes a group of boys – helped by his malice (dating from his days as thief and con man), by a diabolical cynicism, by a lack of any moral sense, and by the vulgarity that stems from his impure relationship with sin. He even succeeds in simulating saintliness. He is believed to be a saint, or something similar. Secretly, he continues to conduct his sexual life of a boy from the working-class suburbs, frequenting pimps, whores, etc. He contracts syphilis. [Then he continues with] [t]he

> clandestine cure, etc. ... and his normal life of pretending saintliness ... Syphilis brings on another serious illness. A terminal illness that causes atrocious suffering. This works out in favour of his fraud of saintliness: he is forced to attend to nothing other than his city of boys and his good works, etc.; and the illness torments him atrociously. In this saintly situation, he dies; in short, as a true saint. (*PPC2*, 2675–6)[56]

The simulation of saintliness produces it. The life gone astray, cynicism, evil: they produce goodness. The saintliness of Sant'Infame is equal parts perversion and ascesis: his fatal illness, provoked by syphilis, brings him closer to the Pauline model. Paul the saint, nevertheless, was authenticity itself, an authenticity consumed by a firm faith and by a tormented awareness of his own weaknesses, experienced as a thorn in his flesh, while he nurtured with his sincere conversion the perversion of his sanctimonious nature, of his (satanic) role of founder and organizer of a Church – a role of which he was unaware, as he was entirely ignorant of the demonic plots of the satanic evangelist Luke. Sant'Infame is instead aware that he is bluffing: he is an ambitious Accattone, thirsting for power. He perverts the chrism of saintliness only to end up tricked by his own behaviour. Pasolini loves paradox, and here the paradox is that he who seeks power and finds saintliness despite himself implies a communitarian result, namely, the spreading of charity. Tormented by the effects of syphilis, Sant'Infame is sanctified by them: suffering redeems him, his *Imitatio Christi* is no less sacred because it is impure.

As the cinematographic critic Serafino Murri has observed on this subject:

> With the barely outlined apologue of *Sant'Infame*, Pasolini demystifies (lowering it to the level of concreteness and human wretchedness) the "social" value of sanctification, but at the same time puts forth a more complex thesis regarding the saintliness "for himself" of the protagonist ... Sant'Infame is the exemplification of the ambiguity of saintliness, of the suspension of the myth of saintliness among vulgar self-exultation ... and the true, concrete suffering, psychological and physical, lived in order to reach, insanely, one's own position of definitive singularity, of moral privilege over others. And, in the end, *Sant'infame* describes the impossibility to discern the mystification of truth, the ambition of factual reality, from the moment that History does not exist, but only its effect on many personal stories, of which, as in this case, only the end counts – death. (1994, 51–2)[57]

A sacred, painful death, a death that rewrites Sant'Infame's destiny and contorts perversion into conversion: at least this is the communitarian effect of this demise. It is not important how a saint becomes a saint: saintliness is an ambiguous undertaking, where St Paul can collaborate with the devil and Sant'Infame can do good works, even if he is merely faking ascesis. Illness marks the simulation of the flesh, at which point it is no longer simulation, but only the sign of suffering Christ that removes the cynical pretences of the game.

With their origins in the archetype of Boccaccio's Ser Ciappelletto, the protagonists of these stories of inverse saintliness end paradoxically by becoming the sanctified object of their very techniques of simulation, or by receiving saintliness from blasphemous rather than divine investitures. One recalls the intellectual protagonist from note 34bis in *Petrolio*, "Prima fiaba sul Potere" ("First Fable on Power"). After a Mephistophelian pact with the Devil, having asked to "reach Power through Sanctity" (*raggiungere il potere attraverso la santità*), he sets into motion a series of "technically" (*tecnicamente*) saintly behaviours and operations that enable him to gain power. Once again we are faced with a simulated rather than a real ascesis. Suddenly, however, real saintliness takes over. His behaviour, born in a demonic context, is turned into a positive awareness of a true imitation of Christ. At the same moment in which he realizes that he has achieved authentic sainthood, the intellectual turns around and sees that it was the Devil who had spoken to him. He immediately becomes aware of a series of paradoxical oppositions:

> Certainly … he had kept his word: it was Sanctity that he had brought him to; Sanctity, not the pretense of Sanctity. Poetry, not Literature.
>
> Possessed by real Sanctity, he realized that that real Sanctity was a gift from the Devil; that the Truth in which he was suddenly living had been the work /of a Lie/; that the Good which he / suddenly, / ineffably enjoyed, was the product of the Evil; that the Revelation / had come about through / his worst sentiments. But all that, thus set forth, was only the letter. Under the series of rational and banal oppositions ran another series of oppositions, not only unspeakable but not even intuitable except as a Joke, / the Theft of the cosmos. Our intellectual gave a shout and fell to the ground … The Devil took advantage of this to open \ to make sure that\… on the palms of his hands were two long, bloody stigmata. (*PETR* 1997, 112–13)[58]

This sort of medieval trick in fact ends with a final, supreme conversation with God, who recounts that he made use of the mask of the Devil to convert the intellectual. When the saint is about to leave, however, violating the just-made pact with the divinity, he turns to look: and so he sees that that very "Luminous Force" (*Forza Luminosa*) that he took to be God has now assumed the physical form of the Devil. Then, hurled like a rock down from the third heaven, he falls into the desert and takes on the form of a mysterious stone, a stone not analysable because it is the objective correlative of "contradictions absolute" (*contradditorietà assoluta*), stone of a thousand substances, of "an infinite variety of materials"[59] where

> each mineral presents contradictory characteristics, both in relation to itself and in relation to the other minerals with which it is amalgamated or compounded: it has not been possible to distinguish in that rock what appeared precious from what appeared to be worthless, or even /toxic/. (*PETR* 1997, 115)[60]

A parody of St Paul's ascension to Third Heaven, the mystical itinerary here regresses to its initial phase, aborting the conversion in the desert, rendering the story's moral a crystallized heap where it is impossible to distinguish good from evil and making saintliness into a monstrous web of perfection and perversion. With the intellectual saint in *Petrolio*, Pasolini displays the comic route of the *ascensus mentis ad Deum*: and yet, in its tragic funniness, it touches the same knot of undecidability between good and evil, between the divine and the demonic, between the sacred and the profane that has marked the pages of the Pauline project. It is the fundamental ambiguity of sacred power and of the sacred as yet another in a long list of configurations of Power: a fascination with a central aspect of civilization and at the same time an awareness of its necessarily contaminated and contaminating nature.

Thus this episode of Pasolinian saintliness closes under the sign of the contamination of power; this trajectory spans the 1950s to the 1960s, with occasional detours into the 1970s. An entire book could be devoted to this final period and to the works that distinguish it: my aim has been to provide an in-depth analysis of the motif of the Incarnation and of the *Imitatio Christi* in Pasolini during the years of the economic boom. Starting points for the following years abound, for instance the desecrated and profaned sacred of *Salò*, its rites, its contemptuous, devastating homosexuality, its martyrdom of a generation sacrificed by cultural genocide. Or we could recall the suburban promenades of *Petrolio*, the mournful and haunted denunciation of the loss of an entire social class, the defeat of the logic of poverty by the complex dynamics of power. In addition, there is *Porno-Teo-Kolossal*'s depiction of a threatening rumble of revolt coming from planet Earth, heard by the angel and the spirit of the deceased Magus King in an already ironically post-apocalyptic heavenless sky. Or we may recall the Hell of the petit bourgeois of *Divina Mimesis*, centred on the most serious Pasolinian sin: bourgeois conformism. More martyrs, apocalypses, hells, and magi, can be found in a heap of Christian themes rearranged in a haunted script full of violence and surreally comic moments. In short, the later works of Pasolini contaminate the "incarnated" Pasolini of the 1960s with the thrust of a clear and bitter disenchantment.

The matrix of the Incarnation and models of saintliness – heretical, criminal, apocalyptic – proposed in his poetry of the 1950s and in his cinema of the 1960s – is overturned by a desecrating and profaning imperative. In reality, however, the invocation at the end of *Lettere luterane* still holds: that return to *agape* is invoked even today by the intellectuals of radical and materialist philosophy as an antidote to the Empire of capital. Pasolini's is an incarnated Marxism: a sacred materialism, profoundly tragic in its "freedom to choose death." Pasolini, however, did not choose his death – even today the world still wonders what happened that November night in 1975. Since then, Pasolini is as *inattuale* as his St Paul: his words resound in the blogs and academic essays as prophesies of biopolitics, globalization, and apocalypse. Although he may appear obsolete, Pasolini, like St Paul, is our contemporary: he is "*here, today, among us* and … he is so almost physically and materially … [It is] our society that he addresses: it is our society which he bemoans and loves, threatens and pardons, attacks and tenderly embraces."[61]

Conclusion

What is the fate and what is the role of the sacred in our culture? Is the sacred still relevant, and why or why not? Does it belong to a transcendent or to an immanent dimension? Can we identify the "wholly other" in our secularized world? How can we interact with this radically separated sphere of human life? Can we integrate it in our history and in our daily existence as an ally in the fight to understand and reinforce our humanity?

Many theorists have raised these questions, from anthropologist Ernesto De Martino to religious historian Mircea Eliade, from theologian Dietrich Bonhoeffer to modern thinkers such as Georges Bataille and René Girard and political philosophers such as Giorgio Agamben, Slavoj Žižek, and Alain Badiou. We must read Pasolini's culturally complex figure and the centrality of the sacred in his films, theoretical works on cinema, poems, novels, and screenplays within the constellation of these crucial protagonists of the history of theories of the sacred. As I have established, Pasolini's meditation on the disappearance of the sacred in our times and its return as a haunting revenant, a threatening disruption of neo-capitalist society, foreshadowed current debates and could contribute substantially to redefining the status of the sacred in our postmodern world.

The sacred in Pasolini has a twofold nature: on the one hand, it is the archaic sacred of the mythical pagan world (*Notes for an African Oresteia, Oedipus Rex, Medea, Pilades*); on the other, it is the Christian sacred with a central focus on the Incarnation (from *Accattone* to *Porno-Teo-Kolossal*). Pasolini's vision of the sacred contaminates both dimensions; his own antiheroes operate outside of both divine and human laws, with no possibility of redemption or any kind of resurrection, nor any opportunity to become agents in history. They are outcasts and *homines sacri*: their death is more an unsanctioned killing than a transcendental sacrificial offer. Since the Incarnation, transcendence has no place in Pasolini's world. Pasolini's Christ is a kenotic figure who emptied himself of his divine nature to fully embrace his humanity, to the point of becoming the remnant – as we have read in *Bestemmia* – of a utopia from the distant past. At the same time, his Christ, like Žižek's Christ, descends among humans to be part of our history and give it a meaning of tragic humanism. The meaning is the fate of the cross, the scandal of the cross. The immanent vision of the sacred in Pasolini derives from this kenotic perspective. Following Michael Hardt's interpretation of Pasolini's poem on the Crucifixion, it is the self-emptying of the God that becomes exposure, the expression of the fullness of the Flesh brought to the point of exhibition.

Pasolini's vision of the sacred is rooted in the lessons of both Ernesto De Martino and Mircea Eliade. Presence is a foundational feature of Pasolini's will to participate in history. At the same time, in his Eliadian stage, Pasolini dismantles any kind of progressive narrative by reading history as humanity's fallen trajectory, precipitated from the archaic ontology of archetypes and of time's eternal return.

A complex web of acceptance and rejection characterized Pasolini's relationship with the Catholic world, from his fierce initial anticlericalism to his collaboration with the Pro Civitate Christiana of Assisi and the dedication of his works to the memory of John XXIII, to his return to anticlericalism at the time of Paul VI's papacy. Nevertheless, his relationship with the Christian legacy goes beyond the Vatican. Incarnation is a central theme in Pasolini's films and scripts in the age of the economic miracle, from *La Ricotta* to *Il Vangelo secondo Matteo* to the long digression on the visionary Passion in the script-in-verse of *Bestemmia*. Pasolini's practice of contamination is a stylistic translation of the incarnational matrix, from the tragic comedy of Stracci's agony to the magmatic, sober rendition of the Crucifixion in *Il Vangelo*. Moving from *Il Vangelo*'s Christ to *Bestemmia*'s Christ, we read *Bestemmia*'s vision of the Passion as a metafilmic meditation, parallel to the theoretical reflections on cinema in *Empirismo eretico*. Pasolini's Passion is a prism through which to investigate the indexicality of cinema, the theology of the image, and the production of presence as an almost tactile proximity between the subject and the real, re-presented in the violent tear of the image, that is, the laceration of the surface of Being down to its abysmal ground.

Adopting the Crucifixion as the *axis mundi* of Pasolini's world, I have traced four different trajectories of *Imitatio Christi*, four different configurations of saintliness. The first is Emilia, the crazy saint of *Teorema,* liquefied in her baptismal tears. She is juxtaposed to the impossible seeding in the desert, in a world deserted by God, in the case of the second saint, the apostate industrialist Paolo. A Franciscan model comes third, caught between the tragic renunciation of saintliness in order to embrace class struggle in *Bestemmia* and the joyful religious turn of a Marxist revolutionary militancy grounded in awareness of social injustice and joy of being in *Uccellacci e uccellini.* The fourth and final configuration of saintliness, the exploration of Pasolini's incarnational sacred, ends with the analysis of another cherished but failed project just like *Bestemmia,* his script *San Paolo. Agape* is there imbued with *eros,* and St Paul's sexual difference is at the root of his saintliness. *Agape* is the ultimate militant virtue in Pasolini's theory of the sacred, as well as in his politics.

Finally, in the last years of Pasolini's production, the need to grasp reality via the cinematic medium and to celebrate the mirroring of cinema and life gave way to a disavowal of his previous myths. He vilified his beloved "subproletarian youth" because of its anthropological mutation into a conformist bourgeois mass, and he completely rejected any kind of transcendence with the farcical disappearance of Heaven in the narrative of *Porno-Teo-kolossal.* While apocalyptic themes took over in his late creative stage, from *Petrolio* to *La Divina Mimesis* to *Porno-Teo-Kolossal,* the need for *agape* was still invoked in his posthumous *Lutheran Letters* and represented one of the strongest prefigurations of contemporary radical theory's debates by Pasolini's theory of the sacred.

By adopting an incarnational matrix and a series of Christian themes and tropes within his corpus with an immanent framework, Pasolini thus anticipated and proposed a political reading of the Christian legacy. His extremely kenotic, heretical interpretation of a barbaric Christology without resurrection and the visceral evangelical turn of his passion for reality help us understand both the political climate that was the context for the dialogue between Marxists and Catholics in the 1960s and our own contemporary discussion of the intersection between the kernel of Christian doctrine in radical theory's critique of global capitalism.

Moreover, Pasolini's theory of the sacred is intertwined with a theory of cinema and of the cinematic sign that invoked a theology of the image and a production of presence, embodied in the image of the Passion. Projecting this inquiry onto the present debate on cinema as a medium and onto future academic debates, I envision Pasolini's "Sacred Flesh" as a decisive point in a trajectory that extends from postwar cinema theory and postwar Italian cinema practice to both a critique and a fulfilment of that same theory and practice. I am referring to Andre Bazin's incarnational vision of cinema – cinema as a "hyperbole of incarnation because of the overwhelming physical presence of the image" (2005, "Grandeur of Limelight," 137). Bazin's incarnational realist cinema – identified now as a death mask, or a moulding of light or Holy Shroud, as a carrier of a physical contact with a corporeal presence – intersects with what Karl Schoonover has defined as "cinepresence" in his *Brutal Vision: The Neorealist Body in Postwar Italian Cinema* (2012). According to Schoonover, the concept of presence becomes amplified in cinema because of a bifurcated temporality that connects the performing bodies and the viewing bodies. In this production of presence, which is medium-specific, we as the spectators "experience the film image both as an account of a presence that once existed or an event that once occurred, and as an account of a presence coming into being or an event unfolding" (2012, 36). Spectatorship thus becomes witnessing: it becomes the experience of the profilmic event as unfolding in the present of its reception. It is a document and a virtual reproduction of the pro-filmic experience in the spectator.

Schoonover employs Bazin's theory in constructing a definition of cinema as "the most immodest of the arts," bordering on pornographic when cinematic images reproduce "a presence so startling as to be potentially prurient, brutal, or crude" (2012, 2). Talking about the documentary of an execution, Bazin calls that cinema "une pornographie ontologique." Schonoover argues that this overwhelming spectacle of violence and realism in cinema – the pornographic image of Bazin, translated into Italian neo-realist cinema's "brutal vision" as the spectacle of war, torture, and injustice waged against partisans, civilians, and children – implies for the spectators an awareness of their status as witnesses. This status triggers a humanistic response of empathy as well as a charitable gaze, which have a global scope and a political impact (culminating historically in the Marshall Plan).

We can transfer this interpretive key to Pasolini's cinema and his own "brutal vision." Pasolini's violent images, rooted in the archaic violence of the sacred as well as in the "pornographic image" represented by the archetypal spectacle of the violence of the Crucifixion, react to their neo-realist antecedents in two ways. On the one hand, they are an Oedipal critique of the neo-realist masters and their naive vision of rebirth (as we have seen in chapter 5); on the other, they act to probe the spectators' empathic response brought to its Pauline extremes. *Agape*, in these violent deaths, comes back as the love for the wretched of the world.

Pasolini's protagonists are the marginalized, the ugly, the poor, the violent, the criminal, the amoral, the brutalized, the innocent bodies of subproletarians. The sacred flesh is the abject flesh: it is pure and impure, cursed and blessed at the same time. By quoting the brutal vision of his neo-realist masters, and challenging the spectators' empathy with a lesson on a charitable gaze that goes beyond the cinematic surface to question the political issues at stake, Pasolini's cinema is the fulfilment of Pauline *agape* on its own terms. It embodies a cinematic vision – of the sacred and of the medium of cinema itself – that shocked the society of the economic miracle with an uncanny, powerful critique.

Pasolini's Sacred Flesh still speaks to our globalized and secularized world. It speaks with the archaic words of myth and rite, it speaks with a "certain realist" vision filtered by a mannerist sensibility and an anti-naturalistic stance. Via an excess of cultural frames and quotations, Pasolini evokes the oneiric, visionary, irrational quality of a cinema that incarnates the *mysterium tremendum* of the sacred in a materialist and immanent way. His cinema acts, in Bazin's words, "like the veil of the Veronica pressed to the face of human suffering" (2005, "Cinema and Exploration," 1:163).

Pasolini speaks, with his incarnational cinema, the words of the Flesh: the emanation of the peasant, subproletarian, Third World body in its vital but agonizing last breaths.

Pasolini, with his own intellectual parable and his own suffering body, with his *parrhesia* and his *agape*, incarnates a different version of the paradox of the cross: scandal for the Christians, and folly for the bourgeois.

Notes

Introduction

1 "Amaro destino, quello degli intellettuali disorganici, i soli intellettuali degni di questo nome: restare pietra dello scandalo per la destra come per la sinistra, pur avendo fornito ad entrambe le armi della critica contro ogni forma di reificazione." The translation is mine, as are all translations unless otherwise indicated.

2 "C'è in Pasolini un legame primordiale, ancestrale, di vita e di linguaggio che trae radicamento e nutrimento da quella misteriosa e oscura fonte da cui fioriscono la corporeità, il sesso ... La traccia che ne emerge è quella di una poesia pensante che nella consapevolezza della perdita del sacro ... ne invoca una nuova venuta, inquietata e sollecitata dalla necessità di ripensarlo quale unità di presenza e assenza."

3 See "Res Sunt Nomina," *EE, SLA1*, 1584–5; *HE*, 255.

4 The parrhesiastes – from the Greek *parrhesia* – is one who feels the obligation to speak the truth for the common good, even at personal risk.

5 Žižek's *The Puppet and the Dwarf* (2003); Badiou's *Saint Paul: The Foundation of Universalism* (2003).

Chapter One

1 *Enciclopedia Einaudi* (Turin: Einaudi, 1981), vol. 12, s.v. "Sacro-Profano," 313.

2 See, for example, Paul Schrader's *Transcendental Style in Film* (1988).

3 "Non c'è un'inquadratura girata col sole: la luce è sempre quella dell'inverno con le nuvole alte e compatte, che, a loro modo, sono assolute come il sereno. E il paese è sempre immobile, in purissimo bianco e nero, e la campagna nuda, disegnata con una punta di ferro ... Piano piano la

suite della vita nel paesello pedemontano, con le sue case di sassi grigi e le sue strade bianche, nella luce accecante dell'aria di neve, diviene iterazione, litania: la serie degli episodi si fa ossessiva, e i significati della povera vicenda umana trapassano a una simbologia tanto più povera di ornamento quanto più ricca di un quasi fisico dolore."

4 "Pasolini non può non credere: egli è una proiezione ancestrale di sua madre, soprattutto! ... E sua madre è popolo, è umanità concepita nata impastata cristiana, come è in realtà la gente friulana da cui proviene – la mia gente, dolorosa e infelice ... Pasolini è un fenomeno escatologico, ecco tutto."

5 *Il sogno del centauro* (*SC*), ed. Jean Duflot with a preface by G.C.Ferretti (Rome: Editori Riuniti, 1983), translated from the French volume *Les Dernières Paroles d'un Impie, Entretiens avec Jean Duflot* (Paris: Belfond, 1981), 2nd expanded ed. of J. Duflot, *Entretiens avec Pier Paolo Pasolini* (Paris: Belfond, 1970). The volume of interviews is here quoted from the collection *Saggi sulla Politica e sulla Società* (*SPS*), ed. Walter Siti and Silvia De Laude for the Meridiani Mondadori (1401–1550). The English translation is mine.

6 This is the title of an important 1965 essay published in *Empirismo eretico* (Milan: Garzanti, 1972), 1242–1639, and later in the first volume of *Saggi sulla Letteratura e sull'Arte*, ed. Walter Siti and Silvia De Laude, 1461–88; henceforth cited as *EE, SLA1*. The English translation by Ben Lawton and Louise Barnett is in Louise Barnett, ed., *Heretical Empiricism*, 167–86 (henceforth *HE*).

7 "Io difendo il sacro perché è la parte dell'uomo che offre meno resistenza alla profanazione del potere, ed è la più minacciata dalle istituzioni delle Chiese ... Mi rendo conto d'altronde che in questa mia nostalgia di un sacro idealizzato, e forse mai esistito – dato che il sacro è sempre stato istituzionalizzato, all'inizio, per esempio, dagli sciamani, poi dai preti – che in questa nostalgia, dicevo, c' è qualcosa di sbagliato, di irrazionale, di tradizionalista."

8 "E quindi che cosa mi resta da fare se non esprimere il riflesso del passato? *[Come costretto alla sincerità].*"

9 From the poem "Poesie Mondane," in the section "La realtà," in *Poesia in forma di rosa* (Milan: Garzanti, 1964), now in the two-volume collection of *Tutte le poesie*, ed. Walter Siti (Milan: Mondadori, 2003); henceforth cited as *TP*. The present quotation is from *TP1*,1099.

10 "La società industriale si è formata in totale contraddizione con la società precedente, la civiltà contadina ... la quale possedeva in proprio il sentimento del sacro. Successivamente, questo sentimento del sacro si è trovato legato alle istituzioni ecclesiastiche, ed è talvolta degenerato fino alla

ferocia, specie quando alienato dal potere. Ecco, in ogni caso, il sentimento del sacro era radicato nel cuore della vita umana. La civiltà borghese lo ha perduto. E con che cosa l'ha sostituito, questo sentimento del sacro, dopo la perdita? Con l'ideologia del benessere e del potere. Ecco. Per ora viviamo in un momento negativo il cui esito ancora mi sfugge. Posso quindi proporre solo ipotesi e non soluzioni."

11 "CENTAURO – Tutto è santo, tutto è santo, tutto è santo. Non c'è niente di naturale nella natura, ragazzo mio, tientelo bene in mente. Quando la natura ti sembrerà naturale, tutto sarà finito – e comincerà qualcos'altro. Addio cielo, addio mare! Che bel cielo! Vicino, felice! Di, ti sembra che un pezzetto solo non sia innaturale? Non sia posseduto da un Dio? E così è il mare, in questo giorno in cui tu hai tredici anni, e peschi con i piedi nell'acqua tiepida. Guardati alle spalle! Che cosa vedi? È forse qualcosa di naturale? No, è un'apparizione, quella che tu vedi alle tue spalle, con le nuvole che si specchiano nell'acqua ferma e pesante delle tre di pomeriggio!

... Guarda laggiù ... quella striscia nera sul mare lucido e rosa come l'olio. E quelle ombre di alberi ... quei canneti ... In ogni punto in cui i tuoi occhi guardano, è nascosto un Dio!

E se per caso non c'è, ha lasciato lì i segni della sua presenza sacra, o silenzio, o odore di erba o fresco di acque dolci ...

Eh sì, tutto è santo, ma la santità è insieme una maledizione. Gli Dei che amano – nel tempo stesso – odiano."

12 Eliade's treatise was first published in Italian in 1954 (Turin: Einaudi) with a preface by anthropologist Ernesto De Martino, from the French 1948 edition, *Traitè d'histoire des religions* (Paris: Payot). Eliade is cited by Pasolini in his 1969 interview with Duflot (*SC*, *SPS*, 1461); in the article "Ho sognato un verso," originally written in the same year for the section *Il caos* of the periodical *Tempo* (*SPS*, 1203–5); and in a book review, "Mircea Eliade, *Mito e realtà*," first collected in the posthumous *Descrizioni di descrizioni* (Turin: Einaudi, 1979), and now in *SLA2*, 2113–18.

13 Pasolini quotes from Eliade 1954, 376:

> "CENTAURO: Ciò che l'uomo, scoprendo l'agricoltura, ha *veduto* nei cereali, ciò che ha *imparato* da questo rapporto, ciò che ha *inteso* dall'esempio dei semi che perdono la loro forma sotto terra per poi rinascere, tutto questo ha rappresentato la lezione definitiva.
>
> La resurrezione, mio caro.
>
> Ma ora questa lezione definitiva non serve più. Ciò che tu vedi nei cereali, ciò che intendi dal rinascere dei semi è per te senza significato, come un lontano ricordo che non ti riguarda più. Infatti non c'è nessun Dio."

14 "Allucinato, infantile e pragmatico amore per la realtà."

15 See *SC, SPS*, 1494: "scoprire gli esseri e le cose come congegni (mondi), macchine cariche di sacralità. Quando giro un film, mi immergo in uno stato di fascinazione davanti a un oggetto, a una cosa, a un viso, gli sguardi, un paesaggio, come se si trattasse di un congegno in cui stesse per esplodere il sacro" (discovering beings and things as mechanisms (worlds), machines loaded with sacrality. When I shoot a film, I immerse myself in a state of fascination with an object, a thing, a landscape, as if they were devices in which the sacred were about to explode).

16 "In *Accattone*, la sacralità era allo stato puro. Bisogna precisare che, quando parlo di questa presenza del sacro, non parlo del film nel suo complesso, delle sue forme interne, degli eventi, delle serie di cause e di effetti, dei lineamenti interiori di un determinato personaggio. Parlo del sacro, cosa dopo cosa, oggetto dopo oggetto, immagine dopo immagine."

17 "È realista solo chi crede nel mito. Il 'mitico' non è che l'altra faccia del realismo." *SLA1*, 1462.

18 "La natura non conosce i 'superamenti.' Ogni cosa in essa si giustappone e coesiste."

19 "L'essere sacro rimane giustapposto all'essere dissacrato. Con questo intendo dire che, vivendo, ho realizzato una serie di superamenti, di dissacrazioni, di evoluzioni. Quello che ero, però, prima di questi superamenti, di queste dissacrazioni, di queste evoluzioni, non è scomparso."

20 "Sono anzi talmente metafisico, mitico, talmente mitologico … da non arrischiarmi a dire che il dato che supera il precedente, dialetticamente, lo incorpori, lo assimili. Dico che si giustappongono."

21 "I superamenti, le sintesi! Sono illusioni, … / La tesi / e l'antitesi convivono con la sintesi: ecco / la vera trinità dell'uomo né prelogico, né logico, / ma reale… . / La storia non c'è, diciamo, c'è la sostanza: che è apparizione." *Trasumanar e organizzar* was originally published by Garzanti in 1971 and is now included in the two volumes of *Tutte le poesie* edited by Walter Siti (Milan: Mondadori, 2003). The present quotation is from *TP2*, 262.

22 See Conti Calabrese 1994, 28.

23 [Duflot]: *Cosicché il sacro, il mito, le civiltà arcaiche, i popoli della terra e della natura, l'uomo preistorico, si seppelliscono […], senza mai scomparire del tutto. Nel cuore dell'uomo permane il bambino. Al centro dei rituali erotici arde l'eros selvaggio. Tutte queste presenze definiscono un'etica profonda, altrettanto, se non più, della morale del progresso e della produzione.*

[Pasolini]: Il tragico è proprio la rottura definitiva di questa continuità.

24 Cf. Pasolini's words in an interview with Pisanelli Stabile: "da una parte, sì la mia formazione razionalistica, il mio atteggiamento razionale e storicistico nell'interpretare il mondo, fa sì che io lotti contro gli idoli, ma, al tempo

stesso, ambiguamente, io continui ad adorare questi idoli perché parte di me stesso è ancora immersa in un mondo mitico e irrazionale." (On the one hand, yes, my rationalistic background, my rational historicist approach to the interpretation of the world, lead me to fight against idols, at the same time, however, I go on adoring these same idols, because part of myself is still immersed in a mythical irrational world.) "L'ultima Medea," originally pubished in January 1970 in *La rassegna* 4.1, 60; now in Subini 2008, 23.

25 The word *tarantismo* alludes to the southern Salento phenomenon of lovestruck young and unmarried women who are supposedly bitten by a tarantula and thus forced to dance until exhaustion in order to exorcise the enchantment.

26 "Una mediazione tecnica che dalla storia ritorna alla storia, e che per questa sua dialettica limita il momento meramente tecnico del mito e del rito, dischiudendo a vari livelli di autonomia e di autocoscienza il mondano e il profano."

27 "Con tale destorificazione viene anzitutto istituito un rapporto con il se stesso alienato (o naturalizzato o destorificato); in secondo luogo per una vitale *pia fraus* si sta nella storia COME SE non ci si stesse: proprio perché le potenze operative dell'uomo non sono nella destorificazione riconosciute nella loro qualità di iniziative umana, quelle potenze sono di fatto permesse e dischiuse, e la cultura come TOTALITA' dei valori è resa possibile."

28 "Il sacro è entrato in agonia e davanti a noi sta il problema di sopravvivere come uomini alla sua morte, senza correre il rischio di perdere – insieme al sacro – l'accesso ai valori culturali umani, o di lasciarci travolgere dal terrore di una storia cui non fa più da orizzonte e da prospettiva la metastoria mitico-rituale. L'alternativa tra umano e divino, che travaglia tutta la storia delle religioni, e che col Cristianesimo è entrata in un drammatico processo di maturazione, si pone oggi nei termini di una decisione attuale alla quale non possiamo sottrarci. Il 'sacro' nei modi tradizionali di un orizzonte metastorico articolato in un nesso organico di miti e di riti, non costituisce una esigenza permanente della natura umana, ma una grande epoca storica che in direzione del passato si perde nella notte delle origini e che giunge sino a noi, eredi della civiltà occidentale: ma per amplissima che sia questa epoca è certo che ne stiamo uscendo, e che il suo tramonto si sta consumando dentro di noi. Il rischio della crisi esistenziale, la esigenza di simbolismi protettivi e reintegratori appartengono certamente alla condizione umana e quindi anche alla civiltà moderna: ma la tecnica dell'orizzonte metastorico è diventata inattuale, onde la civiltà moderna è impegnata ad ordinare una società e una cultura il cui simbolismo esprima il senso della

storia e la coscienza umanistica, senza ricorso all'ambigua politica dei due volti."

29 "Restando su di un piano di comunicazione strumentale come siamo adesso, direi che l'angoscia è un fatto borghese … Il sottoproletariato ha un altro tipo di angoscia quella che studia De Martino facendo ricerche nella poesia popolare in Lucania, per esempio, cioè un'angoscia preistorica rispetto all'angoscia esistenzialistica borghese, storicamente determinata. Io in *Accattone* ho studiato questo tipo di angoscia preistorica rispetto alla nostra … l'angoscia di un contadino lucano che canta un canto funebre su un parente morto, è un'angoscia che ha altre componenti storiche da quelle che prova un borghese come quello della *Noia* di Moravia per esempio … E' tutt'un'altra cosa!" The interview was originally published as "Incontro con Pier Paolo Pasolini" in *Filmcritica* 13.116 (January 1962) and is now included in *PPC2,* 2799–818.

30 "E' chiaro che chi si droga lo fa per riempire un vuoto, un'assenza di qualcosa, che dà smarrimento ed angoscia. E' un sostituto della magia. I primitivi sono sempre di fronte a questo vuoto terribile, nel loro interno. Ernesto De Martino lo chiama "paura della perdita della propria presenza"; e i primitivi, appunto, riempiono questo vuoto ricorrendo alla magia, che lo spiega e lo riempie. Nel mondo moderno, l'alienazione dovuta al condizionamento della natura è sostituita dall'alienazione dovuta al condizionamento della società: passato il primo momento di euforia (illuminismo, scienza, scienza applicata, comodità, benessere, produzione e consumo), ecco che l'alienato comincia a trovarsi solo con se stesso: egli, quindi, come il primitivo, è terrorizzato dall'idea della perdita della propria presenza. In realtà, tutti ci droghiamo. Io (che io sappia) facendo il cinema." "Droga e cultura" ("Drugs and Culture"), originally in "I dialoghi," *Vie nuove* 53, 28 December 1968; collected in *DIAL.*

31 Translation emended.

32 "A differenza dunque che nella vita o nel cinema, in un film un'azione – o segno figurale, o mezzo espressivo, o sintagma vivente riprodotto … – ha come significato il significato dell'analoga azione reale compiuta da quelle persone in carne e ossa, in quello stesso quadro naturale o sociale – ma il suo senso è già compiuto e decifrabile, come se la morte fosse già avvenuta. Ciò vuol dire che nel film il tempo è finito, sia pure per una finzione. Bisogna dunque accettare la favola per forza. Il tempo non è quello della vita quando vive, ma quello della vita dopo la morte: come tale è reale, non è un'illusione e può benissimo essere quello della storia di un film." Pasolini, "Essere è naturale?" ("Is Being Natural?"), 1967, in *HE,* 238–43; *EE, SLA1,* 1569.

33 “O essere immortali e inespressi o esprimersi e morire.” “Essere è naturale?” (“Is Being Natural?”) 1967, *SLA1,* 1569.

34 “Il cinema ... è fondato dunque sul tempo: e obbedisce perciò alle stesse regole che la vita: le regole di un’illusione. Strano a dirsi, ma questa illusione bisogna accettarla. Perché chi ... non l’accetta, anzichè entrare in una fase di maggiore realtà, perde la presenza della realtà: la quale dunque consiste unicamente in tale illusione.” Pasolini, “Perché quella di Edipo è una storia,” in *Edipo re. Un film di Pier Paolo Pasolini* (1967, 12), *PPC1,* 1056.

35 “Alla destorificazione pagana orientata verso la iterazione rituale delle ‘origini’ metastoriche, e alla destorificazione giudaica orientata verso l’attesa del ‘termine’ della storia, si contrappone ora la destorificazione di un evento ‘centrale’ che ha deciso il corso storico: un evento per cui la salvezza è data, e già comincia il Regno che ha reso la morte apparente, sino alla seconda definitiva *parousia.*”

36 Cacitti explains: “L’idea che la religione, come insieme di pratiche e di credenze che presuppongono una trascendenza, sia tramontata, l’impegno del cristiano in un ambito esclusivamente storico, l’insistenza su una forma di fede incentrata sulla passione e crocifissione di Gesù e che prescinde dalla sua resurrezione sono alcuni dei temi che ritroviamo in Pasolini, come presso alcuni esponenti della teologia della morte di Dio” (1997, 12). (The idea that religion, as a system of customs and beliefs that presupposes transcendence, is over; the Christian’s commitment is only to the historical realm; the insistence on a faith that is centred on Jesus’ passion and crucifixion but disregards His resurrection are some of the themes we find in Pasolini as well as in some of theology of the exponents of the death of God.)

37 “Ammirare la natura e gli uomini, di riconoscere la profondità ... delle cose.”

38 “Non mi piace il cattolicesimo in quanto istituzione, non per ateismo militante, ma perché la mia religione, o meglio, il mio spirito religioso – che non ha nulla a che vedere con un’appartenenza fondata sul battesimo – ne viene offeso. Rimane poi questo cripto-cristianesimo, che mi imputano i più aggressivi, quasi fosse una tara vergognosa. Dirò per rispondere loro che difficilmente un occidentale può non essere cristianizzato, se non un cristiano convinto. A maggior ragione un italiano.”

39 “Il mio sentimento del divino è un sentimento informe, psicologico, che ho trovato depositato in me con la nascita, nell’infanzia, e che forse per questo non è tanto forte ... In realtà questa apertura ascetica, questo senso di vita vista sotto il profilo dell’eternità c’è continuamente nelle mie opere, ma non esplode mai fino all’assunzione del divino.“

40 “Religione della sofferenza.”

41 "C'è alla base questa misteriosa, remota ma insopprimibile istanza umanitaria cristiana."

42 "Noi siamo ancora dei figli diretti, gli eredi diretti degli uomini di duemila anni fa. E quindi il momento religioso che c'è in noi è un momento ancora vivo, attualissimo. Eliminarlo non è possibile. Viviamo ancora in quell'ambito culturale che ha prodotto il cristianesimo e ha prodotto le religioni ... Voglio dire che quella religione che noi marxisti rifiutiamo così *in toto,* perché abbiamo scelto un altro tipo di ideologia, in parte scompare nel nostro profondo, nel nostro inconscio, e lì ha una vita che non sappiamo mai determinare, perché non sappiamo cosa succede nel profondo delle viscere nostre; e in parte sopravvive e galleggia nella nostra coscienza assumendo forma di religione disgregata: diventa religiosità. ... Nessuno di noi potrà mai denegare un elemento religioso nel nostro rapporto con il prossimo. Questo sentimento di pietà, di amore ha una radice profondamente religiosa."

43 "Nella concezione generale dell'umanità c'è una profonda differenza, evidentemente, tra un marxista e un cattolico. Il marxista pone completamente la vita e il futuro dell'uomo nell'ambito del tempo, nell'ambito della vita terrena, mentre un cattolico proietta la vita umana nell'aldilà. E questa è una differenza così fondamentale che la cosa sembrerebbe inconciliabile. Però, secondo me, c'è un punto di coincidenza. Ed è appunto quella religione che cacciata dalla porta rientra dalla finestra. Voi sapete che i marxisti ... hanno come base del proprio essere, della propria azione la cosiddetta 'prospettiva': la prospettiva del futuro, quella che per tutti questi anni è stata chiamata la Speranza, con la esse maiuscola. Ora, che cosa è questa prospettiva del futuro, questa Speranza che regge la fede, l'ideologia e l'azione di un comunista? E' una visione, secondo me, profondamente religiosa. Un comunista concepisce la storia come storia della lotta di classe ... Se la storia è concepita come storia della lotta di classe, allora la prospettiva, la speranza dei comunisti implica, postula un momento di astoricità, per lo meno ideale. Al di là del futuro c'è un momento in cui la storia cessa e quindi c'è un momento di metastoricità, di astoricità, anche nel pensiero marxista. Ed è in questo che in fondo il marxista è un uomo religioso. Se fonda tutta la sua azione sugli scioperi e la lotta, e lo fa in nome di una fede che ha come risultato ultimo la vittoria nella lotta dei poveri contro i ricchi, cioè la fine della storia, in questo è un uomo religioso. E' in questo che si può vedere, secondo me, una profonda, sottile possibilità di coincidenza tra la posizione ideologica di un cattolico e quella di un marxista."

44 Post-history is a Pasolinian concept also explored in the collections of poems; cf. "Poesie Mondane" from *Poesia in forma di rosa,* first published in

1964 (Milan: Garzanti) and now in *TP1*, 1099. Pasolini's idea of history created a tension between the personal and lived sense of history and the traces of hierophanies and apparitions of being, with the linear sense of the official history, permeated by his Marxist progressive ideology. Between the idea of a regressive concept of history, based on the memory of myth, and the collective trajectory of a potential revolution, Pasolini created the concept of "post-history" or "new prehistory" as expressing the sense of time in the neocapitalist world, with the end of cyclical and Christian time, the zeroing of sacred apparitions. The development of the concepts of history, post-history, and new history in Pasolini's works has been explored by Santato (2007).

45 See "*Mamma Roma,* ovvero dalla responsabilità individuale alla responsabilità collettiva" ("*Mamma Roma,* or concerning individual and collective responsibility"), an interview with Nino Ferrero originally published in *Filmcritica* 125 (September 1962), 444, now in *PPC2,* 2819–35, in response to an interview with Mario Soldati in *Filmcritica* 124.

46 "Se il cattolicesimo è quello, se il cattolicesimo è l'idea che tutto finirà, cioè se è un elemento di tragedia nell'uomo ...: soltanto che il cattolicesimo non dice che tutto finisce, dice che questo mondo finisce ma poi ce n'è un altro ... e mi pare che la differenza sia sostanziale. Io son d'accordo: c'è dentro di me l'idea tragica che contraddice sempre tutto, l'idea della morte. L'unica cosa che dà una vera grandezza all'uomo è il fatto che muoia ... l'unica grandezza dell'uomo è la sua tragedia: se non ci fosse questa saremmo ancora all'epoca della preistoria. Voglio dire che ho accettato la definizione di Soldati soltanto quando lui mi ha precisato che il cattolicesimo è puro senso della tragedia ... Purtroppo però il cattolicesimo non è questo; il cattolicesimo è la promessa che al di là di queste macerie c'è un altro mondo, e questo invece nei miei film non c'è, non c'è assolutamente! C'è soltanto la morte, ma non l'aldilà."

47 "Il fascino dell'irrazionale, del divino che domina tutto il Vangelo."

48 "Il problema che non posso demistificare è quel tanto di profondamente irrazionale, e quindi in qualche modo religioso, che è nel mistero del mondo. Quello non è demistificabile."

49 "Ciò che non ho fatto, perché è contrario alla mia natura profonda dissacrare sia le cose che la gente. Tendo invece a risacralizzarle il più possibile."

50 "Una caduta da cavallo ... sulla via di Damasco, non si è avuta ...: non sono caduto perché ero già caduto e trascinato da questo cavallo, diciamo, della razionalità, della vita del mondo."

51 "Senza rinunciare alle proprie idee, semplicemente coagulando nelle immagini una propria esperienza confusamente religiosa." *Filmcritica,*" 156–7 (April–May) 1965.

52 "In forma più cosmica che storica."

53 "Fino a oggi la Chiesa è stata la Chiesa di un universo contadino, il quale ha tolto al cristianesimo il suo solo momento originale rispetto a tutte le altre religioni, cioè Cristo. Nell'universo contadino Cristo è stato assimilato a uno dei mille adoni o delle mille proserpine esistenti: i quali ignoravano il tempo reale, cioè la storia. Il tempo degli dei agricoli simili a Cristo era un tempo 'sacro' o 'liturgico' di cui valeva la ciclicità, l'eterno ritorno. Il tempo della loro nascita, della loro azione, della loro morte, della loro discesa agli inferi e della loro risurrezione, era un tempo paradigmatico, a cui periodicamente il tempo della vita, riattualizzandolo, si modellava." For the full text see *SCOR*, *SPS*, 356–61, "6 ottobre 1974. Nuove prospettive storiche: La Chiesa è inutile al potere."

54 "Ma *mai* nel parlare, nel discutere, nel pensare, la gente, anche abbastanza colta, tiene presente, per esempio, che gli ebrei avevano da tempo immemorabile l'idea del *capro espiatorio* su cui trasferire i mali della società e cancellarli col suo sacrificio; oppure che il destino della Madonna e quello di Iside sono identici; come del resto quello di Cristo e quello di Adone; o che, addirittura, prima del sacrificio del capro, presso un'infinità di popoli si usava fare un banchetto (qualche volta orgia), che è adombrato nell'ultima cena; o ancora che la transustanziazione era una nozione diffusa presso decine e decine di popoli, che dunque praticavano il sacramento della comunione ... Insomma, se un raffinatissimo antropologo avesse voluto condensare sincretisticamente tutte le credenze religiose della civiltà contadina, non avrebbe potuto fare di meglio di quello che è raccontato nei vangeli." "L'idea del capro espiatorio" (The Idea of the Scapegoat), originally published in "I dialoghi."

55 See Conti Calabrese's discussion of Pasolini as prefiguring a time when tradition will be erased and replaced only by scientific knowledge and technological myths, and the Catholic Church will be relegated to the Third World (1994, 31).

56 "Finalmente libera da se stessa, cioè dal potere." "Nuove Prospettive Storiche: La Chiesa è inutile al Potere" (New Historical Perspectives: The Church Is Useless to Power), originally published in *Scritti Corsari*, 1975.

57 "Abbracciare quella cultura – da lei sempre odiata – che è per sua stessa natura libera, antiautoritaria, in continuo divenire, contraddittoria, collettiva, scandalosa."

58 "Quel che più m'importa nell'istituzione è il codice che rende possibile la fraternità. Qualsiasi istituzione costituisce un terreno di possibili scambi."

59 "Ricorrerò a San Paolo. Nella Prima Lettera ai Corinti, si legge questa stupenda frase ...: 'restano fede, speranza e carità, queste tre cose: di tutte la migliore è la carità.'

La carità – questa 'cosa' misteriosa e trascurata – al contrario della fede e della speranza, tanto chiare e d'uso comune, è indispensabile alla fede e alla speranza stesse. Infatti la carità è pensabile anche di per sé: la fede e la speranza sono impensabili senza la carità: e non solo impensabili, ma *mostruose*. Quelle del Nazismo (e quindi di un intero popolo) erano fede e speranza senza carità. Lo stesso si dica per la Chiesa clericale.

Insomma il potere – qualunque potere – ha bisogno dell'alibi della fede e della speranza. Non ha affatto bisogno dell'alibi della carità." "Alle soglie di uno scisma" (At the Threshold of a Schism), originally published in "I dialoghi," now in "Da 'Il Caos' sul 'Tempo' 1968," *SPS*, 1121–3.

60 "Informi e cieche forze del potere."

61 "Solo attraverso la Carità si può evitare la disumanità atroce della discriminazione e della repressione: della creazione artificiale e mostruosa dell' 'altro' (con i conseguenti ghetti e le conseguenti terre sante). E solo attraverso la Carità si può debellare la nozione disumana del non-credente, in quanto la Carità può riconoscere anche in esso la Carità (anche se rileva in esso la mancanza di Fede e della Speranza; oppure anche se rileva in esso un'altra Fede e un'altra Speranza)." "Una creazione mostruosa" (A Monstruous Creation), originally published in "I dialoghi," now in "Da 'Il Caos' sul Tempo 1968," *SPS*, 1128.

62 The definition is Ferretti's (1964).

63 "Bastava soltanto un tuo gesto, una tua parola, / Perché quei figli avessero una casa: / Tu non hai fatto un gesto, non hai detto una parola. / Non ti si chiedeva di perdonare Marx! Un'onda / Immensa che si rifrange da millenni di vita / Ti separava da lui, dalla sua religione: / Ma nella tua religione non si parla di pietà? / Migliaia di uomini sotto il tuo pontificato, / Davanti ai tuoi occhi, sono vissuti in stabbi e porcili, / Lo sapevi, peccare non significa fare il male: / Non fare il bene, questo significa peccare. / Quanto bene potevi fare? E non l'hai fatto: / Non c'è stato un peccatore più grande di te." (*La religione del mio tempo*, originally published in 1958, *TP1*, 1008–9)

64 La società italiana si presenta come completamente impregnata di quel marcio che è la corruzione del cristianesimo. In ogni atto, in ogni rapporto, si finisce sempre col mettere la mano su questo pus, su questo resto infetto di ciò che alle origini fu grande e puro. Culto cristiano e piccola borghesia fanno in Italia un'entità sola, che germina la purulenza morale di cui è lordato ogni giorno, ogni atto della nostra vita.

65 "Se io devo dunque affrontare una 'situazione' religiosa, preferisco farlo, ripeto, nell'ambito dello stesso spirito religioso. Mi basta prendere in mano il Vangelo, per poter condannare senza possibilità di dubbi e senza eccezioni, quell'istituzione fredda, arida, corrotta, ignorante che è, oggi, la Chiesa cattolica." Pasolini, "Postilla personale" ("A Personal Post-scriptum"), 3 June 1961, *DIAL*.

66 "Papa Giovanni non è stato semplicemente un buon Papa, un'apparizione angelica nella nostra società e nella nostra storia. E' stato qualche cosa di molto più profondo, di definitivo, secondo me, perché Papa Giovanni è stato il primo uomo della Chiesa, a livello supremo ... che abbia condotto la Chiesa a vivere al massimo livello l'esperienza laica e democratica del nostro ultimo secolo. A vivere cioè quello che la borghesia ha dato di meglio, dalla rivoluzione francese in poi.

... C'è dunque questo fondo di semplicità, di humour manzoniano. E poi c'è tutto un modo di esprimersi, di dire e di essere che è tipico dell'uomo colto, estremamente colto, ad alto livello borghese. Un fatto nuovo nella Chiesa, l'humour, l'ironia ...

Cosa volete immaginare di più rivoluzionario nella Chiesa, nella Chiesa che si è sempre posta come autoritaria, come paternalistica, come dogmatica e come antiliberale e antidemocratica nel fondo? ... Per la prima volta Papa Giovanni ha vissuto all'interno della Chiesa, nel profondo del suo spirito cristiano, la grande esperienza laica e democratica della borghesia. Ha vissuto, cioè, la reale realtà del suo tempo, e nella reale realtà del suo tempo, oltre a questa esperienza fondamentale, laica e democratica della borghesia, ci sono delle nuove realtà, c'è la realtà del socialismo."

"Marxismo e Cristianesimo" (Marxism and Cristianity), in *Le interviste Corsare* (Rome: Liberal Atlantide Editoriale, 1995), 75–7, and *SPS*, 786–824.

67 In his volume *L'eresia cristiana di Pier Paolo Pasolini* (*Pasolini's Christian Heresy*) (2010), Alessio Passeri describes in detail this crucial moment in Pasolini's oeuvre, analysing a series of documents and the pages of *Rocca* (*Fortress*), the group's magazine, and tracing a fundamental line of development of the debate between Marxism and Catholicism mediated by Pasolini's "heretical" figure.

68 "Un accentuarsi dell'evangelismo come religione pura contro la religione di Stato, ufficiale, conformista; o un accentuarsi del moralismo 'protestante.'" "Marxismo e religiosità" ("Marxism and Religiosity"), 30 November 1961.

69 "Una generale protesta contro lo stato di cose precostituite, istituite, divenute insopportabilmente impersonali e soffocanti."

70 "I due primi momenti in una forma d'azione."

71 "Dinamici verso il prossimo."

72 "Io, per me, sono anticlericale ... ma so che in me ci sono duemila anni di cristianesimo: io coi miei avi ho costruito le chiese romaniche, e poi le chiese gotiche, e poi le chiese barocche: esse sono mio patrimonio, nel contenuto e nello stile. Sarei folle se negassi tale forza potente che è in me: se lasciassi ai preti il monopolio del Bene."

73 "Finora Paolo VI è stato dunque vittima di una crisi della Chiesa che, con maggior violenza e rapidità, non poteva esplodere: vittima, ripeto, in quanto diviso in due, lacerato da uno scisma vissuto nella propria persona ... E

sembra di aver capito di avere davanti a sé soltanto due scelte reali, capaci di risolvere una volta per sempre la sua angosciosa impotenza: cioè o compiere il gran rifiuto, e lasciare il Papato, come Celestino V che è stato forse il più grande dei Papi (ma certamente il più santo); oppure scatenare lo scisma, distinguendo, con sé, dal clerico-fascismo la Chiesa Cattolica: ripristinando cioè, secondo l'insegnamento dell'apostolo di cui ha scelto il nome, la funzione primaria della carità." "Ora il Papa si trova disarmato" ("The Pope is now defenseless"), 28 September 1968.

74 "Approvazione di films inammissibili."

75 "Che l'Ufficio Cattolico Internazionale del Cinema si tenga il suo premio e possono riprendersi indietro anche quello che mi diedero per il *Vangelo secondo Matteo.* Sto preparando un film sulla vita di San Paolo, per cui naturalmente continuerò il mio 'dialogo', ma con preti indipendenti e colti e forse un giorno con preti separatisti."

76 "Io sono *completamente solo.* E, per di più, nelle mani del primo che voglia colpirmi. Sono vulnerabile. Sono ricattabile. Forse, è vero, ho anche qualche solidarietà: ma essa è puramente ideale. Non può essermi di nessuno aiuto pratico ... Fatti questi calcoli, se tornano, potrò conservare la mia indipendenza: *la mia provocatoria indipendenza.* E' questa infatti ... che fa nascere contro di me tante ostilità. La mia indipendenza, che è la mia forza, implica solitudine, che è la mia debolezza ... La mia è quindi una indipendenza, diciamo, umana. Un vizio. Non potrei farne a meno. Ne sono schiavo. Non potrei nemmeno gloriarmene, farmene un piccolo vanto. Amo invece la solitudine. Ma essa è pericolosa. Di essa potrei fare gli elogi ... Forse è una nostalgia della perfetta solitudine goduta nel ventre materno. Anzi, sono quasi certo che è questo." "La mia provocatoria indipendenza" ("My Defiant Independence"), January 1969. This reference to the prenatal origins of his solitude, associated with the theme of civic virtue, is typical of Pasolini (i.e., in lying between Freud and Marx).

Chapter Two

1 Alfredo Bini was Pasolini's first producer.

2 When the movie was released in February 1963, the infamous striptease performed in front of the three crosses by of one of the "saintly" women provoked the ire of public prosecutor Giuseppe Di Gennaro. Di Gennaro launched a legal battle against the movie and Pasolini, labelling the film "the Trojan horse of proletarian revolution in the city of God" and condemning the director to a four-month suspended sentence for contempt of state religion. The movie was re-released in November 1963, after several editing cuts (including the striptease scene), with the title *Laviamoci il cervello*

(*Let's get brainwashed*). In May 1964, however, the Italian Court of Appeals absolved Pasolini, ruling that the film did not constitute an offence.

3 "E' probabilmente l'opera che ho meno calcolato, in cui si mescolano molto semplicemente tutti gli elementi di un codice popolare che sognavo di definire: l'umorismo, lo spirito romanesco, la crudeltà e l'egoismo … E' anche il film che ho girato più rapidamente e con meno materiale. C'è poi il metraggio relativamente ridotto (30 minuti), che mi costringeva alla concisione."

4 "Il Santo è Stracci. La faccia di antico camuso / che Giotto vide contro tufi e ruderi castrensi, / i fianchi rotondi che Masaccio chiaroscurò / come un panettiere una sacra pagnotta … / Se vi è oscura la bontà con cui egli si toglie di bocca / il cestino, per darlo alla famiglia che lo mastichi / al suon del Dies Irae; se vi è oscura l'ingenuità / con cui piange sul suo pasto rubato dal cane; / se vi è oscura la tenerezza con cui poi carezza / la colpevole bestia; se vi è oscuro l'umile coraggio / con cui risponde cantando un canto dei nonni ciociari / a chi l'offende; se vi è oscura l'intrepidezza / con cui affronta la sua sorte di inferiore / cantandone la filosofia nel gergo a lui caro dei ladri; / se vi è oscura l'ansia con cui si fa il segno della croce / davanti a uno dei vostri tabernacoli per poveri / filando verso il pasto; se vi è oscura la gratitudine / con cui, dopo un balletto di gioia come Charlot, / si rifà il segno di croce a quello stesso tabernacolo / con cui voi consacrate la sua inferiorità; / se vi è oscura la semplicità con cui muore."

5 "Rispetto ad *Accattone, La ricotta* è una variante della stessa *suite.* Così come può essere l'allegro rispetto all'adagio."

6 "Nella *Ricotta,* al contrario, interviene il mio personale giudizio di critico: non mi sono "perso" in Stracci. Stracci è un personaggio più meccanico di Accattone, perché sono io – e si vede – che aziono i fili. E lo si nota con esattezza nella costante auto-ironia. Ecco perché Stracci è un personaggio meno poetico di Accattone. Ma è però più significativo, più generalizzato. La crisi di cui il film testimonia non è la mia, ma è la crisi di un certo modo di vedere i problemi della realtà italiana. Fino ad *Accattone* i problemi sociali li vedevo unicamente calati nella particolarità e nella specificità italiana, cosa che è diventata impossibile con *La ricotta.* La società è cambiata, cambia. Il solo modo di guardare al sottoproletariato romano è di considerarlo come uno dei molteplici fenomeni del Terzo mondo. Stracci non è più un eroe del sottoproletariato romano in quanto problema specifico ma è l'eroe simbolico del Terzo mondo. Senza alcun dubbio più astratto e meno poetico, ma, per me, più importante." Bertolucci and Comolli, "Le cinema selon Pasolini."

7 "Fellini? He dances" is the director's response to one of the journalist's questions.

8 "In altri termini, Welles, un regista andato oltre le sue antiche convinzioni e diventato cinico, è anche un esteta – cinismo ed estetismo, per un intellettuale, sono quasi sinonimi – e pensa al suo film religioso in chiave, appunto, estetizzante, formalistica, attraverso la ricostruzione squisita di alcuni quadri. Questo, secondo me, è del tutto improduttivo e fondamentalmente insincero per una rappresentazione del Vangelo. Quindi Welles non rappresenta me stesso. Probabilmente è una specie di caricatura di un me stesso andato oltre certi limiti e visto come se, per un processo di inaridimento interiore, fossi diventato un ex comunista... Si spiegano così le sue risposte caustiche e ciniche che aggrediscono il mondo da ogni lato." Originally from "Una discussione del '64" ("A Discussion of 1964,") in AA.VV. 1977, 119–20.

9 "Io sono una forza del Passato. / Solo nella tradizione è il mio amore. / Vengo dai ruderi, dalle chiese, / dalle pale d'altare, dai borghi / abbandonati sugli Appennini o le Prealpi, / dove sono vissuti i fratelli. / Giro per la Tuscolana come un pazzo, / per l'Appia come un cane senza padrone. / O guardo i crepuscoli, le mattine / su Roma, sulla Ciociaria, sul mondo, / come i primi atti della Dopostoria, / cui io assisto, per privilegio d'anagrafe, / dall'orlo estremo di qualche età / sepolta. Mostruoso è chi è nato / dalle viscere di una donna morta. / E io, feto adulto, mi aggiro / più moderno di ogni moderno / a cercare fratelli che non sono più."

10 "Pasolini confesses and problematizes his dilemma as artist conflicted between sincerity and mannerism, total dedication to a 'Living humility' in danger of extinction and 'aesthetic passion'" (Ferrero 1977, 45).

11 See chap. 1, note 44.

12 "Alla fine, deponendo il libro, scoprii che fra il primo brusio e le ultime campane che salutavano la partenza del Papa Pellegrino, avevo letto intero quel duro ma anche tenero, così ebraico e iracondo testo che è appunto quello di Matteo.

L'idea di un film sui Vangeli m'era venuta anche altre volte, ma quel film nacque lì, quel giorno, in quelle ore. E mi resi conto che, oltre alla doppia suggestione, – della lettura e della colonna sonora, di quelle voci e quelle campane, – già c'era nella mia testa anche un vero nucleo e abbozzo di sceneggiatura. L'unico dunque al quale potevo dedicare quel film non poteva essere che lui, Papa Giovanni. E a quella cara 'ombra' l'ho dedicato. L'ombra, che è la regale povertà della fede, non il suo contrario." *Stampa Sera*, Turin, 13 November 1964.

13 "Pensavo a quel dolcissimo Papa contadino che aveva aperto i cuori a una speranza che sembrava allora sempre più difficile, e al quale si erano aperte anche le porte di Regina Coeli, dove era andato a 'guardare negli occhi' ladri e assassini, armato solo di un'immensa ed arguta pietà."

14 "Appena finita la lettura del *Vangelo secondo Matteo* (un giorno di questo ottobre, ad Assisi, con intorno attutita, estranea, e, in fondo, ostile, la festa per l'arrivo del Papa), ho sentito subito il bisogno di 'fare qualcosa': una energia terribile, quasi fisica, quasi manuale. Era l''aumento di vitalità' di cui parlava Berenson ... – l'aumento di vitalità che si concreta generalmente in uno sforzo di comprensione critica dell'opera, in una sua esegesi: in un lavoro, insomma, che la illustri, e trasformi il primo impeto pregrammaticale d'entusiasmo o commozione in un contributo logico, storico. Cosa potevo fare io per il san Matteo? Eppure qualcosa dovevo fare, non era possible restare inerti, inefficienti, dopo una simile emozione, che, così esteticamente profonda, poche volte mi aveva investito nella vita. Ho detto 'emozione estetica.' E sinceramente, perché sotto questo aspetto si è presentato, prepotente, visionario, l'aumento della vitalità." "Una carica di vitalità" ("A charge of vitality"), in *Appendice a "Il Vangelo secondo Matteo," PPC1*, 671–4, 1963.

15 "Vede Don Andrea, la parola spirituale ha per noi due un significato un po' diverso. Quando lei dice spirituale intende soprattutto dire religioso, intimo e religioso. Per me spirituale corrisponde a estetico. Ora, quando io venendo qui ho avuto una delusione pratica, questo non ha nessuna importanza. Però a questa delusione pratica corrisponde invece una profonda rivelazione estetica ..., la mia idea che le cose, quanto più sono piccole e umili, tanto più sono profonde e belle ... Questa cosa è ancora più vera di quanto immaginassi. Quindi, l'idea di questi quattro clivi spelacchiati della predicazione è diventata un'idea estetica, e perciò spirituale." In "Appendice a *Il Vangelo secondo Matteo.*"

16 "A coloro che aspettavano con speranza, cioè ai preti e ai miei amici di Assisi, e a quelli che mi hanno aiutato nelle ricerche filologiche e storiche, rispondo che una caduta da cavallo, come loro speravano, sulla via di Damasco, non si è avuta, per il semplice fatto che io disarcionato da cavallo è da un bel pezzo che ormai lo sono, e trascinato, legato alla staffa, sbattendo la testa sulla polvere, sui sassi e sul fango della strada di Damasco! Quindi non è successo niente: non sono caduto perché ero già caduto e trascinato da questo cavallo, diciamo, della razionalità, della vita del mondo." "Una discussione del '64" ("A discussion of 1964"), 1964.

17 "La mia lettura del Vangelo non poteva essere che la lettura di un marxista, ma contemporaneamente serpeggiava in me il fascino dell'irrazionale, del

divino, che domina tutto il Vangelo. Io come marxista non posso spiegarlo e non può spiegarlo nemmeno il marxismo. Fino a un certo punto della coscienza, anzi in tutta coscienza, è un'opera marxista: non potevo girare delle scene senza che ci fosse un momento di sincerità, intesa come attualità. Infatti, i soldati di Erode come potevo farli? Potevo farli con i baffoni, i denti digrignanti, come i cori dell'opera? No, non li potevo fare così. Li ho vestiti un po' da fascisti e li ho immaginati come delle squadracce fasciste o come i fascisti che uccidevano i bambini slavi buttandoli in aria. La fuga di Giuseppe e di Maria verso l'Egitto come l'ho pensata? L'ho pensata ricordandomi certe fughe, certi sfollamenti di profughi spagnoli attraverso i Pirenei." *Incontro con Pier Paolo Pasolini,* radio broadcast, Radiotelevisione della Svizzera italiana, 5 February 1964.

18 "'Cristo mi chiama, MA SENZA LUCE.' Questi due versi potrebbero essere un'epigrafe che potrei mettere anche oggi al mio *Vangelo.*" Pasolini, "Una discussione del '64" ("A discussion of 1964"), *SPS,* 750, 1964.

19 "La sineciosi è un modo per risalire ancora una volta ad una parola primigenia, parola che contiene la compresenza degli opposti e non può trovare mai fissazione grafica, fin quasi all'autodistruzione." Bazzocchi, "Pasolini e la parola," no. 1.

20 "Il segno sotto cui io lavoro è sempre la contaminazione. Infatti se voi leggete una pagina dei miei libri noterete che la contaminazione è il fatto stilistico dominante, perché io, che provengo da un mondo borghese e non soltanto borghese ma, almeno in gioventù, dalle sedi più raffinate di quel mondo, io lettore degli scrittori decadenti più raffinati eccetera, eccetera, sono arrivato a questo mio mondo. Conseguentemente il *pastiche,* per forza, doveva nascere. E infatti in una pagina dei miei romanzi sono almeno tre i piani in cui mi muovo: cioè il discorso diretto dei personaggi che parlano in dialetto, in gergo, nel gergo più volgare, più fisico, direi; poi il discorso libero indiretto, cioè il monologo interiore dei miei personaggi e infine la parte narrativa o didascalica che è quella mia. Ora questi tre piani linguistici non possono vivere ognuno nella sua sfera senza incontrarsi: devono continuamente intersecarsi e confondersi. Infatti nelle battute dei personaggi, anche in quelle che sembrano le più fisicamente e brutalmente registrate, c'è sempre un *cursus,* un numero spesso, addirittura in endecasillabi, composti anche con delle parolacce. E' quindi la mia educazione di borghese che si inserisce nel discorso fino a trasformare in endecasillabi delle battute fisicamente registrate del mondo reale. Nel discorso libero indiretto poi la contaminazione avviene in maniera chiara, cioè il dialetto, il gergo si contaminano con la lingua parlata. Questa contaminazione avviene anche a livello più alto cioè a livello della parte descrittiva e narrativa." "Una visione

del mondo epico-religiosa" ("An Epic-Religious Vision of the World"), *Bianco e nero,* no. 6, June 1964.

21 "Il *Vangelo* mi poneva il seguente problema: non potevo raccontarlo come una narrazione classica, perché non sono credente, ma ateo. D'altra parte, volevo però filmare il Vangelo secondo Matteo, cioè raccontare la storia di Cristo figlio di Dio. Dovevo dunque narrare un racconto cui non credevo. Non potevo dunque essere io a narrarlo. Così senza volerlo di proposito, sono stato portato a ribaltare tutta la mia tecnica cinematografica e ne è nato questo *magma stilistico* che è proprio del 'cinema di poesia. Perchè, per poter narrare il *Vangelo* ho dovuto immergermi nell'anima di un credente. In questo consiste il discorso indiretto libero: da una parte il racconto è visto attraverso i miei occhi, dall'altra è visto attraverso gli occhi di un credente. Ed è l'uso di questo discorso libero indiretto a causare la contaminazione stilistica, il magma in questione." "Il cinema secondo Pasolini," interview in *Cahiers de Cinema,* no. 169, August 1965, reprinted in *PPC2,* 2890–2907.

22 "C'è un rapporto scandaloso fra me e quest'uomo del popolo che pensa a Cristo. Da parte mia, c'è un atto e uno sforzo di comprensione che non hanno niente di razionalistico, e derivano dagli elementi irrazionali che mi abitano, forse da uno stato latente di religione in me: ma ho vissuto in osmosi con quest'uomo del popolo che crede. Le due nature si erano fuse." "Il cinema secondo Pasolini."

23 "Il *Vangelo* è stato per me una cosa così spaventosa da fare che, mentre la facevo, mi ci aggrappavo e non pensavo a niente. La riflessione è venuta dopo. A dire il vero, il principio della contaminazione, del magma stilistico, del discorso libero indiretto, tutto questo è sopravvenuto senza che io me ne accorgessi." "Il cinema secondo Pasolini."

24 "Una fantasia simile a questa l'ebbi alcuni anni più tardi, ma prima della pubertà. Mi sorgeva, credo, vedendo o immaginando, un'effige di Cristo crocefisso. Quel corpo nudo coperto appena da una strana benda ai fianchi (che io supponevo una discreta convenzione) mi suscitava pensieri non apertamente illeciti, e per quanto spesse volte guardassi quella fascia di seta come a un velame disteso su un inquietante abisso (era l'assoluta gratuità dell'infanzia) tuttavia volgevo subito quei miei sentimenti alla pietà e alla preghiera. Poi nelle mie fantasie affiorava espressamente il desiderio di imitare Gesù nel suo sacrificio per gli altri uomini di essere condannato e ucciso benché affatto innocente. Mi vidi appeso alla croce, inchiodato. I miei fianchi erano succintamente avvolti da quel lembo leggero e un'immensa folla mi guardava. Quel mio pubblico martirio finì col divenire un'immagine voluttuosa e un po' alla volta fui inchiodato col corpo

interamente nudo. Alto, sopra il capo dei presenti, compresi di venerazione, con gli occhi fissi su di me – io mi sentivo [*spazio bianco*] di fronte a un cielo turchino e immenso. Con le braccia aperte, con le mani e i piedi inchiodati, io ero perfettamente indifeso, perduto … Qualche volta [*illeggibile*] stretto con le braccia distese a un cancello o ad un albero, per imitare il Crocefisso; ma non resistevo alla troppo sconvolgente audacia di quella posizione."

25 See poems such as "La Passione," "La Chiesa," "Lettera ai Corinti," and especially "Crocifissione," to which Michael Hardt (2002) devoted an essay in which he explores Pasolini's immanent religiosity.

26 "Ma, ripeto, questo era l'aspetto esterno, stupendamente visuale, dell'aumento di vitalità. Nel fondo c'era qualcosa di più violento ancora, che mi scuoteva.

Era la figura del Cristo come lo vede Matteo. E qui col mio vocabolario estetico-giornalistico dovrei fermarmi. Vorrei però soltanto aggiungere che nulla mi pare più contrario al mondo moderno di quella figura: di quel Cristo mite nel cuore, ma 'mai' nella ragione, che non desiste un attimo dalla propria terribile libertà come volontà di verifica continua della propria religione, come disprezzo continuo per la contraddizione e per lo scandalo. Seguendo le 'accelerazioni stilistiche' di Matteo alla lettera, la funzionalità barbarico-pratica del suo racconto, l'abolizione dei tempi cronologici, i salti ellittici della storia con dentro le 'sproporzioni' delle stasi didascaliche (lo stupendo, interminabile discorso della montagna), la figura di Cristo dovrebbe avere alla fine la stessa violenza di una resistenza: qualcosa che contraddica radicalmente la vita come si sta configurando all'uomo moderno, la sua grigia orgia di cinismo, ironia, brutalità pratica, compromesso, conformismo, glorificazione della propria identità nei connotati della massa, odio per ogni diversità, rancore teologico senza religione." "Una carica di vitalità," in "Appendice a *Il Vangelo secondo Matteo,*" 1963.

27 "'*Non sono venuto a portare la pace ma la spada.*' La chiave in cui ho fatto il film è questa, è questo che mi ha spinto a farlo." "Una discussione del '64" ("A discussion of 1964"), 1964.

28 "Il Cristo di Matteo non parla con dolcezza. Non ha un carattere dolce. La dolcezza è una tipica caratteristica della borghesia e, nel testo di Matteo, davvero questa dolcezza non traspare. La prima impressione che ho avuto – molto forte – è stata l'assoluta e continua tensione del Cristo di Matteo. Se questa tensione fosse venuta a mancare non sarebbe più stato Dio, ma un uomo senza alcun aspetto divino. Attenuare la tensione sarebbe stato come negare il Cristo." Souchon 1965.

29 "In parole molto semplici e povere: io non credo che Cristo sia figlio di Dio, perché non sono credente – almeno nella coscienza. Ma credo che Cristo

sia divino: credo cioè che in lui l'umanità sia così alta, rigorosa, ideale da andare al di là dei comuni termini dell'umanità. Per questo dico 'poesia': strumento irrazionale per esprimere questo mio sentimento irrazionale per Cristo ... Vorrei che le mie esigenze espressive, la mia ispirazione poetica, non contraddicessero mai la vostra sensibilità di credenti. Perché altrimenti non raggiungerei il mio scopo di riproporre a tutti una vita che è modello – sia pure irraggiungibile – per tutti."

30 "Spinta da una tale forza interiore, da una tale irriducibile sete di sapere e di verificare il sapere, senza timore per nessuno scandalo e nessuna contraddizione, che per essa la metafora 'divina' è ai limiti della metaforicità, fino a essere idealmente una realtà." From a letter of June 1963 to Alfredo Bini, the film producer.

31 "Il solo caso di 'bellezza morale' non mediata, ma immediata, allo stato puro, io l'ho sperimentata nel Vangelo."

32 "Frutto di una furiosa ondata irrazionalistica. Voglio fare pura opera di poesia."

33 "Pericoli dell'esteticità (Bach e in parte Mozart, come commento musicale; Piero della Francesca e in parte Duccio per l'ispirazione figurativa; la realtà in fondo preistorica ed esotica, del mondo arabo, come fondo e ambiente)."

34 "Nella fede, nel mito, nella mitologia altrui ..." From a colloquium of March 1964 with the students of the Centro Sperimentale di Cinematografia, published in *Bianco e nero*, no. 6, June 1964.

35 "Ora, questo film può essere veramente nella linea 'nazional-popolare' di cui parlava Gramsci. Ci sono cose raffinate, nei costumi, nella musica, nei paesaggi, ci sono elementi cosiddetti 'squisiti' e forse 'decadentistici', nel senso consueto del termine, con grandi afflati di carattere nazional-popolare. E' un racconto con un fondo favoloso da un lato, ideologico dall'altro, che non ricerca la fedeltà storica, la fedeltà filologica, la ricostruzione, il mondo nazionale ebraico del tempo ... Il San Matteo che ho in mente di fare è un pochino l'esaltazione, ad altro livello, degli elementi che già erano in *Accattone*, in *Mamma Roma* e nella *Ricotta* ... cioè la liberazione dell'ispirazione religiosa, in un marxista ... Il *San Matteo* dovrebbe essere secondo me un violento richiamo alla borghesia stupidamente lanciata verso un futuro che è la distruzione dell'uomo, degli elementi antropologicamente umani, classici e religiosi dell'uomo ... Non ho aggiunto una battuta e non ne ho tolto nessuna, seguo l'ordine del racconto tale e quale come in S. Matteo, con dei tagli narrativi di una violenza e di una epicità quasi magiche presenti nel testo stesso del Vangelo."

36 "Un Cristo frontale, ripreso col 50 o il 75, accompagnato da brevi e intense panoramiche diventava pura enfasi: una riproduzione." Pasolini, "Confessioni tecniche" ("Technical Confessions"), 1966–67.

37 "Ogni frontalità era così sconvolta, ogni ordine, ogni simmetria: irrompevano il magmatico, il casuale, l'asimmetrico: le facce non potevano più essere viste di fronte e al centro dell'inquadratura, ma si presentavano così come capitava, in tutti gli scorci possibili e sempre eccentriche nel fotogramma."

38 "Meno religiosa e più epica, meno ieratica e più moderna, meno romanica e più impressionistica-espressionistica."

39 "Punte magmatiche, espressionistiche, casuali, arbitrarie, asimmetriche, tutte le ... libertà di montaggio, tutte le ... irregolarità: addirittura le citazioni da Dreyer e Ėjzenštejn o i ricordi da Mizoguchi."

40 "L'evocazione ora stranamente prevale sulla rappresentazione. Il caos ha ritrovato una imprevista pacificazione tecnica e stilistica."

41 : "Ho cercato lo scandalo che sempre dà la poesia, attraverso lo scandalo che può dare la sincerità: e invece, ripeto, è chiaro, attraverso il risultato unitario, che non è espressionistico e magmatico, ma a suo modo estremamente ordinato e regolare, mi servivo dello scandalo espressivo per cercare la poesia."

42 "TOTALE con le tre croci, contro il cielo notturno.

PAN. Ai piedi della solita piccola folla: Giovanni, le Marie, Giuseppe di Arimatea, dolenti, atterriti, e muti.

P.P. dei tre crocefissi, che soffrono gli spasimi della morte. (mai crocifissione avrà dato l'insopportabile fisicità del dolore, come questa cinematografica: un naturalismo terribile, da renderne quasi intollerabile la vista.)

...

P.P. di un ladrone che soffre dolori inenarrabili, perduto in essi, senza più voce o sguardo ... P.P. dell'altro ladrone, che soffrendo il soffribile, ha ancora la forza di odiare, e insulta il Cristo:

LADRONE (*insulti?*)

P.P. di Cristo, preso da un dolore fisico la cui vista è intollerabile."

Chapter Three

1 This collection was published a long time before the recent complete publication of the *Bestemmia* screenplay in the author's *opera omnia*, in the second volume of *Tutte le poesie* edited by Walter Siti in 2003 for the *I Meridiani* series by the publisher Mondadori.

2 Greene quotes in translation from Pasolini's letters (1986, *Lettere 1940–1954*, xxiv–xxv): "La cucina era il teatro delle mie sfrenate avventure, mi vedeva chino su quel foglio, assillato semplicemente dal puro problema del rapporto tra il reale e il finto. A me allora si proponeva il fatto della rappresentazione come qualcosa di terribile e primordiale, appunto perché in uno stato di purezza: l'equivalente doveva essere definitivo. Davanti al problema di riprodurre un prato ammattivo. La questione per me era questa: occorre che io disegni tutti i fili d'erba? Non sapevo allora che riempiendo col pastello verde un'intera zona avrei ottenuto la *massa* del prato e che questa sarebbe stata una scusa sufficiente per lasciare negletti i fili d'erba. Tali ipocrisie erano ancora ben lontane da me, ed era con una vera sofferenza che mi sottomettevo a colorire una campitura verde che doveva essere il prato su cui Dio soffiò la vita in Adamo."

3 "Alle origini di un'educazione, fonte di passioni,
non avrei resistito a immaginare
il Cristo d'una visione,
in *qualche stile*,
imponendolo
con la faziosità dei giovani ...
La mia cristologia, ora, più che imberbe
è barbarica; vuol esserlo; teme di fallire
se non suscita un'idea di Cristo
anteriore a ogni stile, a ogni corso della storia,
a ogni fissazione, a ogni sviluppo; vergine;
riprodotta dalla realtà con la realtà
senza un solo ricordo di poemi e pitture;
coi mezzi della realtà che rappresenta sé stessa.
Voglio non solo non conoscere Masaccio,
(il Masaccio di Longhi,
che a lungo ha dominato i miei occhi, il mio cuore,
il mio sesso) ma non voglio
neanche
conoscere la lingua o la pittura.
Voglio che quel Cristo si presenti come realtà.
Non è forse una buona ragione
perché questo sia un film, non un poema?
Nel film ch'io penso, e a cui ti faccio pensare,
lettore,
sono un mago rozzo,

non voglio aver più bisogno dei filtri
evocativi della lingua;
la lingua è uno strumento grossolano, concerto
puerile di campanelli, che il poeta suona
per evocare stregandola la realtà.
Ma è solo quella realtà, che, una volta evocata, *conta*!
Essa è la sola cosa bella e veramente amata!
Quante parole, strumento e stile,
per evocare un'immagine reale di Cristo sulla croce!
Ma io, con un uomo in carne e ossa,
con una vera croce di legno,
con chiodi veri,
e, vorrei, con sangue vero e dolore,
riproduco la realtà con la realtà.
La realtà nuova *assomiglia*,
assomiglia soltanto, alla vera realtà evocata;
ma è a sua volta una realtà.
Il povero mimo di Cristo in carne e ossa
– pagato pochi soldi –
è una realtà come quella fisica del Cristo vero.
Non esco, evocando quella realtà, dal mondo della realtà.
Vivo sempre, non mi distinguo dalla vita, per testimoniarla.
Vivo al di qua del mio bosco di cose apprese e appassite.
Non so scrivere, non so leggere, non so parlare.
La mia grande aspirazione di ragazzo è adempiuta
Sono davanti ai muscoli e alle vene del mio Cristo
che non assomiglia a nessuno di quelli della fantasia
e della storia,
duemila anni di opere sono passati, fortunatamente, invano;
qui ci sono muscoli, vene, legno, la terra dov'è
[conficcata una croce vera,
un respiro presente, un'agonia,
tutte cose che queste mie parole non esprimono,
ma non me ne importa,
perché io qui, in questa sceneggiatura, evoco
[provvisoriamente,
con l'allegria del trionfo,
un Cristo che poi evocherò, nel film, realmente con la
[realtà,

e tu finalmente lo vedrai
vero, fisicamente vero
che ti parla col linguaggio di sé stesso,
anteriore a ogni altro parlare:
con le parole della Carne.
Così Bestemmia vide Cristo – e per forza!
Lo vide com'era lui: un corpo;
non c'è fisica differenza tra Bestemmia e ciò che vede.
Si tratta soltanto di voltare la macchina da presa.
...
Completamente innocente,
come un cane,
come me."

4 "Nessuno, di quel Cristo *che vedeva,* aveva mai scritto,
nessuno l'aveva mai dipinto.
Bestemmia dunque se lo vide davanti come un altro.
Aveva la sua stessa natura, e, tacendo, parlava con lui.
Era prossimo suo; figlio d'un'altra madre; ancora giovane;
ma cosa diceva il linguaggio della sua Carne?
Che moriva.
Lo dicevano gli occhi rovesciati,
le guancie tese e grige di mummia,
i capelli corti di un sudore denso come pus,
il piccolo torace d'uomo sapiente squarciato
con le labbra della ferita orlate di marciume,
le braccia disperatamente tese,
e tutto il corpo tirato giù dal suo peso
come una vittima nuda sul trogolo,
le gambe bagnate di orina
gocciolata giù come alle bestie,
fino sui piedi, a mescolarsi col sangue,
le feci incollate alle coscie e puzzolenti,
le nuove sopra le vecchie, già secche,
perdute dal povero ano senza più volontà."

The brackets indicate that this passage was omitted in the version published by Walter Siti; they indicate an addition to the original text, added by hand to the typescript.

5 "Emerge qui l'identificazione tra il corpo del povero, innocente, ignorante e 'barbarico' santo, con il corpo di Cristo, la cui natura non appare 'indiata'

con l'attribuzione di un carattere trascendente, come in una teologia cristologica. Anzi si direbbe, al contrario, che ci sia una decisiva soppressione del dualismo tra mondo della trascendenza e mondo della realtà. Il Cristo di Pasolini è un uomo che muore secondo una cristologia che si presenta con caratteri fortemente eretici, radicalmente kenotici"; "L'insegnamento che ne deriva è quello di un'eresia cristiana che, propagata e come 'divulgata' in un'epoca desacralizzata, risulta ancor più inquietante e irriducibile, perché detentrice di un sapere antico privo di speranza o di 'fede' ma carico di amore per la vita. Nell'ambito di questa sua religione immanente Pasolini è un cristiano della passione-redenzione più che della passione-resurrezione. 'Una disperata vitalità' lo porta a patire, cioè a riconoscere e a essere riconoscente alla donazione originaria del sacro, la vita che reca sempre nuova vita."

6 Cf. Pasolini, "La lingua scritta della realtà" ("The Written Language of Reality"), *EE, SLA1,* 1503–40.

7 Deleuze 1984, 57.

8 Guattari 2003, 98.

9 "Les gens, écrit Guattari, sont d'abord pris dans un système sémiotique signifiant" qui rend inefficace, précise-t-il, toute entreprise de changement dans l'ordre social, comme de création dans le domaine de l'art. Ces significations contraignantes ... jettent une voile sur la pensée et l'action[:] "...le peintre n'a pas à remplir une surface blanche, il aurait plutôt à vider, désencombrer, débarasser." Dès qu'il est lié à la signification, le désir est bloqué dans son élan.

Les "images significatives" font écran aux ruptures décisives, aux désirs vrais. Il ya un prealable à toute lutte, à toute oeuvre, qui est d'écarter ou de briser le "système d'anti-production"; et celui-ci est d'ordre sémiotique avant tout ... Afin de le condenser en un mot – deux mots plus exactement – ce préalable est le passage, le saut du système signifiant au système d'expression qui est également un système d'expérimentation ... "Le problème, résume Félix Guattari, est de distinguer radicalement une politique de la signification d'une politique de ce que je n'appellerai pas d'information, mais d'expression."

10 "De l'image cinématographique à la realité se passe quelque chose comme une impression, une empreinte, una émanation de nature quasi-physique, ainsi qu'à propos de la photographie l'expose Roland Barthes (un des auteurs affectionnés de Pasolini) dans *La Chambre claire.*

Empreinte ou émanation? En tout cas, immanence certaine de la réalité a ce language, cette langue plutôt, pour la distinguer, comme une expression choise, extraite et composée à partir d'une réalité qui n'a d'autre langage au fond qu'elle-même, qui est celui de sa propre présence à elle-même, tout au cours du 'plan-séquence' continu qu'elle constitue."

11 Ellipsis in original.

12 "Così Bestemmia vide Cristo – e per forza!
Lo vide com'era lui: un corpo;
non c'è fisica differenza tra Bestemmia e ciò che vede.
Si tratta soltanto di voltare la macchina da presa.
... Completamente innocente,
come un cane,
come me.
Vide Cristo nella sua natura.
Un corpo inchiodato ecc... . Quasi che nessuno mai ne avesse parlato,
nessuno mai l'avesse dipinto,
realtà che si ripresentava come realtà nella visione.
Lo riconobbe – un amico, un uomo, sé stesso;
fu perciò che sentì il suo dolore,
e fece quasi per buttarsi su di lui, per aiutarlo,
per salvarlo
come un vivente qualunque,
ferito, o caduto,
come quando l'istinto dice di soccorrere un martire
sconosciuto, che brucia nella sua casa,
o sanguina infilzato dalle lamiere del suo camion;
quell'immagine,
quell'inquadratura
che riproduceva, vivente, fisicamente vivente
un corpo fraterno coperto di sangue
e aveva la stessa natura della natura di Bestemmia,
realtà riprodotte ambedue,
disse col suo solo "essere lì" a Bestemmia
tutto ciò che interi poemi non possono dire.
E Bestemmia altro non seppe se non che "era lì":
ma questo aveva un senso immenso,
aspettava di svolgersi
con una raggiante impazienza...
Era lì, dunque, che fare?
Era lì, che dire?
Era lì: cos'era stata la vita?
Tutto cambiava senso sotto quella luna di sasso,

e sei puttane e un maschietto sporco ancora di sperma
Io non voglio però snaturare Bestemmia.
A ragione la religione non prende sul serio la poesia!
E io peccherei contro la mia teoria stessa
se non vedessi Bestemmia come oggetto che parla
anche senza parlare,
con là sua semplice presenza,
con la sua semplice azione,
con il suo semplice esserci.
Egli è oggetto!
Io non lo creo, ma ho con lui un dialogo,
un vero dialogo,
come con quel ciuffo d'erba su cui posano i suoi ginocchi,
l'erba delle oche e dei moscerini,
che è lei a parlarmi,
a dirmi quello che è:
e se ho un colloquio, come tra pari, con l'erba,
dovrò pure averlo anche con Bestemmia!
– e lo sarò nel film!
– ora non stendo che un progetto.
Ma tu, lettore, collabora con me,
guarda le cose, come presenti, immagini, suoni,
che parlano di sé."

13 "Ricondurre i fatti di cultura a fenomeni di natura." *EE, SLA1,* 1615.
14 "*Portare la Semiologia alla definitiva culturalizzazione della natura.*" *EE, SLA1,* 1615.
15 *EE, SLA1,* 1615 (1967).
16 "I capelli di Jerry Malanga e gli occhi di Umberto Eco appartengono dunque allo stesso Corpo, la fisicità del Reale, dell'Esistente, dell'Essere; e se i capelli di Jerry Malanga sono un oggetto che si 'autorivela' come 'segno di se stesso' agli occhi ricettori di Umberto Eco, non si può dire che si tratti di un dialogo, ma di un monologo che il Corpo infinito della Realtà fa con se stesso." *EE, SLA1,* 1615. Jerry (Gerrard) Malanga is an American poet, filmmaker, artist, and curator who collaborated with Andy Warhol.
17 " L'ho già scritto e riscritto. La realtà non fa altro che parlare con se stessa usando come veicolo l'esperienza umana. Dio, come dicono tutte le religioni, ha creato l'uomo per parlare con Se stesso ..." *EE, SLA1,* 1571. Cf. Pasolini, "I segni viventi e i poeti morti" ("Living signs and dead poets"), *EE, SLA1,* 1574 (1967)

18 "Così succede a chi studia il cinema: siccome il cinema riproduce la realtà, finisce col ricondurre allo studio della realtà. Ma in un modo nuovo e speciale, come se la realtà fosse stata scoperta attraverso la sua riproduzione, e certi suoi meccanismi fossero saltati fuori solo in questa nuova situazione "riflessa."

Il cinema, infatti, riproducendo la realtà, ne evidenzia la sua espressività, che ci poteva essere sfuggita. Ne fa, insomma, una semiologia naturale." Pasolini, "Battute sul cinema" ("Quips on the cinema"), *EE, SLA1*, 1548 [1966–67]).

19 "*Suggerire eideticamente,* attraverso la violenza fisica della sua riproduzione della realtà." Pasolini, "Battute sul cinema," *EE, SLA1*, 1553.

20 Translation emended.

21 "C'è al mondo (!) una macchina che non per nulla si chiama da presa. / Essa è il 'Mangiarealtà,' o l' 'Occhio-Bocca,' come volete. / Non si limita a guardare Joaquim con suo padre e sua madre nella Favela. / Lo guarda e lo riproduce. / Lo parla per mezzo di lui stesso e dei suoi genitori. / Nella riproduzione – su schermetti o schermi – / io lo decifro ... / come nella realtà. / ... Egli sullo schermo o schermetto da laboratorio è linguaggio. / ... Dunque il linguaggio del 'Mangiarealtà' è un linguaggio fratello / a quello della Realtà. / Illusione, sì, illusione, qui e là: ché / chi parla attraverso quel linguaggio è un Essere che c'è e non ama." Pasolini, *Res Sunt Nomina, EE, SLA1*, 1584–5 (1971).

22 "L'ipotetico piano-sequenza puro mette in vista dunque, rappresentandola, l'insignificanza della vita in quanto vita. Ma attraverso questo ipotetico piano-sequenza puro, vengo anche a sapere – con la stessa precisione delle prove da laboratorio – che la proposizione fondamentale che qualcosa di insignificante esprime è: 'Io sono,' oppure 'C'è,' oppure semplicemente 'Essere.'"

Ma essere è naturale? No, a me non sembra, anzi, a me sembra che sia portentoso, misterioso e, semmai, assolutamente innaturale." Cf. Pasolini, "Essere è naturale?" ("Being is natural?"), *EE, SLA1*, 1565 (1967).

23 "Ad allargare talmente l'orizzonte della semiologia e della linguistica da perdere la testa al solo pensiero." Pasolini, "La lingua scritta della realtà" (The written language of reality), *EE, SLA1*, 1513 (1966).

24 Translation amended.

25 "In realtà noi il cinema lo facciamo vivendo, cioè esistendo praticamente, cioè agendo. *L'intera vita, nel complesso delle sue azioni, è un cinema naturale e vivente: in ciò è linguisticamente l'equivalente della lingua orale nel suo momento naturale e biologico.*

Vivendo, dunque, noi ci rappresentiamo, e assistiamo alla rappresentazione altrui. La realtà del mondo umano non è che questa rappresentazione doppia, in cui siamo attori e insieme spettatori: un gigantesco *happening*, se vogliamo." *EE, SLA1*, 1514.

26 Translation amended.

27 Translation amended.

28 Cf. Pasolini, "Il cinema di poesia" ("The cinema of poetry"), *EE, SLA1*, 1463–4 (1965): "La comunicazione visiva che è alla base del linguaggio cinematografico è, al contrario, estremamente rozza, quasi animale. Tanto la mimica e la realtà bruta quanto i sogni e i meccanismi della memoria sono fatti quasi pre-umani, o ai limiti dell'umano: comunque pregrammaticali e addirittura premorfologici ... *Lo strumento linguistico su cui si impianta il cinema è dunque di tipo irrazionalistico*: e questo spiega la profonda qualità onirica del cinema, e anche la sua assoluta e imprescindibile concretezza, diciamo, oggettuale."

29 Green is commenting on Deleuze 1985, 224–5.

30 Translation amended.

31 Cf. Pasolini, "Il cinema di poesia," *EE, SLA1*, 1467–8 (1965): "Il cinema è fondamentalmente onirico per la elementarità dei suoi archetipi (che rielenchiamo: osservazione abituale e quindi inconscia dell'ambiente, mimica, memoria, sogni) e per la fondamentale prevalenza della pregrammaticalità degli oggetti in quanto simboli del linguaggio visivo" (*EE, SLA1*, 1467).

"Perciò per ora il cinema è un linguaggio artistico non filosofico. Può essere parabola, mai espressione concettuale diretta. Ecco dunque un terzo modo di affermare la prevalente artisticità del cinema, la sua violenza espressiva, la sua fisicità onirica" (*EE, SLA1*, 1468).

32 "Come altro parlano i testimoni di Dio se non con l'esempio?
Le parole che io ora dico,
non sono che una parte, l'ultima, dell'esempio
che io testimone di Dio, vi dò con la mia azione,
ossia con la mia vita.
Non gettate il vostro spirito nella lotta!
Gettate il vostro corpo nella lotta!
È con esso che parla il vostro spirito, quello che voi siete.
Quanto ha parlato Cristo!
Eppure niente ha parlato più del suo corpo
inchiodato sulla croce in silenzio.
Non usate parole, non usate immagini,
non usate simboli.
Siate ciò che siete!

Non passate attraverso nessun simbolo!
Siate sempre ciò che siete.
Stracciate con le mani, calpestate sotto i piedi
ogni simbolo: gettate via le croci.
Fate che Cristo parli con sé stesso,
non con le sue parole, non con le parole su di lui.
E dov'è Cristo, è dentro di noi.
...
Ma a differenza della ricchezza che senza l'oro *non è*
Cristo *è* senza l'oro delle parole
Cristo *è*, nella realtà.
Perché dunque non stiamo solo con lui?
Perché usiamo dei simboli di scambio?
Che me ne faccio, io del Cristo
che tu mi vendi con la tua parola o la tua immagine,
ossia coi tuoi simboli
che sono la necessità della vita
e quindi la sua alterazione,
la perdita accettata della sua realtà?
La vita è la sede dell'irrealtà,
eppure io vi dico che c'è solo la vita;
poichè vivere significa vivere soltanto,
e la realtà significa soltanto realtà,
e la vita si vive con sé stessae la realtà si rappresenta con la realtà.
...
Ma voi non ascoltate le mie parole,
seguite il mio esempio!
E ognuno di voi vivrà in Cristo
Non nelle sue parole."

33 "Laudato sie, mi' Signore, co' tutte le tu' creature, / speciarmente fratemo lu sole, / lo quale è giorno, e c'allumini co' llui, / e lui è bellu, e radiante, co' grande splendore: / porta er segno tuo."

34 "Bisogna probabilmente interpretare il nome di "Bestemmia" come una metafora alla quale l'autore ricorre nell'intenzione di postulare una concezione eretica di Cristo negata dalla Chiesa ufficiale, ma corrispondente a quella visione mitico-cosmogonica del redentore compresa e assimilata dalle civiltà arcaico-contadine ... Il ricorso alla bestemmia offre allora la possibilità di affermare che il corpo umano, nella sua integralità, è sacro esattamente quanto quello della divinità cosmogonica a cui viene riferito

nell'invocarla. Sacralità del corpo e del cosmo finiscono per coincidere, in un'unità posta sotto il segno della blasfemia attraverso cui è possibile recuperare una mitica identità antropocosmica. Con il degradare dio ad animale e nel contempo elevando l'animale a dio (cosa che avviene con la bestemmia) l'uomo riconosce di trovarsi in un rapporto di continuità con il cosmo (quale è quella a cui allude la condizione dell'animale), partecipe di una religione immanente che comporta di conseguenza un atteggiamento di perenne consacrazione."

35 "Dunque l'unico linguaggio che potrebbe essere definito LINGUAGGIO e basta è quello della realtà naturale. E quello della realtà umana, nel momento in cui non è semplicemente naturale, ma storica? Cioè: mentre un pioppo parla un linguaggio puro, io, Pier Paolo Pasolini, parlo (stando zitto, con me, con la mia faccia, con la mia azione distribuita in tutti gli attimi, i giorni, gli anni e i decenni della mia vita) parlo un linguaggio puro? No, evidentemente. Questo linguaggio puro è contaminato anzitutto dal patto sociale, ossia dalla lingua, prima parlata e poi scritta: e poi, da tutti gli infiniti linguaggi non scenici, di cui mi fornisce esperienza la mia anagrafe, il mio censo, la mia educazione – la società e il momento storico in cui vivo.

Una sintesi di tutti questi linguaggi integranti uniti al PURO LINGUAGGIO della mia presenza naturale di vivente (come un pioppo), è il linguaggio della mia realtà umana, che è dunque, soprattutto, un ESEMPIO." Cf. Pasolini, "I segni viventi e i poeti morti" (Living signs and dead poets), *EE*, *SLA1*, 1574–5 (1967).

36 "Ognuno di noi (volendo e non volendo) fa vivendo un'azione morale il cui senso è sospeso.

Da ciò la ragione della morte. Se noi fossimo immortali saremo immorali, perché il nostro esempio non avrebbe mai fine, quindi sarebbe indecifrabile, eternamente sospeso e ambiguo."

"O esprimersi e morire o essere inespressi e immortali, dicevo."

"Ma la mia idea della morte, dunque, era una idea comportamentistica e morale: non guardava al dopo della morte, ma al prima: non all'al di là, ma alla vita. Alla vita intesa dunque come adempimento, come tendenza disperata, incerta e continuamente in cerca di supporti, pretesti e relazioni, verso una sua perfezione espressiva." Cf. Pasolini, *I segni viventi e i poeti morti*, *EE*, *SLA1*, 1574–5 (1967).

37 "*Finché siamo vivi, manchiamo di senso*, e il linguaggio della nostra vita … è intraducibile: un caos di possibilità, una ricerca di relazioni e significati senza soluzione di continuità. *La morte compie un fulmineo montaggio della nostra vita*: ossia sceglie i suoi momenti veramente significativi (e non più ormai modificabili da altri possibili momenti contrari o incoerenti), e li mette

in successione, facendo del nostro presente, infinito, instabile e incerto, e dunque linguisticamente non descrivibile, un passato chiaro, stabile, certo, e dunque linguisticamente ben descrivibile (nell'ambito appunto di una Semiologia Generale). *Solo grazie alla morte, la nostra vita ci serve ad esprimerci.*

Il montaggio opera dunque sul film ... quello che la morte opera sulla vita." Cf. Pasolini, "Osservazioni sul piano sequenza" (Observations on the sequence-shot), *EE, SLA1,* 1560 (1967).

38 Cf. Pasolini, "Il cinema impopolare" (Unpopular cinema"), *EE, SLA1,* 1601 (1970).

39 Pasolini, "Il cinema impopolare," 1600.

40 Cf. Pasolini, "Il cinema impopolare," 1601.

41 "Devo ripetere il ritornello: gli spettatori sono feriti dal regista 'cosciente del suo linguaggio,' e a loro volta feriscono il regista (salvo appunto gli spettatori privilegiati che condividono con lui l'idea che lo scandalo estremistico sia necessario) così che il regista può godere equamente del piacere e del dolore del martirio: testimoniando la propria 'libertà dalla repressione' in quanto ebbrezza suicida, vitalità disfattista, auto-esclusione didascalica, esibizione di piaghe significative. Sono questi exempla, quasi agiografici, luoghi di uno scritto reazionario? No: io stesso provo in moviola(o prima, girando) l'effetto quasi sessuale dell'infrazione al codice, come esibizionismo di qualcosa di violato(sentimento che si prova anche scrivendo versi, ma che il cinema moltiplica all'infinito: una cosa è essere martirizzati in camera e una cosa è essere martirizzati in piazza, in una 'morte spettacolare'). (*EE, SLA1,* 1608)

"Solo la morte dell'eroe è uno spettacolo; e solo essa è utile.

I registi-martiri dunque per autodecisione, si trovano sempre, stilisticamente, sulla linea del fuoco: ossia sul fronte delle trasgressioni linguistiche." (*EE, SLA1,* 1609)

42 "La morte consente di inabissarsi nella donazione sacra che è la riserva del continuare a donare. Solo chi ha passione per la vita può veramente morire, poichè vede nella morte la redenzione: il liberarsi di nuova vita. L'eresia cristiana di Pasolini è tutta qui: un Cristo-Uomo patisce e muore; in questo modo, sacrificandosi, dà consapevolezza agli uomini che il sacro, nel sacrificio, è il donarsi nel sottrarsi, e riconoscerlo significa essere partecipi del mistero che il Redentore morendo svela."

Chapter Four

1 "Cosa intende esattamente per film allegorico?

Un'opera in cui ogni cosa significa un'altra cosa, rinvia a un'altra realtà. In *Teorema,* per esempio, il giovane ospite non è solo un ospite venuto a soggiornare in una famiglia di amici milanesi, è l'allegoria di Dio" (*SC, SPS,* 1495). The translation is mine, as for all quotations from Italian texts unless otherwise noted.

2 The six texts are *Orgia, Bestia da stile, Pilade, Calderon, Affabulazione,* and *Porcile.*

3 "L'amore tra questo visitatore divino e questi personaggi borghesi era più bello se silenzioso." Interview with Lino Peroni (1968), in *PPC2,* 2931–6; originally published in *Inquadrature* 15–16 (Autumn 1968), 33–7.

4 "*Teorema* è nato, come su fondo oro, dipinto con la mano destra, mentre con la mano sinistra lavoravo ad affrescare una grande parete (il film omonimo). In tale natura anfibologica, non so sinceramente quale sia prevalente: se quella letteraria o quella filmica."

5 "Spesso le brevi parabole che compongono sveltamente l'insieme del 'sacro esempio' che è *Teorema* ricordano la varia policromia borghese delle predelle tre-quattrocentesche: scene di momentanea vita sacra o paesana, storie di santi, miracoli, leggende, interni di case signorili, paesaggi, episodi fissati con un gusto del vero, una precisione che dà nel nitido realismo favoloso … *Teorema,* abbiamo detto, è un trattamento, un 'film scritto,' … Tutto è già scritto, come nelle fiabe. C'è un film implicito, in *Teorema,* che non è certo quello che vedremo. Questo film è una storia sacra, un esempio, uno 'specchio' medioevale (il fondo oro), contro il quale si defila la stupida storia delle impotenze borghesi che il poeta ci viene via via raccontando. Con un linguaggio candido e ingenuo, addirittura da narratore devoto, come si addice alla povera storia umana, ma anche lussuoso, come si addice al tema ineffabile, Pasolini spiega, commenta, illustra in tante formelle l'essenza di un miracle play."

6 "Un'ipotesi che si dimostra matematicamente per absurdum. Il quesito è questo: se una famiglia borghese venisse visitata da un giovane dio, fosse Dioniso o Jehova, che cosa succederebbe?"

7 "Un borghese, anche se dona la sua fabbrica, in qualsiasi modo agisce, sbaglia. È così?"

8 "Lei mi può rispondere a queste domande? Lei mi può rispondere a queste domande?"

9 Girard writes: "The object is now more desired than ever. Since the model obstinately bars access to it, the possession of this object must make all the difference between the self-sufficiency of the model and the imitator's lack of sufficiency, the model's fullness of being and the imitator's nothingness.

This process of transfiguration does not correspond to anything real, and yet it transforms the object into something that appears superabundantly real. Thus it could be described as metaphysical in character.

... The 'metaphysical' threshold or, if we put it in a different way, the point at which we reach desire properly speaking, is the threshold of the unreal.

... From this point, desire seeks only to find a resistance that it is incapable of overcoming.

To sum up, victory only speeds up the subject's degeneration. The pursuit of failure becomes ever more expert and knowledgeable, without being able to recognize itself as the pursuit of failure" (1987, 296–7).

10 This formula accompanies several titles of chapters dedicated to the downward trajectory of the family members after the visitor's departure, for example chapters 11 or 13.

11 "La rivelazione più piena corrispondeva alla disperazione più assoluta, allo sgomento di un Dio: ... Se la suprema rivelazione e la suprema creazione consistevano nell'incarnazione del Verbo e nella nostra possibilità di riviverne l'esperienza attraverso l' *imitatio Christi*, allora bisognava prepararsi a rivivere non solo i patimenti, ma anche i disperati smarrimenti del Cristo e quel suo distacco dal fondamento."

David Maria Turoldo was a friar and poet who met Pasolini in Udine, in his convent, Santa Maria delle Grazie. The world of Turoldo and Pasolini is the agrarian, archaic Friuli of Pasolini's youth, and the priest and the parrhesiast would share a friendship and a controversial position in the Italian society of those times. Turoldo read his homily at Pasolini's funeral in Casarsa della Delizia (PN) in 1975, when he invited Susanna Pasolini to return, "meeker and more Christian," to her villages and to abandon a Rome where "there is no flower who will blossom in this periphery, not a breath of air which will scatter its fragrance; not a boy with a pure face; not a priest who prays. And the masses in Saint Peter's Square are of little use, neither they persuade many to believe that this is a holy year and that Rome is the city of God" (http://www.terredimezzo.fvg.it/index.php?id=2829).

12 Cf. Alessia Ricciardi's examination of the process of mourning in Pasolini (in the case of *Teorema*, mourning for the death of God) in the context of the end of mourning characteristic of our postmodern age. According to Ricciardi, "Renouncing both the naturalism of sorrow still prevalent in romanticism and the manic denial of grief maintained by the avant-garde, Pasolini's movies constitutes poetic simulacra and allegorizations of loss that ultimately situate his theory of mourning in the territory of a critical postmodernity" (2003, 154).

13 Cf. Žižek: "Here we encounter the third kind of suicide: the 'suicide' that defines the death drive, *symbolic* suicide – not in the sense of 'not dying really, just symbolically' but in the more precise sense of the erasure of the

symbolic network that defines the subject's identity, of cutting off all the links that anchor the subject in its symbolic substance. Here, the subject find itself completely deprived of its symbolic identity, thrown into the 'night of the world' in which is only correlative is the minimum of excremental leftover, a piece of trash, a mote of dust in the eye, an *almost-nothing* that sustains the pure Place-Frame-Void, so that here, 'nothing but the place takes place'" (2000, 30). According to Lacan and Žižek, Paolo here appears to be in a situation similar to that of Antigone, in a condition of *ate*, suspended between two deaths, "still alive, yet excluded from the symbolic community" (Žižek 2000, 156).

14 "Era venuto, non è ritornato, e non tornerà mai più" (*RR2*, 1085). The quotation is from Arthur Rimbaud, *Les Déserts de l'amour*: "Elle n'est pas revenue, et ne reviendra jamais, l'Adorable qui s'était rendue chez moi." In the screenplay it becomes: "he belonged to his own life, and goodness would take more time to come into being than a star. Without me ever hoping for it, the adorable had come, did not come back, and will never return."

15 "When Dionysus arrived in Thebes, under the guise of a handsome mortal boy, with long hair (so long that, even then, Pentheus wanted to cut it), he had a graceful air, full of fun, of youthful laziness ... Little by little, his truly happy presence, a form of liberation ... is revealed as a frightening presence, a form of destruction. 'Dionysus is a god / the kindest and the most terrible of all gods,' he says of himself.

He has come to Thebes in human form to bring love (but not the sentimental love sanctified by convention!), and instead he brings destruction and carnage. He is the irrationality that *changes*, imperceptibly and in total indifference, from sweetness to horror. In it, there is no solution of continuity between God and the Devil, between good and evil ... Whether as 'benign' or 'accursed' apparition, a society based on reason and common sense – which are the opposite of Dionysus, who is irrationality – cannot understand him. But it is exactly its inability to understand irrationality that *irrationally* leads society to its ruin (to the greatest carnage ever described in a work of art)." Cf. Pasolini's "Lettera aperta a Silvana Mangano" ("Open Letter to Silvana Mangano"), from *Il Caos* (1968), *DIAL*, *SPS*, 1142–3.

Pasolini is aware of the power of irrationality, embodied by the emblematic figure of Dionysus, "the kindest and most terrible of all gods," and underlines how denying this power, erasing it from society's horizon of understanding, can provoke the destruction of society itself. Pasolini's words are not far from those of the theorist René Girard about the Dionysiac "sacrificial crisis" in Euripides' play:

The Bacchae begins as a ritual bacchanal. The poet underlines the destruction of distinctions as the god sweeps away all the barriers that usually divide mortals: wealth, age, sex, and so on. Everyone is called on to worship Dionysus; the chorus proclaims that graybeards will now mingle with youth, women will be on a par with men.

The bacchanal portrayed by Euripides involves the women of Thebes. Having established his worship in Asia, Dionysus arrives in his native city in the guise of a young disciple of his own cult who exerts a potent influence over almost everyone who encounters him. Euripides' bacchanal is that of the women of Thebes. After introducing his cult in Asia, Dionysus returns to his native city, in the guise of a young disciple who exerts a strange power of seduction upon most men and women ... The Dyonisiac outbreak spells the disintegration of social institutions and the collapse of the cultural order; both of which disasters are dramatically symbolized by the destruction of the royal palace at the climax of the action. It is futile to attempt to restrain the god of violence. (1977, 126)

Dionysus' destructive component, highlighted by Girard, closely corresponds to the effects exerted by the visitor on the bourgeois family in *Teorema*. Also here all barriers, of gender, status, age are torn down. The only difference is that this Dionysus does not affect the collective fabric but rather each individual. Its objects are not the Menades, but the bourgeois monads represented by Paolo's family members, who, as Pasolini stresses, are all given access to the sacred represented by the visitor – with the notable exception of Emilia and Paolo – each in an absolutely individualized manner unrelated to anything or anyone else.

16 "La dimensione sacrale e dionisiaca affiora nel film soprattutto grazie a un feticismo del dettaglio, e a una poetica del corpo e dello sguardo tipicamente pasoliniana. Il corpo diventa così figura di una sessualità primitiva ed eversiva, che scardina il controllo sociale della famiglia." Fusillo insists on the Dionysian character of the five seductions: "The series of five seductions that follow present some common expressive traits: insistence on nonverbal communication, fetishism for body parts (the eyes, the sex organs) and clothes, the magnetic character of erotic passion, sudden and violent like a sort of possession and revelation" (2006, 216). According to Fusillo, the reactions that follow the abandonment belong to the same Dionysian register: "They are reactions in which the void of communication produced by the perturbing meeting is expressed in an extremely violent and tragic manner (madness, possession, performative creativity, sexual promiscuity, animality)" (219).

17 "In origine, avrei voluto fare di questo visitatore un dio della fecondità, il dio tipico della religione pre-industriale, il dio solare, il dio biblico, Dio Padre. Naturalmente, messo di fronte alla situazione reale, ho dovuto abbandonare l'idea di partenza, e ho fatto di Terence Stamp un'apparizione genericamente ultraterrena e metafisica: potrebbe essere il Diavolo, o una mescolanza di Dio e Diavolo. Quello che importa è tuttavia il fatto che risulta qualcosa di autentico ed inarrestabile." From a 1968 interview with the BBC.

18 "Io non cerco lo scandalo. Dio è lo scandalo, in questo mondo. Il Cristo, se tornasse, sarebbe nuovamente lo scandalo, egli lo è già stato a suo tempo, egli tornerebbe ad esserlo oggi. Il mio sconosciuto … non è Gesù inserito in un contesto attuale, non è neppure Eros in senso assoluto, è il messaggio del dio impietoso, di Jehovah, che attraverso un segno concreto, una presenza misteriosa, toglie i mortali dalla loro falsa sicurezza.

È un dio che distrugge la buona coscienza conquistata a buon prezzo, a riparo della quale vivono o vegetano i benpensanti, i borghesi, chiusi in una falsa idea di se stessi." *La Quinzaine Litteraire*, Paris, 1–15 March 1969, in *Cineforum*, Venice, 9, 85, May 1969.

19 "Questo personaggio non è identificabile con Cristo: è se mai Dio, il Dio Padre (o un inviato che rappresenta il Dio Padre). È insomma il visitatore biblico del Vecchio Testamento, non il visitatore del Nuovo Testamento."

20 See chap. 1, note 44.

21 "E ognuno, nell'attesa, nel ricordo, / come apostolo di un Cristo non crocefisso ma perduto, / ha la sua sorte. / È un teorema: / e ogni sorte è una conseguenza."

22 "Gli Ebrei si incamminarono verso il deserto. Per tutto il giorno, da quando l'orizzonte con le dune oscure di roccia, piatte, o quelle di sabbia, anch'esse oscure, rotonde – si disegnò contro il rosso dell'aurora, a quando si tornò a disegnare uguale, contro il rosso del tramonto, il deserto fu sempre lo stesso.

La sua inospitalità non aveva che una sola forma. Esso si ripeteva uguale in qualsiasi punto gli Ebrei si trovassero, fermi o in cammino. Ad ogni miglio, l'orizzonte si allontanava di un miglio: così tra l'occhio e l'orizzonte, la distanza non cambiava mai. Il deserto aveva i mutamenti del deserto … Il paesaggio del contrario della vita si ripeteva dunque non offuscato o interrotto da niente. Nasceva da se stesso, continuava con se stesso, e finiva in se stesso: ma non rifiutava l'uomo, anzi lo accoglieva, inospitale ma non nemico, contrario alla sua natura, ma profondamente affine alla sua realtà … gli Ebrei cominciarono ad avere l'idea dell'Unicità. L'Unicità del deserto era come un sogno che non lascia dormire e da cui non ci si può risvegliare.

Uno era il deserto, ed era Uno un passo più in là; Uno due passi più in là; Uno per tutti i passi che gli Ebrei potevano compiere ... Era il dolore interminabile di un malato che, spasimando, si rotola ora da una parte ora dall'altra del letto: e da una parte sente il deserto, dall'altra parte sente ancora il deserto, e, nel momento in cui si rotola per cambiare posizione, sente, insieme, il desiderio di dimenticarlo e il desiderio di ritrovarlo."

23 A discussion of the theme of the desert can be found in Jasper 2004.

24 See Vighi: "And could we not argue that *Teorema*, with its circular narrative mapped against the metonymical image of the desert, is precisely a parable on the Real as gaze, the virtual eye of an invisible camera that follows us around everywhere we go, whatever we do? ... The point is that *Teorema* and *Blow-up* manifest an essentially self-reflexive intention by focusing on the void that structures the cinematic image, in other words on the ontological presence of a phantasmatic gaze whose insistence in the visual field, if identified and endorsed, causes the collapse of what we see in terms of the consciousness we derive from it" (2006, 46).

25 "Il deserto ricominciò a riapparire in tutto quello che era: e per rivederlo così – deserto e nient'altro che deserto – bastava solamente *esserci.* Paolo andava, andava, e ogni suo passo era una conferma. Scomparsi gli ultimi ciuffi di palme, ... ricominciò l'ossessione, ossia il procedere restando sempre allo stesso punto ... Qualsiasi cosa Paolo pensasse, era contaminata e dominata da quella presenza. Tutte le cose della sua vita ... erano unificate da quella Cosa, che egli sperimentava sempre allo stesso modo, perché era sempre la stessa.

Non poteva impazzire perché, in fondo, il deserto, in quanto forma unica, in quanto solamente se stesso, gli dava un profondo senso di pace: come se fosse tornato, no, *non nel grembo della madre, ma nel grembo del padre.*

Infatti, come un padre, il deserto lo guardava da ogni punto del suo orizzonte sconfinatamente aperto. Non c'era niente che riparasse Paolo da quello sguardo: in qualunque punto egli fosse – cioè sempre nello stesso punto – attraverso le distese oscure della sabbia e delle pietre, quello sguardo lo raggiungeva senza nessuna difficoltà: con la stessa profonda pace, naturalezza e violenza con cui splendeva il sole, inalterabile ...

Paolo percorreva quella strada senza storia, in quella identificazione completa tra la luce del sole e coscienza di star vivendo."

26 "Dell'uscita dall'Eden materno e felice." See Rinaldi 1982, 256ff.

27 "Il primo Paradiso, Odetta, era quello del padre.

C'era un'alleanza dei sensi, nel figlio
– maschio e femmina –
dovuta all'adorazione di qualcosa di unico.
E il mondo, intorno,
Aveva un lineamento solo: quello del deserto.
In quella luce oscura e senza fine,
Nel cerchio del deserto come un grembo potente,
Il bambino godeva il Paradiso.
Ricordati: c'era un Padre soltanto (non la madre).
La sua protezione
Aveva un sorriso adulto ma giovane,
E lievemente ironico, come ha sempre chi protegge
Il debole, il tenerino – maschio o femminuccia."

28 "PIENO DI UNA DOMANDA A CUI NON SO RISPONDERE."
29 "Come già il popolo d'Israele o l'apostolo Paolo, / il deserto mi si presenta come ciò / che, della realtà, è solo indispensabile. / O, meglio ancora, come la realtà / di tutto spogliata fuori che della sua essenza / così come se la rappresenta chi vive, e qualche volta, / la pensa, pur senza essere un filosofo. / Non c'è infatti, qui intorno, niente / oltre a ciò che è necessario: / la terra, il cielo e il corpo di un uomo. / … Ma cosa prevarrà? L'aridità mondana / della ragione o la religione, spregevole / fecondità di chi vive lasciato indietro dalla storia?"
30 "Un urlo fatto per invocare l'attenzione di qualcuno / o il suo aiuto: ma anche, forse, per bestemmiarlo."
31 "Destinato a durare oltre ogni possibile fine."
32 "Emilia è una ragazza senza età, che potrebbe avere otto anni come trentotto; un'alto-italiana povera; un'esclusa di razza bianca. (È molto probabile che venga da qualche paese della Bassa, non lontano da Milano, eppure ancora completamente contadino: magari dal Lodigiano stesso, dai posti che hanno dato i natali a una santa che probabilmente le somigliava, santa Maria Cabrini.)"
33 "Ti saluto male, in fretta e per ultima, / perché io so che il tuo dolore è inconsolabile / e non ha neanche bisogno di chiedere consolazione. / Tu vivi tutta nel presente. / Come gli uccelli del cielo e i gigli dei campi, / tu non ci pensi, al domani. Del resto, / ci siamo mai parlati? Noi non abbiamo / scambiato parole, quasi gli altri / avessero una coscienza, e tu no. / Invece, evidentemente, anche tu, / povera Emilia, ragazza di basso costo, / esclusa, spossessata dal mondo, / una coscienza ce l'hai. / … Non hai un'anima bella, tu. Per tutto questo, / la rapidità e la mancanza di solennità / nei

nostri saluti, non sono che l'indice / di una misteriosa complicità tra noi due. / Il taxi è arrivato … / Tu sarai l'unica a sapere, quando sarò partito, / che non tornerò mai più, e mi cercherai / dove dovrai cercarmi."

34 See Bynum 1987.

35 "*Emilia, mangia, mangia, l' è buono … devi mangiare, su…*" (film dialogue).

36 "Si tratta di una santa pazza; nel testo romanzesco, essa è 'una pazza che porta la sua valigia come un'infanticida.'" Emilia is the hagiographic figure of the "holy fool" presented in a naturalistic fashion.

37 "Nel suo fondo ha qualcosa dell'Apocalisse, e dentro è biblica, capace di maledizioni potenti come di travolgenti benedizioni." See De Giusti 1983, 94.

38 Pasolini introduces the notion of the free indirect point-of-view shot in *Heretical Empiricism* (2005; *EE*, 1972). See in particular his statements in the essay "The 'Cinema of Poetry'" (*HE*, 167–86):

"That nevertheless a free indirect discourse may also be possible for cinema is certain. Let us call this process a 'free indirect point-of-view shot' ... In the first place, it cannot be an actual 'interior monologue,' since cinema does not have the possibilities of interiorization and abstraction that the word has. It is an 'interior monologue' of images, that's all. In other words, it lacks the entire abstract and theoretical dimension which is explicitly involved in the evocative and cognitive act of the character's monologue." (*HE*, 176–7)

"Thus, the fundamental characteristic of the 'free indirect point-of-view shot' is not linguistic but stylistic. And it can therefore be defined as an interior monologue lacking both the explicit conceptual element and the explicit abstract philosophical element." (*HE*, 178)

"This, at least in theory, causes the 'free indirect point-of-view shot' in cinema to imply the possibility of an extreme stylistic articulation. In fact, it causes it to free the expressive possibilities compressed by the traditional narrative convention through a sort of return to the origins, until the original oneiric, barbaric, irregular, aggressive, visionary quality of cinema is found through its technical devices. In short, it is the 'free indirect point-of-view shot' which establishes a possible tradition of the 'technical language of poetry' in cinema." (*HE*, 178)

For a more extensive discussion of indirect speech and the free indirect point-of-view shot, see chapter 2, section entitled "*Il Vangelo secondo Matteo.*"

39 "Chi resta a guardare in piedi, chi cade in ginocchio, chi tace, chi prega; chi è inebetito e chi commosso fino alle lacrime. La stupefacente presenza di quella piccola figura nera, sospesa sull'orlo del tetto, contro un cielo

vertiginoso, pieno delle malinconiche nubi del tramonto listate di luce, è una visione che non riesce a saziare e ad esaurire la folle felicità di cui riempie."

40 Ernesto De Martino, famous Italian anthropologist and author of, among other works, *Il mondo magico* (1948) and *Sud e magia* (1953), was certainly an important point of reference for Pasolini, as I noted in chapter 1.

41 "I miracoli disturbano la nostra cosiddetta visione oggettiva e scientifica della realtà. Ma la realtà 'soggettiva' del miracolo esiste. Esiste per i contadini del mezzogiorno italiano, così come esisteva per quelli di Palestina. Il miracolo è l'innocente e ingenua spiegazione del mistero reale che abita l'uomo, del potere che si nasconde in lui ...A prescindere dal suo aspetto teologico, la rivelazione del miracolo partecipa altrettanto della magia.

In ogni caso, ho volutamente preso una distanza tecnica dalla realtà dei miracoli per dare pieno rilievo al fatto che appartengono realmente a una mentalità, a una cultura che non sono più totalmente le nostre." From a 1968 interview with the BBC.

42 "Non aver paura, non sono venuta qui per morire, ma per piangere ... e le mie non sono lacrime di dolore, no, saranno una sorgente ... che non sarà una sorgente di dolore." See the passage of *Teorema*, the novel (*RR2*, 1090).

43 "Ma la serva diventa, invece, una santa matta, / va nel cortile della sua casa sottoproletaria, / tace, prega e fa miracoli, / guarisce gente, / mangia ortiche soltanto, finché i capelli le divengono verdi, / e infine, per morire, / si fa seppellire piangendo da una scavatrice, / e le sue lacrime rampollando dal fango / divengono una fonte miracolosa."

44 "Témoin privilégié de l'humanité, de la sensibilité du Dieu-homme."

45 "L'image de la *source* est une métaphore centrale du cheminement magdalénien et de la voie proposée aux fidèles. Le couple *source de miséricorde/ source des larmes*, désignant le Christ et la femme, apparaît dans la plupart des textes; c'est la source des larmes qui permet à la Madeleine d'en venir à la source de miséricorde qui est le Christ; à l'inverse, c'est la source de miséricorde qui lui donne la source des larmes. ... La *source de miséricorde* a toutes le caractéristiques d'une forme d'eau spirituelle: elle lave les péchés et, comme l'eau de source, apaise la soif, irrigue l'âme aride. Enfin grâce à sa faculté d'effacer les péchés et de convertir, le fluide de la miséricorde et sa forme matérielle principale – l'eau des larmes – s'assimilent à l'eau du baptême." Nagy 2000, 262–3.

46 "A gridare è, straziata
... la vecchia scavatrice: ma, insieme, il fresco
sterro sconvolto, o, nel breve confine

dell'orizzonte novecentesco,
tutto il quartiere… È la città,
sprofondata in un chiarore di festa,

è il mondo. Piange ciò che ha
fine e ricomincia. Ciò che era
area erbosa, aperto spiazzo, e si fa

cortile, bianco come cera,
chiuso in un decoro che è rancore;
ciò che era quasi una vecchia fiera

di freschi intonachi sghembi al sole,
e si fa nuovo isolato, brulicante
in un ordine ch'è spento dolore.

Piange ciò che muta, anche
per farsi migliore. La luce
del futuro non cessa un solo istante

di ferirci: è qui, che brucia
in ogni nostro atto quotidiano,
angoscia anche nella fiducia

che ci dà vita, nell'impeto gobettiano
verso questi operai, che muti innalzano,
nel rione dell'altro fronte umano,

il loro straccio di speranza." (*TP1*, 848–9)

(Who screams, torn
… is the old excavator: but, together, the cool
stunned dug-up earth or, within the close confines

of the twentieth-century horizon,
the whole neighbourhood … It is the city,
immersed in a festive light,

it is the world. It cries what has an end and a new beginning.
What was grassy area, open field, and becomes

courtyard, as white as wax,
wrapped in a decorum that is rancor;
what was almost an old festival

of crooked fresh plaster in the sun,
and becomes again isolated, swarming
in an order that is dull pain.

What changes cries, even if
to become better. The light of the future
does not stop for an instant

to hurt us: it is here, burning
in our every daily action,
anguish even in faith

that gives us life, in the Gobettian impetus
toward these workers, who silently raise,
in the neighborhood of the other human front,

their red rag of hope.)

Ryan-Scheutz points out: "The excavator's doleful plea thus preceded the saint's purifying tears and the father's bestial cry, portending their role as relics of authenticity in modern times" (2007, 159).

47 Cf. Pasolini's vision of Rome as palimpsest in Jewell, 1992.

48 "[Duflot]: *Quale significato deve essere attribuito al momento in cui la serva seppellisce se stessa in fondo a un cantiere edilizio?*

[Pasolini]: Pure qui, l'allusione è relativamente semplice. Intendo rammentare come le civiltà anteriori alle nostre non sono affatto scomparse ma si seppelliscono soltanto. Cosicchè la civiltà contadina permane seppellita sotto il mondo operaio, sotto la civiltà industriale. In realtà, può darsi che sia questo l'unico momento di ottimismo nel film."

49 See Brown 1981.

50 "Lava la ferita al polso e alla mano del compagno" ...; l'acqua comincia a lavare la carne dal sangue, comincia anche a guarirne la ferita: in pochi istanti il taglio si chiude, e il sangue cessa di scorrere.

Prima che gli operai, com'è naturale, comincino ad alzare le loro grida di stupore – abbandonandosi nelle manifestazioni ingenue e un po' sciocche, che gli uomini non sanno trattenere davanti alle cose di cui non hanno esperienza – c'è un momento di profondo silenzio. Le loro povere facce, scavate, dure e buone, sono volte verso quella pozzetta, che scintilla, inconcepibile, sotto il sole."

51 "Ora questa illusione gramsciana è oggettivamente caduta, non ce l'ho più. Perché è oggettivamente cambiato il mondo di fronte a me. Mentre al

tempo di Gramsci e al tempo in cui pensavo le mie prime opere e covavo la mia prima ideologia una distinzione nettamente classica tra classe popolare e classe borghese era ancora possibile, oggi oggettivamente non lo è più. Cioè quello che diceva Gramsci quarant'anni fa e ciò che pensavo io dieci anni fa non è più lecito, non è più attendibile, perché l'Italia è entrata in una nuova fase storica. Questo fa sì che la distinzione tra popolare nel senso gramsciano della parola e borghese non sia più possibile … sarebbe illecito che io avessi in testa un popolo ideale a cui rivolgermi con le mie opere … In seguito ... anzichè tentare un'opera epico-popolare, la quale avrebbe rischiato di diventare sincrona con un'opera tipica della cultura di massa (in quanto la nozione di popolo è venuta a coincidere con la nozione di massa), ho cercato dei film che reagissero a questo, che fossero difficili e quindi inconsumabili ..., adesso punto sull'inconsumabilità.

E quindi sulla difficoltà, sull'enigmaticità, sulla complessità stilistica, ecc. È questo il primo goffo tentativo, individualistico e in parte anarcoide, di lottare contro le determinazioni della cultura di massa."

52 "Un gruppo di persone intelligenti e disposte a combattere questa cultura di massa."

53 "Se scrivessi dei versi apposta per essere capito dal bracciante calabrese farei della retorica, del pedagogismo, della propaganda - magari anche nobile, in buona fede - ma tradirei me stesso in quanto scrittore. Cioè, all'ingiustizia del bracciante calabrese che non capisce, opporrei l'ingiustizia dello scrittore che tradisce se stesso."

54 See Murri 1994, 69–70: "Il vero antagonista di questa società non va più visto nel 'popolo' occidentale, ormai massificato e scomparso, ma in una realtà altra, molto più semplice, più etnologicamente basilare. Pasolini pensa con sempre maggiore ossessività alla verità, per quanto cruda e contraddittoria, delle poco tecnologicamente sofisticate società del Terzo Mondo." (The true antagonist of this society can no longer be found in the western "people," by now massified and vanished, but in another reality, much simpler, more ethnologically basic. Pasolini thinks with ever growing obsession about the reality, however crude and contradictory, of the not so technologically sophisticated societies of the Third World.)

55 See Fusillo 1996, particularly the chapter entitled "Medea: Un conflitto di culture" (Medea: A Conflict of Cultures), 127–79.

56 "Medea e Giasone sono infatti due personaggi simbolici, che rappresentano da una parte una cultura primitiva, magica e sacrale, dall'altra una cultura moderna, razionalistica e borghese (vista comunque nel suo formarsi); a questa bipolarità culturale se ne sovrappone una psicoanalitica tra Es ed Ego (Pasolini affermava fra l'altro di aver concepito Giasone e Medea come

un unico personaggio), e una politica fra Occidente e Terzo Mondo (come sarà ancora più nettamente negli *Appunti per un'Orestiade africana*."

57 "A volte scrivo la sceneggiatura senza sapere chi sarà l'attore. In questo caso sapevo che sarebbe stata la Callas, quindi ho sempre calibrato la mia sceneggiatura in funzione di lei. Ha contato molto nella creazione del personaggio ... La barbarie, sprofondata dentro, che vien fuori nei suoi occhi, nei suoi lineamenti, non si manifesta direttamente, anzi. Lei appartiene a un mondo contadino, greco, agrario, e poi si è educata per una civiltà borghese. Dunque in un certo senso ho cercato di concentrare nel suo personaggio la complessa totalità di Medea." Pasolini, 1970, "Intervista con Pisanelli Stabile."

58 According to Viano, the choice of Callas was a colossal mistake: "Medea (Maria Callas) represents, instead, 'the archaic, hieratic, religious universe,' the barbaric and prehistoric elements of civilization. Considering that this is the world whose disappearance Pasolini regretted, he failed to create a powerful and compelling Medea. He chose Callas because of her 'barbaric features' and it was, in my opinion, the biggest casting error in his career. Callas brought to the character of Medea all the glamour of her public image – something which Pasolini, aware as he was of what actors are in real life, should have taken into account ... The obsessive close-ups of her expressionless face ... and the stiffness of her movements, encumbered by heavy costumes, evoke the immobility of someone asking herself one question too many ... And Callas fails to convey the sense of passion that, after all, Medea had to signify, especially in view of her opposition to Jason" (1993, 241). In reality, the priestly element seems to prevail over the passional one. Medea is a priestess before being a woman, a priestess who has lost her powers due to her passion but who proposes herself as the officiant in sacrificial rites throughout the movie. The first sacrifice we see is the *sparagmos* meant to protect her own community and guarantee a good harvest. The second is the desecrating instrumental sacrifice of her brother Apsyrtus to protect Jason and the Argonauts as they escape with the golden fleece. The third is the ultimate sacrifice of her own children, meant to break the bond that ties her to Jason, that is, to a culture to which she does not belong, that does not understand her, and that has alienated her from the sacred.

59 "GIASONE È una visione?
(A rispondergli è il Centauro, umano e razionale, mentre quello mitico tace e guarda ridendo).

CENTAURO Se lo è, sei tu che la produci. Noi due siamo infatti dentro di te.
GIASONE MA io ho conosciuto un solo Centauro ...

CENTAURO No: ne hai conosciuti due; uno sacro, quando eri bambino, uno sconsacrato, quando sei divenuto adulto. Ma ciò che è sacro si conserva accanto alla sua nuova forma sconsacrata. Ed eccoci qua, uno a fianco all'altro!

GIASONE Ma qual è la funzione del vecchio Centauro, quello che ho conosciuto da bambino, e che tu, Centauro Nuovo, se ho ben capito, hai sostituito, non facendolo scomparire, ma aggiungendoti a lui?

CENTAURO Esso non parla, naturalmente, perché la sua logica è così diversa dalla nostra, che non si potrebbe intendere… Ma posso parlare io, per lui. È sotto il suo segno che tu – al di fuori dei tuoi calcoli e della tua interpretazione – in realtà, ami Medea.

GIASONE Io amo Medea?

CENTAURO Sì. E inoltre hai pietà di lei, e comprendi la sua … catastrofe spirituale… il suo disorientamento di donna antica in un mondo che non crede in nulla di ciò in cui lei ha sempre creduto … La poverina ha avuto una conversione alla rovescia, e non si è più ripresa."

60 "Conversione alla rovescia – o folgorazione negativa –/ una Saula credente che cade da cavallo e non crede più."

61 "Violazione di un universo arcaico da parte di un universo moderno e pragmatico."

62 "Non si possono piantare le tende così, a caso; bisogna prima rivolgersi agli Dèi, pregarli: consacrare il luogo, perché ogni luogo dove l'uomo pianta le sue tende è sacro, ripete la creazione del cosmo, diviene un *centro*: e questo centro deve essere segnato da una pietra, da un albero; da un segno qualsiasi, *sacro*. Questo è tutto ciò che Medea sa, e che le sembra sacrilego non sapere, non applicare. E lo dice con frasi rotte, incomprensibili … Così dapprima gli Argonauti la ascoltano e la osservano strabiliati; ma subito i loro occhi si velano di ironia (anche, e soprattutto Giasone) e l'ascoltano con beffarda pazienza ...

Medea allora li lascia, li abbandona alla loro follia, cerca di stare sola (come una bestia ferita ecc.).

Cosa cerca in questa terra sconosciuta? Cerca il "sacro." Che ha abbandonato nella Colchide, e il cui sentimento è cessato di colpo con l'apparizione 'carnale' di Giasone, proprio nel Centro, nell'Omphalos in cui era custodito il vello d'oro.

... Nella luce del tramonto atrocemente dolce, tra le ombre lunghissime delle cose, Medea cerca un albero, che sia *albero sacro*. Ce ne sono tanti, intorno, alberi: pioppi, sambuchi, cespugli di more, fichi: ma nessuno di essi è l'albero che essa cerca. Sono tutti poveri, comuni, umili alberi nella gloria dell'estate.

Medea come in un folle monologo, mormora tra sé – per vincere la sordità delle cose – un Inno alla vegetazione (da inventare, mescolando frammenti di Inni di varie religioni antiche ecc.) …

Medea cerca disperatamente una roccia, ora. Un *sasso sacro.* Ce n'è molti, intorno, in quella costa mediterranea. Ma, come gli alberi, non rispondono alla supplica di Medea: restano quello che sono, insignificanti e bellissime pietre. Anche ad esse, monologando, Medea rivolge un Inno (cfr. sopra)."

63 "Medea seduta su una pietra tace: come tace il mondo intorno a lei, puramente fisico, come un'atroce e stupenda apparizione irreale … Essa è come inebetita: è inespressiva, ma con la grandiosità di una gigantesca cavalletta, o di una divinità di pietra. Non sa cosa fare di se stessa e si è chiusa nel suo silenzio come in una teca."

64 "La propria atonia di bestia disorientata: nell'amore trova, di colpo (umanizzandosi) un sostituto della religiosità perduta: nell'esperienza sessuale ritrova il perduto rapporto sacrale con la realtà ... possedendo a sua volta in lui [Giasone] la rigenerazione della vita."

65 "Riassumendo grossolanamente, potremmo dire che l'eros è amore come desiderio, tende verso l'alto, spinge l'uomo a divinizzarsi, ama ciò che è bello e riconosce che solo ciò che ha valore è amabile; l'agàpe è sacrificio, si spende per ciò che gli è inferiore, ama soprattutto ciò che non ha valore, e quindi è immotivata e umanamente inconcepibile. L'eros è l'amore dell'uomo che riconosce nell'uomo la divinità, l'agàpe è l'amore che viene da Dio …

L'amore come sacrificio mormora un'altra verità: 'peccatores sunt pulchri, quia diluguntur, non diliguntur, quia sunt pulchri,' dice Lutero. Niente si può dedurre dalla bellezza, i poveri devono essere amati per uno slancio immotivato, o motivato da ragioni indipendenti dal soggetto singolo. Credo si possa dire che per Pasolini la scoperta dell'oggettività storica coincide con l'inserimento del motivo dell'agàpe sull'originario eros."

66 "Dal conflitto fra cultura arcaica e cultura moderna Pasolini non vuole far trionfare la prima, irrimediabilmente perdente, né demonizzare la seconda, ma solo mostrare l'unilateralità ingenua di una società che crede di aver superato il sacro, di aver controllato le passioni."

67 "Quando vediamo Emilia sepolta, o quasi in atto di autoseppellirsi, con quel pianto che esce da tutto il suo volto, in una specie di sudorazione sanguigna 'cristiana' che si trasforma in qualcosa di più limpido, e anche di più accettabile, per il senso di stellarità e di bellezza presente in tutto il film, riandiamo all'idea di una fonte viva promanante appunto dalla parte della realtà umana che forse non è ancora stata contaminata, che forse non lo è mai stata, e che probabilmente, magari in vitro, magari su un altro pianeta,

riuscirà a salvarsi e a salvare. In definitiva vale di più quella pozza d'acqua, quella pozza di pure lacrime che fuoriescono dallo sguardo cancellato di Emilia, che non forse il grido nel deserto, in cui termina il film, quel grido che continua all'infinito, ed è così tremendamente gremito di intenti e di simboli, di umanità che non potendo veramente 'transumanare' (verbo che Pasolini doveva sempre più fare suo), si ritrova ferina, e sempre più oscura a se stessa."

68 From the poem "Poesie mondane," in the section "La realtà" of Pasolini's *Poesia in forma di rosa* (1964), now *TP1*, 1079–1270.

69 "Non piango perché quel mondo non torna più, ma piango perché il suo tornare è finito." "Il canto delle campane" ("Ciant da li Ciampanis," *NG*, *TP2*, 426). See also stanza "III (variante)" from "Tornant al país": "Il più grande dolore era la più grande consolazione: sapere cioè che 'il tempo non si muove' e che 'il riso dei padri sta, come la pioggia nei rami, negli occhi dei loro bambini'; sapere che non finisce una forma del mondo, morire dentro quel mondo pieno di semi e di gemme." *NG*, *TP2*, 421. (The greatest sorrow was also the greatest consolation: knowing, that is, that "time does not move" and that "the smile of the fathers lingers, like rain on branches, in the eyes of their children"; knowing that a form of the world does not end; dying inside that world full of seeds and gems.)

70 "Poi, per amore di quelli che erano ragazzetti come lui – fino a poco prima che sul suo capo le stelle cambiassero la loro luce – avrebbe voluto dar la sua vita per tutto il mondo sconosciuto – lui, sconosciuto, piccolo santo, granello perduto nel campo.

E invece ha scritto poesie di santità, credendo così che il cuore gli si ingrandisse. I giorni sono passati a un lavoro che ha rovinato la santità del suo cuore: il granello non è morto, e lui è restato solo."

71 "Il motivo conduttore, il tema dominante, la 'Todestriebe' che caratterizza, esplicitamente o implicitamente, tutta l'opera pasoliniana."

72 "La morte è in Pasolini non già, o non tanto, il biochimico concludersi dell'esistere biologico, quanto la legge caratterizzante dell'esistenza, la pulsione sovrana, la conclusione obbligata e definitiva (la sola definitiva e perciò la sola veramente necessitata) di ogni discorrere e di ogni esistere: e dunque la sola, dominante, tensione della realtà."

73 "Il salto dalla Preistoria alla Dopostoria non può essere che un presente, la Storia, fatto di inesorabile morte."

74 "Il film della pienezza cristiana di Pasolini."

75 "Apostolo di un Cristo non crocefisso ma perduto."

76 "*Un reale sentimento del sacro.*"

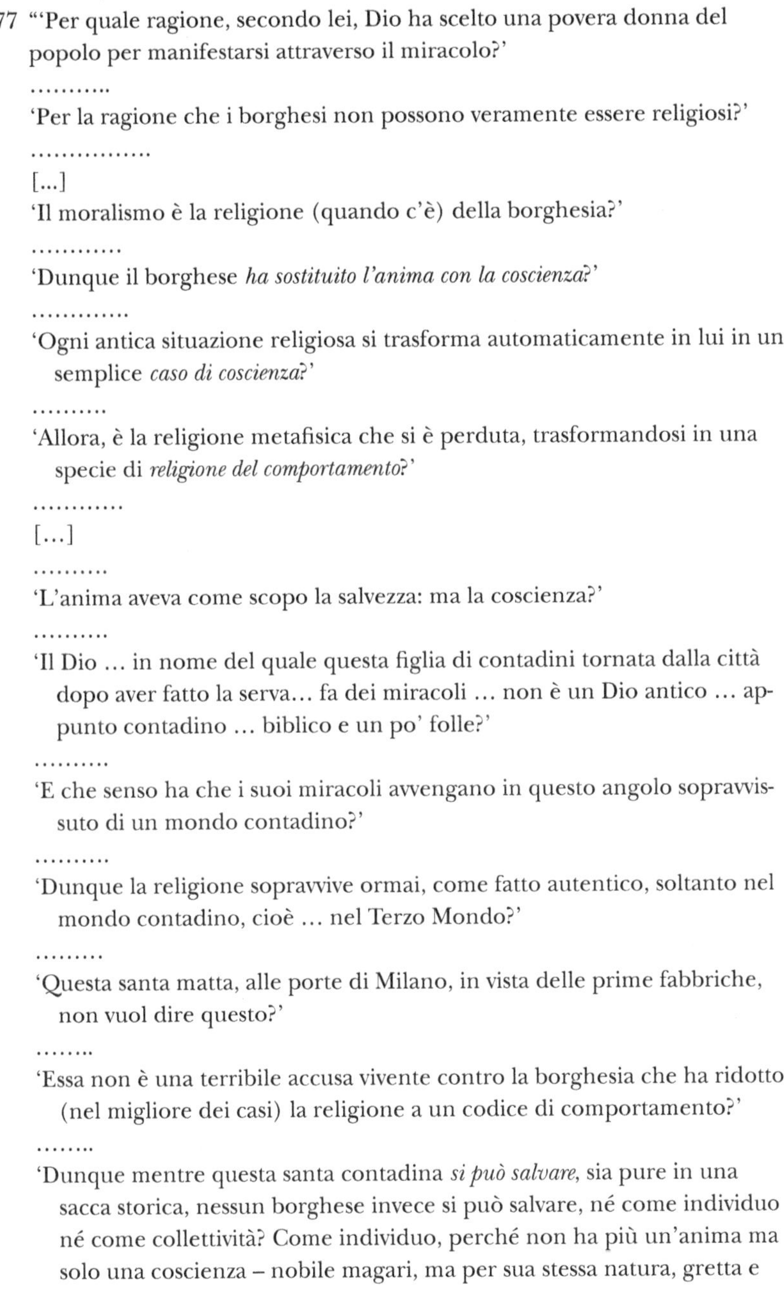

77 "'Per quale ragione, secondo lei, Dio ha scelto una povera donna del popolo per manifestarsi attraverso il miracolo?'

....

'Per la ragione che i borghesi non possono veramente essere religiosi?'

....

[...]

'Il moralismo è la religione (quando c'è) della borghesia?'

....

'Dunque il borghese *ha sostituito l'anima con la coscienza?*'

....

'Ogni antica situazione religiosa si trasforma automaticamente in lui in un semplice *caso di coscienza?*'

....

'Allora, è la religione metafisica che si è perduta, trasformandosi in una specie di *religione del comportamento?*'

....

[...]

....

'L'anima aveva come scopo la salvezza: ma la coscienza?'

....

'Il Dio ... in nome del quale questa figlia di contadini tornata dalla città dopo aver fatto la serva... fa dei miracoli ... non è un Dio antico ... appunto contadino ... biblico e un po' folle?'

....

'E che senso ha che i suoi miracoli avvengano in questo angolo sopravvissuto di un mondo contadino?'

....

'Dunque la religione sopravvive ormai, come fatto autentico, soltanto nel mondo contadino, cioè ... nel Terzo Mondo?'

....

'Questa santa matta, alle porte di Milano, in vista delle prime fabbriche, non vuol dire questo?'

....

'Essa non è una terribile accusa vivente contro la borghesia che ha ridotto (nel migliore dei casi) la religione a un codice di comportamento?'

....

'Dunque mentre questa santa contadina *si può salvare*, sia pure in una sacca storica, nessun borghese invece si può salvare, né come individuo né come collettività? Come individuo, perché non ha più un'anima ma solo una coscienza – nobile magari, ma per sua stessa natura, gretta e limitata –; come collettività perché la sua storia si sta esaurendo senza lasciare tracce, trasformandosi da storia delle prime industrie a storia della completa industrializzazione del mondo?'

....

'Ma il nuovo tipo di religione che allora nascerà (e se ne vedono già nelle nazioni più avanzate i primi segni) non avrà nulla a che fare con questa merda (scusi la parola) che è il mondo borghese, capitalistico o socialista, in cui viviamo?'

..........."

Chapter Five

1 "Ognuno di noi (volendo e non volendo) fa vivendo un'azione morale il cui senso è sospeso." Pasolini, "I segni viventi e i poeti morti" (Living signs and dead poets), *EE*, in *SLA1*, 1575 (1967).
2 "Vivendo, dunque, noi ci rappresentiamo, e assistiamo alla rappresentazione altrui. La realtà del mondo umano non è che questa rappresentazione doppia, in cui siamo attori e insieme spettatori: un gigantesco *happening*, se vogliamo." Pasolini, "La lingua scritta della realtà" (The written language of reality), *EE*, *SLA1*, 1514 (1966).
3 "Francesco si è messo *fuori del testo* e concepiva la propria vita, così come quella di ogni buon cristiano e *in primis* dei confratelli, come una 'performance rivoluzionaria,' un'azione che cambia la vita di tutti coloro che vi prendono parte e la rende, da pura reazione alle contingenze, un evento capace di assimilarla al divino. Il suo obiettivo dichiarato era quello di riattualizzare e reincarnare i comportamenti di Gesù e di concretizzare un'idea di comunità cristiana, ma, come è proprio di ogni riattualizzazione, la questione andava ben aldilà del produrre o riprodurre un testo, si trattava di interpretare il senso delle azioni di Cristo affinché le proprie fossero efficaci nel presente."
4 Cf. Subini 2007, 41n3.
5 Peter Brunette, http://www.criterion.com/current/posts/379-the-flowers-of-st-francis-gods-jester, 22 August 2005, accessed 19 December 2013.
6 "Il rifiuto del razionalismo critico."
7 "Un realismo che illuminava e documentava una realtà spirituale piuttosto che oggettuale."
8 *The Catholic Encyclopedia*, http://www.newadvent.org/cathen/06078b.htm, accessed 19 December 2013.
9 "*Una nozione non realistica di realismo* coincideva dunque con la capacità antropologica di rinunciare alle categorie scientifiche positivistiche, per mantenersi poeticamente fedele alla verità spirituale di un'altra epoca."

10 "Ma, accostandomi alla figura di Francesco, non ho preteso di dare una vita del Santo. In *Francesco giullare di Dio*, io non racconto né la sua nascita né la sua morte, né ho preteso di raggiungere l'esposizione completa del messaggio e dello spirito francescano o di accostarmi direttamente ala formidabile e complessa personalità di Francesco. Ho creduto invece opportune mostrarne i riflessi sui suoi seguaci, fra i quali, pertanto, hanno acquistato grande rilievo frate Ginepro e frate Giovanni il semplice, che rivelano fino al paradosso lo spirito di semplicità, di innocenza, di letizia che dallo spirito di Francesco promanano.

In sostanza, come già dice il titolo, il mio film vuole essere l'esposizione dell'aspetto giullaresco del francescanesimo, di quella giocosità, di quella 'perfetta letizia,' della liberazione che lo spirito trova nella povertà, nell'assoluto distacco dalle cose materiali.

E questo aspetto particolare del grande spirito francescano io ho pensato di ridarlo sulla falsariga dei *Fioretti* dove, secondo me, si conserva intatto il profumo del francescanesimo primitivo.

... Riproporre oggi certi aspetti del francescanesimo primitivo mi pare sia la cosa che meglio risponda alle aspirazioni profonde e ai bisogni dell'umanità che, per aver dimenticato la lezione del Poverello, schiava dell'ambizione di ricchezza, ha perduto persino la gioia di vivere." Originally published as "Il messaggio di Francesco," *Epoca*, 18 November 1950, 54.

11 See Brunette 1987, 133.

12 Quoted from Cavani's comments in Pasti, "Bello, asciutto, estatico: E' il santo che fa scena," *La Repubblica*, 26 September 1981, 4.

13 "Devo dire che, per quanto mi riguarda, la cosa è del tutto casuale. Non ho pensato prima a Francesco e, dopo, ho fatto un film su Francesco; ho pensato agli uccelli e, siccome Francesco predicava agli uccelli, ho poi tirato in ballo il santo di Assisi. Mentre giravo il mio ultimo film, non è che mi interessasse in modo particolare la figura di San Francesco. Certo, la cosa può essere nata da una serie di coordinazioni interne; due anni fa progettai un film su una specie di san Francesco. Si intitolava *Bestemmia*. Il protagonista era una sorta di San Francesco, però miserabile, non figlio di un borghese o di un piccolo industriale, ma figlio proprio del popolo, soprannominato Bestemmia perché 'sacrilego.' Da questo nasceva una storia analoga a quella del santo di Assisi. Può darsi che le cose si siano poi mescolate dentro di me. Il mio Francesco è comunque una figura simbolica, da favola, che rappresenta la Chiesa in un periodo di grande progresso. Le parole, da lui pronunciate, sono le stesse dette da Paolo VI all'ONU."

14 "Di inserire il cattolicesimo in una mentalità piccolo-borghese."

15 "Direi che a un non credente, piace di più un san Francesco che parla agli uccelli e fa i miracoli. La religione occidentale, impermeata di laicismo che essa crede rivoluzionario rispetto al proprio spirito clericale e si sbaglia, tende a mostrarsi scettica e ironica rispetto ai miracoli. Ma i miracoli sono la religione. Un santo che non voli, che non sparisca, che non determini i fatti naturali magicamente non è un santo; oppure, è un santo occidentale.

Certo, anch'io talvolta sono scettico di fronte ai miracoli. Ma non escludo che essi avvengano. Quelli di Cristo sono effettivamente avvenuti. Tornando all'immagine del santo dato dalla Cavani, mi sembra che la regista si è guardata bene, secondo le regole e non secondo lo scandalo, di far fare a Francesco dei miracoli. Ha 'occidentalizzato' il più possibile Francesco … Ha staccato gli elementi orientali (fame, morte, sporcizia, mancanza di speranza, ferocia), che erano nel mondo di Francesco, e vi ha immesso elementi piccoloborghesi …

Per quanti sforzi faccia il Francesco della Cavani, non riesce ad essere diverso, diverso e cioè santo … non si può dire che abbia molto da fare con la folle e sublime aristocraticità della religione: "Molti sono i chiamati e pochi gli eletti." ... La riduzione di *Francesco* ha, per me, un canone di irrazionalismo religioso e di pauperismo sociale e, più che rappresentare un santo, descrive un anima bella."

16 Concerning miracles, interpreting them in an immanent rather than transcendent key, Pasolini writes: "I miracoli disturbano la nostra cosiddetta visione oggettiva e scientifica della realtà. Ma la realtà 'soggettiva' del miracolo esiste. Esiste per i contadini del mezzogiorno italiano, così come esisteva per quelli della Palestina. Il miracolo è l'innocente e ingenua spiegazione del mistero reale che abita l'uomo, del potere che si nasconde in lui … A prescindere dal suo aspetto teologico, la rivelazione del miracolo partecipa altrettanto della magia." *SC, SPS,* 1423. (Miracles upset our so-called objective and scientific vision of reality. But the 'subjective' reality of miracles does exist. It exists for the peasants of southern Italy like it existed for those in Palestine. A miracle is the innocent and naïve explanation of the real mystery that lives in humanity, of the power that hides in man … Regardless of its theological side, the revelation of the miracle participates also in magic.)

17 These are Paul VI's words used in *Uccellacci e uccellini:* "The human community needs justice; Christ wants us to hunger and thirst for justice. We know, however, that justice advances gradually and that, as society progresses, our souls realize that it is not perfect and whole, and the evident discriminations by which humanity is still afflicted and that must be remedied come to the fore. Don't these discriminations among the citizens' classes and

their nations put peace in the gravest danger?" Aula Conciliare, *Discorso del sommo Pontefice Paolo vi ai padri conciliari riguardo la sua visita all'onu*, 5 October 1965, http://www.vatican.va/holy_father/paul_vi/speeches/1965/documents/hf_p-vi_spe_19651005_resoconto-viaggio_it.html, accessed 19 December 2013.

18 "Il film su San Francesco è ancora una progetto lontano che non so se realizzerò o meno ... Ma poi non si tratta proprio di San Francesco, si tratta di un santo completamente inventato che somiglia vagamente al santo di Assisi – ma è inutile nemmeno farlo questo nome, se mai lo si potrà fare dopo che ho finito il film, perché in realtà questo santo inventerà *Il cantico delle creature* – però con un linguaggio ancora più rozzo che san Francesco – diventerà eretico e verrà addirittura ucciso dai soldati del papa, come è successo in infiniti casi nel Medioevo ... Ma questo, ripeto, è un progetto talmente lontano che è inutile parlarne." Originally published as "Intervista di N. Ferrero e D. Mignano," *Filmcritica* 125 (September 1962).

19 Siti, *Note e Notizie sui testi, Bestemmia, TP2*, 1723. The information on *Bestemmia* was taken from the appendix to Walter Siti's text, 1723–42.

20 "Ho poi intenzione di raccogliere tutti i miei racconti, che sotto forma di 'racconti da farsi' (del '50, '51) o sotto forma di sceneggiature sono andato scrivendo in questo decennio. L'ultima che sto scrivendo sotto il curioso cartello di *treatment in versi*, si intitola 'Bestemmia': e sarà appunto 'Bestemmia' il titolo di questo volume, che spero esca entro l'anno." "Inchiesta sui lavori futuri degli scrittori," in *Corriere della Sera*, 29 December 1963.

21 "Mi rifaccio cattolico, nazionalista/romanico, nelle mie ricerche per 'BESTEMMIA,' / o 'LA DIVINA MIMESIS.'"

22 "Primavera medioevale. Un Santo eretico / (chiamato Bestemmia, dai compari. / Sarà un magnaccia, al solito. Chiedere / al dolente leonetti consulenza / su prostituzione Medioevo). / Poi visione. La passione popolare / (un'infinita carrellata con Maria / che avanza, chiedendo in umbro / del figlio, cantando in umbro l'agonia). / La primavera porta una coltre / di erba dura tenerella, di primule ... / e l'atonia dei sensi mista alla libidine. / Dopo la visione (gozzoviglie / mortuarie, empie – di puttane), / una 'preghiera' negli ardenti prati. / Puttane, magnaccia, ladri, contadini / con le mani congiunte sotto la faccia / (tutto con il cinquanta controluce). / Girerò i più assolati Appennini."

23 "*Bestemmia* è un racconto in versi ambientato in un medioevo ideale dell'Italia centrale, immagino durante il periodo delle invasioni normanne, a Salerno e in Puglia, che racconta la storia di un tipo profondamente simile ad Accattone, un magnaccia che vive in mezzo alle prostitute alla periferia di quella cosa incredibile che doveva essere Roma in quegli anni. E

come Accattone ha una vena mistica che, dati i tempi, ha delle soluzioni. E la soluzione prima è una visione. Questa specie di Accattone dell'anno 1100 immagina la Passione, una Passione popolare con le Marie che seguono Cristo, ecc. Da quel momento, da magnaccia, turpe individuo qual è, diventa santo. Ma al tempo stesso diventa anche rivoluzionario. Cioè fonda un ordine di tipo eretico che io inventerò, ma su basi storiche abbastanza precise. E di qui la lotta contro il papato del tempo. Bestemmia viene ucciso dopo aver ripredicato il Vangelo secondo la riscoperta, che sarà poi francescana, dei sacri testi. Questo racconto era nato con l'idea di essere un film, ma non mi andava di scriverlo così, normalmente, e l'ho scritto in versi, anzi lo sto scrivendo." "Intervista alla Radio Televisione Svizzera Italiana," 5 February 1964, now included in *TP2.*

24 "Vado avanti a lavorare a una strana cosa, che ho cominciato quattro o cinque anni fa, che si chiama 'Bestemmia': una sceneggiatura che ho scritto in versi e che ho portato dentro di me, trasformandola man mano che cambiavo le mie idee sul cinema." "Intervista a Gaetano Stocchi," *Sette Giorni,* 27 August 1967.

25 "Il titolo di questo volumone sarebbe Bestemmia, perché vi comprenderei anche un lungo frammento inedito intitolato appunto così." Pasolini 1988, *Lettere 1955–1975,* 624.

26 The fragment was published for the first time in *Cinema e film,* 1.2 (1967), 225.

27 "La Shangay di un secolo/ dopo l'Anno Mille."

28 "Mucchi di tuguri aggrappati all'Acquedotto."

29 "Mandrie di bambini / con la pancia grossa e il tracoma – tra capannelli di donne nere come <salme>."

30 Cf. Walter Siti, in *TP2,* 1730.

31 "Bestemmia par fatto col vapore / di fave e fagioli, con rami di viti: / un mucchio di foglie grige e peste per zigomo, / e sopra, l'occhio marroncino, che cova / rabbia con pianto; e i capelli / son quelli del malandrino, venditore d'acqua / o rapinatore, cresciuto, dalla grazia / del ragazzino figlio bastardo o orfanello, / a quella del giovane. La forza, l'altezza / non toglie al corpo le curve / del servitorello meridionale: ed è, / per forza e altezza, una tigre, un bandito: / Musolino e Giuliano ancora innocente, / dedito solo al sogno / di una vita fuori dalla legge: / nato per realizzare quel sogno."

32 "Fior de limone / – ora ch'è in mezzo alle spianate solitarie – / fior de limone, / mamma me ce fece de carnevale: / me fece d'allegria no de passione! / Ma tutto è passione / nel suo colore grigio carico di salute. / ' Arzanno l'occi ar celo vide stellato, / e vidde Ggesù mio tutto ferito: / e l'ho

ferito io co'r mi peccato.' / Non ha mai pensato / una sola volta a Gesù e al peccato, intento / solo a essere dritto tra i dritti."

33 "Una belva nera, fetida, / che non conosce padrone né Dio, / ma ha gloria di un solo fratello, Bestemmia."

34 "Le bocche aperte dovettero restare a lungo aperte. / Ma i poveri sono sempre pronti ad accettare la pazzia. / Le sei sorelle puttane e il puttanino Nicolino / Si abituarono subito a ciò che / Davanti ai loro occhi bene aperti, si svolgeva. / E come i pazzi sanno subito come essere pazzi, / Così i poveri sanno subito cosa fare con i pazzi. / Bestemmia, pazzo, piangente, / Con due occhi come due tristi fontane piene d'acqua, / Alzò il testone greve dalla spalluccia di Nicolino, / E, con la sicurezza dei pazzi, prese la porta. / Là dietro sfavillava, blu come il mare, la luna."

35 "Le sei puttane e il puttanino."

36 "Ii poveri sanno subito cosa fare con i pazzi."

37 "E guarda un po' alla volta quelle faccie, / di cui il buon borghese ha paura, / rivelare la loro forza sacra: / i grandi occhi d'animale del popolo cattivo, / gli zigomi nobili, la pelle incontaminata, / le bocche e i menti appena abbozzati con un sublime / colpo di pollice: / guarda, guarda, e dimmi / se Bestemmia non ha trovato subito un degno seguito di / [santità. / E nulla è cambiato in loro, non illuderti! / Non succedono miracoli nelle anime! / Sono le stesse, / le stesse puttane che si sono strette tra sorelle, / pancia di troia contro pancia di troia, / che hanno giaciuto insieme in un'orgia che non sapeva / [di esserlo, / che hanno dato Nicolino a Bestemmia come una / [cavallina allo stallone, le stesse: / le stesse che hanno riso con le bocche contadine / un po' sdentate sotto le guancie rosse, / gli stessi occhi con luce liquida delle ragazze / che passano per strada di sera, già peccatrici, / e profondamente innocenti. / È questa innocenza che è la stessa; i cari a Dio / possono anche peccare; se cari Gli sono, cari Gli saranno; / dipende solo da qualche suo disegno / misterioso come fuoco nel fuoco, / che qualcosa nella vita di quei suoi cari / possa mutare – *senza però mutarli!* / Le sante puttane diventano sante, nient'altro che sante; / cominciano a pregare intorno a Bestemmia, / e cantano il rosario, / con voci all'unisono, / cui Nicolino aggiunge la sua voce più rauca; / e altra gente esce dalle case, / nel cuore della notte."

38 "Lo imitavano solo come potevano / stando in ginocchio accanto a lui. / Imitavano il miracolo, povere scimmie/in quell'estate del mondo, generosi come bambini … / Attraverso lui adoravano ciò che lui adorava."

39 "Cagne inferocite per amore di Dio."

40 "In cui ricominciava il tradimento di Dio."

41 "Col suo nasone / e la sua cadoppa di vecchio contadino."

42 “Fantoccio di Dio / fatto per essere usato / in quel lavoro senza prodotto / che è la preghiera in comune.”

43 In the character’s death, we see a clear reference to Angelo Roncalli, that is, Pope John XXIII, the Bergamasque pope of peasant origin who had been the protagonist of the Second Vatican Council: “I’m dying … / He looked around almost with irony, as if to bid adieu: … but it was an adieu, an adieu with no pain” (cf. *Bestemmia,* 1040). The dying pope alluded to his imminent departure with the ironic image of his “very ready suitcase.”

44 “A vivere in Cristo, non nelle sue parole.”

45 “Cristo parli con se stesso, / non con le sue parole, non con le parole su di lui.”

46 “I simboli: / le immagini della Madonna e di Cristo / e le Croci.”

47 Cf. Pasolini, *Bestemmia, TP2,* 1055: “dove Bestemmia e i suoi fedeli *adoravano Dio vivendolo.*”

48 The leader’s name is Di Gennaro, the same as that of the prosecutor who charged Pasolini with “contempt of state religion” in the trial against *La ricotta* that followed the confiscation of the film in 1963.

49 “Insomma essi erano banditi / dalla città *dove Dio si rappresenta e si nomina / e dove le sue lodi si cantano.*”

50 “Che cosa diceva la luce dei suoi occhi / se non che la morte era una domanda / e il corpo martoriato una risposta?”

51 “Il mondo tornò mondo” in una “delusione straziante e meravigliosa.”

52 “Come i cani intorno alla tavola.”

53 “Mucchietto / di stracci.”

54 “‘Altissimu, onnipotente, bon Signore,
so’ tua le lauda, la gloria, l’onore e ogni benedizione!’” …
‘Ad te solo, altissimu, se konfano,
e nissun omo è degnu de mentovatte.’ …
‘Laudato sie, mi’ Signore, co’ tutte le tu’ creature,
speciarmente fratemo lu sole,
lo quale è giorno, e c’allumini co’ llui,
e lui è bellu, e radiante, co’ grande splendore:
porta er segno tuo.’
Poi si accorge, il contadino che non sa dire
le cose, come un bambino, se non nominandole,
che c’è la luna, sul bosco nel cielo.”

55 “Noi li ammazzeremo tutti” … “poi Dio dividerà / le anime degli innocenti da quelli dei rei.”

56 “Legato a un tronco, in fondo a una valletta … / morto di fame e ferite, le carni annerite dalle corde.”

57 "In fondo al fosso, lacerata nel petto nudo, con la testa / affondata nell'acqua e nel fango. / Era una sorgente d'acqua santa, / che continuava tranquilla a sgorgare/ e a scorrere tra i morti."
58 "Ma nella grazia di Dio, cosa non è grazia? /Anche un membro gonfio e odorante come un'acacia. / Così il santo, col peso della sua gioventù, / che fu del male e del male innocente, e ora era di Dio, / s'era alzato a cercare la pace sotto le acacie."
59 "Il teatro della morte."
60 "Chi deve andare va, chi deve restare, resta … / Chi se ne va è colpevole, chi resta è sconfitto."
61 "Coi loro carri come poveri altari di legno."
62 "Tra i poveri colpevoli che vanno, / i poveri perduti che rimangono: ma niente / muta negli atti, nei gesti, nei silenzi dell'addio."
63 "Qua e là, i fratelli, chi accampato / per uccidere, chi per essere ucciso, / per puro caso vittima o assassino, / per puro caso angelico o infernale."
64 "Sui loro cavallini matti, col gran collo nero / la culatta lucida, gli occhi colti in aranceti."
65 "Piero non ha dipinto ancora per lui / l'elmo morello o lilla a catino / né il giubbetto di terra verde … / Né Giotto gli ha tagliato i mantelli / o le cioce – e in altri paesi, lontani come Asie, / ci sono guerrieri stellati, su fondi d'oro: / egli, incondito come una bestia / (il millennio da cui dura la morte / della sua patria imperiale / è breve come un decennio, o dieci mesi, egli / ne ha la delicatezza alessandrina, intatta) / vive di sola vita, / inimmaginabile, / appunto come una bestia, / che nulla può mendicare / se non il vivere."
66 "L'opera si divide in tre parti: ognuna finisce con l'apparizione dell'angelo che avverte Bestemmia che Dio lo lascia solo e libero (ed egli si trova dunque nella realtà e le faccende – l'empirismo, il pragmatismo del mondo): la I volta appena egli ha annunciato la sua prima frase eretica e ha dei seguaci (le suore che gettano i veli); per cui egli si trova nella necessità di riorganizzare la vita dei perseguitati in una terra di nessuno comunistica ecc.; la seconda volta, nella pace di questa sua organizzazione (le sue meditazioni filosofiche ecc.) ed egli si trova ad amare carnalmente e umanamente la ragazza e ad affrontare la morte di Agonia; la terza volta alla fine, quando è già pronto alla morte, e quindi egli si trova nella necessità di lottare."
67 "Bestemmia, disse l'angelo – tu preghi e ascolti, / e sai di morire con la carne. / Mi ha mandato Dio. / Egli ha altrove i suoi santi / come tu volevi essere. Vengono soldati a ucciderti. / Ma non a uccidere te solo. Questi sono fatti della terra. / Sei libero, Bestemmia. Altra è la strada, / dice il Signore, della tua santità. / Quanto ti è stato vicino! / Egli ti ha toccato mentre le puttane / si amavano carnalmente tra sorelle / E violentavano, le

innocenti, un bambino. / Ti è stato vicino ad aiutarti a fingere miracoli. / Ti è stato vicino quando studiavi il modo di farli davvero. / Ti è stato vicino quando hai dovuto occuparti degli uomini / anzichè di lui. A ogni uomo il suo cuore, / a ogni santo la sua santità. Sei libero! / Il Signore ora si allontana da te. Ti lascia solo. / Con lo stesso alto e inaspettato amore / con cui ti si è avvicinato, ora se ne va. / … Dio, abbandonandoti, ti lascia ben chiara / l'ultima verità – essa è qui, con la luce, ma non ha parole."

68 "'Mi risveglio, mi trovo giovane di misera madre, malandato,
feroce: coi suoi occhi da vipera, i denti di cane,
nel momento in cui Cristo mi aveva denudato
come un condannato a morte. Basta. Ora sono qui.
Abbiamo poche ore di vita.
L'alba di domani ci vedrà cadaveri già vecchi.
Dei giovani come noi vengono per massacrarci:
perché non è fra loro il nostro posto?

Quale caso ci ha fatto martiri anzichè assassini?

Sono nato in fondo all'Occidente:
quindi mi sono trovato in mano, durante la santità
voluta da Dio, una zappa: e ora un'arma.

Sono tra i martiri. Finchè il Signore ha voluto
sono stato Santo come ho potuto. Adesso egli mi ha abbandonato.
Ho parole da bandito, da dirvi. …
Aspettiamoli come uomini: siamo nati dallo stesso popolo,
affamato, siamo fratelli e cugini,
per un caso non siamo compagni d'arme. …

Fate quello che volete:
potete fuggire. Io non vi chiedo più,
come fanno i santi, il martirio. Essi sorridendo
sono ben più spietati del diavolo!
Non voglio umiliare così, con un tale sorriso,
i miei assassini.
D'altra parte è giusto che poiché la mia morte,
ormai, non gli può insegnare più niente,
gl'insegni qualcosa la mia vita: voglio dire
gli ultimi atti della mia vita. …
Gli insegnerò che si può lottare per Dio,
contro i fascisti che se ne dicono servi;

i servi del potere, con quella loro maledetta forza,
di cui possono sempre giustamente vantarsi! Ché s'essi
fossero deboli, la nostra vittoria non avrebbe dolore!
...
Stamattina voglio la nostra vita.
Se decidete di stare qui e di lottare,
dovete desiderare veramente di vivere, di vivere
a costo di ammazzare loro, i sicari,
i padroni di un mondo che non vuole nulla:
... Ma noi dobbiamo veramente desiderare, invece, di ucciderli.
Migliaia e migliaia di morti come loro per molti secoli,

e la vita finalmente sarà salva. Cominciamo!'
I compagni di Bestemmia dissero che volevano
restare lì e combattere.

'Io – continuò a dire Bestemmia – non so più nulla.
Dio se n'è andato con la mia santità:
mi ha lasciato qui nudo. Lo ripeto perché ancora non credo.

E tuttavia la santità mi ha lasciato la sua luce.
Che abbandono è mai questo?
Sono incerto. Prima di morire, o di far morire,
forse non pregherò nemmeno. Sono incerto, incerto ...
Nessuno potrà mai scrivere alla nostra storia la parola Fine.'"

69 "Alla fine Bestemmia – con la partenza di Maria e dei suoi, destinati a rientrare nella vita normale ecc. Senza speranza, a ripiombare nella storia a loro nemica (quella di una classe superiore) che li vuole solo vivi, nient'altro ecc., rassegnati, vinti ecc. Servi, lieti servi, generazioni di animali che passano sulla terra, inferiori, innocenti e malvagi, con le loro sere, i loro giorni, le loro emigrazioni, le loro pesti ecc. La loro religione senza verità, come semplice obbedienza e conformismo ecc. Di gente umile ecc. ecc. – alla fine Bestemmia ritorna al mondo, e anziché dare la sua morte, al ricordo di quella gente che l'avrebbe subito mitizzato, esorcizzato facendolo santo, inserito nella lamentosa agiografia ecc., allontanato da sé nell'adorazione superstiziosa e estranea ecc. Decide di offrire la sua lotta. Opporre la vita alla vitalità ecc, la rabbia della fede contro la rabbia mercenaria, i diritti della povertà contro la prepotenza della ricchezza. Prende le armi in mano – le armi delle rivoluzioni popolari, falci e forche, e coi pochi suoi, aspetta e affronta i fascisti. Il poema finisce su questa lotta ancora senza esito, su questa lotta pura, l'eterna lotta."

70 "Con *Uccellacci e uccellini* si chiude definitivamente il sogno da cui tutta l'avventura cinematografica di Pasolini aveva avuto origine: quello di elaborare un linguaggio in grado di parlare a tutti, rivolto ad un popolo inteso nel senso gramsciano del termine, come 'altro' dalla borghesia. Constatato l'avvento, al posto di quel popolo, di una massa costruita *ad hoc*, dall'alto, ad opera della classe borghese, una massa la cui semplicità apparente è in realtà volontà di disimpegno e di volgarizzazione, Pasolini epura gradualmente i suoi film da quella che poteva esserne fino ad allora ritenuta la 'cifra': il carattere popolare.

... Il destinatario del messaggio filmico non viene più dato per scontato, ma, al contrario, è un destinatario da costruire (così come costruito è l'antagonista-massa)."

71 "'Uccellacci e uccellini' di Pier Paolo Pasolini si allinea, con caratteri particolari propri dell'autore, nella categoria dei film sulla 'crisi.' Quale sia questa crisi è ormai noto: la fine degli anni cinquanta, Suez e Budapest, il riflusso dell'impegno e la vittoria del disimpegno, la sconfitta delle ideologie, l'albeggiare di una civiltà dei consumi, così a Oriente come a Occidente, fatta di masse consumatrici e produttrici e di quadri tecnologici. Per quanto riguarda poi l'Italia, a queste spiegazioni ne va aggiunta una a parte: l'avanzata neocapitalista ha incluso tra i paesi 'che hanno' anche un paese come il nostro nel quale molti ancora 'non hanno.' Donde una contraddizione che non può non riflettersi anche nella letteratura."

72 Cesare Zavattini was one of the most important screenwriters and theorists of neo-realist cinema. The names are names of common people, workers, the unemployed, and the like.

73 "Non pensi però, signor Totò, che io pianga sulla fine di quello in cui credo. Sono convinto che qualcun altro verrà e prenderà la mia bandiera per portarla avanti. Oh, io piango solo su me stesso. E' umano, no, quando senti di non contare più."

74 "I funerali di Togliatti, un frammento di qualche minuto incastonato nel film":la politica e la morte, unite da una solenne, grave, infinita violenza." Sono immagini di cine-giornali d'attualità, montate al ritmo ieratico di una Passione Bachiana. Pugni chiusi, segni di croce di gente addolorata che rende l'ultimo omaggio cioè le esequie di un capo rivoluzionario "visto anche come un santo." Ancora una sequenza a doppio taglio, di significato complesso, commovente, e, insieme, imbarazzante per la sua turgida retorica avulsa dalla storia dei personaggi: comemmorazione e distacco da un avvenimento che, poeticamente, segna la fine di un'epoca, e l'inizio di un'altra stagione, dalla moralità "aperta," ricca di squilibri, d'incertezze, di confusione di cui lo stesso *Uccellacci e uccellini*, favola d'oggi, è testimonianza e confessione."

75 "FRATE CICCILLO: Ecco, frate Francesco, noi i falchi l'avemo convinti, e mo' i falchi come falchi l'adorano, er Signore; e pure li passeretti, l'avemo convinti, e pure ai passeretti, per conto loro, je sta bene, l'adorano, er Signore. Ma er fatto è che fra de loro ... se sgrugnano (*con immneso dolore*) s'ammazzano, a frate Francè ... Che ce posso fà io se ce sta la classe dei falchi e la classe dei passeretti, che nun ponno annà d'accordo fra loro? Che ce posso fà?

SAN FRANCESCO: Che ce puoi fà? Ma tutto ce puoi fà, co' l'aiuto del Signore!

FRATE CICCILLO: Come sarebbe a dì?

SAN FRANCESCO: Sarebbe a dì che dovete insegnà ai falchi e ai passeretti tutto quello che nun hanno capito, e che voi dovevate faje capì!

FRATE CICCILLO: Come?

SAN FRANCESCO: Coraggio, fratelli. Dovete ricomincià tutto daccapo ...

...

FRATE CICCILLO: Ma i falchi so' falchi, e i passeri so' passeri ... Nun c'è niente da fà, è la fatalità der monno ...

SAN FRANCESCO: Bisogna cambiarlo, er monno, frate Ciccillo: è questo che nun avete capito! Andate, e ricominciate tutto, in lode del Signore!"

76 "And, while in many ways drawing inspiration from the 'figurative fulguration' of *Vangelo*, also the missionary friars' refined and emotional apologue-intermezzo in Roman dialect emphasizes its rapt and composed religiosity as it empties it, however, of its intense Christian violence and anger." ("E anche il raffinato e commosso apologo-intermezzo romanico dei frati evangelizzatori, mentre si rifà per tanti versi alla "folgorazione figurativa" del *Vangelo*, ne accentua la raccolta e composta religiosità svuotandola, però, della sua intense violenza e collera cristiana." Ferrero, "Uccellacci e uccellini," in *Mondo Nuovo*, 6 June 1966.)

77 "Il corvo, ci dice l'autore, è il razionalismo ideologico superato dal messaggio giovanneo."

78 "Io per nascita, per formazione e per cultura sono un borghese, anzi un piccolo borghese. Allora sono, da una parte razionalista – laico, liberale, razionalista – come tradizione, e dall'altra sono un irrazionalista. Il mio senso religioso si innesta sul mio irrazionalismo di borghese, di borghese angosciato che è una figura tipica della cultura europea, credo anche nel Nord Europa. Quindi, quando io ho scelto l'ideologia marxista per interpretare la realtà, per capire quello che sta intorno a me, è chiaro che il mio marxismo è stato intriso di irrazionalismo e quindi di religiosità. Anzi, poichè penso che tutto sommato la piccola borghesia sia esattamente il contrario dello

spirito religioso, sia incapace del sentimento del sacro nel senso più alto e sublime della parola, credo che la religione sia un'arma formidabile di lotta contro lo spirito piccolo borghese, angusto, meschino, retrivo, egoista, ipocrita, ecc. Quindi in me naturalmente marxismo e religione si alleano nella mia polemica contro la borghesia." Typescript of interview, Cannes, 13 May 1966, Fondo Pasolini, Bologna.

79 "Una strada non frequentata ma aperta."

80 "In questo estremo confronto, in questo estremo 'scandalo': attraverso la 'scandalo' di questa sincerità (la politica è mortale) allo 'scandalo' della poesia (l'amore è eterno)."

81 Lucien Goldmann (1913–1970) was a French Marxist philosopher and sociologist of Romanian origins.

82 This is the formulation of the novel as the "demonic search for the hero," according to Lukács.

83 "Due 'personaggi veri' occupati, *direttamente e esplicitamente*, in una 'ricerca degradata di valori autentici in un mondo degradato.' *Questo è l'oggetto stesso del mio film.* E non per nulla il corvo parlante, verso la fine, cita una frase di Lukàcs: 'il cammino comincia, e il viaggio è finito.' Non accetto insomma di arrendermi all'ecolalia, all'imitazione della 'realtà' (la scomparsa dell'individuo problematico, per il prevalere definitivo dei valori di scambio sui valori d'uso): il mio marxismo degli anni Cinquanta mi porta a continuare a credere, sempre parafrasando Goldmann, a una 'ricerca che progredisce.' Naturalmente senza ottimismo, anzi, nel più nero pessimismo. Nell'allegoria di queste tre favole, la trama di fondo è la crisi e la necessità di rinnovamento del marxismo ... Su questa trama di fondo si fondano moltissimi altri motivi: prima di tutto la condanna alla tendenza del pensiero borghese a 'negare ogni sacralità, che si tratti del sacro celeste delle religioni trascendentali o del sacro immanente dell'avvenire storico.'"

84 "FRATE CICCILLO (*euforico*)
Altissimo, onnipotente, bon Signore,
quanto so' contento che c'è er sole!
E quanto so' contento che c'è pure l'acqua,
perché chi è sozzo ce se lava la faccia.
Laudato sii mi' Signore per 'sto somaro
per tutte 'ste pecore e 'sto pecoraro.
Il somarello è là che raglia; e il pecoraro tra le sue bestie, con la sua vecchia faccia piena di bitorzoli.
E Ninetto che ogni tanto, tutto allegro, dice amen.
FRATE NINETTO Amen ... amen ...

FRATE CICCILLO (*irresistibile nella sua santa allegrezza*)
Laudato sii mi' Signore per 'sto santo monno
che ce ponno campa' tutti, pure quelli che nun ponno ...
Sta passando uno sciancato, che come faccia a camminare, non si sa.
FRATE CICCILLO
Beata l'erba fresca, l'ortica e la cicoria,
e chi se la magna che Dio l'abbia in Gloria.
Una vecchietta, poverina, sta raccogliendo infatti la cicoria.
FRATE CICCILLO
Guai a quelli che morranno ne li peccata mortali
che me dispiace tanto a vede' 'sti brutti funerali!
Laudato sii mi' Signore per la contentezza che sta nei cori,
perché tutto quello che ciai intorno so' rose e fiori."

85 See the analysis of the Passion in *Bestemmia* in chapter 3.

86 Cf. Viano 1993: "At its best, Pasolini's realism is the result of the interaction between two fundamental semiotic attitudes which I will define as (1) ideological and (2) mystical. Fueled by Marxism and Freudian psychoanalysis, the ideological attitude does not trust the world of appearances and therefore treats reality suspiciously" (61).

> "But one cannot be suspicious all the time. Reality is also what is visible, the realm of appearance and the sense that there is no unmasking that will get us to the core of things" (62).

> "Fueled by Jung's and Eliade's works on myth as well as by his own readings in existential phenomenology, Pasolini's mystical attitude eschews logical thinking, exalts the enigmatic quality of life, and celebrates death as the purveyor of *the* mystery that 'makes Man great.' ... it values myth and the sacred, for they both rely on metaphor, bear witness to the multiplicity of meaning, and enhance the subject's disposition to wondering. And wandering" (63).

> Rather than in the name of an omnipotent textuality, referentiality should be questioned in order to better mime reality ... The text must somehow evoke reality, albeit within the framework of a problematic referentiality, which is what most of Pasolini's films do" (66).

87 "We know that justice is progressive and we know that, as society progresses, the awareness of its imperfect composition awakens, and the strident inequalities that afflict mankind come to the surface": These are the pope's words to the United Nations.

88 "Dai falsi miti dell'ottimismo razionale o mistico."
89 "Sarà solo con le proprie mani che l'uomo potrà forse spezzare le proprie catene."

Chapter Six

1 "Ho l'impressione che, a chi lo legga impreparato, questo progetto faccia venire un po' il capogiro: ma in realtà è scritto, per ora, a suo uso. Quanto a me, comincio a sentire verso questo progetto quell'amore esclusivo e invasato che mi lega alle mie opere, quando il farle comincia a diventare intrattenibile."
2 "Tutta la mia gioventù è stata affascinata da film americani, cioè da un'America violenta, brutale. Ma non è questa l'America che ho ritrovato: è un'America giovane, disperata, idealista. V'è in loro un gran pragmatismo e allo stesso tempo un tale idealismo. Non sono mai cinici, scettici, come lo siamo noi. Non sono mai qualunquisti, realisti: vivono sempre nel sogno e devono idealizzare ogni cosa ... Vieni in America e scopri la sinistra più bella che un marxista, oggi, possa scoprire. Ho conosciuto i giovani dello SNCC, sai gli studenti che vanno nel Sud a organizzare i negri. Fanno venire in mente i primi cristiani, v'è in loro la stessa assolutezza per cui Cristo diceva al giovane ricco: 'Per venire con me devi abbandonare tutto, chi ama il padre e la madre odia me.' Non sono comunisti né anticomunisti, sono mistici della democrazia: la loro rivoluzione consiste nel portare la democrazia alle estreme e quasi folli conseguenze. M'è venuta un'idea, conoscendoli: ambientare in America il mio film su San Paolo. Voglio trasferire l'intera azione da Roma a New York, situandola ai tempi nostri ma senza cambiar nulla. Mi spiego? Restando fedelissimo alle sue lettere. New York ha molte analogie con l'antica Roma di cui parla San Paolo. La corruzione, le clientele, il problema dei negri, dei drogati. E a tutto questo san Paolo dava una risposta santa, cioè scandalosa, come gli Sncc."
3 The manuscript gives two dates: 22–28 May 1968 (first draft) and 31 May–9 June 9 (revision). May 1968 was marked by civil unrest and general strikes, with the occupation of French universities and factories by students and workers protesting against capitalism and the state.
4 "Caro Don Cordero, ... Sono certo che sia lei che Don Lamera sarete, come si dice, choccati, da questo abbozzo. Infatti qui si narra la storia di due Paoli: il santo e il prete. E c'è una contraddizione, evidentemente, in questo: io sono tutto per il santo, mentre non sono certo molto tenero con il prete. Ma credo che la Chiesa, proprio con Paolo VI, sia giunta al punto

di avere il coraggio di condannare tutto il clericalismo, e quindi anche se stessa in quanto tale (dico, nei suoi termini pratici e temporali).

Qui, in questa lettera introduttiva accentuo, per onestà, questo punto: nella sceneggiatura, come vedrà, la cosa è trattata con meno schematismo e rigidità, lasciando libero lo spettatore di scegliere e di risolvere le contraddizioni: e di stabilire se questo FILM TEOLOGICO sia un inno alla Santità o alla Chiesa."

5 "Nella faccia di Paolo si legge qualcosa di peggio che la cattiveria: si legge la viltà, la ferocia, la decisione a essere abbietto, l'ipocrisia che fa sì che tutto questo avvenga in nome della Legge, o della Tradizione – o di Dio. Tutto ciò non può non rendere quella faccia anche disperata."

6 "Il contrasto tra la domanda 'attuale' rivolta a Paolo e la sua risposta 'santa.'"

7 In this respect, it is useful to refer to a passage from "I Dialoghi" of the same period: "I read in an issue several weeks ago about Rome's 'Potere Operaio.' The article, like all the others, was unsigned, and contained this idea: 'Only he who dedicates himself to the practical matter of "organizing" the struggle, subordinating all the other moments to the organizational moment, will truly find himself on a revolutionary path' ... As soon as I read this sentence, I thought, 'There's a sentence that St. Paul could have uttered.' I immediately understood what today's 'Student Movement' is: it is political movement whose ascesis is doing [*il fare*] ... Now, for the first time that I know of in the story of Believing, Doing is born. While in the time of the Bible, through St. Paul up until today, Doing was nothing but the other face of Believing. One can suppose that a Belief (unadorned, removed, not confronted, distained) directs this entire operation: and that it is not the case of a return to it, through the discovery of Doing (of Organizing). While I write, a meeting is taking place at the University of Rome ... Naturally, it is an organizational, practical meeting. And nonetheless I feel a rigidly mystical air hanging over it. I don't say this as a negative – quite the opposite. If the connection between mysticism and organization were finally discovered, I'd become a passionate organizer."

("Leggo in un numero di qualche settimana fa di 'Potere Operaio' di Roma, in un articolo non firmato, come tutti gli altri, questo concetto: 'Solo chi si dà praticamente a "organizzare" la lotta, subordinando al momento organizzativo tutti gli altri momenti, si trova veramente nel corso rivoluzionario' ... Appena letta quella frase ho pensato: 'Ecco una frase che avrebbe potuto pronunciare San Paolo.' Ho capito di colpo che cosa è oggi il 'Movimento Studentesco.' Esso è un movimento politico la cui ascesi consiste nel fare ... Ora, per la prima volta, che io sappia, nella storia il Credere nasce dal Fare: mentre dal tempo della Bibbia, attraverso San Paolo fino ai giorni nostri, il Fare non era che l'altra faccia del Credere. E' da supporsi che un Credere (incondito, rimosso, non affrontato, spregiato) presieda a tutta questa operazione: e che non si tratti che di un ritorno ad esso, attraverso la scoperta del Fare (dell'Organizzazione). Mentre scrivo, all'Università di Roma ... si sta svolgendo una riunione ... E' una riunione organizzativa, pratica, naturalmente. E tuttavia sento incombere su essa un'aria rigidamente mistica. Non lo dico come un fatto negativo, anzi! Nel caso che scoprissi finalmente il nesso tra misticismo e organizzazione diverrei un organizzatore appassionato." "Fare e pensare," *DIAL*, 734-5.

8 "Lei sa che sto preparando un film su San Paolo, sull'ideologia religiosa del suo tempo, cioè grosso modo sulla *Gnosi* attraverso le diverse correnti di pensiero del periodo ellenistico. E vado scoprendo sempre più in proposito, man mano che studio i mistici, che l'altra faccia del misticismo è proprio il 'fare,' l' 'agire,' l'azione.

Del resto la prossima raccolta di poesie che pubblicherò si intitolerà *Trasumanar e organizzar*. Con questa espressione voglio dire che l'altra faccia della 'trasumanizzazione' (la parola è di Dante, in questa forma apocopata), ossia dell'ascesa spirituale, è proprio l'organizzazione. Nel caso di San Paolo, l'altra faccia della santità, del rapimento al 'terzo cielo,' è l'organizzazione della Chiesa. Ci sarebbe molto da dire sui popoli che, secondo noi, agiscono solo al livello pratico, pragmatico: sono sempre ascetici e profondamente religiosi."

9 "Uno si chiama *Bestemmia*, ed è la vita di San Paolo, quello che avevo scritto 5 o 6 anni fa ma che adesso ho ripensato, nel senso che l'ho reso più radicale e violentemente anticlericale. Mentre prima lo era polemicamente, adesso il senso del film è una cosa violentissima, come non si è mai fatto, contro la Chiesa e contro il Vaticano, perché faccio un San Paolo doppio, cioè schizofrenico, nettamente dissociato in due: uno è il santo (evidentemente San Paolo ha avuto un'esperienza mistica – dalle lettere risulta chiaro – ed anche autentica), l'altro invece è il prete, exfariseo, che recupera le sue situazioni culturali precedenti e che sarà il fondatore della Chiesa. Come tale lo condanno; come mistico va bene, è un'esperienza mistica come altre, rispettabile, non la giudico, e invece lo condanno violentemente come fondatore della Chiesa, con tutti gli elementi negativi della Chiesa già pronti: la sessuofobia, l'antifemminismo, l'organizzazione, le collette, il trionfalismo, il moralismo. Insomma, tutte

le cose che hanno fatto il male della Chiesa sono già tutte in lui." Pasolini, "La perdita della realtà e il cinema inintegrabile," in De Giusti 1979, 156–7.

10 "L'idea poetica – che dovrebbe diventare insieme il filo conduttore del film – e anche la sua novità – consiste nel trasporre l'intera vicenda di San Paolo ai nostri giorni ... Qual è la ragione per cui vorrei trasporre la sua vicenda terrena ai nostri giorni? E' molto semplice: per dare cinematograficamente nel modo più diretto e violento l'impressione e la convinzione della sua attualità. Per dire insomma esplicitamente, e senza neanche costringerlo a pensare, allo spettatore, che 'San Paolo è *qui, oggi, tra noi*' e che lo è quasi fisicamente e materialmente. Che è alla nostra società che egli si rivolge: è la nostra società che egli piange e ama, minaccia e perdona, aggredisce e teneramente abbraccia."

11 "Così il film rivelerà attraverso questo processo la sua profonda tematica: che è contrapposizione di 'attualità' e 'santità' – il mondo della storia, che tende, nel suo eccesso di presenza e di urgenza a sfuggire nel mistero, nell'astrattezza, nel puro interrogativo – e il mondo del divino, che, nella sua religiosa astrattezza, al contrario, discende tra gli uomini, si fa concreto e operante."

12 On this point, see chapter 1's comparison between Eliade's phenomenological theory of the sacred and De Martino's historicist theory.

13 "Ci sono troppi problemi da risolvere, qui e ora, Duflot! Dobbiamo vivere, qui e ora!" Pasolini, *SC, SPS*, 1144. (There are two many problems to resolve, here and now, Duflot! We have to live, here and now!)

14 "Le cose, i personaggi, gli ambienti parleranno da sé. E da qui nascerà il fatto più nuovo e forse poetico del film: le 'domande' che gli evangelizzati porranno a San Paolo saranno domande di uomini moderni, specifiche, circostanziate, problematiche, politiche, formulate con un linguaggio tipico dei nostri giorni; le 'risposte' di San Paolo, invece, saranno quelle che sono: cioè esclusivamente religiose, e per di più formulate col linguaggio tipico di San Paolo, universale ed eterno ma inattuale (in senso stretto)."

15 "Questa mia violenza contro la Chiesa è profondamente religiosa, in quanto accuso San Paolo di aver fondato una Chiesa anzichè una religione."

16 "Aggiungere scena infernale in cui Satana incarica il suo mandante di incarnarsi in Luca, che, finito di scrivere il Vangelo, si accinge a scrivere gli *Atti* (e Satana si raccomanda di scriverli con stile falso, eufemistico e ufficiale)." Pasolini, *Abbozzo di sceneggiatura per un film su San Paolo.*

17 "La sua parola politica si costruisce secondo precisi nessi di causa ed effetto, procede sicura, agisce sul senso di colpa, discrimina ragione e irrazionalità, si apre a 'serie discussioni,' si organizza in dibattiti e richiede obbedienza

ai suoi modelli ... La critica pasoliniana è qui radicale: non solo verso il linguaggio della politica, ma verso tutto il linguaggio tecnico rigidamente comunicativo ... La parola tecnico-politica è 'dura,' decisa, 'quasi autoritaria,' oppure è caratterizzata da una 'dolcezza eufemistica,' dal trionfalismo e dall'ironia. All'opposto, la parola sacra o poetica è pronunciata come in delirio, fa soffrire nel corpo e nella mente ed è un monologo senza destinatario."

18 "39. CONTROCIELO
Esterno. Giorno.

Compare misteriosamente, in *dissolvenza*, contro il cielo profondamente azzurro, il viso segnato, dolce e inafferrabile, dell'Autore degli *Atti*, che lascia cadere sullo spettatore – come astrattamente e da lontano, improvvisando – queste parole:

'Con ogni istituzione nascono le azioni diplomatiche e le parole eufemistiche.
Con ogni istituzione nasce un patto con la propria coscienza.
Con ogni istituzione nasce la paura del compagno.
L'istituzione della Chiesa è stata *solamente* una necessità.'
Diavoli" (Pasolini, *Abbozzo di sceneggiatura per un film su San Paolo*)

19 "The author of a saint's life does not invent from scratch; rather, he turns what is known about a holy person's existence into a recognizable example of devotional biography ... Like a hagiography, Acts would be a 'falsified' account of real events and written in an 'official' style because this narrative details the birth of an 'official' Church" (Maggi 2009, 50–1).

20 Parmeggiani writes: "Analogamente, e torniamo al *San Paolo*, la parola sacra che Pasolini sceglie a proprio modello, è campo dinamico di tensioni linguistiche, incessante movimento d'infrazione ad un ordine te(le)ologico che rigenera costantemente se stesso. Nel dinamismo formale del San Paolo in quanto sceneggiatura, Pasolini riproduce il senso dinamico della parola sacra, parola che fa del suo *poter-essere* la propria caratteristica strutturale. Come parola in movimento, che ri-significa costantemente se stessa, anch'essa esige da parte di chi la recepisce un atto interpretativo che comprenda sia il Verbo rivelato e assoluto dell'originale, sia la temporalità della nostra lingua, della nostra esistenza umana" (1996, 200). (Analogously, and turning back to *San Paolo*, the sacred word that Pasolini chooses for his own model is a dynamic field of linguistic tensions, of incessant infractions against a theo-/teleological order that is constantly regenerating itself. In the fundamental dynamism of St. Paul to the extent that it

is a screenplay, Pasolini reproduces the dynamic sense of the sacred word, a word that makes its own power-to-be its own structural characteristic. Like a word in movement, that resignifies itself constantly, it also demands from the recipient an interpretive act that includes both the revealed, absolute Word of the original and the temporality of our language, of our human existence.")

21 Pasolini, "La sceneggiatura come 'struttura che vuol essere un'altra struttura'" (1965), *EE, SLA1*, 1489–1502.

22 "Written words, images evoked, and the imaginary of the reader, who is called to put together different temporalities, different genrès, different realities – in particular history, recent events, and the Bible – participate in this rewriting of history throughout the whole text" (Mariniello 1999, 78).

23 "Dobbiamo ora completare questa osservazione iniziale, precisando che il cinèma, così accentuato e funzionalizzato, come dicevamo, non è un mero elemento, sia pur dilatato, del segno, ma è il segno di un altro sistema linguistico. Non solo dunque il segno della sceneggiatura esprime *oltre che la forma 'una volontà della forma a essere un'altra,' cioè coglie 'la forma in movimento'*: un movimento che si conclude liberamente e variamente nella fantasia dello scrittore e nella fantasia collaboratrice e simpatetica del lettore, liberamente e variamente coincidenti: tutto questo avviene normalmente nell'ambito della scrittura, e presuppone solo nominalmente un'altra lingua (in cui la forma si compia). E' insomma una questione che mette in rapporto metalinguaggio con metalinguaggio, e le forme reciproche.

Ciò che è più importante notare è che la parola della sceneggiatura *è, così, contemporaneamente il segno di due strutture diverse*, in quanto il significato che esso denota è doppio: *e appartiene a due lingue dotate di strutture diverse*." Pasolini, "La sceneggiatura come 'struttura che vuol essere altra struttura,'" *EE, SLA1*, 1497.

24 "San Paolo subirà il martirio in mezzo al traffico della periferia di una grande città, moderna fino allo spasimo, coi suoi ponti sospesi, i suoi grattacieli, la folla immensa e schiacciante, che passa senza fermarsi davanti allo spettacolo della morte, e continua a vorticare intorno, per le sue enormi strade, indifferente, nemica, senza senso. Ma in quel mondo di acciaio e di cemento è risuonata (o è tornata a risuonare) la parola 'Dio.'"

25 "Avrà i caratteri mitici e simbolici di una rievocazione, come già la caduta nel deserto." In the screenplay it is Luke who speaks of Paul's time in the desert. Once again, it is the ambiguous Luke of the 1968 version, suspended before he takes the route of satanic silence and of the euphemistic drafting of the falsified Acts under the demonic dictation of the 1974 rewriting.

"21 CONTROCIELO
Esterno. Giorno.
Un uomo anziano, nobile, misterioso, col viso segnato dalle fatiche fisiche e gli occhi chiari ed estremamente miti, parla direttamente allo spettatore del film.
'Nessun deserto sarà mai più deserto di una casa, di una piazza, di una strada dove si vive millenovecentosettanta anni dopo Cristo. Qui è la solitudine. Gomito a gomito col vicino, vestito nei tuoi stessi grandi magazzini, cliente dei tuoi stessi negozi, lettore dei tuoi stessi giornali, spettatore della tua stessa televisione, è il silenzio.
'Non c'è altra metafora del deserto che la vita quotidiana.
'Essa è irrappresentabile, perché è l'ombra della vita: e i suoi silenzi sono interiori. E' un bene della pace. Ma non sempre la pace è migliore della Guerra. In una pace dominata dal potere, si può protestare col non voler esistere.
...
'Io sono l'autore degli *Atti degli Apostoli.*'

Discorsi diavoli
(passaggio di tre anni nel deserto)"
Cf. *Abbozzo di sceneggiatura, PPC2,* 1900–1.

[AGAINST THE SKY
Outside. Day.
An ancient man, noble, mysterious, with a face distinguished by physical strain and clear and extremely soft eyes, speaks directly to the spectator.

"No desert will be more deserted than a house, than a square, than a street where you live 1,970 years after Christ. Here is the solitude. Elbow to elbow your neighbour, clothed from the same big stores as you, client of the same stores as you, reader of the same papers as you, spectator of the same television as you, [this] is the silence.

"There is no other metaphor for the desert than daily life.

"It is not representable, because it is the shadow of life: and its silences are internal. It is one good thing of peace. But peace is not always better than war. In a peace dominated by power, one can protest using the desire not to exist.

...

"I am the author of the *Acts of the Apostles.*"

Conversations of devils
(passage of three years in the desert)].

This is a mythical-symbolic re-evocation of the desert and of the mysterious angelic-satanic interlocutor who recalls the ambivalence of the visitor in *Teorema.*

26 "'Tutti mi hanno abbandonato ...,' scrive Paolo assalito dalla malattia e chino sulla branda della prigione; ma, immediatamente dopo, aggiunge: '... mi hanno portato alle catene ... ma la parola di Dio non è incatenata.' Il senso dell'abbandono si muta nell'opposto sentimento della vicinanza di dio: questo, che è il centro della psicologia della *theologia crucis,* tipica tanto della mistica tedesca quanto dell'esperienza luterana, è anche la dominante della 'religiosità' particolare di Pasolini."

27 "*La porta* del cesso sta ancora muovendosi su e giù: l'uomo che ha sparato è appena scomparso.

Paolo si abbatte sul ballatoio, immobile sul suo sangue. Ha una breve agonia. E ben presto si perde in lui ogni segno di vita. Il pavimento del ballatoio è sconnesso. Il sangue si raggruma in una fessura, e comincia a gocciolare giù, sul lastricato del cortile. E' una piccola pozza rosea, su cui continuano a cadere le gocce del sangue di Paolo" (1968–74).

28 Armando Maggi (2009,106) has underlined a Franciscan link between the "little rosy puddle" of Paul and the "vermilion rose" of Francis's stigmata in a poem by Jacapone da Todi: Laude 61, "O Francesco povero – partiarca novello" (Oh poor Francis, new patriarch).

29 Catherine greets her confessor Raymond of Capua: "I, Caterina ... send you my greetings in the precious blood of God's Son. I long to see you engulfed and drowned in the sweet blood ..., which is permeated with the fire of his blazing charity ... I am saying that unless you are drowned in the blood you will not attain the little virtue of true humility ... [S]hut yourself up in the open side of God's Son ... There the dear bride [the soul] rests in the bed of fire and blood." Caterina da Siena, Letter 31, quoted in Bynum 2007, 164.

30 "The sprinkling of which St. Peter is speaking (and which is signified by this sprinkling [baptism]) is none other than preaching [c. I Pet. 1:1–2] ... The tongue of the preacher or Christian is the aspergillum. He dips into the rosy red blood of Christ [*tunkt er in des Herrn Christi rosenfarb blut*] and sprinkles the people with it [*besprenget damit das volck*], that is, he preaches to them the gospel, which declares that Christ has purchased the forgiveness of sins with his precious blood, that he has poured out [*vergossen*] his blood on the cross for the whole world, and that he who believes this has been sprinkled with this blood." Luther, "Sermon at the Baptism of Bernhard von Anhat," in *Werke, kritische Gesamtausgabe,* 49.132; quoted in Bynum 2007, 227.

31 "Abandon me! Incarnation is all about abandonment – abandonment to the flesh. Paul writes that in becoming flesh Christ abandoned the form of God; he emptied himself by taking on a limited materiality. This self-emptying is the exposure of the flesh. It is a kind of slavery that appeared to Paul in prison as liberation. What exactly did Christ abandon when he emptied himself? Certainly he did not abandon divinity as such; rather he emptied the transcendental *form* and carried divinity into the material. From one perspective this abandoned being might seem precarious, foundationless, cast over the abyss, but really this abandonment testifies instead to the fullness of the surfaces of being. The self-emptying or *kenosis* of Christ, the evacuation of the transcendental, is the affirmation of the plenitude of the material, the fullness of the flesh." Hardt 2002, 78.

32 "Take me now! Pasolini is fascinated with the immodest offering of Christ's body on the cross. His wounds are open. His entire body – breast, belly, sex, and knees – is burning under the gazes of the crowds and the elements. At the point of death, Christ is all body, an open piece of flesh, abandoned, exposed. This when Christ's emptied divinity, its radiant surfaces shine forth most brightly." Hardt 2002, 80.

33 "Exposed flesh is not transgression but scandal. In other words, exposure does indeed oppose and negate the norms of propriety, but its effect does not depend on that opposition as a support. Violation of the norm is not primary to exposure; the negation is secondary, an afterthought, an accident. It turns its back on the norm – that is its great offense. Exposure operates in ignorance of the norm, and thus conducts, in the only way possible, its real destruction. Christ's body testifies to the scandal, the scandal of the cross." Hardt 2002, 80–1.

34 See Foucault 1999, "The Meaning and Evolution of the Word Parrhesia," http://foucault.info/documents/parrhesia/foucault.DT1.wordParrhesia.en.html.

35 Bisogna esporsi (questo insegna
il povero Cristo inchiodato?),
la chiarezza del cuore è degna
di ogni scherno, di ogni peccato
di ogni più nuda passione ...
(questo vuol dire il Crocifisso?
sacrificare ogni giorno il dono
rinunciare ogni giorno al perdono
sporgersi ingenui sull'abisso).
Noi staremo offerti sulla croce

alla gogna, tra le pupille
limpide di gioia feroce,
scoprendo all'ironia le stille
del sangue dal petto ai ginocchi,
miti, ridicoli, tremando
d'intelletto e passione nel gioco
del cuore arso sul fuoco,
per testimoniare lo scandalo. (*USI, TP1*, 467–8)

36 "Vorrei accentuare la parola esibizione. La vocazione alle piaghe del martirio che l'autore fa a se stesso nel momento in cui trasgredisce l'istinto di conservarsi, sostituendolo con quello di perdersi – non ha senso se non è resa esplicita al massimo: se non è appunto esibita. In ogni autore, nell'atto di inventare, la libertà si presenta come esibizione della perdita masochistica di qualcosa di certo. Egli nell'atto inventivo, necessariamente scandaloso, si espone – e proprio alla lettera – agli altri: allo scandalo, appunto, al ridicolo, alla riprovazione, al senso di diversità, e perché no? all'ammirazione, sia pure un po' sospetta. C'è insomma il 'piacere' che si ha in ogni attuazione del desiderio di dolore e di morte." *EE, SLA1*, 1601.

37 "Libertà di scegliere la morte." *EE, SLA1*, 1600.

38 "Un grande o un piccolo martirio." *EE, SLA1*, 1601.

39 "GODERE DELLA LIBERTA' ALTRUI." *EE, SLA1*, 1603.

40 "Lo spettatore, in quanto tale, gode l'esempio di tale libertà, e come tale lo oggettiva: lo reinserisce nel parlabile. Ma ciò avviene al di fuori di ogni 'integrazione': in un certo senso al di fuori della società (la quale infatti non integra solo lo scandalo dell'autore ma anche la comprensione scandalosa dello spettatore). E' un rapporto tra singolo e singolo, che avviene sotto il segno ambiguo degli istinti e sotto il segno religioso (non confessionale) della carità." *EE, SLA1*, 1604.

41 "Il crocifisso, tramite Paolo, diverrà metafora per giustificare le proprie debolezze."

42 "Lo scandalo altro non è che l'ostentazione delle proprie debolezze."

43 "Mi attrae nel sottoproletario la sua faccia, che è pulita (mentre quella del borghese è sporca); perché è innocente (mentre quella del borghese è colpevole), perché è pura (mentre quella del borghese è volgare), perché è religiosa (mentre quella del borghese è ipocrita), perché è pazza (mentre quella del borghese è prudente), perché è sensuale (mentre quella del borghese è fredda), perché è infantile (mentre quella del borghese è adulta), perché è immediata (mentre quella del borghese è previdente), perché è gentile (mentre quella del borghese è insolente), perché è indifesa (mentre

quella del borghese è dignitosa), perché è incompleta (mentre quella del borghese è rifinita), perché è fiduciosa (mentre quella del borghese è dura), perché è tenera (mentre quella del borghese è ironica), perché è pericolosa (mentre quella del borghese è molle), perché è feroce (mentre quella del borghese è ricattatoria), perché è colorata (mentre quella del borghese è bianca)."

44 "Secondo: anche la 'realtà' dei corpi innocenti è stata violata, manipolata, manomessa dal potere consumistico: anzi, tale violenza sui corpi è diventato il dato più macroscopico della nuova epoca umana.

Terzo: le vite sessuali private (come la mia) hanno subito il trauma sia della falsa tolleranza che della degradazione corporea, e ciò che nella fantasie sessuali era dolore e gioia, è divenuto suicida delusione, informe accidia." *SPS*, 600.

45 "Ma oggi la degenerazione dei corpi e dei sessi ha assunto valore retroattivo. Se coloro che *allora* erano così e così, hanno potuto diventare *ora* così e così, vuol dire che lo erano già potenzialmente: quindi anche il loro modo di essere di *allora* è, dal presente, svalutato. I giovani e i ragazzi del sottoproletariato romano … se *ora* sono immondizia umana, vuol dire che anche *allora* potenzialmente lo erano: erano quindi degli imbecilli costretti a essere adorabili, degli squallidi criminali costretti a essere dei simpatici malandrini, dei vili inetti costretti a essere santamente innocenti, ecc. Ecc. Il crollo del presente implica anche il crollo del passato. La vita è un mucchio di insignificanti e ironiche rovine." *SPS*, 601.

46 Maggi writes: "As *Saint Paul* confirms, for Pasolini homosexuality is the mark of sickness and division. It is the sign of mortality, the sign of man's 'original sin.' In Walter Siti's world, Pasolini had had the intuition that in him a homosexual and a monster coexisted. 'For Pasolini, the (homosexual) man is a monster also because his monstrosity reveals the monstrous "derealization" of reality, as Rumble says. He is a sort of Sadean creature, victim and spectator of his crime (crime in the sense of an act against the nature of things). Nico Naldini, Pasolini's cousin, puts it very clearly: 'For Pasolini, homosexuality was something foreign, something to fight, something to resist.' Homosexuality, as far as the man Pasolini is concerned, is the sign of foreignness, of the expulsion from the original family due to an original sin. For Pasolini, the homosexual signifies both the beginning of time (the exile from the mother's land) and the end of time (the apocalypse within contemporary society)" (2009, 83–4).

47 "7 To keep me from becoming conceited because of these surpassingly great revelations, there was given me a thorn in my flesh, a messenger of Satan, to torment me. 8 Three times I pleaded with the Lord to take it

away from me. 9 But he said to me, 'My grace is sufficient for you, for my power is made perfect in weakness.' Therefore I will boast all the more gladly about my weaknesses, so that Christ's power may rest on me. 10 That is why, for Christ's sake, I delight in weaknesses, in insults, in hardships, in persecutions, in difficulties. For when I am weak, then I am strong" (2 Cor. 12:7–10).

48 "C'è insomma il "piacere" che si ha in ogni attuazione del desiderio di dolore e di morte." *EE, SLA1*, 1601.

49 "In Pasolini's screenplay, the apostle Paul is the sodomite whose primary role in society is to speak annihilation. Paul's apocalyptic message is in direct contrast with his febrile effort to construct a new religious repression. In *Saint Paul*, the apostle experiences his private recognition of his homosexual desire as a mystical insight. We could say that Paul lives his homosexuality as the apprehension of a new idiom that in actuality has been lying dormant inside of him. This idiom translates into a physical disease that contradicts his other language of law and domination (the creation of the Church as a repressive order). Homosexuality, we could infer, is a language that undoes his speaker. Pasolini's Saint Paul paradoxically envisions the new 'flesh' arising at the end of time as 'the flesh that dies.' The apocalyptic flesh theorized by Pasolini's St. Paul is a physical presence (Paul's flesh) whose primary and exclusive idiom is death. This is the sodomitical flesh (the flesh of those who practice death), as the apostle emphasizes in his *Letter to the Romans.*" Maggi 2009,11–12.

50 "SOGNO DI PAOLO. TARSO

Paolo sogna frammenti della sua infanzia.

Il suo allattamento.

Il padre un giorno che nel giardino lo alza verso il cielo.

Una scappata dalla scuola (che abbiamo visto nel suo soggiorno a Tarso). Con alcuni compagni vaga nei dintorni della città e giunge in un incantato luogo campestre (che abbiamo visto apparirgli durante il rapimento al Terzo Cielo).

Infine coi compagni giunge allo stadio. Dei ragazzi più grandi fanno delle gare. Poi dentro gli spogliatoi si spogliano nudi davanti agli occhi dei ragazzini e di Paolo.

Al ritorno a casa Paolo si sente male. E' preso dalle convulsioni. Le stesse che lo perseguiteranno per tutta la vita."

51 Translation emended.

52 "In quel periodo di Belluno, appunto dai tre anni ai tre anni e mezzo, ho provato le prime morse dell'amore sessuale: identiche a quelle che avrei provato finora (atrocemente acute dai sedici ai trent'anni): quella dolcezza

terribile e ansiosa che prende alle viscere e le consuma, le brucia, le contorce come una ventata calda, struggente, davanti all'oggetto dell'amore. Di tale oggetto d'amore ricordo, credo, solo le gambe – e precisamente l'incavo dietro il ginocchio coi tendini tesi – e la sintesi delle sue fattezze di creatura sbadata, forte, felice e protettrice (ma traditrice, sempre chiamata altrove): tanto che un giorno sono andato a cercare tale oggetto del mio struggimento, tenero-terribile, a casa sua ... Io non sapevo naturalmente di che si trattasse sentivo solo la fisicità della presenza di quel sentimento, così densa e cocente da torcermi le viscere. Mi sono dunque trovato nella necessità fisica di 'nominare' quel sentimento, e, nel mio stato di parlante solamente vocale, non di scrivente, ho inventato un termine. Tale termine era, lo ricordo perfettamente, TETA VELETA." Pasolini, "Dal Laboratorio," 1965, in *EE, SLA1,* 1350.

53 "Maxime hermétique, formule quasiment magique, 'abraxas' gnostique du corps pasolinien."

54 On the death drive of Pasolinian characters and mostly in *Accattone,* see Vighi 2003.

55 "E' un fatto ontologico; la grazia, il dono del sublime, lo si ha o lo si acquista ... Dapprincipio è un fatto meramente morale, la trasmutazione di se stesso in un senso idealistico, in altre parole la bontà, la sincerità, tutte le qualità morali portate al grado più alto di esaltazione.

In seguito, la santità può prendere, col tempo, il senso del rifiuto del mondo, dell'ascesi, dell'esercizio della crudeltà nei propri confronti, della ricerca di un approfondimento irraggiungibile di sé."

56 "Mandato controvoglia, con uno stratagemma, dai genitori in seminario (raccontato in osteria tra ladri). Scappa dal seminario, e torna nell'ambiente da cui è venuto: un ambiente di miseria e perversione (una borgata di una grande città). Il seminario l'ha peggiorato, involgarito, in quanto gli ha fatto perdere l'innocenza del suo rapporto col male. Il vizio e la delinquenza sono perciò veramente sporchi: egli vi cade fino in fondo. Arricchisce un po', poi la miseria. Prospettive di un futuro di miseria. Finge il pentimento: finge un rinnovarsi della vocazione religiosa. Si fa riprendere nel seminario. Ne esce prete. Attua la sua ambizione di successo e di miglioramento economico, nell'assurda idea di diventare un santo o qualcosa di simile. Organizza – con la pazienza dei santi, e aiutato dalla sua malizia di ex-ladro e truffatore, dal suo cinismo diabolico, dalla sua mancanza di ogni senso morale, e dalla volgarità derivante dal suo rapporto impuro col peccato – , riesce a organizzare una città di ragazzi: e, insieme, a simulare la santità. Viene creduto un santo, o qualcosa di simile. Egli, di nascosto, continua a fare la sua vita sensuale di ragazzo di borgata, frequenta magnaccia,

puttane ecc. Prende la sifilide. La cura clandestinamente ecc. ... e nella vita normale continua a fingere la santità ... La sifilide gli porta un'altra grave malattia ecc. Una malattia mortale che gli causa sofferenze atroci. Questo torna a favore del suo inganno di santità: è costretto a non occuparsi altro che della sua città di ragazzi e delle sue opere di bene, ecc.; e la malattia lo tormenta atrocemente. In questa situazione di santo, muore; in tutto come un santo vero."

57 "Con l'apologo appena abbozzato di *Sant'Infame*, Pasolini demistifica (abbassandolo al livello della concretezza e della meschinità umana) il valore 'sociale' della santificazione, ma nello stesso tempo espone una tesi più complessa, che riguarda la santità 'per sé' del protagonista ... Sant'Infame è l'esemplificazione dell'ambiguità della santità, della sospensione del mito della santità tra la volgare autoesaltazione ... e la vera, concreta sofferenza, psicologica come fisica, vissuta per raggiungere, follemente, la propria posizione di singolarità definitiva, di privilegio morale sugli altri. E, in fin dei conti, in *Sant'infame* viene descritta l'impossibilità di discernere la mistificazione dalla verità, l'ambizione dalla realtà di fatto, dal momento che la Storia non esiste, ma esiste soltanto l'effetto della Storia sulle tante storie personali, delle quali, come in questo caso, conta unicamente la fine, la morte."

58 "Certo, ... egli aveva mantenuto la parola; era la santità che gli aveva fatto raggiungere: la Santità, non la finzione della Santità. La Poesia, non la Letteratura! Posseduto da tale santità reale, egli si rese conto che tale Santità reale era stata un dono del Diavolo; che la Verità in cui di colpo viveva era stata opera della [Menzogna]; che il Bene di cui, ineffabilmente, [di colpo], godeva, era prodotto del Male; che la Rivelazione [era avvenuta attraverso] i suoi peggiori sentimenti. Ma tutto questo, così enunciato, non era che la lettera. Sotto questa serie di opposizioni razionali e banali, scorreva un'altra serie di opposizioni, non solo non parlabili, ma neanche intuibili, se non come Scherzo [Sottrazione del cosmo. Il nostro intellettuale lanciò un urlo e cadde per terra ... Il Diavolo ne approfittò per aprirgli ... sulle palme delle mani due lunghe, sanguinose stimmate." *RR2*, 1318.

59 "Un'infinita varietà di materie." *RR2*, 1318.

60 "Ogni materiale presenta caratteri contraddittori, sia in rapporto a se stesso che in rapporto agli altri minerali con cui è amalgamato e composto: non è stato possibile separare in quella pietra ciò che appariva prezioso da ciò che appariva privo di ogni valore o addirittura venefico." *PETR*, *RR2*, 1321–2.

61 "*Qui, oggi, tra noi* e ... lo è quasi fisicamente e materialmente ... [E'] alla nostra società che egli si rivolge: è la nostra società che egli piange e ama, minaccia e perdona, aggredisce e teneramente abbraccia." *PPC2*, 2023.

Bibliography

AA.VV (various authors). 1966. "Lo scandalo di Francesco." *Orizzonti*, June 5.

AA.VV (various authors). 1977. *Pier Paolo Pasolini nel dibattito culturale contemporaneo*. Amm.ne Provinciale di Pavia, Comune di Alessandria.

Agamben, Giorgio. 1993. *The Coming Community*. Minneapolis: University of Minnesota Press.

– 1998. *Homo Sacer: Sovereign Power and Bare Life*. Stanford: Stanford University Press.

– 2005. *The Time That Remains: A Commentary on the Letter to the Romans*. Stanford: Stanford University Press.

– 2007. *Profanations*. New York: Zone Books.

– 2011. *The Kingdom and the Glory: For a Theological Genealogy of Economy and Government*. Stanford: Stanford University Press

– 2011. "Angels." *Angelaki: Journal of the Theoretical Humanities*, 16.3, 117–23.

Alcoff, Linda, and John Caputo, eds. 2009. *St. Paul among the Philosophers*. Bloomington: Indiana University Press.

Allen, Beverly. 1982. *Pier Paolo Pasolini: The Poetics of Heresy*. Saratoga, CA: Anma Libri.

Angelini, Franca. 2000. *Pasolini e lo spettacolo*. Rome: Bulzoni.

Antonello, Pierpaolo. 2013. *Dimenticare Pasolini*. Milan: Mimesis.

Argento, Dario. 1965. "Opera 'ideo-comica' con tema religioso." *Paese Sera*, 29 October.

Asor Rosa, Alberto. *Scrittori e popolo*. Rome: Samonà e Savelli.

Attisani, Antonio. 2003. "La rivoluzione inimitabile di Francesco." In *L'invenzione del teatro*, 113–58. Rome: Bulzoni Editore,

Auerbach, Erich. 1953. *Mimesis: The Representation of Reality in Western Literature*. Princeton: Princeton University Press.

Bachmann, Gideon. 1979. "La perdita della realtà e il cinema inintegrabile" (Chia, 13 September 1974). In *Il cinema in forma di poesia,* edited by Luciano De Giusti, 152–66. Pordenone: Cinemazero.

Bachtin, Michael. 1982. *The Dialogic Imagination.* Austin: University of Texas Press.

Badiou, Alain. 2003. *Saint Paul: The Foundation of Universalism.* Stanford: Stanford University Press.

Baldelli, Pio. 1951. "Falsificazione umana di un giullare di Dio." *Cinema,* no. 55, 1 February.

– 1978. "Il 'caso' Pasolini e l'uso della morte." In *Perché Pasolini,* edited by Gualtiero De Santi, Lenti Maria, and Rossini Roberto, 153–68. Florence: Guaraldi.

Baldoni, Adalberto, and Borgna, Gianni. 2010. *Una lunga incomprensione. Pasolini fra destra e sinistra.* Firenze: Vallecchi.

Baranski, Zigmunt G. 1999. "The Texts of *Il Vangelo Secondo Matteo.*" In *Pasolini Old and New,* edited by Baranski, 281–320. Dublin: Four Court Press.

Bataille, George. 2004 [1970]. *Visions of Excess: Selected Writings 1927–1939.* Minneapolis: University of Minnesota Press.

– 1988. *Inner Experience.* Albany: SUNY Press.

Baugh, Lloyd. 1997. *Imaging the Divine: Jesus and Christ – Figures in Film.* Kansas City: Sheed and Ward.

Bazin, Andrè. 2005. "Cinema and Exploration." In *What Is Cinema?,* 1:154–63. Berkeley: University of California Press.

– 2005. "De Sica: Metteur en Scène." In *What Is Cinema?,* 2:61–82. Berkeley: University of California Press.

– 2005. "The Grandeur of Limelight." In *What Is Cinema?,* 2:128–39. Berkeley: University of California Press.

– 2005. "Marginal Notes on *Eroticism in the Cinema.*" In *What Is Cinema?,* 2:169–75. Berkeley: University of California Press.

– 2005. "Painting and Cinema." In *What Is Cinema?,* 1:164–69. Berkeley: University of California Press.

Bazzocchi, Marco Antonio. 1995. "Pasolini e la parola." *Bollettino '900: Electronic Newsletter of '900 Italian Literature* 2–3.1 (December 1995–96). http://www.comune.bologna.it/iperbole/boll900/bazzocc2.htm.

– 1998. *Pier Paolo Pasolini.* Milan: Bruno Mondadori.

– 2007. *I burattini filosofi: Pasolini dalla letteratura al cinema.* Milan: Bruno Mondadori.

Benedetti, Carla. 1995. "Per una letteratura impura." In *A partire da "Petrolio." Pasolini interroga la letteratura,* 9–13. Ravenna: Longo.

– 1998. *Pasolini contro Calvino.* Turin: Bollati Boringhieri.

Benedetti, Carla, and Giovanni Giovannetti. 2012. *Frocio e basta.* Milan: Effigie.

Benedetti, Carla, and M.A. Grignani, eds. 1995. *A partire da "Petrolio". Pasolini interroga la letteratura.* Ravenna: Longo.

Benjamin, Walter. 2008 [1936]. *The Work of Art in the Age of Its Technological Reproducibility, and Other Writings on Media,* ed. Michael W. Jennings, Brigid Doherty, and Thomas Y. Levin. Cambridge, MA: Belknap.

Bernardi, Sandro. 1997. "Pasolini, la storia e il mito." In *Scrittori e cinema fra gli anni '50 e '60,* ed. Francesco Falaschi, 26–36. Florence: Giunti.

– 2010. "Pasolini, Marilyn e la partenza degli dei dalla Terra." *Fata Morgana, Quadrimestrale di Cinema e Visioni, Il Sacro,* 10 (January–April): 115–38.

Bernardini, Aldo. 1969. "Religiosità e sacralità nel teorema di Pasolini." *Cineforum* 85 (May): 310–15.

Bertelli, Pino. 2000. *Pier Paolo Pasolini: Il cinema in corpo.* Rome: Edizioni Croce.

Bertini, Antonio. 1979. *Teoria e tecnica del film in Pasolini.* Rome: Bulzoni.

Bertolucci, Bernardo, and Jean-Louis Comolli. 1965. "Le cinéma selon Pasolini." *Cahiers du Cinéma* 169: 22–5.

Betti, Laura, and Michele Gulinucci, eds. 1996. *Le Regole di un'illusione.* Rome; Associazione Fondo Pier Paolo Pasolini. Cited in the text as *RILL.*

Biasin, Gian Paolo. 1975. *Literary Diseases.* Austin: University of Texas Press.

Bini, Daniela. 2009. "Intersezioni culturali: Pasolini tra cinema e sceneggiata, tragedia classica e teatro dei pupi, Modugno e Pirandello." In AA.VV [various authors], *Geografie d'Italia. Atti del XIX Convegno dell'Associazione di Lingua e Letteratura Italiana.* Padua: University of Padua.

Blanton, Ward. 2010. "Reappearance of Paul, 'Sick'": Foucault's Biopolitics and the Political Significance of Pasolini's Apostle." *Journal of Culture and Religious Theory,* 11.1: 52–77.

Boscalijon, Daniel R. 2010. "Žižek's Atheist Theology." *International Journal of Žižeck Studies,* 4.4: 1–14. http://zizekstudies.org/index.php/ijzs/article/view/271/346.

Brown, Peter. 1981. *The Cult of Saints.* Chicago: University of Chicago Press.

Brunette, Peter. 1987. "God's Jester." In *Roberto Rossellini.,* 128–37. New York: Oxford University Press,

Bruno, Giuliana. 1994. "The Body of Pasolini's Semiotics." In *Pier Paolo Pasolini: Contemporary Perspectives,* edited by Patrick Rumble and Bart Testa, 88–105. Toronto: University of Toronto Press.

Bruno, Marcello Walter. 2008. "Corpus Christi Pasolini." In *Corpus Pasolini,* edited by Alessandro Canadè, 85–102. Cosenza: Pellegrini.

Bynum, Caroline Walker. 1987. *Holy Feast and Holy Fast: The Religious Significance of Food to Medieval Women.* Berkeley: University of California Press.

– 2007. *Wonderful Blood: Theology and Practice in Late Medieval Northern Germany and Beyond.* Philadelphia: University of Pennsylvania Press.

Cacitti, Remo, Giuseppe Conti Calabrese, Marzio Manenti,and Natale Spineto, eds. 1997. *Pasolini e il sacro.* Udine: DARP Edizioni Friuli.

Calabretto, Roberto. 1999. *Pasolini e la musica.* Pordenone: Cinemazero.

Caminati, Luca. 2010. *Il cinema come happening. Il primitivismo pasoliniano e la scena artistica italiana degli anni Sessanta.* Milan: Postmedia.

Campani, Ermelinda. 2003. *Cinema e sacro. Divinità, magia e mistero sul grande schermo.* Rome; Gremese Editore.

Cappabianca, Alessandro. 1998. *Il cinema e il sacro.* Genoa: Le mani.

Carotenuto, Aldo. 1985. *L'autunno della coscienza. Ricerche psicologiche su Pier Paolo Pasolini.* Turin: Boringhieri.

Caruso, Lucio Settimio. 1966. "Uccellacci e uccellini di Pier Paolo Pasolini." *Il Mattino,* 9 June.

– 1988. "Il Cristo severo di Pasolini." *Avvenire,* 2 September.

Casi, Stefano, ed. 1990. *Desiderio di Pasolini.* Turin: Sonda.

Casiraghi, Ugo. 1966. "Una favola ideo-comica." *L' Unità,* 5 May.

Chiesa, Lorenzo. 2005. "Pasolini, Badiou, Žižek and the Legacy of Christian Love." in *HTVNews,* 60: 8–12.

Chiesa, Lorenzo, and Alberto Toscano. 2007. "*Agape* and the Anonymous Religion of Atheism." *Angelaki,* 12.1: 113–25.

– 2011. "The Bio-Theo-Politics of Birth." *Angelaki: Journal of the Theoretical Humanities,* 16:3, 101–15.

Chiesi, Roberto, and Andrea Mancini. 2007. *Poet of Ashes.* San Francisco: Citylights.

Colombo, Furio, and Gian Carlo Ferretti. 2005. *L'ultima intervista di Pasolini.* Rome: Avagliano.

Conti Calabrese, Giuseppe. 1994. *Pasolini e il sacro.* Milan: Jaca.

Dagrada, Elena. 1985. "Sulla soggettiva libera indiretta." *Cinema e cinema* 12.1: 48–55.

De Ceccatty, René. 1998. *Sur Pier Paolo Pasolini.* Paris: Editions du Scorff.

– 2005. *Pasolini.* Paris: Gallimard.

De Gaetano, Roberto. 2008. "L'epico-religioso e il comico-popolare." In *Corpus Pasolini,* edited by Alessandro Canadè, 75–83. Cosenza: Pellegrini.

De Giusti, Luciano, ed. 1979. *Il cinema in forma di poesia.* Pordenone: Cinemazero.

– 1983. *I film di Pier Paolo Pasolini.* Rome: Gremese.

Deleuze, Gilles. 1981. *Francis Bacon, Logique de la sensation.* Paris: Éditions de la Différence.

– 1985. *Cinema II: L'Image-Temps.* Paris: Minuit.

– 1989. *Cinema 2: The Time-Image.* Minneapolis: Minnesota University Press.

De Martino, Ernesto. 1958. *Morte e Pianto Rituale delmondo antico.* Turin: Einaudi.

– 1959. "Mito, scienze religiose e civiltà moderna." *Nuovi Argomenti* 37 (March–April): 4–48.

– 1995. "Fenomenologia religiosa e storicismo assoluto." In *Storia e metastoria: I fondamenti di una teoria del sacro*, edited by Marcello Massenzio, 47–74. Lecce: Argo.

– 2002. *La fine del mondo. Contributo all'analisi delle apocalissi culturali.* Turin: Einaudi.

– 2007. *Sud e magia.* Milan: Feltrinelli.

Depoortere, Frederiek. 2008. *Christ ian Postmodern Philosophy: Gianni Vattimo, René Girard and Slavoj Žižeck.* London: T & T Clark.

– 2009. *Badiou and Theology.* London: T & T Clark.

Derrida, Jacques. 1993. *Memoirs of the Blind: The Self-Portrait and Other Ruins*, translated by Pascale-Anne Brault and Michael Naas. Chicago: University of Chicago Press.

De Santi, Gualtiero, Maria Lenti, and Roberto Rossini, eds. 1978. *Perché Pasolini.* Florence: Guaraldi.

Dottorini, Daniele. 2010. "La dialettica del sacro." *Fata Morgana, Quadrimestrale di Cinema e Visioni, Il Sacro* 10 (January–April): 39–53.

Eliade, Mircea. 1954. *Trattato di Storia delle religioni.* Turin: Einaudi.

– 1959 [1956]. *The Sacred and the Profane.* New York: Harvest/HBJ.

– 2005 [1954]. *The Myth of the Eternal Return: Cosmos and History.* Princeton: Princeton University Press.

Escobar, Renato. 1978. "Pier Paolo Pasolini: Progetto per un film su San Paolo." *Cinemasessanta* 121 (May): 19–25.

Fabbri, Paolo. 1994. "Free/ Indirect/Discourse." In *Pier Paolo Pasolini*, edited by Patrick Rumble and Bart Testa, 78–87. Toronto: University of Toronto Press.

Felice, Angela, and Giampaolo Gri, eds. 2013. *Pasolini e l'interrogazione del sacro.* Venice: Marsilio.

Ferrero, Adelio. 1966. "Uccellacci e uccellini." *Mondo Nuovo*, 6 June.

– 1977. *Il cinema di Pier Paolo Pasolini.* Padua: Marsilio.

Ferretti, Gian Carlo. 1964. *Letteratura e ideologia.* Rome: Editori Riuniti.

– 1976. *L'universo orrendo.* Rome: Editori Riuniti.

Fink, Guido. 1966. "Prosa e crisi dell'ideologia nell'ultimo film di Pier Paolo Pasolini." *Cinema Nuovo*, November.

Finotti, Fabio. 1993. "Una poetica del verbo." In *Testimonianza e Poesia. David Maria Turoldo.*, edited by Armando Fiscon and Enrico Grandesso, 93–130. Camposanpiero: Edizioni del Noce.

– 2000. "Itinerario di Rebora, dai *Frammenti Lirici* ai *Canti Anonimi.*" In *Il sacro nella poesia contemporanea*, conference proceedings, Florence, 28–29 October 1997, edited by Giuliano Ladolfi and Marco Merlin, 31–43. Florence: Interlinea Edizioni.

– 2007. "I *Frammenti Lirici* e la consacrazione della parola." In *Bellezza, filosofia, poesia nel 50° della morte di Clemente Rebora*, edited by Pier Paolo Ottonello, 71–84. Stresa: Edizioni Rosminiane:.

– 2007. "I segni e la storia. Le biografie letterarie di Francesco d'Assisi tra '800 e '900." In *Giovanni Jorgensen e il Francescanesimo*, Atti del 35 Convegno internazionale, Assisi, 28–31. Assisi: Società Internazionale di Studi Francescani. Centro Universitario di Studi Francescani.

Fortini, Franco. 1993. *Attraverso Pasolini.* Turin: Einaudi.

Foucault, Michel. 1999 [1983]. "The Meaning and Evolution of the Word Parrhesia." In *Discourse and Truth: The Problematization of Parrhesia.* Edited by Joseph Pearson. http://foucault.info/documents/parrhesia/foucault.DT1.wordParrhesia.en.html.

Francione, Fabio, ed. 2010. *Pasolini sconosciuto.* Alessandria: Falsopiano.

Frugoni, Chiara. 1998. *Francis of Assisi.* London: SCM.

Fusillo, Massimo. 1996. *La Grecia secondo Pasolini.* Florence: La Nuova Italia.

– 2006. *Il Dio Ibrido. Dioniso e le "Baccanti" nel Novecento.* Bologna: Il Mulino.

Galimberti, Umberto. 2000. *Orme del sacro.* Milan: Feltrinelli.

Galluzzi, Francesco. 1994. *Pasolini e la pittura.* Rome: Bulzoni.

Garboli, Cesare. 1969. *La stanza separata.* Milan: Mondadori.

Girard, René. 1977. *Violence and the Sacred.* Baltimore: Johns Hopkins University Press.

– 1987. *Things Hidden since the Foundation of the World.* Stanford: Stanford University Press.

Golino, Enzo. 1985. *Pasolini: Il sogno di una cosa. Pedagogia, eros, letteratura dal mito del popolo alla società di massa.* Bologna: Il Mulino.

Gordon, Robert. 1996. *Pasolini: Forms of Subjectivity.* Oxford: Clarendon.

Greene, Naomi. 1990. *Cinema as Heresy.* Princeton: Princeton University Press.

– 1994. "*Salò*: The Refusal to Consume." In *Pier Paolo Pasolini*, edited by Patrick Rumble and Bart Testa, 232–42. Toronto: University of Toronto Press.

Gregor, Brian, and Jens Zimmermann, eds. 2009. *Bonhoeffer and Continental Thought: Cruciform Philosophy.* Bloomington: Indiana University Press.

Guattari, Félix. 2003. *Chimères* 50: 98.

Guidi, Alessandro, and Pier Luigi Sassetti. 2009. *L'eredità di Pier Paolo Pasolini.* Milan: Mimesis.

Gumbrecht, Hans Ulrich. 2004. *Production of Presence.* Stanford: Stanford University Press.

Gumbrecht, Hans Ulrich, and K. Ludwig Pfeiffer. 1994. *Materialities of Communication.* Stanford: Stanford University Press.

Hardt, Michael. 2002 [1997]. "Exposure: Pasolini in the Flesh." In *A Shock to Thought: Expression after Deleuze and Guattari*, edited by Brian Massumi, 77–84.

London: Routledge. Originally published in *Canadian Review of Comparative Literature* 24.3: 579–87.

Hardt, Michael. 2008. "L'esposizione della carne." In *Corpus Pasolini*, edited by Alessandro Canadè, 61–74. Cosenza: Pellegrini.

Hardt, Michael, and Toni Negri. 2001. *Empire*. Cambridge, MA: Harvard University Press.

Harrison, Robert. 2003. *The Dominion of the Dead*. Chicago: University of Chicago Press.

Kotsko, Adam. 2008. *Žižeck and Theology*. London: T & T Clark.

Jameson, Fredric. 1991. *Postmodernism, or the Cultural Logic of Late Capitalism*. Durham: Duke University Press.

Jansen, Katherine Ludwig. 2000. *The Making of the Magdalen: Preaching and Popular Devotion in the Later Middle Ages*. Princeton: Princeton University Press.

Jasper, David. 2004. *The Sacred Desert: Religion, Literature, Art and Culture*. Malden, MA: Blackwell.

Jewell, Keala. 1992. *The Poiesis of History*. Ithaca, NY: Cornell University Press.

Jori, Giacomo. 2001. *Pasolini*. Turin: Einaudi.

Lawton, Ben. 1980–81. "The Evolving Rejection of Homosexuality, the Sub-Proletariat, and the Third World in the Films of Pier Paolo Pasolini." *Italian Quarterly* 82–83 (Fall–Winter): 167–75.

Lawton, Ben, and Maura Bergonzoni, eds. 2009. *Pier Paolo Pasolini: In Loving Memory*. Washington, DC: New Academia.

Macciocchi, Maria Antonietta, ed.1980. *Pasolini*. Paris: Grasset.

Maggi, Armando. 2009. *The Resurrection of the Body*. Chicago: University of Chicago Press.

Magrelli, Enrico, ed. 1977. *Con Pier Paolo Pasolini*. Rome: Bulzoni.

Mancini, Michele, and Perrella Giuseppe, eds. 1981. *Pier Paolo Pasolini: Corpi e luoghi*. Rome: Theorema.

Marchesini, Alberto. 1994. *Citazioni pittoriche nel cinema di Pasolini: da* Accattone *al* Decameron. Florence: La Nuova Italia.

Marchi, Donatella. 2006. "*San Paolo* (Epeisòdion)," *Poetiche*, no. 1, 81–94.

Marcus, Millicent. 1986. "Pasolini's *Teorema*: The Halfway Revolution." In *Italian Film in the Light of Neorealism*, 245–62. Princeton: Princeton University Press.

– 1993. *Filming by the Book: Italian Cinema and Literary Adaptation*. Baltimore: Johns Hopkins University Press.

Mariniello, Silvestra. 1999. "*St. Paul*: The Unmade Movie." *Cinémas* 9.2–3: 67–84.

Marrone, Gaetana. 2000. *The Gaze and the Labyrinth*. Princeton: Princeton University Press.

Martellini, Luigi. 1989. *Introduzione a Pasolini*. Bari: Laterza.

– 2006. *Ritratto di Pasolini.* Bari: Laterza.

Micciché, Lino. 1966. "*Uccellacci e Uccellini.*" *L'Avanti,* 12 May.

– 1975. "La morte e la storia." *Cinema Sessanta,* September–October.

– 1975. *Il cinema italiano degli anni '60.* Venice: Marsilio.

Miconi, Andrea. 1998. *Pier Paolo Pasolini.* Milan: Costa & Nolan.

Morandini, Morando. 1966. "Pasolini e le ceneri di Togliatti." *L'osservatore politico letterario* 8 (6 June).

– 1991. "Introduzione." In Pier Paolo Pasolini, *Il Vangelo secondo Matteo, Edipo re, Medea,* i–viii. Milan: Garzanti.

Moravia, Alberto. 1966. "Un corvo che ha letto Marx." *L'Espresso* 12.20 (15 May).

Morefield, Kenneth R., ed. 2008. *Faith and Spirituality in Masters of World Cinema.* Cambridge: Cambridge Scholars.

Moscati, Italo. 1995. *Pasolini e il teorema del sesso.* Milan: Il Saggiatore.

Murri, Serafino. 1994. *Pier Paolo Pasolini.* Milan: Il Castoro.

– 2001. *Pier Paolo Pasolini: "Salò o le 120 giornate di Sodoma."* Turin: Lindau.

Nagy, Piroska. 2000. *Le don des larmes au Moyen Âge.* Paris: Albin Michel.

Naldini, Nico. 1994. *Pier Paolo Pasolini. Vita attraverso le lettere.* Turin: Einaudi.

Nancy, Jean-Luc. 1991. *The Inoperative Community.* Minneapolis: University of Minnesota Press.

– 1993. *The Birth to Presence.* Stanford: Stanford University Press.

– 2005. *The Ground of the Image.* Fordham: Fordham University Press.

– 2008. *Dis-Enclosure: The Deconstruction of Christianity.* New York: Fordham University Press.

Novello, Neil, ed. 1999. *Al trionfo dell'esserci: Teoria e prassi nell'ultimo cinema di Pier Paolo Pasolini.* Florence: Manent.

– 2007. *Il sangue del re: L'opera di Pasolini.* Cesena: Il ponte vecchio.

– 2007. *Pier Paolo Pasolini.* Napoli: Liguori.

Ogletree, Thomas W. 1966. *The Death of God Controversy.* Nashville, TN: Abingdon.

Palmer, Michael. 1997. *Freud and Jung on Religion.* London: Routledge.

Panicali, Anna. 1995. "Paolo e San Paolo." In *Il mistero della parola. Capitoli critici sul teatro di Pier Paolo Pasolini,* edited by Gualtiero De Santi and Massimo Puliani, 79–85. Rome: Il Cigno Galileo Galilei Edizioni di Arte e Scienza.

Parmeggiani, Francesca. 1996. "Pasolini e la parola sacra." *Italica* 73.2: 195–214.

Pasolini, Pier Paolo. 1946–47. *Quaderni Rossi.* Booklet. *RR1,* 131–57.

– 1948–49. "La crocifissione." Poem. In *USI, TP1,* 467–8.

– 1956. "Il pianto della scavatrice." Poem. In *Le Ceneri di Gramsci, TP1,* 833–49.

– 1957. *Le ceneri di Gramsci.* Book. *TP1,* 763–867.

– 1958. *L'usignolo della Chiesa Cattolica.* Book. Milan: Longanesi. In *TP1,* 381–503.
– 1961 (May). "Lotta al Fariseismo (che è dappertutto)." Article. *DIAL,* 118.
– 1961 (June). "Postilla personale." Article. *DIAL,* 134.
– 1961 (November). "Marxismo e religiosità." Article. *DIAL,* 206–7.
– 1961. "A un Papa." Poem. In *La Religione del mio tempo.* Milan: Garzanti. In *TP1,* 1009.
– 1961. *La Religione del mio tempo.* Book. Milan: Garzanti. *TP1,* 889–1060.
– 1962 (January). "Incontro con Pier Paolo Pasolini." Interview. *Filmcritica* 116. In *PPC2,* 2799–2818.
– 1962 (September). "*Mamma Roma,* ovvero dalla responsabilità individuale alla responsabilità collettiva." Interview. *Filmcritica* 125. In *PPC2,* 2819–2835.
– 1962–67. *Bestemmia.* Script. *TP2,* 995–1115.
– 1963. "Una carica di vitalità."Article. *Il giorno,* 6 March. In *PPC1,* 671–4.
– 1964 (5 February). "Intervista alla Radio Televisione Svizzera Italiana." Interview. In TP2, 1724, and *RILL,* 103–4.
– 1964 (February). Press release no. 95 of 27 October 1964, Ritz Cinema d'Essai with the cultural sponsorship of the Milanese Group of Cinema Critics; from a letter to Dr Lucio S. Caruso of Pro Civitate Christiana. Assisi.
– 1964 (December). "Marxismo e Cristianesimo." Interview. *L'Eco di Brescia.* In *SPS,* 786–824.
– 1964. *Poesia in forma di rosa.* Book. Milan: Garzanti. In *TP1,* 1079–2056.
– 1964. "Una discussione del '64." Interview. In AA.VV. 1977 and *SPS,* 748–85.
– 1964. "Una visione del mondo epico-religiosa." Interview. Originally in *Bianco e nero,* no. 6, June 1964. Now in *PPC2,* 2844–79.
– 1965 (April–May). "Intervista rilasciata a Maurizio Ponzi." Interview. *Filmcritica* 156–7. In *PPC2,* 2880–9.
– 1965. "Dal Laboratorio." Essay. In *EE, SLA1,* 1307–42.
– 1965. "Il cinema di poesia." Essay. In *EE, SLA1,* 1461–88.
– 1965. "La sceneggiatura come struttura che vuol essere un'altra struttura." Essay. In *EE, SLA1,* 1489–1502.
– 1965. *Alì dagli occhi azzurri.* Book. Milan: Garzanti.
– 1966. Interview. Cannes, 13 May. Fondo Pasolini, Bologna (typescript).
– 1966. "La lingua scritta della realtà." Essay. In *EE, SLA1,* 1503–40.
– 1966. "Progetto per un film su San Paolo." Script. In *PPC2,* 2023–30.
– 1966. "Un marxista a New York." Interview. *L'Europeo,* 13 October. In *SPS,* 1597–1606.
– 1966–67. "Battute sul cinema." Essay. In *EE, SLA1,* 1541–54.
– 1966–67. "Confessioni tecniche." Essay. In *PPC2,* 2768–84.
– 1967. "Il codice dei codici." Essay. In *EE, SLA1,* 1600–10.

– 1967. "Una lucida passione. Intervista a Gaetano Stucchi." Interview. *Sette Giorni,* 27 August.
– 1967. "I segni viventi e i poeti morti." Essay. In *EE, SLA1,* 1573–81.
– 1967. "Essere è naturale?" Essay. In *EE, SLA1,* 1562–9.
– 1967. "Osservazioni sul piano sequenza." Essay. In *EE, SLA1,* 1555–61.
– 1967–68. "Sant'Infame." Film treatment. In *PPC2,* 2673–6.
– 1967–75. *Porno-Teo-Kolossal.* Film treatment. In *PPC2,* 2695–2753.
– 1968. "Alle soglie di uno scisma." Article. *SPS,* 1121–3.
– 1968. "Droga e Cultura." Article. *Vie Nuove,* 53 (28 December). *DIAL* 549–50.
– 1968. "Lettera aperta a Silvana Mangano."Article. In *SPS,* 1140–3.
– 1968. "Ora il Papa si trova disarmato." Article. In *DIAL,* 495.
– 1968. "Il PCI ai giovani." Poem. In *EE, SLA1,* 1440–50.
– 1968. "Intervista rilasciata a L. Peroni." Interview. *Inquadrature,* 15–16 (Fall). In *PPC2,* 2931–6.
– 1968. *Teorema.* Book. In *RR2,* 891–1067.
– 1968. *Teorema.* Script. In *PPC2,* 1079–90.
– 1968. "Una creazione mostruosa." Article. *SPS,* 1128.
– 1968–74. "Abbozzo di sceneggiatura per un film su San Paolo." Script. In *PPC2,* 1883–2020.
– 1969. "La mia provocatoria indipendenza." Article. In *DIAL* 557–8.
– 1969. "L'idea del Capro espiatorio." Article. In *SPS,* 1219.
– 1970. "Il cinema impopolare." Essay. In *EE, SLA1,* 1600–10.
– 1970. "Intervista con Pisanelli Stabile. L'ultima Medea." Interview. In *La Rassegna,* 1 January .
– 1970. *Medea.* Milan: Garzanti. Script. In *PPC1,* 1205–88.
– 1971. "Res sunt nomina." Essay. In *EE, SLA1,* 1584–91.
– 1971. *Trasumanar e organizzar.* Book. Milan: Garzanti. In *TP2,* 3–389.
– 1972. *Empirismo eretico.* Book. Milan: Garzanti. In *SLA1,* 1401–1550.
– 1974. (September). "La perdita della realtà e il cinema inintegrabile." Interview with Gideon Bachmann. In De Giusti 1979.
– 1974. "6 ottobre 1974: La Chiesa è inutile al potere." Article. In *SCOR, SPS,* 356–61.
– 1975 (15 June). "Abiura dalla *Trilogia della Vita.*" Article. In *Corriere della Sera,* 9 November 1975; and in *Lettere luterane,* in *SPS,* 599–603.
– 1975. *La nuova gioventù. Poesie friulane 1941–1974.* Book.Turin: Einaudi. In *TP2,* 391–527.
– 1975. *Scritti Corsari.* Book. Milan: Garzanti. In *SPS,* 265–535
– 1975. "Quasi un testamento." Article. In *Gente,* 17 November, and in *SPS,* 853–71.
– 1979. *Descrizioni di descrizioni.* Book. Turin: Einaudi.

– 1983. *Il sogno del centauro.* Edited by Jean Duflot. Interview. First ed. Rome: Editori Riuniti. In *SPS,* 1403–1545.
– 1986. *Pier Paolo Pasolini. Lettere 1940–1954.* Letters. Edited by Nico Naldini. Turin: Einaudi.
– 1988. *Pier Paolo Pasolini. Lettere 1955–1975.* Letters. Edited by Nico Naldini. Turin: Einaudi.
– 1991. *Il Vangelo secondo Matteo, Edipo re, Medea.* Book. Milan: Garzanti.
– 1992. *Petrolio.* Book. Turin: Einaudi. In *RR2,* 1159–1830.
– 1997. *Petrolio.* Book. New York: Pantheon.
– 2005. *Heretical Empiricism.* Edited by Louise Barnett. Translated by Ben Lawton and Louise Barnett. Book. Washington, DC: New Academia.
Passannanti, Erminia. 2009. *Il Cristo dell'eresia. Rappresentazione del sacro e censura nei film di Pier Paolo Pasolini.* Novi Ligure: Joker.
Passeri, Alessio. 2010. *L'eresia cristiana di Pier Paolo Pasolini. Il rapporto con la cittadella di Assisi.* Milan: Mimesis.
Pasti, Daniela. 1981. "Bello, asciutto, estatico: E' il santo che fa la scena." *La Repubblica,* 26 September.
Patti, Emanuela, ed. 2009. *La nuova gioventù: L'eredità intellettuale di Pier Paolo Pasolini.* Novi Ligure: Joker.
Perolino, Ugo. 2012. *Il sacro e l'impuro.* Cesena: Società Editrice "Il Ponte Vecchio."
Repetto, Antonino. 1998. *Invito al cinema di Pasolini.* Milan: Mursia.
Restivo, Angelo. 2002. *The Cinema of Economic Miracles.* Durham: Duke University Press.
Rhodes, John David. 2007. *Stupendous, Miserable City: Pasolini's Rome.* Minneapolis: University of Minnesota Press.
Ricciardi, Alessia. 2003. *The Ends of Mourning.* Stanford: Stanford University Press.
Ricoeur, Paul. 2009. "The Non-religious Interpretation of Christianity in Bonhoeffer." In *Bonhoeffer and Continental Thought: Cruciform Philosophy,* edited by Brian Gregor and Jens Zimmermann, 156–76. Bloomington: Indiana University Press.
Rimini, Stefania. 2006. *La ferita e l'assenza. Performance del sacrificio nella drammaturgia di Pasolini.* Acireale: Bonanno Editore.
Rinaldi, Rinaldo. 1982. *Pier Paolo Pasolini.* Milan: Mursia.
Rohdie, Sam. 1995. *The Passion of Pier Paolo Pasolini.* Bloomington: Indiana University Press.
– 1999. "Neo-realism and Pasolini: The Desire for Reality.' In *Pasolini Old and New,* edited by Zigmunt G. Baranski, 163–83. Dublin: Four Court Press.
Rossellini, Roberto. 1987. *Il mio metodo, scritti e interviste.* Edited by Adriano Aprà. Padua: Marsilio.

Rumble, Patrick. 1996. *Allegories of Contamination*. Toronto: Toronto University Press.

Rumble, Patrick, and Bart Testa, eds. 1994. *Pier Paolo Pasolini: Contemporary Perspectives*. Toronto: University of Toronto Press.

Ryan-Scheutz, Coleen. 1999. "Salvaging the Sacred: Female Subjectivity in Pasolini's *Medea*." *Italica* 76.2: 94–103.

– 2007. *Sex, the Self and the Sacred: Women in the Cinema of Pier Paolo Pasolini*. Toronto: Toronto University Press.

Salvini, Laura. 2004. *I frammenti del tutto: Ipotesi di letture dell'ultimo progetto cinematografico di Pier Paolo Pasolini, "Porno-Teo-Kolossal."* Bologna: Clueb.

Santato, Guido. 1983. *Pier Paolo Pasolini: L'opera e il suo tempo*. Padua: Cleup.

– 2007. "'L'abisso tra corpo e storia': Pasolini tra mito, storia e dopostoria." *Studi Pasoliniani* 1: 15–36.

Sapelli, Giulio. 2005. *Modernizzazione sneza sviluppo: Il capitalismo secondo Pasolini*. Milan: Bruno Mondadori.

Savoca, Giuseppe, ed. 2002. *Contributi per Pasolini*. Florence: Olschki.

Schérer, Renè, and Giorgio, Passerone. 2006. *Passages pasoliniens*. Villeneuve d'Ascq: Presses Universitaires du Septentrion.

Schoonover, Karl. 2012. *Brutal Vision: The Neorealist Body in Postwar Italian Cinema*. Minneapolis: University of Minnesota Press.

Schrader, Paul. 1972. *Transcendental Style in Film*. Berkeley: University of Califiornia Press.

Siciliano, Enzo. 1978. *Vita di Pasolini*. Milan: Rizzoli.

Siti, Walter. 1984. "Pier Paolo Pasolini." In *Un'idea del '900*, edited by Paolo Orvieto, 141–56. Rome: Salerno Editrice.

– 1989. "Il sole vero e il sole della pellicola, o sull'espressionismo di Pasolini." *Rivista di Letteratura Italiana* 7.1: 97–131.

– 1994. "Pasolini's Second Victory." In *Pier Paolo Pasolini: Contemporary Perspectives*, edited by Patrick Rumble and Bart Testa, 56–77. Toronto: University of Toronto Press.

– 1998. "Tracce scritte di un'opera vivente." In *RR1*, ix–xcii.

Snyder, Stephen. 1982. *Pier Paolo Pasolini*. Boston: Twayne.

Souchon, Paul. 1965. "Entretiens avec Pier Paolo Pasolini." *Revue et fiches du cinema*, 28 February.

Spackman, Barbara.1989. *Decadent Genealogies: The Rhetoric of Sickness from Baudelaire to D'Annunzio*. Ithaca: Cornell University Press.

Stack, Oswald. 1969. *Pasolini on Pasolini: Interviews with Oswald Stack*. Bloomington: Indiana University Press.

Steimatsky, Noah. 2008. *Italian Locations: Reinhabiting the Past in Postwar Cinema*. Minneapolis: Minnesota University Press.

Subini, Tomaso. 2004. "La caduta impossibile: San Paolo secondo Pasolini." In *Il Dilettoso Monte*, edited by Massimo Gioseffi, 227–74. Milan: Edizioni Universitarie di Lettere, Economia, Diritto.
– 2007. "Il Medioevo di Francesco Giullare di Dio." In *Un medioevo per il cinema*, special issue of *Doctor Virtualis* (January): 23–50.
– 2008. *La necessità di morire. Il cinema di Pier Paolo Pasolini e il sacro*. Rome: Edizioni Fondazione Ente dello Spettacolo.
– 2009. *Pier Paolo Pasolini. La Ricotta*. Turin: Lindau.
– 2010. *Tre Studi su* Il Vangelo Secondo Matteo. Milan: Raffaello Cortina Editore.
Taviani, Ferdinando. 1966. "Uccellacci e uccellini." *Civitas*, June, 101–5.
Taylor, Mark C. 1987. *Altarity*. Chicago: University of Chicago Press.
– 1992. *Disfiguring: Art, Architecture, Religion*. Chicago: University of Chicago Press.
– 2007. *After God*. Chicago: University of Chicago Press.
Tong, Janice. 2001. "Crisis of Ideology and the Disenchanting Eye: Pasolini and Bataille." *Contretemps* 2 (May): 74–91.
Tricomi, Antonio. 2005. *Pasolini: Gesto e maniera*. Catanzaro: Rubbettino.
– 2005. *Sull'opera mancata di Pasolini*. Rome: Carocci.
– 2011. *In corso d'opera. Scritti su Pasolini*. Massa: Transeuropa.
Verdone, Mario. 1966. "Uccellacci e uccellini." *Bianco e nero*, 11 November, 76–79.
Viano, Maurizio. 1993. *A Certain Realism: Making Use of Pasolini's Theory and Practice*. Berkeley: University of California Press.
Vighi, Fabio. 2001. *Le ragioni dell'altro. La formazione di Pasolini tra saggistica, letteratura e cinema*. Ravenna: Longo.
– 2003. "Pasolini and Exclusion: Žižeck, Agamben and the Modern Sub-Proletariat." *Theory Culture Society* 20.5: 99–121.
– 2006. *Traumatic Encounters in Italian Film: Locating the Cinematic Unconscious*. Bristol: Intellect Books.
Wagstaff, Christopher. 1999. "Reality into Poetry: Pasolini's Film Theory." In *Pasolini Old and New*, edited by Zygmunt Baransky, 185–227. Dublin: Four Courts Press.
Ward, David. 1995. *A Poetics of Resistance: Narrative and the Writings of Pier Paolo Pasolini*. Madison, NJ: Farleigh Dickinson University Press.
Watkin, Christopher. 2011. *Difficult Atheism: Post-Theological Thinking in Alain Badiou, Jean-Luc Nancy and Quentin Meillassoux*. Edinburgh: Edinburgh University Press.
Willemen, Paul, ed. *Pier Paolo Pasolini*. London: British Film Institute.

Wyschogrod, Edith. 1990. *Saints and Postmodernism.* Chicago: University of Chicago Press.

Zanzotto, Andrea. 1983. "Pasolini nel nostro tempo." In *Pier Paolo Pasolini. L'opera e il suo tempo,* edited by G. Santato, 235–9. Padua: Cleup Editore.

– 1994. "Su *Teorema.*" In *Aure e disincanti nel Novecento letterario,* 161–6.Milan: Mondadori.

Zigaina, Giuseppe. 1995. *Hostia. Trilogia della morte di Pier Paolo Pasolini.* Venice: Marsilio.

Zingari, Guido. 2006. *Ontologia del rifiuto: Pasolini e i rifiuti dell'umanità in una società impura.* Rome: Le nubi edizioni.

Žižek, Slavoj. 2000. *The Fragile Absolute.* London: Verso.

– 2003. *The Puppet and the Dwarf: The Perverse Core of Christianity.* Cambridge, MA: MIT Press.

– 2007. "Towards a Materialist Theology." *Angelaki* 12 (1 April): 19–26.

– 2011 (8 August). "The Only Church That Illuminates Is a Burning Church." ABC Religion and Ethics. http://www.abc.net.au/religion/articles/2011/08/08/3287944.htm.

Žižek, Slavoj, and Boris Gunjevic. 2012. *God in Pain: Inversions of Apocalypse.* New York: Seven Stories Press.

Žižek, Slavoj, and John Milbank. 2009. *The Monstrosity of Christ: Paradox or Dialectic?* Cambridge, MA: MIT Press.

Index of Names

Terms appearing in italics are names of fictional or filmic characters.

Accattone, 6, 9, 57, 58, 158
Adorno, Theodor, 11
Agamben, Giorgio, 7, 57, 213, 221
Agonia, 161, 168
Altizer, Thomas J.J., 7, 36
Antamoro, Giulio, 151
Artaud, Antonin, 97, 98
Auerbach, Erich, 64

Bach, Johan Sebastian, 72, 175
Bachmann, Gideon, 194, 197
Badiou, Alain, 7, 14, 186, 213, 214, 221, 227
Barthes, Roland, 87
Bataille, George, 5, 20, 141, 144, 204, 221
Bazin, Andrè, 149, 179, 224, 225
Benjamin, Walter, 11, 25
Berenson, Bernard, 63
Bertolucci, Bernardo, 56
Betti, Laura, 53, 128
Bini, Alfredo, 53, 64
Boccaccio, Giovanni, 218
Bonhoeffer, Dietrich, 7, 36, 44, 221
Borges, Jorge Luis, 104
Brelich, Angelo, 32

Callas, Maria, 27, 136, 271
Carraro, Andrea, 64
Caruso, Lucio Settimio, 143
Cavani, Liliana, 14, 151–5, 172
Cefis, Eugenio, 15
Celestine V, 49
Chaplin, Charlie, 53, 55, 56
Cicognani, Giovanni Amleto, 49
Colussi, Susanna, 70, 129, 260n11
Commendatore, the, 54, 59
Cordero, Don Emilio, 187, 188

De Martino, Ernesto, 5, 7, 11, 29, 30, 31, 32, 33, 35, 75, 129, 196, 221, 222
De Sica, Vittorio, 179
Deleuze, Gilles, 13, 96–9, 101, 102, 104, 204
Derrida, Jacques, 91, 130
Dionysus, 114, 119
Dostoevski, Fëdor, 141
Dreyer, Theodor, 55, 74
Duccio da Boninsegna, 72
Durkheim, Emile, 18

Eco, Umberto, 93
Ėjzenštejn, Sergej Michajlovič, 74

Eliade, Mircea, 5, 7, 11, 18 , 19, 20, 24, 26 27, 28, 29, 30, 31, 39, 41, 140, 221, 222
Emilia, 14, 75, 112–16, 122, 125–36, 138, 144, 146, 154, 166, 223
Euripides, 70

Fellini, Federico, 58, 148, 150
Fortini, Franco, 10, 26, 66
Foucault, Michel, 70, 211
Frazer, James, 24
Freud, Sigmund, 239
Friar Ciccillo, 151, 154, 155, 164, 175–86,
Friar Ginepro, 148, 150
Friar Giovanni, 150
Friar Ninetto, 151, 154, 155, 175–9

Garboli, Cesare, 114, 119
Garzanti, Livio, 158, 159
Giasone, 137–9
Giotto, 55, 56, 83, 167
Girard, René, 18, 20, 116, 221
Godard, Jean Luc, 52
Goldmann, Lucien, 177
Gramsci, Antonio, 72, 134
Gregoretti, Ugo, 52
Guattari, Félix, 86, 87
Gumbrecht, Hans Ulrich, 10, 91

Halliday, Jon, 189
Hjelmslev, Louis Trolle, 99

Innocenti Ninetto, 174
Innocenti Totò, 174

Jacobus de Varagine, 131
Jason, 23, 24, 135, 136
Jehovah, 114, 120
Jesus, 76, 69, 71, 76, 77, 83, 92, 148, 160
John XXIII (Angelo Roncalli), 11, 12, 44, 45, 46, 47, 48, 62, 155, 164, 176, 188, 222
John, 76
Judas, 76, 150
Jung, Carl Gustav, 18, 20, 38

Kant, Immanuel, 34
King, Martin Luther Jr, 202,

Lacan, Jacques, 261
Lenin (Ul'janov Vladimir Il'ič), 74
Levi, Primo, 185
Levy-Bruhl, Lucien, 18, 19, 24
Little Tramp/Charlot, 53, 56
Longhi, Roberto, 80, 192
Lucia, 112–18
Lukàcs, György, 177
Luther, Martin, 139, 203

Malanga, Jerry, 93
Mangini, Cecilia, 32
Manzoni, Alessandro, 47
Mao Tse-tung, 174
Maria, 166–7, 171
Mario Cipriani. *See* Stracci
Marx, Karl, 45, 57
Mary Magdalen, 130, 131
Masaccio, 55, 56, 80, 83, 159
Mattei, Enrico, 15
Matthew. *See* Saint Matthew
Mauss, Marcel, 18
Medea, 24, 135–40
Menard, Pierre, 104
Mizoguchi, Kenji, 74
Monroe, Marilyn, 111, 112
Mozart, Wolfgang Amadeus, 12, 72

Nancy, Jean-Luc, 7, 13, 34, 82, 99, 100, 119, 125

Negri, Antonio, 14, 48, 154, 176, 186
Nicolino, 161–3, 165
Ninetto, Davoli, 151

Odetta, 112, 113, 117, 118, 124, 127
Office Catholique International du Cinéma (OCIC), 49
Otto, Rudolf, 18, 19, 29

Paolo, Uccello, 167
Paolo, 75, 112–46, 223
Pasolini, Susanna, 70, 129, 260n11
Paul VI (Giovanni Battista Montini), 12, 45, 48, 49, 153, 155, 176, 186, 188, 189,194, 222
Pedote, 53, 59
Pelosi, Pino, 15
Piero della Francesca, 72, 83, 151, 167
Pietro, 112, 113, 116–18
Pius XII (Eugenio Maria Pacelli), 12, 45, 46
Pompeius Festus, 57
Pontormo, Jacopo, 54, 55, 60, 79
Pro Civitate Christiana, 47, 62, 64

Rebora, Clemente, 9, 21
Riccetto, 160
Ricoeur, Paul, 36, 44
Rimbaud, Arthur, 112, 119
Roncalli, Angelo. *See* John XXIII
Rossellini, Roberto, 14, 52, 53, 62, 148–155, 172, 179, 180, 186
Rosso, Fiorentino, 60, 79

Saint Catherine of Siena, 149, 203
Saint Damian, 165
Saint Francis, 175, 176, 211
Saint Francis of Assisi, 116, 119, 141, 147–65
Saint Maria Cabrini, 126
Saint Matthew, 4, 63, 68, 70–5, 150, 186
Saint Paul, 43, 44, 49, 123, 155, 193–220
Saint Peter, 64, 97, 112
Sant'Infame, 215, 218
Snow, Edgar, 174
Soldati, Mario, 40
Stack, Oswald, 53, 75, 184, 189
Stamp, Terence, 120
Stracci, 12, 53–9, 61, 78, 79, 159, 222

Taylor, Mark, 118
Togliatti, Palmiro, 174, 175
Totò, 151
Turoldo, David Maria, 9, 21, 117

Van der Leeuw, Gerardus, 19
Verdi, Giuseppe, 54
Vico, Giambattista, 132

Warhol, Andy, 253
Welles, Orson, 53, 59, 60, 79

Zanzotto, Andrea, 140, 142, 199
Zavattini, Cesare, 286
Žižek, Slavoj, 7, 8, 12, 14, 36, 48, 58, 65, 85, 88, 122, 155, 176, 187, 213, 214, 221, 222, 227
Zucchetto, 46

Index of Films and Screenplays

Accattone, 6, 9, 11, 25, 32, 56, 57, 73, 74, 78, 157–9, 221

Appunti per un'Orestiade Africana/Notes for an African Oresteia, 135

Bestemmia/Blasphemy, 10, 14, 37, 78–110, 148, 153, 155–72, 185, 187, 193, 194, 222, 223

Decameron, 91

Edipo Re/Oedipus Rex, 189, 212

Il Vangelo secondo Matteo/The Gospel According to Matthew, 11, 12, 21, 40, 45, 47, 49, 52, 53, 62–77, 78, 82, 83, 86, 87, 130, 150, 151, 156, 158, 164, 167, 176, 186, 187, 189, 222

I Racconti di Canterbury/Canterbury Tales, 91

La rabbia/Rage, 111

La Ricotta/Ricotta, 45, 52–62, 73, 78, 82, 83, 156, 157, 159, 182, 222

Mamma Roma, 11, 52, 73, 74, 78

Medea, 11, 23, 27, 32, 98, 135, 137, 142, 221

Porno-Teo-Kolossal, 50, 215, 220, 221, 223

RoGoPag, 52

Salò o le 120 giornate di Sodoma/Salò or a Hundred Days of Sodom, 50, 51, 167, 215, 219

San Paolo/Saint Paul, 70, 119, 194

Sopralluoghi in Palestina/Location Hunting in Palestine, 47, 64

Teorema/Theorem, 11, 13, 17, 23, 49, 75, 111–46, 154, 161, 166, 171, 178, 201, 215, 223

Trilogia della vita/Trilogy of Life, 182

Uccellacci e uccellini/The Hawks and the Sparrows, 10, 14, 75, 143, 148, 151, 152, 155, 156, 164, 172–87, 223

Index of Subjects

abandonment, 12, 29, 168, 202, 204, 210, 213
abject, 58, 85, 105, 225
abjuration, 77, 86, 164
aesthetic emotion, 63
aestheticism, 59, 72
acheiropoietic icon, 9, 83, 87–8
afterlife, 63, 65
agape or *caritas*, 7, 8, 10, 11, 14, 36–7, 38, 43–4, 48, 49, 65, 85, 88, 121, 131, 135, 139, 140, 141, 143, 155, 186, 203, 205, 206, 207, 208, 209, 210, 211, 213, 214, 215, 216, 220, 223, 224, 225
allegory, 111, 129, 177
altarity, 118
America, 187, 188, 192, 201
analogy, 121, 189, 200
anchorite, 13, 14, 111, 112, 116, 187
angst, 5, 30, 32, 33, 113
animal, 23, 30, 53, 56, 96, 105, 138, 139, 154, 162, 166, 171, 172, 178
anthropological: mapping, 16; mutation, 110, 207, 223
anticlericalism, 63, 194, 195, 197, 222
anti-naturalism, 60, 180, 225
apocalypticism, 6, 7, 16, 17, 29, 50, 74, 111, 116, 120, 128, 130, 142, 191, 202, 207, 211, 213, 215, 220, 223
apparition, 4, 27, 46, 138, 169
archetypes, 20, 28, 29, 30, 39, 42, 88, 83, 88, 92, 99, 109, 130,131, 218, 222, 224
artifice, 180, 186
artist, 13, 113, 116, 186, 210, 217
askesis, 121, 128, 130, 216, 218
atheism, 35, 36, 37, 41, 44, 63, 68, 69, 71
atonement, 139
attualità, 195, 196, 197, 200, 201, 213
auraticity, 215
authenticity, 6, 40, 116, 185, 217
axis mundi, 24, 137, 222

baptism, 37, 73, 131, 132, 144, 223
barbarity, 24, 37, 71, 85, 136, 155, 156, 180, 181
beauty, 19, 72, 104, 112, 117, 118, 139, 140, 166; and ethos 72
believer, 4, 8, 12, 44, 47, 63, 65, 67–8, 71, 72, 101, 135, 153, 197

Bestemmia, 13, 78, 80–2, 84, 88–93, 102–5, 106, 109, 153–72, 178
best of youth, 50, 207, 215
biopolitics, 220
blood, 8, 33, 82, 84, 85, 90, 98, 133, 140, 191, 202, 203, 204, 211, 215, 218
body, 5, 8, 9, 10, 13, 22, 25, 30, 69, 71, 76, 79, 82, 83, 84, 85, 87, 89, 90, 93, 97, 98, 102–3, 105, 110, 117, 118, 119, 120, 122, 125, 126, 135, 138, 140, 141, 158, 160, 162, 163, 164, 165, 182, 183, 184, 185, 195, 198, 202, 204, 207, 208, 210, 211,213, 215, 224, 225; Pasolini's, 3, 4, 15, 16, 49, 51, 225; performing and viewing, 224; throw one's body into the fight, 102–4, 106, 155, 171, 193
bourgeois, 16 23, 28, 32, 37, 38, 47, 55, 57, 58, 59, 67, 71, 100, 112, 113, 114, 115, 116, 119, 122, 126, 128, 134, 135, 136, 137, 144, 145, 147, 152, 153, 162, 176, 177, 178, 206, 215, 220, 223, 225
bourgeoisie, 14, 46, 47, 48, 73, 110, 115, 116, 119, 120, 134, 142, 143, 144, 145, 146, 173, 177, 190, 206, 214
Byzantine icon, 151

cannibalization, 94, 174, 185
canone sospeso, 134, 146, 171, 201
canonization, 144, 146
capital, 59
capitalism, 7, 17, 86, 154, 176, 223; short-circuit of 65
Carnival, 91, 160
carnivalizations, 54, 58, 60, 79, 160
catatonia, 127–8
Catholicism as institution, 10, 37, 40, 41, 42, 45, 47, 49, 50, 62, 79, 101, 111, 153, 156, 175, 176, 187, 214, 222
centaur, 23, 24, 136, 137
Christ, 6, 7, 8, 9, 10, 12, 13, 15, 20, 36, 40, 41, 42, 43, 44, 50, 52, 53, 57, 59, 63, 64, 65, 66, 67, 68, 69, 70, 71, 72, 73, 74, 75, 76, 77, 78, 79, 80, 81, 83, 84, 85, 86, 87, 88, 89, 92, 98, 100, 101, 102, 103, 105, 110, 112, 117,119, 120, 121, 122, 129, 131, 143, 147, 148, 149, 150, 151, 152, 155, 158, 160, 161, 162, 164, 165, 169, 176, 178, 181, 185, 186, 188, 191, 203, 204, 208, 209, 211, 215, 218, 222
Christian: paradox, 208, 209, 214, 225; political legacy, 8, 155, 214, 223
Christianity, 7, 12, 29, 30, 31, 36, 37, 38, 39, 41, 42, 44, 46, 48, 83, 85, 86, 143, 162, 174, 177
Christological figure, 52, 174, 203
Christology, barbaric, v, 12, 78, 80, 85, 102, 104, 172, 178, 223
Church, 12, 13, 14, 15, 26, 37, 41, 42, 43, 44, 46, 47, 48, 49, 60, 69, 105, 111, 118, 121, 127, 144, 147, 153,155, 164, 176, 178, 189, 191, 193, 194, 195, 197, 198, 199, 203, 213, 217; schism 43, 48, 49, 194
cinema: as life, living cinema, 95–6, 223; as magic and drug, 33; of poetry, 22, 25, 74, 96, 111, 181; vs. film, 34, 95, 147, 180; as written language of reality/praxis, 35, 52, 86, 94, 95, 96, 147, 172
cinema d'elite, 11, 134, 172
cinèma verité, 114
cinepresence, 224

coincidentia oppositorum, 26, 160, 200, 205, 213
commodification, 11
communion, 42, 179
communism, 154, 207, 213, 214
community, 20, 21, 59, 65, 113, 116, 119, 122, 127,128, 129, 134, 135, 137,139, 147, 148, 154, 161, 162, 163, 164, 167, 192, 193
compliance, 191
conflict of cultures, 135, 137, 139, 140, 142
conformity or comformism, 59, 70, 71,171, 195, 209, 214, 220, 223
conscience, 16, 66, 71, 119, 120, 126, 128, 145, 172, 174, 181, 186, 198
consciousness, 31, 38, 44, 56, 94, 124, 180,183
consumerism, 11, 25, 51, 207
contagion, 18, 163
contamination, 10, 18, 67, 68, 105, 119, 156, 219, 222
conversion, 22, 41, 47, 65, 66, 78, 89, 111, 112, 117, 121, 123, 124, 125, 126, 131, 137, 161, 162, 192, 211, 217, 218, 219; backward conversion, 137
"corona, la," 61
corporeality, 3, 4, 5, 8, 9, 11, 13, 17, 87, 93, 98, 101, 181, 182, 183, 184, 224,
cosmos, 87, 105, 137, 218
covenant, 122
creation, 8, 30, 44, 50, 83, 104, 117, 124,136, 137, 154, 173, 179, 180, 186, 203, 213
creatures, 104, 155, 156, 165, 166, 178, 184, 186
criminal, 10, 15, 52, 57, 102, 159, 160, 162, 197, 208, 220, 225
crisis films, 173
crisis of signs, 115, 144
cross, vi, 9, 10, 12, 13, 15, 21, 36, 41, 53, 54, 56, 57, 58, 59, 61, 69, 70, 77, 79, 81, 85, 88, 101, 103, 121, 122, 155, 164, 165, 167,175, 190, 203, 204, 206, 209, 210, 214, 222, 225
crow, 174, 175, 176, 177
Crucifix, 69, 165, 118, 159, 165, 204
Crucifixion, 6, 9, 10, 12, 52, 54, 58, 64, 69, 77, 78, 82, 84, 86, 87–8, 102, 109, 121, 143, 156, 162, 181, 201, 203, 206, 208, 210, 222, 224; scenes 12, 13, 36, 69, 76, 203
crypto-Christianity, 37
cultural genocide, 29, 50, 219
culture, 3, 9, 16, 30, 34, 35, 37, 43, 46, 59, 80, 91, 93, 94, 101, 129, 132, 134, 135, 139, 140, 142, 161, 177, 180, 181, 222; culture industry, 25, 59

death, 3, 6, 7, 9, 10, 12, 13, 17, 20, 27, 31, 32, 33, 34, 35, 37, 38, 40, 42, 46, 56, 57, 58, 59, 61, 70, 76–7, 79, 83, 88, 106–8, 109, 110, 119, 121, 133, 141, 143, 144, 146, 147, 150, 153, 165, 166, 167, 168, 170, 171, 172, 174, 175, 181, 182, 183, 185, 201, 202, 203, 204, 205, 206, 210, 211, 217, 218, 222; culture of, 34; drive, 15, 108, 109, 191, 205, 210, 213; social, 113, 144; of God, debate, 7, 36, 44; as montage, 13, 34, 40, 107, 142, 210
degeneration, 208
degradation, 207, 209, 210
de-historicization, 30, 33, 35
demonicità, 194
desecration, 6, 26, 28, 41, 215

desert, 14, 112, 113, 115, 116, 117, 119, 121, 122, 123, 124, 125, 131, 140, 141, 144, 146, 178, 201, 219, 223
desire, 3, 14, 15, 23, 58, 69, 79, 86, 87, 101, 113, 116, 118, 121, 123, 125, 129, 139, 147, 150, 173, 181, 182, 184, 186, 190, 195, 204, 205, 206, 209,210, 211, 212, 213,
Devil, the, 120, 170, 198, 199, 218, 219
Dies Irae, 56, 61
difference, 6, 9, 14, 15, 17, 32, 39, 40, 53, 55, 82, 86, 117, 151, 154, 155, 181, 184, 190, 205, 206, 208, 209, 210, 223
Dionysus, 114, 119
disfiguring, 118
disorganic intellectuals, 3
dissent, 49, 112, 152, 172
diversity, radical, 71, 148, 153
divine, 4, 7, 19, 28, 31, 36, 37, 38, 40, 57, 66, 71, 72, 75, 83, 85, 95, 102, 104, 105, 113, 118, 119, 125, 127, 131, 139, 148, 157, 162, 168, 196, 201, 207, 209, 218, 219, 221, 222
divinization of the world, 7
Dopostoria or Post-history, 39, 60, 62, 115, 121, 125, 141, 143, 174, 178, 234–5n44
doubt, 37, 46, 144, 174, 180, 186, 203
dream, 22, 59, 81, 96, 99, 123, 160, 169, 173, 180, 188, 190, 192, 211, 212
drowning, 161

Ecclesia, 43, 47, 48, 194
Eloi, Eloi, Lama Sabachtani?, 65, 76, 77
empathy, 88, 224, 225
eros, 8, 14, 20, 27, 69, 116, 120, 136, 137, 139, 181, 182, 183, 184, 211; and *agape*, 140, 205, 208, 209, 213, 215, 223; and *pathos*, 108
eroticism, 13, 69, 204, 210
eschatological phenomenon, Pasolini as, 21
eschaton, 15, 50
esthétique relationelle, 96
Eucharist, 82, 84, 91, 92, 127, 174, 203
evangelization, 151, 178
excavator, 130, 132, 133, 268–9n46
excess, 56, 57, 58, 79, 152, 181, 196, 225
exclusion, 19, 57, 58, 65, 110
exemplum, 106, 108, 114, 152
exhibition, 108, 110, 205, 210, 222
expenditure, 20
exposure, 9, 13, 89, 101, 102, 149, 204, 205, 222
expulsion, 13, 116, 146
Eye-Mouth device, 10, 94

faith, 12, 28, 37–8, 39, 43–4, 50, 55, 58, 59, 62, 64, 66, 72, 85, 88, 97–8, 109, 117, 134, 171, 190, 192, 217
farce, 54, 57
father's loins, 123
fellatio, 161
female sphere, 6, 131
film: vs. cinema, 34, 95, 147, 180; theological, 188, 189. *See also* cinema
finitude, 8, 88, 211
fisicità, 98, 99
flesh, 1, 6, 8, 9, 10, 13, 15, 33, 58, 76, 77, 81, 84, 87, 89, 91, 93, 97–8, 99, 101–2, 105, 122, 133, 147, 154, 156, 166, 168, 181, 182, 183, 203, 204, 206, 209, 211, 213, 215, 217, 218,

222, 223; sacredness of, 9, 58, 104, 211, 215, 225
foolishness/folly, 138, 161, 202, 203, 225
"forza del Passato" (force of the Past), 22, 53, 60, 127
found footage, 111
Franciscanism, vi, 14, 62, 147, 148, 150, 151, 155, 156, 159, 193; Rossellini's, didactic value of, 148; Rossellini's, jester-like quality of, 150, 180
Franciscan Marxism, 178
freedom to choose death, 8, 13, 58, 108, 205, 210, 220
free indirect: discourse or speech, 10, 61, 67, 68, 69; point-of-view shot, 10, 12, 61, 67, 76, 128; silence, 128, 144
funeral, 174, 175, 179

Gandhism, 149
Ganz Andere (the Wholly Other), 19, 29, 30, 221
gaze, 55, 66, 67, 74, 76, 77, 84, 116, 118, 120, 122, 123, 128, 130, 136, 137, 140, 160, 167, 179, 190, 224, 225
genealogy of sacred images, 9, 86, 102
genius loci, 133
global capitalism, critique of, 15, 17, 50, 176, 223
globalization, 50, 220
God, 4, 6, 7, 8, 9, 10, 12, 13, 14, 15, 19, 20, 24, 25, 35, 36, 44, 54, 58, 61, 63, 64, 65, 66, 68, 71, 77, 79, 83, 84, 85, 86, 87, 88, 89, 91, 92, 93, 102, 104, 105, 109, 111, 114, 115, 117, 118, 119, 120, 121, 122, 124, 125, 126, 127, 131, 132, 133, 137,139, 141, 144, 145, 146, 161, 162, 163, 164, 165, 166, 168, 169, 170, 171, 172, 179, 183, 190, 201, 202, 209, 210, 211, 218, 219, 222, 223
gods, 24, 28, 132, 137
Gospel, v, 4, 11, 21, 36, 40, 42, 44, 46, 52, 53, 62, 63, 64, 68, 72, 73, 74, 75, 121, 150, 195, 206, 207
grace, 9, 21, 121, 131, 159, 162, 163, 166, 191, 216
Gramscian: identity, 59; illusion, 134, 135, 172
grave, 132, 165, 166

hagiography, 6, 92, 104, 106, 108–9, 111, 112, 127, 128, 129, 134, 144, 149, 160, 171, 172, 174, 175, 199; and Pasolini's scholarship, 16; subversive, 10, 15, 48, 75, 78, 110, 150, 154, 156, 172, 186, 187
happening, 95–6, 147
hate, 71, 205, 206
hawks, 10, 148, 151, 172, 175, 176
heaven. *See* Paradise/Heaven
hedonism, 214
heresy, 9, 10, 11, 15, 37, 44, 47, 50, 52, 69, 85, 86, 101–2, 105, 109, 110, 111, 112, 143, 154, 155, 156, 157, 158, 165, 168, 171, 172, 193, 215, 220, 223
hierophanies, 7, 20, 23, 24, 25, 27, 28, 75, 142, 161
history, v, 3, 6, 8, 16, 18, 20, 23, 27, 28, 29, 30, 31, 33, 34, 35, 36, 39, 40, 41, 43, 46, 58, 60, 61, 62, 80, 81, 86, 88, 101, 111, 115, 124, 125, 129, 143, 145, 146, 171, 172, 176, 179, 181, 183, 184, 185, 186, 189, 195, 196, 197, 199, 202, 217, 221, 222; end of 39, 115, 123, 124, 145; as tragedy 28, 40

holiness, 23, 24, 165
holy cards, 129
holy madness, 150, 152, 161, 180
Holy Spirit, 8, 174, 190
homogenization, 17, 23, 115, 146, 153
Homo historicus, 37
homophobia, 208
Homo religiosus, 28, 37, 38–9
Homo sacer, 57–8, 222
homosexuality, vi, 6, 14, 112, 161, 190, 203, 208, 209, 210, 211, 212, 213, 219
hope, 9, 12, 15, 37–8, 39, 43–4, 47, 61, 63, 65, 74, 85, 88, 124, 125, 132, 140, 146, 153, 157, 171, 188, 194, 211
hunger, 8, 54, 55, 56, 58, 153, 166

iconoclasm, 102, 164
iconology, 203
idealism, 149, 188, 192
ideology, 23, 28, 38, 39, 41, 65, 98, 134, 143, 144, 174, 176, 177, 193, 196
illness, 113, 193, 202, 208, 210, 211, 213, 217, 218
Imitatio Christi, 10, 48, 69, 92, 102, 109, 117, 121, 125, 216, 217, 219, 222
immanence, 4, 8, 9, 11, 12, 13, 15, 19, 20, 29, 40, 58, 61, 64–5, 72, 74, 75, 85, 87, 89, 101, 102, 105, 118, 143, 178, 183, 196, 201, 204, 206, 211, 221, 222, 223
Inattualità, 197, 200, 216, 220
Incarnation, the, v, 4, 6, 7, 9, 10, 12, 13, 15, 21, 35, 36, 52, 64, 65, 68, 77, 79, 82, 84, 87–9, 98, 99, 101, 105, 111, 117, 119, 121, 122, 155, 158, 181, 184, 186, 187, 198, 203, 204, 210, 219, 220, 221, 222, 223, 224, 225
inconsumability, 134
indexical link between image and referent, 9, 83, 222
infraction of the code, 108
inner experience, 141
innocence, 16, 69, 76, 82, 84, 85, 110, 112, 129, 149, 150, 151, 154, 160, 162, 166, 169, 171, 206, 207, 216, 225
institution, vii, 15, 22, 23, 37, 42, 43, 45, 46, 48, 49, 105, 121, 127, 132, 154, 163, 164, 187, 192, 193, 196, 197, 198, 199, 209, 213
interpretation, 5, 6, 8, 9, 11, 12, 15, 16, 19, 20, 21, 29, 36, 40, 44, 51, 57, 85, 86, 91, 96, 119, 120, 142, 172, 184, 191, 209, 211, 213, 222, 223
irony, 47, 53, 57, 71, 79, 138, 143, 198, 204, 206, 208
irrationalism/irrationality, 48, 72, 135, 153, 177, 178, 180, 192, 198

jacquerie, 172
Jehovah, 114, 120
jouissance, 8, 214
joy, 101, 130, 154, 155, 160, 178, 179, 184, 204, 206, 207, 223; politics of, 154

kairos, 146
kenosis, 7, 8, 13, 36, 77, 85, 88, 89, 98, 102, 109, 178, 209, 222, 223
kronos, 146

language: Pentecostal, 199; of praxis, 106, 182
laughter, 27, 161

law, 70, 108, 109, 143, 160, 190, 204, 205, 209, 210, 213, 221
levitation, 113, 128, 131, 144
liquefaction, 14, 131, 140
liquidity, 140, 146,
long take, 181
love, 8, 24, 25, 38, 43, 44, 50, 53, 60, 65, 85, 86, 95, 101, 112, 116, 131, 137, 139, 142, 147, 154, 155, 166, 169, 176, 177, 179, 186, 187, 188, 195, 206, 207, 208, 209, 212, 214, 217, 220, 224; politics of, 155, 214

mad: saint, v, 10, 13, 52, 111, 112, 127, 130, 134, 139, 144, 145, 187; woman, 116, 127
magma, stylistic, 67, 68, 73, 74, 207, 222
mana, 19
mannerism, 53, 60, 61, 79, 83, 129, 181, 186, 225
martyrdom, v, 6, 12, 17, 58, 69, 101–2, 106, 108–9, 165, 168, 170, 192, 202, 205, 210, 215, 219
Marxism *en poète*, 38, 154, 177
Marxist-Catholic debate, 10, 11, 40, 44–5, 47, 49, 50, 63, 67, 156, 175, 176, 177, 214, 223
mass: audience, 173; media, 144
materialism: bourgeois, 176; Marxist, 192; sacred, 220
messianism, 21, 65, 119, 152
militancy, communist, 8, 154, 155, 223
mimetic desire, 14, 116, 125, 139
miracle play, 114
miracles, 10, 11, 33, 74–5, 82, 85, 102, 113, 114, 128, 129–30, 131, 133, 135, 142, 144–5, 146, 149, 153, 154, 162, 163, 164, 169, 178, 179, 190, 191, 222, 225
mirror, 79, 114, 116, 119
monologue of infinite Body of Reality, 93
morality, 175, 194
mourning, impossibility of, 125, 146
movement vs. institution, 193, 196
multitudes, 154
mysterium tremendum, 19, 110, 225
mystery, 23, 40, 64, 84, 85, 102, 110, 119, 129, 162, 186, 196
mysticism, 10, 43, 192, 193, 194, 197, 202, 203, 206, 213, 219
mystics of democracy, 188
myth, 6, 20, 23, 24, 25, 26, 27, 29, 30, 31, 34, 35, 36, 41, 61, 72, 73, 74, 86, 101, 105, 111, 112, 113, 116, 124, 135, 136, 139, 141, 171, 180, 186, 197, 201, 207, 208, 212, 215, 217, 221, 223, 225

national-popular cinema, 11, 72, 73, 172
naturalism, 77, 185, 186
neo-capitalism, 8, 10, 14, 15, 39, 43, 50, 51, 58,59, 65, 173, 185, 194, 211, 215, 221; triumph of, 51, 59
neo-realism, 14, 16, 62, 148, 150, 179, 180, 181, 184, 224; "brutal vision" of, 224, 225
New Testament, 60, 62, 120, 121, 158
nostalgia, 11, 16, 17, 22, 23, 50, 180, 186, 207; revolutionary use of, 17
nostos, 127
numinous, 19, 20

Oedipal: fixation, 113; scene, 212
Old Testament, 64, 115, 116, 119, 120, 121, 122
ontology, archaic, 27, 28, 39, 41, 42, 222

oppositions, 164, 218
optimism, 177, 186
orgy, 13, 42, 71, 109, 160, 161, 162, 166
origin, 28, 31, 35, 82, 84, 104, 114, 123, 144, 156, 186, 201, 202, 218
origins, return to, 11, 27, 39, 41, 104, 127, 138, 141, 169
oxymoron, 66, 79, 216

pain, 8, 21, 65, 76, 77, 81, 82, 83, 88, 101, 108, 109, 123, 126, 170, 175, 181, 182, 185, 205, 206, 207, 209, 210, 218
palimpsest, 132
palingenesis, 62, 186, 194, 224
palinodes, 86, 87, 104, 164
pan-semiosis vs. resistance to semiosis, 93, 104, 183
Paradise/Heaven, 29, 50, 54, 74, 124, 139, 160, 190, 191, 193, 194, 198, 211, 212, 215, 219, 223
parody, vi, 6, 15, 75, 79, 126, 127, 129, 130, 142, 144, 215, 216, 219
parousia, 35, 146, 200, 202
parrhesia, 70, 72, 204, 206, 225
Parrhesiastes, 12, 216
Pasolini, legacy of, 3, 13, 16, 17
Passion, v, 4, 5, 7, 8, 9, 11, 12, 13, 15, 41, 52, 53, 54, 55, 57, 58, 59, 60, 61, 64, 76, 77, 78–9, 80, 83, 84, 85, 86, 87, 88, 89, 91, 92, 101, 109, 110, 112, 119, 122, 127, 139, 140, 157, 158, 160, 162, 175, 178, 181, 182, 183, 184, 192, 203, 204, 207, 209, 215, 222, 223
pastiche (postmodern), 62, 67, 156, 180
pathos, 85, 88, 101, 108, 181, 182
pauperism, 153
paupertas, 151, 154
peace, 71, 123, 124, 154, 166, 168, 176, 186, 202
penance, 130–1
people vs. mass, 135, 173, 174, 175
performance, revolutionary, 147, 148
perspectivism, 38–9, 47, 48
pessimism, 29, 177
petrifaction, 131
phallus, 160
pietas, 43, 46, 101
planctus Mariae, 76
poetry, 5, 21, 32, 60, 66, 69, 71, 72, 74, 90, 144, 117, 132, 142, 144, 159, 177, 193, 198, 213, 218, 220
politics, 8, 31, 87, 98, 154, 155, 175, 177, 191, 196, 211, 214, 220, 223; of expression, 87
popes, v, 12, 44, 45, 46, 47,48, 49, 62–3, 153, 155, 156, 164, 165, 166, 168, 176, 188, 189, 194, 195
"pornographie ontologique," 224
postmodernism, 17, 62, 92, 115, 154, 159, 221
poverty, politics of, 8, 155, 214
power, 15, 16, 18, 19, 20, 22, 23, 24, 26, 30, 43, 48, 59, 64, 88, 91, 94, 97, 101, 104, 122, 129, 132, 137, 147, 154, 155, 169, 170,174, 185, 191, 192, 193, 194, 195, 199, 202, 207, 213, 214, 215, 217, 218, 219, 220, 225
pragmatism, 168, 184, 188, 192, 194
prayer, 69, 105, 106, 125, 141, 157, 164, 165
praxis, 39, 83, 95, 96, 106, 147, 155, 181, 182, 183, 184, 186, 193
presence, 3, 4, 8, 9, 10, 13, 24, 25, 27, 30, 34, 35, 55, 82, 85, 86, 87, 88, 89, 90–1, 92, 93, 95, 96, 97, 99, 100,

101, 102, 104, 106, 108, 110, 118, 120, 122, 123, 127, 128, 129, 130, 132, 135, 147, 148, 155, 158, 164, 169, 177, 181, 182, 186, 196, 197, 202, 212, 222, 223, 224; crisis of, 6, 29, 30–3, 196; vs. meaning, 91–2; production of, 10, 13, 52, 82, 83, 84, 88, 91, 92, 100, 148, 155, 181, 182, 185, 186, 222, 223, 224
pres-ence (*pres-entia*), 100
presence-absence, 5, 118
presentification, 185
priest, 14, 21, 22, 47, 48, 49, 65, 135, 136, 137, 163, 164, 189, 194, 197, 208, 209, 213, 214, 216
profanation, 22, 208, 215
pro-filmic, 26, 180, 181, 222, 224
prostitutes/whores, 90, 116, 157, 158, 161, 162, 163, 164, 168, 169, 216
purgatorial motion, 146

rationalism, 28, 48, 149, 176, 177
realism, 14, 26, 64, 65, 66, 79, 100, 114, 149, 150, 184, 185, 224, 225; mystical, 149; non-realistic, 149, 150
reality, 3, 4, 5, 8, 10, 11, 15, 17, 20, 25, 26, 28, 31, 34, 35, 47, 52, 57,64,65, 66, 68, 72, 79, 80, 81, 82, 83, 84, 85, 86, 87, 88, 89, 93, 94, 95, 96, 97, 98, 100, 102, 103, 104, 106, 111, 112, 113, 119, 120, 123, 124, 125, 129, 137, 139, 140, 141, 143, 146, 148, 149, 150, 152, 168, 177, 179, 180, 181, 182, 183, 184, 185, 186, 207, 211, 217, 223; reality as language, 4, 5, 93, 94, 95, 106, 179, 182; as little sister, 179
rebellion, 147, 152, 154, 171, 185
redemption, 9, 61, 65, 85, 110, 114, 117, 121, 143, 144, 191, 221
regime of signs, 86
relevance to the present, vi, 195
religion, 4, 12, 18, 19, 23, 24, 26, 29, 30, 31, 32, 36, 37, 38, 39, 42, 43, 44, 45, 48, 70, 71, 90, 93, 105, 120, 125, 127, 138, 141, 145,147, 153, 157, 161, 167, 171, 176, 177, 178, 196, 197; of behavior, 145; traditional, 6
religiosity, v, 36, 37, 38, 41, 42, 43, 63, 65, 127, 149, 176, 177, 202
representation, 5, 10, 16, 60, 64, 69, 74, 78, 79, 82, 83, 92, 95, 100, 101, 102, 104, 109, 112, 115, 147, 155,156, 181, 182, 185, 199; vs. evocation, 74; polemic against, 5, 78, 79, 82, 83, 92, 104, 109, 155, 165, 181
re-presentation, 82, 92
repudiation, 207, 208
resistance, 16,179, 189, 190
resurrection, 5, 6, 8, 9, 10, 12, 25, 42, 61,70, 75, 79, 85, 117, 121, 141, 185, 195, 208, 211, 221, 223
revelation, 20, 64, 85, 100, 113, 116, 117, 119, 121, 129, 135, 137, 143, 180, 201, 209, 218
revolution, 11, 12, 15, 17, 46, 47, 49, 50, 61, 71, 74, 76, 86, 87, 115, 117, 125, 128, 132, 143, 147, 148, 152, 153,154, 155, 158, 171, 172, 174, 175, 176, 178, 184, 185, 188, 192, 193, 196, 207, 213, 214, 223
ritual and rite, 6, 20, 27, 29, 30, 31, 33, 34, 35, 42, 50, 87, 91, 108, 116,191, 215, 219, 225
ruins, 40, 53, 56, 60, 127, 208

sacrality, 25, 42, 54, 61, 99, 105, 139, 155, 178; technical, 73, 74
sacratio, 57, 58

sacred, v, 4, 5, 6, 7, 8, 9, 10, 11, 12, 13, 14, 15, 16, 17, 18, 19, 20, 21, 22, 23, 24, 25, 26, 27, 28, 29, 30, 31, 32, 33, 34, 35, 36, 37, 38, 39, 40, 41, 42, 44, 50, 51, 53, 54, 55, 58, 61, 62, 66, 67, 68, 83, 85, 86, 88, 93, 98, 99, 101, 102, 105, 109, 110, 111, 112, 114, 115, 116, 117, 119, 120, 121, 125, 127, 128, 129, 132, 133, 134, 135, 136, 137, 138, 139, 140, 141, 142, 143, 144, 146, 150, 154, 155, 156, 158, 160, 161, 162, 163, 164, 169, 172, 176, 177, 178, 189, 192, 193, 195, 196, 197, 198, 199, 200, 201, 202, 206, 207, 211, 213, 214, 215, 217, 218, 219, 220, 221, 222; archaic, 11, 16, 17, 26, 33, 35, 42, 50, 99, 105, 127, 135, 137, 146, 206, 221, 224; as language, 4, 5, 22, 25, 198; centrality, 214; Christian, 35, 36, 37, 38, 42, 48, 88, 117, 174, 177, 188, 206, 221; definition, 18, 23; denial of, 178; dual nature of, 119, 195, 219; etymology of, "sacred" 18; immanent vision of, 4, 8, 31, 85, 101, 105, 178, 222, 225; irrelevance of, 22, 110; loss of, 5, 23, 24, 29, 31, 42, 58, 137, 138, 139, 143, 202, 221; Pascoli's, 127; presence, 25, 156, 158, 161, 163, 192, 193, 202, 213; and profane, 19, 20, 23, 26, 28, 67, 136, 138, 196, 197, 219, 223, 224, 225; as reality, 26; sense of, 144, 177; sources of Pasolini's interpretation, 5; as a technical process, 31; as tragedy, 28, 40; visitation of, 55, 114, 116, 119

sacrifice, 9, 13, 15, 19, 20, 42, 57, 65, 69, 72, 77, 87, 109–10, 112, 113, 122, 125, 133, 134, 135, 139, 140, 142, 143, 185, 204, 219

saintliness and sainthood, vi, 10, 14, 15, 106, 111–12, 127, 128, 133, 134, 135, 142, 144, 155, 162, 168, 169, 170, 172, 189, 193, 194, 196, 197, 208, 213, 214, 215, 216, 217, 218, 219, 220, 223

saints, v, 4, 6, 13, 14, 42, 43, 52, 53, 54, 56, 58, 63, 73, 75, 78, 85, 88, 92, 93, 101, 102, 104, 111, 112, 113, 114, 116, 119, 126, 127, 128, 130, 133, 141, 142, 144, 145, 147, 148, 149, 150, 152, 153, 154, 155, 156, 157, 158, 160, 162, 163, 164, 165, 166, 168, 169, 170, 171, 172, 174, 175, 176, 179, 187, 189, 192, 193, 194, 197, 199, 201, 202, 208, 209, 211, 217, 218, 219, 223; cult of, 42, 133; mad saint, v, 10, 13, 52, 111, 112, 127, 130, 134, 139, 144, 145, 187

salvation, 9, 35, 61, 140, 143, 145, 209

sanctus, definition of, 18, 203

scandal, vi, 3, 9, 13, 15, 22, 43, 61, 68, 70, 71, 72, 74, 108, 109, 110, 120, 148, 153, 163, 176, 177, 188, 190, 202, 203, 204, 205, 206, 209, 211, 214, 222, 225

scapegoat, 3, 6, 20, 42, 49

schism of the Church, 43, 48, 49, 194

secularization, 30, 50, 153, 221, 225

seed, paradigm of the, 24, 25, 98, 140, 141, 142, 174, 193, 223

semiology of reality, 11, 93, 94, 95, 97

"senso della terra" (sense of the earth), 22, 141

sex, 5, 6, 14, 27, 54, 57, 80, 98, 100, 108, 113, 118, 135, 139, 161, 165, 194, 212, 213

sexism, 194
sex phobia, 194
sexuality, 20, 120, 137
shame, 209, 210
sickness, vi, 15, 203, 211, 212
signs, 4, 13, 24, 86, 94, 96, 98, 99, 104, 115, 119, 144, 145, 174, 175, 182, 183, 184
simulacra, 55, 58, 59, 61, 62, 118
simulation, 217, 218
sin, 45, 46, 90, 131, 132, 160, 162, 179, 204, 208, 216, 220
slapstick, 191
sodomitical flesh, 6, 211, 213
solitude, 15, 50
soul, 63, 68, 101, 119, 126, 132, 137, 144, 145, 153, 162, 166, 203, 210; sparrows, 10, 148, 151, 172, 175, 176
spirituality, aesthetic, 12, 64, 67, 70, 72
spring, 130, 131, 132, 133, 140, 144, 157, 166, 189
spring of mercy, 131
stage-text, 197, 199, 200
stigmata, 209, 211, 218
sting of the flesh, 209, 217
stornelli, 160
"stracci" as rags, 55, 59
subjactivity, 183, 184
sublime, 19, 23, 64, 65, 122, 153, 162, 177, 202, 208, 213, 216
subproletarian: flesh, 8, 9, 12, 15, 16, 58, 76, 215; heroes, 12, 29, 55, 56, 59, 61, 65, 110, 142, 172, 181, 185, 206, 215, 223, 225
subproletarians, anthropological difference of, 17, 32
subproletariat, 32, 57, 126, 139, 142, 172, 199, 206, 207, 208, 225
suicide, 112, 119, 122, 134; symbolic, 119, 122
syncretism, religious, 35, 42, 119, 143
synoeciosis, 10, 26, 66, 213
system of signs, 86, 96

tableaux vivants, 55, 60, 61, 79
tarantismo, 29
tears, 14, 35, 53, 56, 113, 129, 130, 131, 132, 133, 140, 141, 144, 146, 159, 166, 167, 180, 223
telelology, 146
"teta veleta," 212, 213
text, sacred, 150, 189, 197, 200
thanatos, 8, 20, 142, 182, 183, 184, 185
theologia crucis, 202
theologian *en poète*, 196
theology: atheist, 7; of image, 9, 52, 82, 83, 85, 222, 223; of the flesh, 122; radical, 7
theorem, 23, 111, 115, 118, 121, 134, 186
Third World, 16, 36, 57, 135, 145, 159, 174, 176, 215, 225; Third World heroes, 57, 135
time: cyclical, 27, 42, 123; finite, 133
tolerance, sexual, 207
tragedy, 9, 28, 38, 40, 55, 57, 61, 63, 113, 119, 135, 200, 207
tragic, vi, 8, 10, 12, 14, 16, 17, 27, 28, 35, 38, 40, 54, 55, 56, 61, 62, 64, 65, 79, 108, 116, 165, 220
tragic humanism, 222
transcendence: immanent, 13, 58, 72, 89, 101, 102, 178, 183, 204, 206; vs. immanence, 196; refuse of, 28, 65, 222
transfiguration, 74, 129
trans-historicism, 28

transhumanize, 27, 37, 140, 141, 19
transubstantiation on film, 9, 82, 83, 84, 87–8, 92, 98, 118, 181
truth, search for, 151

universalism, 50, 214, 227
universality, 57, 58, 85
utopia, 17, 82, 202, 211, 222

Vatican, 11, 12, 45, 47, 74, 152, 165, 187, 194, 195, 222
Veronica, the, 83, 98, 225
violence, 6, 11, 13, 16, 20, 35, 48, 71, 73, 88, 91, 92, 94, 99, 100, 124, 140, 149, 162, 163, 169, 172, 175, 197, 207, 215, 220, 224; of the image, 99, 224; pathological images of, 100
vitality, 9, 13, 16, 56, 63, 70, 85, 108, 109, 110, 169, 171, 206, 210, 213

weakness, 15, 50, 191, 193, 206, 209, 217
West, the, 31, 37, 78, 101, 135, 153, 154, 170, 173, 270n54
word, the, sacred vs. technical/historical, 196, 197, 198, 199, 200, 201, 202
words of the Flesh, v, 12, 13, 78, 81, 93, 97, 98, 99, 103, 156, 181, 182, 225
working class, 122, 132, 133, 134, 139, 141, 142, 143, 144, 152, 216

youth, 15, 16, 50, 67,69, 79, 80, 128, 166, 169, 188, 192, 207, 208, 215, 223

www.ingramcontent.com/pod-product-compliance
Lightning Source LLC
LaVergne TN
LVHW090149080826
844660LV00013B/733/J

* 9 7 8 1 4 4 2 6 4 8 0 6 7 *